Religion and the Political Imagination

T0382490

The theory of secularisation became a virtually unchallenged truth of twentieth-century social science. First sketched out by Enlightenment philosophers, then transformed into an irreversible global process by nineteenth-century thinkers, the theory was given substance by the precipitate drop in religious practice across Western Europe in the 1960s. However, the re-emergence of acute conflicts at the interface between religion and politics in the later twentieth century confounded such assumptions. It is clear that ideas about secularisation must be rethought. Yet, as this important collection of essays reveals, not everything contained in the idea of secularisation was false. Analyses of developments since 1500 reveal a wide spectrum of historical processes: partial secularisation in some spheres has been accompanied by sacralisation in others. Utilising new approaches derived from history, philosophy, politics and anthropology, *Religion and the Political Imagination* offers new ways of thinking about the urgency of religious issues in the contemporary world.

IRA KATZNELSON is Ruggles Professor of Political Science and History at Columbia University and Research Associate at the Centre for History and Economics, King's College, Cambridge. A fellow of the American Academy of Arts and Sciences and the American Philosophical Society, Professor Katznelson has published widely on the history of the western liberal tradition.

GARETH STEDMAN JONES is Professor of Political Thought in the Faculty of History at the University of Cambridge. A fellow of King's College, Cambridge, he is also Director of the Centre for History and Economics. Professor Stedman Jones has written widely on the history of nineteenth- and twentieth-century European political thought.

Religion and the Political Imagination

Edited by

Ira Katznelson and Gareth Stedman Jones

CAMBRIDGE
UNIVERSITY PRESS

CAMBRIDGE
UNIVERSITY PRESS

University Printing House, Cambridge CB2 8BS, United Kingdom

Cambridge University Press is part of the University of Cambridge.

It furthers the University's mission by disseminating knowledge in the pursuit of education, learning and research at the highest international levels of excellence.

www.cambridge.org
Information on this title: www.cambridge.org/9780521147347

© Cambridge University Press 2010

First published 2010

A catalogue record for this publication is available from the British Library

Library of Congress Cataloguing in Publication data

Religion and the political imagination / edited by Ira Katznelson and Gareth Stedman Jones.
   p.   cm.
   Includes bibliographical references and index.
   ISBN 978-0-521-76654-8 (Hardback) – ISBN 978-0-521-14734-7 (Pbk.)
   1. Secularization–History.   2. Religion and politics–History.
I. Katznelson, Ira.   II. Jones, Gareth Stedman.   III. Title.
   BL2747.8.R455 2010
   211'.609–dc22

                                                            2010017812

ISBN 978-0-521-76654-8 Hardback
ISBN 978-0-521-14734-7 Paperback

Contents

Contributors

KAREN BARKEY Professor of Sociology and History, Columbia University

CALLUM G. BROWN Professor of Religious and Cultural History, University of Dundee

CHRISTOPHER CLARK Professor of Modern European History and Fellow, St Catharine's College, Cambridge

INGRID CREPPELL Associate Professor of Political Science, George Washington University

GEOFFREY HOSKING Emeritus Professor of Russian History, University College London

HUMEIRA IQTIDAR Research Fellow, Centre of South Asian Studies and King's College, Cambridge

IRA KATZNELSON Ruggles Professor of Political Science and History, Columbia University

SUDIPTA KAVIRAJ Professor, South Asian Politics, Columbia University

JYTTE KLAUSEN Lawrence A. Wien Professor of International Cooperation, Brandeis University Affiliate, Center for European Studies, Harvard University

HUGH McLEOD Professor of Church History, University of Birmingham

MICHAEL O'BRIEN Professor of American Intellectual History, University of Cambridge

JONATHAN PARRY Professor of Modern British History, University of Cambridge

EMILE PERREAU-SAUSSINE Late Newton Trust Lecturer, Department of Politics and International Studies, University of Cambridge

ANAT SCOLNICOV Director of Studies and College Lecturer in Law, Lucy Cavendish College, Cambridge

GARETH STEDMAN JONES Professor of Political Thought and Fellow, King's College, Cambridge

DAVID M. THOMPSON Emeritus Professor of Modern Church History, Fitzwilliam College, Cambridge

Acknowledgements

We wish to acknowledge the general support and financial assistance given to this project by the Edmond de Rothschild Foundation. With the help of the Foundation we were able to organise several productive colloquia from which the ideas in this book emerged. The Foundation also provided support to the Centre for History and Economics at King's College, Cambridge, in editing the book. In this connection we would particularly like to thank Mary-Rose Cheadle for all the dedicated work she contributed. We would also like to acknowledge the friendly encouragement given to us by Firoz Ladak, the Executive Director of the Edmond and Benjamin de Rothschild Foundations.

Sadly, one of our authors, Dr Emile Perreau-Saussine, died suddenly during the production of this volume. We should like to record our deep regret at the passing away of someone who contributed so fruitfully to this project.

Introduction: multiple secularities

Ira Katznelson and Gareth Stedman Jones

The brilliant sculptor Pietro Torrigiano mutilated a terracotta Pietà he had executed in early sixteenth-century Spain. He was convicted by the Inquisition for defiling a sacred image, and was imprisoned in Seville until he died in 1528.[1] There are moments and places where artists can still be persecuted for violating religious norms. That, for instance, is the situation of Maqbool Fida Husain, a leading nonagenarian and Muslim Indian contemporary painter who lives in Dubai, afraid to return home because of the controversy that surrounds his nude depictions of Hindu goddesses. Think also of the Taliban's wilful destruction of the monumental Buddhas of Bamyan in 2001, said to be idols forbidden by sharia law. But such instances are in the main shocking exceptions.

This book treats religion and the political imagination in the period spanning this transformation. Until quite recently, a rather simple story prevailed. 'Secularisation' purported to describe a universal transition from a traditional religious picture of the world to a rational conception. Every society was thought to be caught up in this global trajectory, even if each progressed along it at different speeds. In this approach, the division and differentiation of church and state into separate spheres was identified with a progressive separation of politics from religion, an overall shift from a religious to a rational and scientific mentality, and a waning acceptance of religious authority. This perspective has, for some time, lost its capacity to persuade. And yet, something profound did happen. How should it be understood, studied and analysed?

Just as it used to be asked, if capitalism was of a piece why were the working classes it called into life so diverse?,[2] so it may also be wondered

---

[1] Sir William Stirling Maxwell, *Annals of the artists of Spain*, vol. 1 (London: John Nimmo, 1891), pp. 125–7. Vasari gives the date of Torrigiano's death as 1522, but it is more conventionally given as 1528.

[2] Aristide Zolberg, 'How many exceptionalisms?', in Ira Katznelson and Aristide Zolberg (eds.), *Working-class formation: nineteenth-century patterns in western Europe and the United States* (Princeton: Princeton University Press, 1986), p. 397. See also the chapters by Klausen and Scolnicov in this book.

why the supposedly universal process of secularisation has generated such varied relationships between religion and the political imagination. Liberated from the constraints imposed by this once-prevalent linear theory, this book presents a portrait of multiple forms of secularity by investigating a wide spectrum of interactions between religion and politics. Focusing on this borderland, the case histories found in this volume probe its shifting locations, character and permeability, paying particular attention to the implications of what John Rawls once termed 'fair terms of social cooperation between citizens' who are 'divided by profound doctrinal conflict' involving 'a transcendent element not admitting of compromise'.[3]

I

History has played a joke upon once-vibrant expectations that religion would wane as modern life advanced. Religion still possesses a powerful hold upon political imaginations. Ever since the Iranian Revolution of 1979, questions concerning the relationship between religion and politics have acquired an urgency unknown during the preceding century. This may be the result of a discernible global bifurcation in the pattern of relations between church and state. Throughout much of North Africa, the Middle East, South Asia and North America, secular forms of polity have been under pressure. The terrorist attacks of 2001 in New York, 2005 in London and Bali, and 2008 in Mumbai have highlighted a worldwide resurgence of extreme theocratic forms of Islamism. These events have been accompanied by the growth of aggressive forms of Hindu nationalism and by the religious extremism of some Jewish settlers in Palestine. During this period, the Christian right rose to become a formidable policy-making force in the United States. At the same time, important North American social movements, notably those that have concerned civil rights and the environment, have also found important support in both mainstream and evangelical churches; while in Latin America an analogous role has been played by radical movements inspired by liberation theology.

By contrast, in much of western and southern Europe, religious observance and compliance with church doctrine, whether in Catholic or Protestant regions, has continued a decline, visible since the 1960s and not as yet showing any clear signs of reversal. In these areas,

---

[3] John Rawls, *Political liberalism: expanded edition* (New York: Columbia University Press, 2005), pp. xxv, xxvi.

churches have steadily lost power and influence, and the trend has been one of loosening ever further the residual ties that connect states with the inherited Christian cultures over which they preside. Most European countries now proclaim their pluralist rather than their Protestant or Catholic identities. Those regions, in which large parts of the population still define themselves in confessional terms, Ulster Protestants or Polish Catholics for example, appear aberrant or anachronistic.

But even in those parts of Europe most marked by a historic decline in the attractiveness, influence and robustness of the region's historic churches, the reduction of religion to a dwindling private commitment has been accompanied by its vivid reappearance in the public sphere. No longer just a legacy of times past, the arrival of newcomers with different and deep religious commitments has raised questions long thought dormant, including issues about public dress, the content of schooling, offensive imagery or speech, and religious architecture. There has also been pointed disagreement about the admission of a non-Christian state into the European Community, and about references to Christianity in the preamble to the proposed constitution of the European Union.[4] Even here, the current century cannot be identified as fully secular.

The rise of political forms of militant religious sectarianism, the stubborn resistance of religion to predictions of an ineluctable disappearance, the patently incorrect ideas about a necessary linear religious falling off, and the vibrant presence of religious issues in public life as subjects of political dispute have manifestly put into question an inherited and once virtually unchallenged set of historical and comparative assumptions that equated modernity with secularisation. The historical narrative underpinning this assumption that religion ultimately could not thrive, or even survive, was built upon sweeping post-Enlightenment expectations put forward in the theories of nineteenth-century Positivists, especially Auguste Comte, with roots going back to the beginnings of the Enlightenment criticism of revealed religion – to Spinoza, Bayle, Voltaire, Hume and others. These thinkers had targeted supernatural belief as forms of superstition and ecclesiastical institutions as unwanted rivals to secular state authority. Science and the secularisation of everyday assumptions about the world, it was assumed, were progressively replacing religion and magic, just as

---

[4] For a thoughtful overview of recent trends, including the role religion continues to play in the life of Europe's Christian majority, see Grace Davie, 'Religion in Europe in the 21st century: the factors to take into account', *European Journal of Sociology* 47/2 (2006), 271–96.

knowledge supplanted superstition and dogma. Religion originated in mankind's fear of the unknown. Science was the hallmark of disciplined curiosity about the world. Religion would recede as knowledge increased.

From the late nineteenth century this interpretation of the world was carried forward by social scientists. It was thought to be associated with the West's rise to global dominance through the rationalisation of its commercial transactions, its social relations and its governmental forms. By the early twentieth century, this orientation to religion within the emerging social sciences had become familiar. Variants of Comte's position were shared by most of the era's leading thinkers, including Karl Marx, John Stuart Mill and Herbert Spencer. In the form in which it was depicted by Émile Durkheim, the first truly modern sociologist of religion, the process of social differentiation and its impact on the reduction of religion became the prevailing orthodoxy. In the most influential account of this process, Max Weber's *The Protestant ethic and the spirit of capitalism* of 1904, the meticulous Calvinist accounting of time and expenditure, originally tethered to the promise of salvation, was said to provide underpinnings for the abstinent and calculative mentality of early capitalism. That in turn supplied the crucial psychic component at the core of the extraordinary expansion of commercial and industrial capitalism in the eighteenth and nineteenth centuries.[5] A half-century later, theories that projected a further, even inevitable, compartmentalisation and decline of religion in an increasingly disenchanted and differentiated world had achieved nearly canonical status.[6]

---

[5] When canon law held sway in the West, secularisation referred 'to the legal (canonical) process whereby a "religious" person left the cloister to return to the "world" and its temptations, becoming thereby a "secular" person'. In analogous fashion, secularisation for Weber entailed the migration of such a religious calling to the worldly sphere. José Casanova, *Public religions in the modern world* (Chicago: University of Chicago Press, 1994), p. 13.

[6] So much so, Casanova comments, that 'the theory of secularization may be the only theory which was able to attain a truly paradigmatic status within the modern social sciences... Indeed, the consensus was such that not only did the theory remain uncontested but apparently it was not even necessary to test it, since everybody took it for granted.' Casanova, *Public religions*, p. 17. An account of this intellectual history linking antagonism to religion and the birth of modern social science is provided by Jeffrey K. Hadden, 'Towards desacralizing secularization theory', *Social Forces* 65 (1987), 587–611. A fascinating intellectual history that lies just to the side of this book is the debate between Karl Löwith and Hans Blumenberg about the status of secularisation in the birth of modernity: See Karl Löwith, *Meaning in history* (Chicago: University of Chicago Press, 1949); Hans Blumenberg, *The legitimacy of the modern age* (Cambridge, MA: MIT Press, 1983). For Löwith, the modern idea of progress represents a 'secularisation' of biblical eschatology. For Blumenberg, this central modern idea was not an extension of traditional religious positions but a novel departure, a secular answer to the same zone of questions once answered by religion. 'What mainly occurred in the process that is interpreted as secularization', Blumenberg wrote, '... should be described

The chapters brought together in this volume have been written by historians, sociologists and analysts of politics. All move well beyond the formerly influential ideas about religion and society, church and state, prevalent in the human sciences up until a generation ago.[7] These chapters put forward not one grand historical sweep, but a diversity of paths; not one narrative, but many. They resist even residual inclusive claims, those, for example, which argue that religion has lost its efficacious capacity to motivate thought and action under modern conditions, that religion has been permanently reduced to the zone of the private outside the public sphere in much of the world, or that religion has come to reflect deeper and more important causal factors like material patterns, the diffusion of scientific knowledge, or the growing capacity of human beings to control their natural and social environments. These chapters point in fresh directions to suggest how comparative and historically informed studies of religion and politics might help us understand the interplay between religion and the political imagination under modern conditions.

But the aim of this book is not to replace unconvincing theory by a demonstration of empirical diversity. To be sure, the instances discussed penetratingly call into question the position Charles Taylor has called 'mainstream secularisation'.[8] Much of the raw material upon which that thesis was built was a stylised history of the seventeenth-century scientific revolution (pre-eminently the story of Galileo) and the discredit or abandonment of 'sacred history' which followed during the time of the Enlightenment. But even within its own terms this story is contradictory. In England, for example, from the seventeenth to the nineteenth century, there developed a strong alliance between science and a Christian-based natural philosophy, and there proved to be many ways there, and elsewhere, for Darwinism and Christianity to coexist. The United States shows how it is possible for an explicitly secular order, grounded not in divine right but in popular sovereignty, to house an

---

not as the *transposition* of authentically theological contents into secularized alienation from their origin, but rather as the *reoccupation* of answer positions that had become vacant and whose corresponding questions could not be eliminated', p. 65. See also the influential argument put forward by Carl Schmitt, that all political concepts are derived from theology. Carl Schmitt, *Political theology: four chapters on the concept of sovereignty* (Chicago: University of Chicago Press, 2005).

[7] The book's chapters make no pretence of covering the whole world. There is no discussion of East Asia, the Middle East, Latin America or Africa. Full coverage, though, is not the book's purpose.

[8] See Charles Taylor, *A secular age* (Cambridge, MA: Harvard University Press, 2007), p. 431, for the position entailing claims that religious faith and practice have weakened and that there has been a contraction to the capability, ambition and effects of religious institutions as a consequence of social differentiation, rationalisation and social knowledge associated with modernity.

uncommonly religious population and to be exceptionally hospitable to religious vitality. This is the case despite the existence of strong distinctions between the public and the private, the religious and the secular, and despite an arguably increasing commitment to the modern values of individualism, voluntarism and pluralism grown over time. Unlike France, and much of Europe, where 'the Enlightenment has been configured as a *freedom from belief* . . . in the United States, the Enlightenment became something very different . . . a *freedom to believe*'.[9] This predominantly, but not exclusively, American experience has enabled the emergence of worlds in which doctrines, organisations, forms of worship and religious practices are only loosely coupled, with the effect that the meaning of religion itself becomes open to a plethora of possibilities.

Recognising the inadequacy of once-dominant views, the chapters in this volume press forward with a critique that has been proceeding ever since David Martin famously objected to secularisation theory as inherently facile, distorting and ideological, suggesting the concept should be purged from the lexicon of social science.[10] The challenge he posed is now well advanced. Many historical studies have now offered caveats and correctives to the mechanical and one-dimensional view.[11] Our purpose is less to bury older unsupportable claims than it is to point to more productive theory and to help advance more persuasive ways of

---

[9] Davie, 'Religion', 289.

[10] David Martin, 'Towards eliminating the concept of secularisation', in J. Gould (ed.), *Penguin survey of the social sciences* (Harmondsworth: Penguin, 1965); reprinted in David Martin, *The religious and the secular: studies in secularization* (New York: Schocken Books, 1969). The effort to rethink secularisation was motivated in part by new empirical work that raised questions about the adequacy of traditional views. Especially important was Gerhard Lenski's *The religious factor* (Garden City, NY: Doubleday, 1961). For a contemporaneous overview, identifying six different meanings and calling for a moratorium on the use of the term, see Larry Shiner, 'The concept secularization in empirical research', *Journal for the Scientific Study of Religion* 6 (1967), 202–20.

[11] An important instance is Hugh McLeod's *Religion and the people of western Europe, 1789–1970* (Oxford: Oxford University Press, 1981). McLeod stresses how variations to relationships among churches, urbanisation, clerical and anti-clerical impulses, and political disputations shaped the variety of outcomes. Three years later, an influential collection edited by Philip Hammond, *The sacred in a secular age* (Berkeley: University of California Press, 1985), called for a reassessment as 'in a period of religious decline the sacred seems remarkably alive' (p. 4). A similar point has been made by José Casanova, who asks, 'who still believes in the *myth* of secularization', in the simple form of the steady and sure subsumption of the secular by the profane? *Public religions*, p. 11. Writing in this spirit, the sociologist of religion Rodney Stark has offered 'final words . . . as secularization is laid to rest'. Rodney Stark, 'Secularization, R.I.P.', *Sociology of Religion* 60 (1999), 249–73.

bringing together studies of religious change in the post-medieval world with accounts of political developments.

Such a venture, though, cannot proceed without grappling with the issues designated by secularisation and the predicaments for religion that it has identified. Not without a touch of irony, just over a decade after he counselled doing away with the concept, David Martin published a 'general theory of secularization' arguing that however much the too standard version fails to account for the array of modern experiences and forms, secularisation should be considered as a contextual variable, a feature of modern life that helps constitute a diversity of patterns. The religious universe of faiths, theologies and institutions did not remain constant; it developed – sometimes receding, marked by a with-drawal from churches and denominations, and sometimes marked by distinctly increased commitments and participation – within the ambit of the varieties of modern politics, economics and society. The aim, from this vantage-point, is not to decide whether secularisation exists or not, but to better specify the factors that affect the particular characteristics of religion at different times and places.[12]

This book, likewise, does not abjure any and all notions of secularisa-tion. Rather than abandon the term and its questions entirely, it accepts as a point of departure Taylor's observation that 'belief in God isn't quite the same thing in 1500 and 2000'. With belief and religious practice having lost their compulsory status, we have been taken 'from a society in which it was virtually impossible not to believe in God, to one in which faith, even for the staunchest believer, is one human possibility among others ... Belief in God is no longer axiomatic. There are alternatives.'[13] These changes, moreover, came not only from outside religion, but from inside as well, especially through impulses towards reform. After the Reformation, all Christian faiths, including Catholi-cism against its own fierce preferences, became denominations.

It is this epochal change in the standing and character of religion in the western world – a change that transcended the way medieval thinkers conceptualised the division between the religious and the secular, and

---

[12] David Martin, *A general theory of secularisation* (Oxford: Blackwell, 1969). For a discussion of the development of his views, see David Martin, 'The secularisation issue: prospect and retrospect', *British Journal of Sociology* 42 (1991), 465–74. A notable contribution Martin makes is that of insisting that theory focus on differences despite similarities, rather than merely the other way around. A more recent overview along these lines building on Martin's work is David Lyon, 'Rethinking secularization: retrospect and prospect', *Review of Religious Research* 26 (1985), 228–43.

[13] Taylor, *Secular age*, pp. 13, 3.

modified the profound capacity religious organisations and doctrines possess to organise, manage and control patterns of life, thought and behaviour in the worldly realm – that orients Taylor's magisterial rumination on what he calls 'the secular age'. This era is distinct from times past because religion and belief have become options among other possibilities even in the most stringently devout of places, if sometimes only by means of personal withdrawal and private affirmation. While the chronology of this shift distinguishing between then and now is not fixed or the same across locations, and while religious cultures were heterogeneous before and after, the distinction between 'yesterday' and 'today' broadly holds. And there is no turning back, no prospect of a return to yesterday.

The instances the chapters chronicle lie inside this movement starting off from what Taylor calls a 'naïve' circumstance, in which it was not necessary to think about religion as a distinct set of commitments and practices, and where a penumbra of faith existed as a background condition for all, and ending with a 'reflective' framework in which God, belief, and the encompassing and directive powers of religion no longer could be taken for granted. With this transformation, claims of religious organisations, clergy and doctrines largely came to be confined to a distinct domain, but not one ever entirely divorced from nation states and their politics.[14] This grand change, moreover, affected the status of religion not only in the West, but in areas of the globe touched by western conquest, by opening new options and patterns of contestation.

Before the transformation designated by secularisation was set in train, Christians, Muslims and Jews in Europe, North Africa and the Ottoman Empire had no option but to live encompassing and distinctively Christian, Muslim and Jewish lives, while conversion could rightfully move only in one direction. The existence of other faiths could be recognised, but in any given location and political space only one faith could dominate, separated by high walls from the others. After the transformation, plurality and the growth of choice became hallmarks of religious life, not in a manner that was identical across instances, and with no necessary diminution of private and public religious life.

Religion was supplanted in many places by other bases for political legitimacy. Across a range of regimes, modern states asserted their distinctive standing, rejecting claims of supremacy or control by the church over the state. Of course such claims had often been resisted by

---

[14] *Ibid.*, p. 13.

kings and courts, but with the Reformation's insistence on voluntarism and liberty of conscience, the impulse towards separate or at least highly distinctive spheres was significantly strengthened. Modern states of all kinds ordinarily do not utilise religion or the clergy to ground their claims to be sovereign over people and territory, to recruit personnel, to organise their ensemble of institutions, or motivate their normative stories. In this way, the frontiers of religion and politics became more varied and more open, and more charged as sites of conflict and uncertainty. Even in the first explicitly secular constitutional state in North America, the status of Christianity in public life has been a subject of controversy and division ever since its foundation.

An affirmation of a specific historical conjuncture and a large-scale adjustment to the condition, place and possibilities for religion designated by secularisation need not imply a 'once upon a time' fixed treatment of the pre-modern period anterior to the vast changes of modern life. Such an orientation is present, for example, in the idea that once there was a moment when to be a Christian and to be a citizen was the same thing. This wooden supposition is undermined and complicated, among many circumstances, by the diversity of beliefs in late Antiquity, by the presence of the Jews in various parts of medieval Europe and by the continual battle against heresy which preoccupied the medieval church. Indeed, the idea that all citizens were Christian was always more of a brute political imposition (the continuity between Christianity and the imperial cult of Antiquity) than a sociological reality. What this suggests more generally is that 'secularisation' should not be understood as a dominant and all-encompassing trajectory, but rather as one component of a larger and more contradictory history, which contains moments of sacralisation as well.

In rejecting one-directional views of secularisation and in recognising the vast expansion of possibilities, Taylor rightly takes care to reject its mirror image – the idea that religion has remained a constant despite massive transformations to how people live. 'On the contrary', he writes:

the present scene, shorn of earlier forms, is different and unrecognisable to any earlier epoch. It is marked by an unheard of pluralism of outlooks, religious and non- and anti-religious, in which the number of possible positions seems to be increasing without end. It is marked in consequence by a great deal of fragilisation, and hence movement between different outlooks. It naturally depends on one's milieu, but it is harder and harder to find a niche where either belief or unbelief go without saying ... Religious belief now exists in a field where there is also a wide range of other spiritual options. But the interesting story is not simply one of decline, but also of a new placement of the sacred or spiritual in relation to individual and social life.[15]

This, too, is secularisation, but secularisation with a difference. Spiritual life was not slain by modern conditions. It was reconstituted, reformed and recomposed in a field of possibilities that range from self-conscious and powerful reassertions of orthodox religion at one pole to militant unbelief and laicism at the other. The large space in-between has been occupied by once unheard-of combinations and configurations of lived religion.[16]

At issue is not whether but how religion survives, acts and influences. Understanding secularisation to compose not a single and global trajectory, but a congerie of mechanisms and social processes, the authors of the chapters in this book specify what happened, and consider the particular conditions, pressures and actions that shaped those results. By encouraging historically grounded ways to approach religion as a contingent and variable political phenomenon, they do more than call simple linear understandings into question, though they do that sharply. By constructing these instances analytically, the chapters widen the scope of our understanding of secularisation as a heterogeneous process, and encourage a more precise and more comparative approach to studies of religion and the political imagination that appreciates how secularisation broadened religion's variety. Located at the junction of history, social science and political thought, the chapters privilege questions that link the dynamics of religious change and diversity to the character and actions of political regimes, and they assess the implications of those relationships for key outcomes, especially prospects for toleration.

---

[15] *Ibid.*, p. 437. Taylor's reflective history, which reminds us that secularity does not imply the absence but the diversification of religion and religious possibility, stops short of offering guidelines that might shape comparative-historical research. *A secular age,* moreover, is concerned in the main with themes of immanence and transcendence, with religious experience and questions about human convictions, with gains and losses for cultures as religious life has shifted in tone and character, and with the narrowing of the self and the flattening of the good under modern conditions. It is concerned less with matters that concern politics and the state, or the consequences of a variety of patterns of interaction between religious ideas and institutions and political regimes for religious persecution and intergroup toleration, each of which is a central theme of this book.

[16] This process also eroded older possibilities. As religious plurality advanced with the Reformation, the central ritual of the Mass was abolished for millions of Europeans; dance, drama and music associated with worship were suppressed; and various rites of passage were downgraded. New churches insisted on more demanding tests of religious adherence. Catholicism became less open, and more doctrinaire. Impulses of reason and control established tests for valid thought, tolerable practices and acceptable forms of material and symbolic expression.

II

Among the unpersuasive features of the older approach to secularisation was a vagueness about timing and a lack of focused empirical investigation into its particular circumstances. But starting with the Reformation there were important milestones that stood out clearly, including the two earliest instances of the separation of church and state accomplished during the American and French Revolutions, followed half a century later by a supposedly terminal crisis of Christian belief provoked by the appearance of Charles Darwin's *The origin of species* in 1859, whose theory of evolution left nothing for God to do. The process of secularisation understood in this way was seen to be well on its way to completion by the end of the nineteenth century. For by then, the impact of doctrinal crisis had become intertwined with major social and economic changes, which were thought to have shattered inherited habits of religious adherence. Industrialisation meant families massed together in factory towns with few churches and little of the traditional influence or control formerly exercised by the clergy. Mass migrations from country to city after 1850, it was argued, resulted in an increasingly close association between the church and a reactionary rump of landowners and aristocrats.

Leaving aside the many points of historical detail on which this narrative might be questioned – what stands out most obviously is its acceptance of two fundamental and now certainly unsustainable assumptions. The first is that an allegedly global process can be equated with an overwhelmingly European story. The second, an assumption that goes back to the beginning of the positivist approach, is that politics is a second-order phenomenon, an effect rather than a cause of the intellectual, or social and economic developments which precede it.

In the first case, that of the European story that underpins the supposed universalism of the secularisation process, it is clear that in present circumstances not only does it not apply to most of the world of Islam, but equally that it fails to capture what is most distinctive about the religious and political culture of the United States. The conviction that there was an identity between (western) Europe, North America and modernity was strikingly exemplified by the case of Max Weber. For it was on the occasion of a visit to the industrial abattoirs of Chicago that Weber was inspired to put forward the vision of rationalisation found in *The Protestant ethic*. This idea of the New World as extension or culmination of the Old is problematic, most especially in relation to religion.

The inadequacy of the second assumption is strikingly highlighted by the different circumstances and effects attending the two earliest instances of the separation of church and state, the United States in

1791, with the First Amendment to the Constitution which forbade a religious establishment and protected the right to free religious expression unencumbered by the state,[17] and France with the Constitution of 1795 guaranteeing free worship, and specifying that the Republic would not pay for any expenses of religion. Politics, above all that concerning the different inherited relationships between church and state, played a central part in explaining contrasts between Europe and North America. It is no less crucial in accounting for the diversity of religious relationships in other parts of the world.

In the United States, the division between church and state, which took place soon after the framing of the American Constitution, was, as Michael O'Brien's chapter reveals, relatively unconflictual. It arose, not from a desire to secularise the Constitution, but in order to placate the opposition to church establishments from the religious themselves. It is important to remember that separation only applied at a federal level; twelve out of the thirteen states retained religious tests for office through into the 1830s, and the country was widely regarded normatively and practically as Christian.[18] In effect, the Federal Constitution represented a stand-off between different religious groups; in the nineteenth century, between Protestant groups. In the course of the twentieth century, it came gradually to encompass Catholics and Jews into the polity; and towards the end of the century and much more tentatively, other faiths as well. But even now, political leadership is virtually confined to declared believers; a public admission of the lack of a faith is effectively a disqualification for office. From the beginning, separation proceeded upon the virtually unquestioned assumption that America was and would remain a Christian commonwealth, and, for the majority of Americans, it still does. It remains the 'City on the Hill', still so often invoked by American presidents. Far from marginalising religion, therefore, the effect of the separation of church and state in United States, as

---

[17] On the persistent and inescapable tension between these two requirements, see Jesse H. Chopper, 'The religion clauses of the First Amendment: reconciling the conflict', *University of Pittsburgh Law Review* 41 (1980), 673–701.

[18] An important summary of this matter is Carl Zollman, 'Religious liberty in American law, I', *Michigan Law Review* 17 (1919), 335–77; Zollman discusses the consequences in such then legitimate practices as laws against blasphemy and Sunday closings in 'Religious liberty in American law, II', *Michigan Law Review* 17 (1919), 456–78. A more recent treatment of the same issues can be found in Philip Hamburger, *Separation of church and state* (Cambridge, MA: Harvard University Press, 2002). For a discussion of religious tests for office, see Daniel Dreisbach, 'The constitution's forgotten religion clause: reflections on the Article VI religious test ban', *Journal of Church and State* 38 (1996), 261–95.

both Marx and Tocqueville were to note, was to produce an unparalleled flourishing of religion in American civil society.

As Ingrid Creppell emphasises in her chapter, a clear distinction should be made between 'political' secularisation and what she calls 'existential' secularisation. It was as often the religious themselves who pressed for political secularisation – the removal of a specific confessional foundation for the authority and legitimacy of government and the state. But pressure to separate civil from ecclesiastical establishments did not mean the separation of religion from politics. In Britain, as Jonathan Parry's chapter reveals, the movement for the disestablishment of the Church of England, ultimately unsuccessful but particularly strong between the 1830s and 1880s, was similarly led by Protestant Dissenters, not as a means of producing a secular society, but as a way of freeing religion from the corrupting trappings of power. This was a demand made by religious radicals, which went back to Wycliffe and the Lollards in the fourteenth century. For this reason, the demand for the separation of church and state, conventionally seen as a sign of secularisation in general, was often no such thing.

In France, a country, in which the separation of church and state also raised the question of the separation of religion and politics (although this had not been the original intention), or even the replacement of Christianity by a post-Christian creed (republicanism or the Cult of the Supreme Being), the question was altogether more traumatic and intractable. The attempt to reform the church by decreeing that the clergy be elected by the people and that their loyalty to the new civil constitution of clergy be reinforced by an oath was the main reason for the crown's resistance to the revolution and became the justification of its rallying call to its supporters in the country. Louis XVI was strongly opposed to the reforms in the status of the church between 1789 and 1791. In June 1791, he and the royal family attempted to escape across the borders of France, but he was halted at Varennes. He left behind a document denouncing all the changes in the relation between church and state since the storming of the Bastille in 1789. The royal family's escape and recapture helped to provoke the declaration of the republic, the intervention of foreign powers and the radicalisation of the revolution. It led to civil war and the execution of the monarch. Thereafter, Christianity itself was displaced and in 1793–4 the Cult of Reason was celebrated in Notre Dame. Robespierre's Cult of the Supreme Being of the summer of 1794 was conceived as a moderate alternative to the Cult of Reason.

In the aftermath of Robespierre's fall, church and state were wholly separated and an uneasy truce proclaimed. But it was only with

Napoleon's Concordat of 1801 renewing the relationship between the
state and the Catholic Church, that the issue was temporarily stilled.
As the chapter by Gareth Stedman Jones suggests, socialism in France
was one offshoot of this conflict; Catholic ultramontanism, as Emile
Perreau-Saussine argues, was another. The place of the church in
French national life and the possibility of its coexistence with a
French Republic dominated French politics through to the Third
Republic, to the definitive separation of church and state in 1905,
and arguably through to the fall of France and Pétain's Vichy regime
during World War II.

After 1848, the church turned its back on liberalism, rationalism
and its former participation in the administration of the nation state.
In its place, the church publicly proclaimed its ultramontanism, its
celebration of the miraculous (both at Lourdes and on the question
of the Immaculate Conception), and its support for ecclesiastical
hierarchy and papal infallibility. France was now polarised between a
positivist or socialist-based republicanism and an explicitly dogmatic
and anti-liberal church. Looked at from the perspective of conventional theories of secularisation, the church's reaction might have been
construed as disastrous. But as the chapters by Chris Clark and Emile
Perreau-Saussine both in different ways argue, the church's response
was far from ineffective. In large parts of France, the reforms of
the Revolution, the church's changing political status and its militant opposition to rationalism and republicanism did not fundamentally damage its position in French society. At a village level, its
newfound endorsement of local folk culture noticeably helped it in
the 1850–1950 period. Furthermore, its unambiguously reactionary
stance in theological terms was accompanied by the development of
modern means of communication, the founding of new confessional
parties and an active engagement with organised labour. In France
as elsewhere in western Europe, there was a precipitate decline in
religious observance from the 1960s. But before that, in the twenty
years following World War II, the French Church, forced to adopt a
more positive stance towards political democracy, had shared in the
growth of Christian Democratic mass parties.

Attempts to redraw the boundaries between religion and politics,
church and state in other European states were sometimes no less
bloodthirsty, and scarcely less conflictual, than in France. The Russian
Revolution of 1917, as Geoffrey Hosking recounts, followed the pattern
of the French, and more remotely the English, in its violent overthrow
of sacred kingship and its attempt to repress the former priesthood.
Furthermore, like the first French Republic, though much more

systematically, it tried to create a new Communist priesthood of its own, detailed to propagate an officially sanctioned 'dialectical materialism', which lasted right down to its collapse at the end of the 1980s. In southern Europe, Spain in particular, the pitting of republican sentiment against the church resulted in a succession of violent episodes, especially the burning of churches in Catalonia in 1909, and culminated in a vicious and bloody civil war in the 1930s. In Italy, the antagonism between the papacy and the newly united state produced an uneasy truce between the religious and liberals or socialists, comparable to that between Catholics and supporters of *démocratie sociale* in France.

In Germany, brought together in 1871 in the newly united Second Reich, Bismarck intensified earlier Prussian attempts to marginalise Catholics in the so-called *Kulturkampf* of the 1870s and 1880s. Secularisation of the constitution only occurred in Germany and the Austro-Hungarian Empire in 1918. Even so, the pattern of confessional politics defensively established in the nineteenth century survived into the post-World War II period in the Catholic regions of central and southern Europe. Finally, in Britain, the site of the first overthrow of quasi-sacerdotal kingship, the post-revolution compromise negotiated in 1660 and readjusted in 1689, 1707 and 1827–8 survived. Constitutionally, Britain remains a confessional state.

The danger of applying a decontextualised model of intellectual change on its own is also exemplified in traditional treatments of the place of Darwin in the secularisation story. Popular historians are still apt to make Darwin's *Origin* responsible for a terminal crisis in Christian belief. After Darwin, so the accusation goes, it had to be accepted that men were descended not from angels, but apes. Most of this story is legend, which originated in the polemics of fundamentalist Christian preachers in the southern United States. It is a product of the parochialism of the historiography of the English-speaking world that ignores the fact that Darwin did not cause a crisis of belief in Europe, that he was buried in Westminster Abbey, and that most liberal Christians at least did not find it difficult to reconcile Darwin with their religious beliefs. This is also suggested by the fact that religious observance in Britain reached its peak, not in the Victorian, but in the Edwardian age, 1901–10.

Such an interpretation also fails to take account of a more fundamental challenge to a Christian polity, which had become manifest long before the debate about evolution, and was at its height, not in the 1860s, but in the 1790s. This was the felt threat to Christianity during the period of the French Revolution and Napoleonic Wars. During that time, faced by the rise of 'infidelism', dramatised by Tom Paine's pamphlet, *The age of reason*, religious revival spearheaded by the evangelical movement had been responsible for a large-scale moral and political reformation. It was that period of the evangelical crusade and counter-revolutionary polemic, which had ushered in 'Victorianism' and 'the age of atonement'. Looked at, therefore, in a larger time frame, what Darwin and Darwinism threatened was not an undisturbed and age-old Christianity, but a faith which had been energetically reconstructed in the face of the rationalist and secularist threat posed by the Enlightenment and the French Revolution.

Traditional accounts of secularisation as a global process appeared to be triumphantly confirmed by the developments of the 1960s. The 1960s were indeed an extraordinary decade. Between 1958 and 1974 religious observance dropped precipitately all over western Europe. According to Hugh McLeod, the importance of the 1960s in the religious history of western Europe can only be compared with that of the 1520s. In this volume, he stresses the centrality of an emphasis upon individual emancipation, the right of individuals to decide for themselves in matters of belief, morals and lifestyles without reference to state, church, employers, parents or neighbourhoods. Fundamental to these changes in behaviour were migration to better-paid employment in the towns, and the general prosperity of wage earners resulting in better-quality housing, new forms of consumer spending and new leisure patterns (holidays abroad, the family as the focus of leisure). Equally, Callum Brown discusses fundamental shifts which occurred in the behaviour of women, not only the impact of the Pill, but the growing participation of married women in the labour market, increasing time spent with a spouse and a corresponding decrease in the importance of neighbourhood activities and accompanying pressures to conform. In village life, rising levels of education challenged religious authority, while the increasing earning power of the young weakened the disciplinary sanctions available to parents and employers.

Finally, there were political and institutional changes of matching importance. Students, in the 1950s still a rather conservative and religiously observant group, were radicalised both by the counter-culture which the new prosperity made possible and by destabilising political events like the Vietnam War. In Britain and elsewhere, the 1960s witnessed a series of liberalising reforms affecting divorce, homosexuality, abortion, school discipline and capital punishment. In the Catholic world, there were even more momentous changes presaged by Vatican II. But by angering conservatives (through the abolition of Latin Mass and a renewed distancing from folk culture), while at the same time thwarting liberal expectations (especially on the questions of clerical marriage and contraception), the Council reforms provoked serious splits in the Catholic world.

The changes of the 1960s were fundamental, and forty to fifty years later show little sign of being reversed. But the relationship between these changes and conventional conceptions of secularisation is less straightforward than might at first appear. In no European state has there been a complete separation of church and state. Instead, individual states have negotiated pacts with dominant national confessions. In return for compliance with or support for existing constitutional and political arrangements, national churches have continued to discharge important social and educational functions and enjoy a privileged position within the state. However strong the principle of *laïcité* in France, the state continues to pay the salaries of all teachers in religious schools. Similarly, in the Netherlands, now one of the most secular of European states, welfare services continue primarily to be the responsibility of religious denominations. Moreover, as Anat Scolnicov demonstrates in her chapter, the European Court has been extremely anxious not to disturb existing relationships between church and state in particular member countries. To a surprising extent, except where the immigration of non-Christian peoples has significantly modified pre-existing residential patterns, the religious map of Europe remains that established by the Peace of Augsburg in 1555. According to Jytte Klausen, Europeans do not think that the church should decide their values, but their behaviour nevertheless remains Christian. Her statistics suggest, for example, that while only 20 per cent of the European population attend a place of worship, 88 per cent belong to a religious denomination. Similarly, in Sweden, while fewer than 50 per cent believe in God, 83 per cent belong to a church. Even when not religious themselves, a large majority of Europeans expect churches to continue to preside over rites of passage, especially weddings and funerals. The growth of a non-Christian population, particularly Hindus and Muslims, in recent times has put these arrangements under increasing pressure. But so far, whether because of conservatism or fear of the electoral consequences, governments have acted with great circumspection and have been reluctant to do more than deal with individual issues as they arise.

Far from presaging the next universal stage in the progress of secularisation, the 1960s really tell us more about a history specific to western Europe. In the period between 1848 and the 1950s, communities based upon confession and class became differentiated from one another by means of churches, political parties, trade unions, religious groups and neighbourhood organisations. Family relationships were crucial for the securing of work, and women played essential roles in tying together neighbourhoods, establishing local forms of reciprocity and enforcing customary expectations. Newfound prosperity, less insecurity of employment and unanticipated opportunities for mobility, both geographical and social, were primarily responsible for the decline of the various forms of collectivist ethos, whether political or religious, that became visible in the 1960s.

The changes and clashes of the 1960s were also related not so much to questions of religious belief as to questions of religious, moral and political authority. Such questions, as David Thompson's chapter reminds us, had accompanied the history of the Christian Church in Europe, ever since the bishop of Rome had assumed the Roman title of Pontifex Maximus after the proclamation of Christianity throughout the Roman Empire under the Emperor Constantine in AD 364. The relative powers of popes and kings, magistrates and bishops produced recurrent conflict in the Middle Ages, leaving aside crusades against the infidel, growing repression of heresy and periodic violence against the Jews. Luther's emphasis upon scripture rather than the church as the source of truth, and his insistence that there were no intermediaries between God and the individual soul (hence, the priesthood of all believers), brought these conflicts to the centre of the stage.

During the French Revolution, these questions were posed again in the attempt of the National Assembly to place the government of the French Church in the hands of the people. It was the disastrous failure of the revolutionary attempt at reform that helped to generate civil war, de-Christianisation, the Terror and European war. Hence the search for a new *pouvoir spirituel* (spiritual power) capable of replacing the role played by the church under the *Ancien Régime*. The chapter by Gareth Stedman Jones on the place of socialism in the history of religion in Europe argues that the attempt to replace religious and political authority by the authority of science, signalled by the advent of socialism and positivism in the early nineteenth century, was a direct response to this revolutionary crisis.

In Europe, socialism, ultramontane Catholicism and nationalism were three of the most distinctive and lasting responses to the French Revolution, together with various combinations among them. In France after 1848, a particular combination between socialism and republican nationalism, *démocratie sociale*, dominated the politics of the left. In Ireland and Poland where nationalist movements were bent upon breaking away from large multinational empires, Catholicism became the primary form of national identity. Socialism was also notable because of its ability to enlist mass support for creeds which ignored the boundaries of the nation state. For this reason, it is not surprising that both these creeds clashed with major nineteenth-century programmes of state building: in Germany and Italy for example. The conflict was particularly clear in the post-1871 German Reich, where Bismarck waged an open battle against Catholics and socialists as *Reichsfeinde* (enemies of the Reich). Bismarck's principal parliamentary allies were the National Liberal Party, of which Max Weber was a prominent and committed member. Weber's equation between Protestantism, rationality and modernity was very much in tune with the secular liberal and Protestant assumptions, which underpinned the arguments of the *Kulturkampf*.

The supposedly global developments of the 1960s, therefore, were the outcome of the crumbling of distinctively European antagonisms and polarities. Once the rest of the world is taken into account, there is a strong case for turning this argument on its head. Far from providing the embodiment of a universal model, the Christian religion and the history of Christianity in Europe is one particular and rather unrepresentative case. The emphasis upon creed found in Christianity is not shared by many other religions, in which practices and rituals are considered more important. As Sudipta Kaviraj argues in discussing the 'thick' religion of his grandfather in Bengal, a formalised credal list does not capture either what his religion was about or what it meant to him. In some religions, worship is polytheistic, in others the existence or non-existence of God is not a salient question. Similarly, in other religions, in Islam or Judaism for example, there is nothing comparable to the Christian ecclesiastical hierarchy, an inheritance from the ancient Roman Empire. For these reasons, most religions have not produced comparable tensions between church and state. What was crucial in the relationship between western Europe and the rest of the world was not the inherent superiority of its religious institutions and beliefs, but the fact of conquest, domination and empire building on the part of European powers from the early modern period onwards.

Arguments in defence of the values of 'the free world' during the period of decolonisation and the 'cold war' often treated religious toleration as an intrinsic part of the liberal inheritance of the West. But as Karen Barkey demonstrates, the most successful and enduring forms of peaceful coexistence between confessions in the pre-modern age were to be found among the Ottomans rather than in Christendom. As Ira Katznelson argues in the case of the changing treatment of the Jews in England, there was no intrinsic connection between liberalism and toleration. *De facto* toleration existed in some periods for pragmatic reasons, but it remained reversible. In the British Empire in the eighteenth, nineteenth and twentieth centuries, there were also shifts in attitudes towards toleration taken for similar reasons of expediency. From the chapters by Humeira Iqtidar and Sudipta Kaviraj on South Asia, it seems clear, moreover, that forms of religious codification introduced by the British for administrative reasons helped to reshape the religions of the Indian subcontinent, both Hinduism and Islam, along the lines of the credal religions of Europe, and helped to provoke an array, not a single set, of responses. Furthermore, whatever its reputation in Europe, secularism in colonial and non-European contexts could play an intolerant and authoritarian role. In these ways, the colonial experience helped to produce the 'thin' but fundamentalist versions of Islamism and Hindu nationalism, which play such powerful roles in South Asia today.

III

Scholarship about religion and politics, these chapters counsel, should worry less about whether an older meaning of secularisation is 'true' – manifestly it is not – than about developments inside the boundaries of a revised conception of secularisation. In this book, secularisation as a complex and multiple process has been characterised by a wide spectrum of convictions and practices that range from an overwhelming religiosity to a biting rejection of God. Understood in this way, the term designates a distinctive field marked by heterogeneous forms of religion (and irreligion), including a host of revivals, which often place religion at the centre of the thoughts, convictions and feelings of modern people across the globe. In this sense, 'secularisation' makes this continuum possible, and exerts pressures that become constitutive of each of the options. Each of these situations, moreover, is rich with implications for toleration, and for the fate of minority religions and the security and liberty of their adherents.

These chapters also trigger questions about how a comparative approach to religion and the political imagination might be further developed. Such questions suggest that the drift in direction that has taken place over the past half-millennium has been far more permissive and less determinative of particular outcomes than the straightforward and uncomplicated single pathway designated by traditional theory. As the overarching meaning and context for religious beliefs, theologies, institutions and behaviour changed both in the West and more globally, each key site of analysis considered in this book became more heterogeneous, especially with regard to the relationships that link political regimes to religious institutions, doctrines and practices. Significant outcomes like the character of toleration have been shaped by an array of factors and mechanisms, including matters of sequence and timing, the character of governance and the degree of religious pluralism.

It is this multiple secularity that these chapters explore. They do more than complicate, contradict or revise teleological accounts of secularisation. Rather, they propose a richer and more complex deconstruction and reconstruction of the idea of secularisation – not so much the abandonment of the concept *tout court*, as a rethinking of the cluster of approaches and assumptions that have generally accompanied it. These include a flat and unchanging portrayal of religion, an overly integrated picture of modern political thought and the separation of a history of ideas concerning religion from the analysis of religion as an institutional site in a field of power and influence. What these discussions offer is the treatment of key terms – whether secularisation, religion, political regimes or toleration – as conceptual variables, with each characterised by a spectrum of alternatives. Each particular situation is constituted by a combination of these elements.

Much is at stake in pursuing the openings offered by these case histories and by the wider approach to secularisation they authorise – not just better history and social science, but better prospects for religious comity, free expression and social peace. Mainstream secularisation theory projected the growth of toleration as a result of the reduction of faith from truth to opinion, of the loss of passion for religious worship and doctrine, and of the growth of scepticism and pluralism. By diminishing the thrust and appeal of religion, it was thought, the harm perpetuated by intolerance would diminish. Of course, we know better. The chapters in this book help us understand why, by providing materials that bring together both a particular focus on things political and an orientation to research that constructs individual cases in ways which make possible meaningful comparison.

Regrettably, a comparative orientation has been notably missing in regard to crucial areas of inquiry. These include the movement out of the seemingly fixed status of religion in the western medieval world. It is striking how few comparative historical studies of secularisation there are.[19] Another concerns the effects of cross-cultural colonial contact. Here the terms of interaction also varied considerably, and resulted in

[19] In *Public religions*, pp. 24–5, Casanova underscores how, if one views secularisation as a modern historical process and accepts the view that, above all, these four simultaneous developments – the Protestant Reformation, the rise of the modern state, the rise of modern capitalism and the rise of modern science – set in motion the dynamics of the process by undermining the medieval system and themselves became at the same time the carriers of the processes of differentiation of which secularisation is one aspect, then it follows that one should expect different historical patterns of secularisation. As each of these carriers developed different dynamics in different places and at different times, the patterns and the outcomes of the historical processes of secularisation should vary accordingly. Intuitively, even a superficial knowledge of the various histories tells one that this is the case.

a spectrum of different patterns of exchange, ranging from learning to rejection, syncretism to purity.

Both in Europe and beyond, a crucial boundary line invites comparative study – the frontier of religion and political regimes (including their norms, patterns of justification, institutional ensembles and rules of transaction with civil society). This is an especially significant zone where a comparative approach has been insufficiently present. If we are to better understand not just why, but how, diverse emplacements and patterning of religion, across instances and within the dynamics of individual cases, came to characterise different post-medieval times and settings, we have to attend to points of contact and conflict between religion and political regimes, with each understood as complex constellations of elements, without making the European experience a global model based on a supposed linear decline of religion.[20]

Once simple secularisation is set aside, systematic comparative analysis becomes not just inviting but obligatory. A key aim of the book is to suggest that future work should further develop an analytical template that both directs and draws from the cases it considers. Such scholarship would seek to advance ideas and propositions about how a determinate number of characteristics concerning the qualities of religion, the degree of confessional pluralism, and institutional rules governing transactions between religion and the state within specific types of political regime shape relationships linking religion and politics. Such characteristics in turn shape the content of secularisation and the possibilities and extent of toleration. Bearing in mind the alleged last words of the 'utopian socialist' Henri de Saint-Simon in 1825, 'religion never dies out; it only changes its form', much remains to be accomplished.

---

[20] Defying spatial provincialism, the criticism is not simply of an underlying and often unexamined Eurocentrism, but questioning how much of the original platform of secularism was targeted against eighteenth- and nineteenth-century forms of Christian fundamentalism, and therefore might have only a tangential relevance to other locations and different creeds. The chapters dealing with circumstances outside the West reject any simple effort to transpose the assumptions of *Kulturkampf* liberal nationalism through to the rest of the world, where the context for such struggle was not present.

1 Secularisation: religion and the roots of innovation in the political sphere

Ingrid Creppell

Many of the great social theorists – Hume, Marx, Durkheim, Weber and Freud among them – predicted the loss of religious belief as society developed in wealth and complexity and humans grew more rational and scientific. Perhaps one day they will be vindicated, but so far, their projections are strikingly inadequate, as people continue to seek religious experience, espouse religious beliefs, and embrace religious community. Nevertheless, important changes did happen to religion and the predictions of the grand theories have served as the basis for the secularisation thesis – the conjecture that modernity brings with it a decline in belief at the individual level and religious power at the institutional one. The continuing power of religion as well as the clear change in its role justifies continued interest in this field.

A large literature on secularisation developed mainly in the fields of sociology and history.[1] This scholarship is now also enriched with Charles Taylor's major study of the rise of the secular age, a grand, detailed and integrated story, in which he traces changes in the nature and sensibility of spiritual believing through intellectual history and philosophy.[2] Yet, even

---

[1] This literature has recently grown even larger in light of fundamentalisms around the globe, the idea of a 'clash of civilisations' and events like 9/11. Lines of debate include questions about how secularisation should be defined; its existence or non-existence; stronger and weaker versions of change, and sociopolitical or geographical variations; European exceptionalism versus American exceptionalism; causes of personal versus political secularisation, and so forth. Three notable recent contributions are Charles Taylor, *A secular age* (Harvard: Harvard University Press, 2007); Pippa Norris and Ronald Inglehart, *Sacred and secular* (Cambridge: Cambridge University Press, 2004); Steve Bruce, *God is dead, secularization in the West* (Oxford: Blackwell, 2002).

[2] Charles Taylor defines three types of secularity. In secularity 1, common institutions and practices including the state can function with no reference to God or a transcendent realm; in secularity 2, people no longer believe and practise religious faiths. Secularity 3 refers to the condition of belief in which a multiplicity of beliefs as well as unbelief exist side by side – faith in God is just one option and 'frequently not the easiest to embrace' (p. 3). He argues that the evolution of this 'condition of belief' required a complex interplay of factors, the most important being the development of 'exclusive humanism'. To counter the 'subtraction' story, which focused on the disappearance of God, Taylor presents another

in light of the wealth of detail from these fields of study, specific aspects of the secularisation story need further understanding.

In this chapter, I examine changes in the political realm once the dominance of religious authority began to come apart. This well-worn story may not seem to need retelling: cycles of religious war led to fatigue, the agreement to disagree, and the separation of church and state. But the nutshell version of political secularisation as the institutional separation of church and state obscures more than it reveals. In the post-Reformation period (late sixteenth to early eighteenth century), a fundamentally new historical path opens up, leading to secularisation in western political regimes. How did it happen that people moved from a world in which religion (and one's connection to it) served as the ultimate moral arbiter to a world in which political membership took precedence as the public and normative reference point for power? To describe the large-scale institutional transformation as one mainly of realignment of regimes of power glides over the underpinnings and mechanisms of this change, which depended upon the mental and cultural capacity of persons to live in such a new arrangement. An account must be given of the value structure and habits of mind making it possible at the level of peoples' collective allegiances and beliefs to sustain a world where public religious uniformity no longer prevailed. What was required was a rebalancing of public allegiance and a normative basis for political authority; these two were related. To treat political membership as superseding religious membership, persons had to accept political authority as sustaining normative legitimacy.

The connection between innovation in the political realm during the post-Reformation period and the process of secularisation as a reduction in religion's power is often presented as definitional: separation of church/ state constitutes an essential modern western political development, and incarnates one version of secularism. However, this won't do for an understanding of the rebalancing of religion and politics. Through what adjustments did subjects/citizens come to accept this reshaped allegiance? How did the political sphere achieve an autonomous political legitimacy? On the one hand, it may look as if removing the aegis of divine status from the secular ruler would render secular power a realm of pure Machiavellian realpolitik. This was one option, but not the most stable in the long run. On the other hand, the loss of religion's pre-eminent authorising public status

'pole of moral or spiritual aspiration' arising as an alternative form of fullness and affirmation. Moral and spiritual need is now filled by an appreciation of aspects of distinctly human existence and of human construction. There has been a large response to Taylor's book since this chapter was written. See M. Warner, J. Vanantwerpen and C. Calhoun (eds.), *Varieties of secularism in a secular age* (Cambridge, MA: Harvard University Press, 2010).

did not usher in a secular power naturally legitimated by law and justice-seeking or automatically carrying an ancient Greek civic ideal. The legitimacy of the political realm had to be constructed, specifically *in relation to* religious power and activism not separately from it. Pragmatic power – to succeed in garnering support – must be more than a strict calculation of force in so far as it protected and made possible what mattered to people: order, peace and the space to maintain religious faith. Eventually, political power and the political community it protected came to be valued independently as a sphere of human self-making, though this valuation took many years to build.

Three key points of origination of the modern form of politics demonstrate the continued power of religion and the shape that political institutions and values assumed in response to it. These origins are: toleration, democracy and national identity. Each form of political innovation was, in its beginning, tied to religion and religious believers, for toleration and democracy in particular; the manner and success of the treatment of conflicting religious groups conveyed independent legitimating value to the political realm. For secular political legitimation to grow, people learned new modes of perception, of felt allegiance, and organisation and action as social and political beings. I examine these three aspects of modernising politics in this chapter. The origins of modern political institutions – self-government, the neutral state and nationalism – can in part be found in early modern struggles of political rulers to manage religious activism and of the people's acceptance of this practical and theoretical elaboration of the state's purpose in relation to and beyond religion once endogenous religious change began. In the course of responding to religious vitality, political power in the West built an independent normative legitimacy.

The chapter begins by considering the concept of secularisation, developing a simple distinction between existential and political secularisation. I then sketch out an ideal-typical view of a 'medieval' pre-secularised political world in which religion invested state power with ideological justification, and consider tensions embedded in that perspective, which set the stage for major shifts. I then turn to the early modern, post-Reformation period to examine changes that took place in the political realm given religious conflict and activism among the general population.

The concept of secularisation

The concept of secularisation has a long and contentious history. The main lines of debate are between those who claim it never did capture social reality and those defenders who insist on it as an obvious feature of modernity. Bryan Wilson, a leading defender of the thesis, observes 'that religion once provided legitimacy for secular authority; endorsed, at times even sanctioned, public policy; sustained with a battery of threats and blandishments the agencies of social control; was seen as the font of all "true learning"; socialised the young; and even sponsored a range of recreative activities. The loss of these functions is the core of the secularization thesis.'[3] Rodney Stark, on the other hand, argues that the secularisation thesis should be declared dead and buried, because it blatantly fails when applied to religious *beliefs* today and is otiose when applied to institutional separation. He comments: 'One definition ... identifies secularization as *de-institutionalization*. This refers to a decline in the social power of once-dominant religious institutions whereby other social institutions, especially political and educational institutions, have escaped from prior religious domination. If this were all that secularization means, there would be nothing to argue about.'[4]

Both of these positions fail to recognise the complexity of the change that undoubtedly took place. On the one hand, it seems highly unlikely that if secularisation as a decline in religious belief has proven false there is nothing left to argue about: the current reassertion of religion's role in politics should alert us to the fact that we know too little about the attitudinal underpinnings of the macro-institutional changes Stark claims are uncontroversial. On the other hand, there are important limitations to Wilson's approach. To equate a loss of the functions he lists (and not all of them were lost) with a decline in religion's social significance is wrong. The *church's* loss of its legitimising authority as an ideological trump card should not be equated with a loss of *religion's* social significance. Wilson also leaves completely unexplored the direct connection between this change in the status of religion and correlative changes in politics. To simply say that a 'separation' between church and state emerged, relegating religion to a lesser, private or social sphere, fails to account for the intricate ties between these two in their very separation. The assumption generally has been that secularisation is something that happened to religion's status because of changes in 'society' – atomisation brought about by industrialisation, urbanisation, rationalised bureaucratisation; or changes in knowledge and ideas – science, progress, individualism, and a more historical and empirical consciousness. From this sociological approach, the political causes and consequences of changes to religion are secondary. Completely left out of Wilson's depiction of the Reformation's effect is its deeply

---

[3] Bryan Wilson, *Religion in secular society* (London: C. A. Watts, 1966), p. 200.
[4] Rodney Stark, 'Secularization, R.I.P.', *Sociology of Religion* 60/3 (1999), 249–73 (quote on 251–2).

political character: these and other religious movements brought about change not simply because of their individualist orientation, that is, because of the *form* of faith, but because they were radical religious *movements* that led to political conflict and the need for a public political response.[5] Wilson asserts the need to study denominationalism and sectarianism as 'responses' to secularisation, when in fact these should be viewed as 'causes' of secularisation before emerging as subsequent developments. The failure to consider the political dimension of the causes, consequences and essential nature of the transformation has left this literature fairly unhelpful in making sense of its origins and of religion's resurgence today.

José Casanova provides a useful description of three interpretations of the meaning of secularisation: (a) secularisation as the decline of religious beliefs and practices in modern societies (the most common usage); (b) secularisation as the privatisation of religion; and (c) secularisation as the differentiation of the secular sphere (state, economy, science), or as 'emancipation' from religious institutions and norms.[6] We can reduce this trichotomy to two types: secularisation as a diminishment in personal religious faith (a), and as an institutional development (b and c) – the separation of the private and public spheres, religion/politics, and church/state. I will call these, respectively, existential secularisation and political secularisation. The latter is the focus of this chapter. While the emergence of existential secularisation and its connection to political secularisation and to modernisation is of great interest, I will not discuss that here, though a very brief comment on existential secularisation seems in order.

'Existential secularisation' proposes that people in rationalist cultures will gradually shed their mental and emotional bondage to belief in a higher force or spiritual realm. The prospect of the disappearance of religious faith raises deep questions about the nature of the human psyche and condition.[7] It appears unlikely that human beings, as we now understand our psychological, cultural and sociological make-up, are capable *en masse* of living without a conception of some transcendent force or spiritual reality and which for most is attached to a religious faith. The structure of human consciousness may include an impulse towards an Archimedean point from which to examine earth and human existence; and this might naturally lead to a projection of an idea of 'God' or a transcendent reality. Or, the inexplicable mystery of existence calls for reflection on its source:

---

[5] Wilson, *Religion*, p. 26.
[6] José Casanova, 'Rethinking secularization: a global comparative perspective' *The Hedgehog Review* 8/1–2 (Spring/Summer 2006), 7.
[7] The definition of 'religion' is also notoriously elusive and controversial.

science reduces the domains of the unexplained but the very condition of 'being' does not seem amenable to scientific explanation. Finally, the experience of human inequality facilitates belief in a God who gives dignity and worth to the lives of billions of downtrodden. In Orhan Pamuk's novel *Snow* a character asks: 'If God does not exist, that means heaven does not exist either. And that means the world's poor, those millions who live in poverty and oppression, will never go to heaven. And if that is so, then how do you explain all the suffering of the poor? What are we here for, and why do we put up with so much unhappiness, if it's all for nothing?'[8] But even with universal equality would universal atheism reign? Any consideration of secularisation must acknowledge the power that religion continues to hold on the human mind. Despite predictions, rationality has not displaced contemplation of God or faith communities. Still, we need not take a position on the prospects of existential secularisation to understand political secularisation, to which I now turn.[9]

Political secularisation can be viewed as both a process of change and a relatively stable condition. In the latter form, we find it embodied in institutions and beliefs that ground collective power in a non-religious legitimating authority, yet one that takes religion seriously and continues to be cognisant of it. 'Secular' has sometimes been taken to imply hostility to religion, as indicated by the current Pope who condemns secular society for its denial of religion. Chris Clark's analysis of the secular political parties who adopted vehemently anti-clerical, nationalist positions in France in the second half of the nineteenth century also exemplifies this. Yet an emphasis on positive hostility to religion and the church skews the meaning and significance of the concept of secularity and its

---

[8] Orhan Pamuk, *Snow* (New York: Knopf, 2004), p. 103.
[9] A number of attacks on the religious mindset have appeared recently. See, for instance, Sam Harris, *The end of faith: religion, terror, and the future of reason* (London: Free Press, 2005); Daniel Dennett, *Breaking the spell: religion as a natural phenomenon* (London: Penguin, 2006); Richard Dawkins, *The God delusion* (London: Black Swan, 2006); and Christopher Hitchens, *God is not great: the case against religions* (London: Atlantic, 2007). These works offer spirited hatchet jobs on the immaturity and delusional nature of religious believers. A major problem leaps out, however: it's hard to imagine that these critics would have launched attacks if religious believers had gone about quietly, though delusionally, believing in God, obeying the Ten Commandments and not disturbing public life. Because religion now plays such a major *political* role, these authors have been provoked to write these books. But political factors play no part in their explanations or understanding of the causes of religious belief and activism; they are only a consequence. This seems a significant omission for understanding the power of mentalities and the role of religion. The explanation for religion's current bellicosity must be found in something other than simply 'religion'. See David Martin's *Does Christianity cause war?* (Oxford: Clarendon Press, 1997) in general and his attack on Dawkins in particular, pp. 21–49.

history and condition. Clearly, hatred of the church and of specific religions and believers developed. But secular signifies something else: I would argue we ought to define it as consciously non-religious (as in practically, humanly constructed) or as alert to the non-religious nature of one's position. Essentially, secularity implies the relationship *between* religion and the worldly realm, the continual adjustment of the political and religious foundations of collective meaning and identity. As a condition, secularisation is mindful of the continued importance but changed status of religion.

Political secularisation also connotes a historical, institutional and normative *process* by which collective public power developed a justification separate from a religious foundation. Political power acquired normative stability on a basis of more mundane values and achievements, again with a recognition of religion as an important element of social and political interaction. The process depends on the positive coming to terms with the de-authorisation or retraction of religious powers and a corresponding legitimation of political authority. This description of the process contrasts with the more conventional one, which has emphasised separation of spheres and the privatisation of religion. In emphasising separation and privacy, we misleadingly remove religion from the domain of politics. As a number of chapters in this volume show, the process and stable endpoint do not result in the disappearance of religion.

To reconstruct a logic of how the secularisation process unfolded, we should begin with a cursory depiction of the medieval world in which the supremacy of religious authorisation over political power prevailed.

Political allegiance under religious hegemony

Secularisation must be viewed in terms of a preceding period and institutional context in which religious authority presided over political power in so far as it guaranteed the rightfulness of force and violence and the civic status of persons as members of a significant community. Lines of religion's ideological and moral authority before fragmentation of the church's monopoly can be pictured as follows:

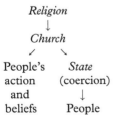

A necessary condition of secularisation consists in the breaking of this religion → church → state lineage. That relationship was broken in fact long before its logic was rejected and theoretically superseded. Tension between the church and secular authorities pre-dated the onset of the Reformation. While the church occupied an ultimate ideological position, it constantly worked in competition with political rulers. But the ideational sources available to substantiate a secular authority's normative position were minimal in the face of the intellectual apparatus justifying the church's special status. Brian Tierney explains: 'the widespread acceptance of [St Augustine's] view that the state was rooted in human sinfulness impeded for centuries the development of any adequate *theory* of the intrinsic dignity and excellence of the temporal power as an answer to prelates who regarded themselves as the only true spokesmen for the City of God'.[10] The church's public normative role prevailed until the Reformation, when it began to collapse due to its inability to enforce universal orthodoxy. That breakdown was set in motion by the inherent dynamism and natural plurality of religious belief itself and the resulting fragmentation in the church. But this situation remained unstable and ungovernable, as it opened a vacuum of authority.

How were people to reconceive their membership when two different collective allegiances could no longer work according to the expected integrated and complementary functions? Religious groups made claims against the majority among whom they lived; the majority suppressed and persecuted minority groups. The political authority could either take sides and become a party to the disputes or attempt to stand above and enforce an unstable peace. The major problem remained the expectation that earthly authority required and traditionally found its justification on a religious basis, yet without a unity of true beliefs protected by the authorising force of a church to whom political power paid ideological obeisance, that status quo idea brought more chaos than order.

The empirical reality of a sundered church undermined claims to unitary, normative authority; however, in the absence of an alternative ideological defence of secular rule, religious and political thinkers continued to argue for religion's pre-eminence and its sanctifying role in relation to secular rulers. Various ideological roads were tried; these did not uniformly move from religiously based to secular. Indeed, the swings in power's justification (and the often meandering ideological

[10] Brian Tierney, *The crisis of church and state 1050–1300* (Toronto: University of Toronto Press, 1988), p. 10.

consequences of the varied proposals) emerge when we recall that long
before the Reformation, Marsilius of Padua developed perhaps the first
defence of secular legitimacy against pontifical authority in his *Defensor
pacis* in 1324, while the legitimation of earthly rule tied to God through
the doctrine of the divine right of kings found prominent voice in
Filmer's *Patriarcha* more than three centuries later in 1680. In between
these extremes of early secularity and late divinity, we find writers
continuing to struggle to clarify the ruler's relationship to sanctioning
authority. Calvin insisted in 1559: 'the end of secular government ...
while we remain in this world, is to foster and protect the external
worship of God, defend pure doctrine and religion and the good condition of the Church' and later: 'The first duty of subjects towards their
magistrates is to hold their office in the highest possible regard; that is, to
recognise it as a commission delegated (so to speak) by God, and on this
account to revere them as God's ministers and representatives.'[11] While
Calvin recognised a separation of secular and religious authority, he
simultaneously, in principle, subordinated the secular to the religious
realm. An alternative ideational defence of secular rule reflective of
political change emerged most starkly and powerfully in Hobbes's work
in the mid 1600s.

The gradual, stop–start process of political secularisation unfolded
through relocating normative power to a basis other than religion.
Where was that to come from? The capacity of the state to move into
an alternative role pre-existed in the elaborate legal tradition of the West.
But the law could be viewed as a cold scalpel, a tool to divide up and
enforce agreements, or it could be viewed as an institutional basis of a
common life characterised by justice. That basis will develop out of:
justice through toleration and a conception of the authorising force of
the people's will. The perception and acceptance of the changed status
of the political realm came from the needs and experiences of religious
believers in conflict (religious difference and the security dilemma) as
well as the ideological means available for reinterpreting the meaning of
political life. In this lineage of change, outlined below, religion splinters
into two sharply distinguished forms: beliefs held and mobilised by
people at both a group and an individual level and beliefs protected
and represented in the church. The emotional and ideational legitimacy
that religion provided was in part transferred to and transformed by the
sphere of politics, contributing to its unique moral legitimacy. Thus we

[11] Jean Calvin, 'On civil government', in Harro Hopfl (ed.), *Luther and Calvin on secular
authority* (Cambridge: Cambridge University Press, 1991), pp. 49, 74. From Calvin's
Institutio Christianae Religionis, book IV, ch. 20, 1559.

should construct a second diagram delineating the changed status of the political sphere in relation to religious and ideational change. Here religion is no longer the sole reigning public authority.

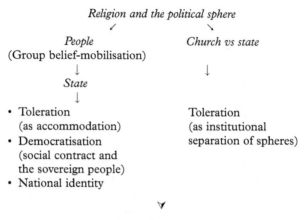

Religion and the political sphere

People	Church vs state
(Group belief-mobilisation)	
↓	↓
State	
↓	
• Toleration	Toleration
(as accommodation)	(as institutional
• Democratisation	separation of spheres)
(social contract and	
the sovereign people)	
• National identity	

Political experiences

- State as protector of religion and religious pluralism
- State as responsive to mobilised groups/persons
- State as representative of a sovereign people

- Development of normative legitimacy of political realm

= secularisation

This general description of secularisation as the necessary rise of an autonomously legitimated political realm does not project a single line of development but it does direct those studying secularisation as a historical process and as a possibility for religiously constituted societies today to focus on the bases of state and national legitimacy and power, in particular as these must be responsive to religion, not hostile to it.

Consolidating state power depends on people being willing to give their allegiance and trust to the state (however minimally at first). Consolidation can be pursued through a monopoly on violence and force, or through a longer-term process of normative legitimation of state-building. I am arguing that secularisation as a process and stable endpoint emerges through the latter. Even in the classic case of realpolitik, Machiavelli's drive for Italian unity underlay his appeal to force and violence. But as I discuss in the section on national identity, an exclusive focus on nationalism will not produce political experience and habits among a people conducive to secularisation.

In another type of case – Germany – the initial political–religious settlement of the Peace of Augsburg (1555) did not generate a process of political secularisation and ruler legitimation, because each prince continued to maintain a monopoly on his subjects' religious beliefs within his territory. Neither the prince nor the people were challenged to conceptualise a new form of the justification of power; a basic medieval model served to guide obedience. Religious diversity may have been a feature of the broader Holy Roman Empire, but diversity across political boundaries did not translate into a political experiment among the population living within one political domain, confronting a plurality among themselves or the prospect of obedience to a sovereign whose religious beliefs differed from their own. The situation changed abruptly in Prussia when Elector John Sigismund converted to Calvinism in 1613, thus adopting a faith at odds with the general population and most elites (and even his own wife), all of whom resisted the imposition of Calvinism. As Clark notes, the tension generated by the Lutheran–Calvinist confrontation produced more than 200 books during the most intense period – 1614–17 – and eventually rendered Brandenburg-Prussia a biconfessional state in its public symbolism and ceremonies.[12] These and subsequent changes in the 1660s under Frederick William's implementation of policies of tolerance allowed a Prussian experience of confessional diversity within one polity. With the conclusion of the Thirty Years' War and the Peace of Westphalia in 1648, principles of toleration (for all three great religious confessions within the Holy Roman Empire) were implemented across the board and grounds for the political experience of pluralism publicly ratified.

In France, England and the Netherlands, the demands of living with a plurality of religions under one political ruler began early. These initial experiences with highly activated religious publics vying as confessional combatants produced a type of change we do not find in Prussia, a change not only in some measure of a people's civic education and its investment in the state as an ideological locus, both of which we do find in the later Prussian case, but in the nature of state power itself. Certainly, experiments with religious pluralism and demanding, activated publics did not unfold in a smooth, upward trajectory. While France had initially led the way with the Edict of Nantes in 1598 protecting Huguenot worship, Louis XIV dramatically rescinded this protection in 1685, brutally upending whatever tentative

---

[12] See Christopher Clark, *Iron kingdom, the rise and downfall of Prussia, 1600–1947* (Cambridge, MA: Harvard University Press, 2006), pp. 115–25ff.

accommodation had developed, a move that shocked the conscience of many at the time and provoked Pierre Bayle, a French Huguenot, to attack the intolerance and absurdity of it.[13] This looks like a clear diversion from the secularisation path, as indeed it was. It demonstrates, however, not that secularisation might not have happened but that the construction of the legitimacy of the state would take a variety of paths. Here Louis XIV used the tack of confessional uniformity to consolidate his absolute control over the state; while France under this regime cannot be classified as a modern 'secular' state, the components of French national identity began to coalesce. Religion became a political tool and this in itself indicates the complex path to secularity. The revolutions of 1848–9 in France, as Clark's chapter in this volume shows, did not obviate religion but accentuated its cleavage-producing power. These revolutions also produced one of the first republican, rabidly anti-clerical, self-consciously secular parties. England and France followed two sharply contrasting processes of secularisation in part as a result of the type of political and ideological mobilisation generated by a fight against absolutism in the French case. All cases exhibit the effects of the experiment with pluralism, but the French, English and Dutch cases of subject/citizen activism reveal the forces that shifted the base of power in the state more fully than the situation in Germany.

Innovation in the political sphere: building allegiance to political community

As I have stressed, secularisation should not be defined as the disappearance of religion nor even its quiescence as a political force. Rather, secularisation is a retraction of religion as the sole normative source of public political allegiance and the emergence of a concept and a felt commitment to an autonomous political realm. Secularisation requires that persons (not just rulers) invest emotionally and ideationally in the political sphere and that religious persons be able to be distinctly political persons as well. The growth of political value came from human needs to protect the religious self and from needs to find a solution to collective security. The tradition of legal adjudication in the West was not sufficient to accomplish an elevation of the political sphere because the framework of law did not originally

---

[13] The public outrage at Louis XIV's revocation is telling in Charles Taylor's story, because it signals a massive shift in expectations and sensibilities by the late seventeenth century in favour of religious freedom. See Taylor, *A secular age*, pp. 224, 236.

serve as representative of the interests of the population as a whole nor was it imbued with an ideological dimension. The public's conception of government and the political sphere began to change through three main avenues: arguments and experiments of toleration, which contributed to the state as justice-producing; democratic agitation and the conceptualisation of the state as representative of the sovereign people; and in some ways through the construction of national identity. I briefly examine each of these to show how they grew out of and brought about changes in the manner in which persons (re)balanced religious and political allegiance and led to a new view of political power. The following discussion should not be taken as an adequate synopsis (much less micro-history) of each type of innovation, but we will recognise in these developments (experiential and theoretically elaborated) the roots of a modern conception of political legitimacy, which, we should emphasise, certainly did not only lead to peace and justice. Our present ideal of the liberal democratic secular state justified as well many actions in the West's violent modern history.

Toleration

Tolerance – as the permission by an authority to allow divergent religious practice within one political body – existed in non-liberal and non-democratic regimes, for example, the Roman and Ottoman Empires and contemporary authoritarian and autocratic states. Tolerance granted by empires or absolute powers remains, however, a concession on the part of the power; it neither repositions that power vis-à-vis the demands for religious freedom coming from below, nor does it require an accommodation among the vying religious groups themselves within society. In contrast, the situation in post-Reformation Europe set the stage for a new way of thinking about the purpose of political power and expectations of treatment among diverse and conflicting groups. Perez Zagorin has emphasised the essentially religious nature of the foundations of toleration,[14] rightly stressing the non-strategic arguments used to justify it, but in doing so he does not adequately account for the *human* capacities that enabled conflicting religious groups to move out of situations of conflict. Toleration becomes a possibility because it can be justified from within a religious point of view. But it becomes a

---

[14] Perez Zagorin, *How the idea of religious toleration came to the west* (Princeton: Princeton University Press, 2003), pp. 13, 289.

solution when religiously driven persons are also able to perceive themselves and their needs from another point of view: the political perspective standing for a more encompassing pluralist human perspective. Religious change instigated policies of toleration that generated change in the status of the state and diverse groups through the working out of regimes and policies of toleration. In this section, I present some features of the development of toleration as it contributed to the enhancement of unique political principles and practices.

Toleration in its modern form is the norm to accept a diversity of commitments and to provide social space for differences of belief and worship in order that persons can live together. This norm is housed in public and private values and in public law. Historically, the implementation of such policies by political rulers and the testing of them by believers had an effect on politics by contributing to its status as something beyond a purely strategic or pragmatic power. Implementation had a direct (feedback) effect on politics itself.[15] How did that work?

First, toleration was initially a top–down initiative: when uniformity failed, political rulers struggled to find a way to protect the space for religion (belief and worship) within conditions of diversity and conflict. To impose order and peace within the realm many adopted policies of coexistence. This implementation of toleration makes law a focus of the common resolution of emotionally laden conflict. Fights over religion imbue politics with emotion and need, and therefore the political solution emerges as something more than a purely practical, strategic settlement. Furthermore, for the state to be capable of implementing toleration and hope to have it survive as public policy,

---

[15] The complex causality of toleration depended on endogenous changes in religious beliefs about conscience, heresy and the community of believers on earth (along with other internal doctrines); exogenous changes in the accumulation of ideological and concrete power by secular rulers; and finally, changes in conceptions of the self and allegiance. Specifically, the emergence of the state, a public realm and groups' connection to it proved the crucial resolution. While the appeal of toleration became stronger with both religious and political changes, I focus on the latter because, ultimately, I believe the capacities of the political realm were the driving force, though in normative not in simple strategic terms. For decades an unmixable amalgam of traditional ideas about faith and implementing God's will on earth, new ideas about faith and God's relation to human life and the individual, and old ideas about the duties of the political magistrate, or of the relative value of the earthly realm coexisted uneasily. Not until new ideas about the nature and value of the political realm and its connection to human life could be formulated did a possibility emerge that toleration would become a stable principle or practice. See my *Toleration and identity, foundations in early modern thought* (London: Routledge, 2003).

elites and the people would need to believe the state could protect them. This was not just a question of coercive power but essentially one about risking faith in the state. The state can only serve the religious need for protection when people have risked and thereby tentatively invested themselves in the political realm. The more competing groups took a risk and relinquished power to the state, the more that state could actually protect the diverse groups within it. This iterated process (repeated efforts at coexistence collapsing back into violence and chaos) took decades to achieve a relatively stable regime of tolerance in France, England and the Netherlands. The continued belief that 'The duty of the magistrate is to enact the dictates of the Church's orders' called for a type of implementation of religion in the world. This command does not appear verbatim in the Old or New Testament but served complex political–religious (indeed social–cultural) purposes, one of which eventually legitimated the normative authority of the secular ruler. With implementation of tolerant policies, political power moved out of a purely derivative status into its own unique role.

The principle of toleration actually creates an identification with the political process, a political identity, one not necessarily linked to any particular national identity, though hostility to 'outsiders' could contribute to an inner consolidation, as I discuss later. This political role exists not solely as a juridical condition, rather, the practice and commitment to toleration among people and groups enables an abstract understanding of oneself as a political person to emerge, one of the distinctive features of liberal politics. In this process, the political identification of the people with the state or polity might appear initially to have been purely strategic and provisional: as long as the sovereign could protect them, the people would go along with him or her. But this inadequately describes the people's growing allegiance to the political sovereign and the community that the sovereign protects. The nature of political normativity comes to rest on its own rationale through toleration providing the state with a secular point of view, or even a common political-moral identity through participating in the 'impartial' sphere of the public. Some of the ethos of this rebalancing of the political self can be seen in the opening lines of the Toleration Act of 1689: 'Forasmuch as some ease to scrupulous consciences in the exercise of religion may be an effectual means to unite their Majesties Protestant subjects in interest and affection' and then continues by delineating the penalties lifted (along with other provisions as well as stipulations) for those Dissenting religious groups previously suppressed. The purpose of the

Act is explicitly stated as *uniting* citizens in interest and affection.[16] It is quite natural to ridicule the rhetoric of this Act and others like it, exposing the underlying interests served, and the fact that parties were left unprotected by it. Nevertheless, the historical and ethical meaning of such legal documents cannot be reduced to the level of individual calculation but should be viewed through the larger concrete consequences these ideological proclamations of 'unity' eventually enabled.

In more concrete terms, practices of toleration among the population constituted a minimal civic education. Outward edicts may force hostile and recalcitrant religious groups to accede to the ruler's imposition of toleration; they may do so grudgingly for any number of reasons, but in the process, the experience might bring confirmation of the value of a common life and in any case, the physical reality that one is not destroyed by living next to 'dangerous heretics'. This concrete experience helped dislodge some of the original fear of diverse belief and believers. An element of moral universalism thereby becomes embedded in the essence of the state: people come to conceive part of who they are as members of such a community, a unity premised upon diversity.

Theorists attempted to make sense of the foundations of the shifting nature of political power and of modern allegiance to the state. Sovereign rulers worked to reinforce the justice-providing features of the state. Jean Bodin, for example, as the theorist of the absolutist state, was also a firm supporter of toleration. He depicted the function and nature of the sovereign as a neutral and depersonalised power, not as a paternalistic oligarch. Hobbes, while not a supporter of freedom of worship, did support freedom of belief. His depiction of sovereign power can be interpreted as constitutive of the rule of law. Finally, Locke extended the concept of political power as the realm of secular law accountable to the people. These theoretical innovations helped create the beginnings of ideas such as 'liberal neutrality' and 'impartiality'.

Democracy and the seeds of a sovereign people

We are accustomed to situating the origins of modern democracy in the radical popular demands for political rights of the French Revolution.

---

[16] The fact that 'unity' was premised upon excluding Catholics might be taken to undercut the moral significance of this partial universalism. But normative change happens in different ways. The language of impartiality eventually came to be used to critique the partiality of the initial settlement.

What began then came to fruition in the twentieth-century idea of the right of every adult regardless of gender, property or educational status to participate in government, either directly or indirectly, through the election of representatives. But the origins of democracy began earlier.[17] In the early modern years, people and groups were highly mobilised around religious goals; this mobilisation can be read as generating two main types of outcomes, one liberal and the other democratic. Liberalism's genesis in this period is proverbial and well analysed, but that of democracy much less so.

In this section I highlight the seeds of democracy at this time and argue for its relationship to secularisation. Certainly, mobilisation in the name of religion does not demote religion; rather, the logic is that mobilisation for religion accentuates the importance of political mobilisation in general and generates new experiences, habits and responses among the general population and at the governmental and institutional level. Below two trajectories of change are laid out in a very schematic way:

> Religious needs → people act against king, and/or minority/ majority → king grants rights; protects religious interests (liberal settlement)
>
> Religious needs → people act against king, and/or minority/ majority → push back by other groups → people experience/ gain political activity (origins of modern democracy)
> → habits of politicisation and institutional responses develop
> → political life itself gains intrinsic worth

Thus, the connection between the formation of democracy and secularisation makes sense historically in that demanding a say in power against an absolute monarch, even if the 'peoples' voice' originally sought religious rights as its goals, contributed to practices and ideas of political involvement and participation. The Reformation and post-Reformation mobilisation of religious believers, therefore, ought

---

[17] As David Wootton notes: 'In the early seventeenth century nearly all English people saw the king as an absolute ruler governing a nation of Christians by divine right. By the end of the century it was generally recognized that one could argue about politics without relying on religious premises; it was widely maintained that tyrants were answerable to their subjects; and it was even proposed that rulers and constitutions should be assessed in terms of their ability to ensure prosperity rather than godliness.' David Wootton (ed.), *Divine right and democracy* (New York: Penguin, 1986), p. 18. See also the very suggestive and helpful analysis of 'The sovereign people', in Taylor, *A secular age*, pp. 196–211.

to be seen as crucial in establishing the basis for the politicisation of modern consciousness.

Hobbes's writing provides direct evidence of the connection between religious agitation and the origins of democracy. His work is of interest at two levels: first, his analysis explicitly draws the linkage, and he is highly critical of the dynamism and what he considers irrationality of religious democratic mobilisation; second, the innovation of his political theory provides a substantive contribution to the elevation of the political sphere itself. Hobbes examined the link between religious belief, political agitation and the minds of the people. The centrality of Hobbes's concern with the activist nature of religion is demonstrated throughout *Leviathan*; the latter half of the book is devoted almost entirely to alternative interpretations of scripture. But much of his concern with the destabilising yet inexorable forces of democracy can be found in *Behemoth*, a study of the causes of rebellion, sedition and political breakdown in the English Civil War, which he completed in 1668.

In *Behemoth*, Hobbes details the ways in which religious actors embodied democratic development through what they did and in how they justified themselves. The book is an extended plea for the importance of obedience to the sovereign, an attitude that the people had completely lost in their competition for power and in demanding religious freedoms against the sovereign's imposition of religious uniformity. Democratic impulses emerged not only as an unintentional consequence of religious activism, but also as a conscious ideological objective among the Levellers and the Dissenters more generally in their fight against the King during the Civil War. In *Behemoth*, Hobbes constantly emphasised the connection between, on the one hand, the seditious interpretations of scripture justifying rebellion against the King and in favour of freedom and Parliament and, on the other, those doctrines often propagated by Schoolmen from 'the Universities' inspired by ancient democracy. One of the interlocutors in the dialogue of the text remarks:

They must punish then the most of those that have had their breeding in the Universities. For such curious questions in divinity are first started in the Universities, and so are all those politic questions concerning the rights of civil and ecclesiastic government; and there they are furnished with arguments for liberty out of the works of Aristotle, Plato, Cicero, Seneca, and out of the histories of Rome and Greece, for their disputations against the necessary power of their sovereigns.[18]

---

[18] Thomas Hobbes, *Behemoth or the long parliament* (Chicago: University of Chicago Press, 1990), pp. 55–6; see also pp. 95, 109.

He concludes that 'The mischief proceeded wholly from the Presbyterian preachers, who, by a long practiced histrionic faculty, preached up the rebellion powerfully ... To the end that the State becoming popular, the Church might be so too, and governed by an Assembly; and by consequence (as they thought) seeing politics are subservient to religion, they might govern.'[19]

Hobbes sought to overcome these dangerous democratic impulses because he viewed them as leading to incessant competition, violence and anarchy. Still, he accepted a key tenet of the democratic impulse: '[T]he power of the mighty hath no foundation but in the opinion and belief of the people.'[20] If that opinion is attached to 'religion' as dictated by clerics with their own divisive intentions, then the people will necessarily be led to self-defeating ends. What he diagnoses in *Behemoth*, he attempts to remedy in *Leviathan*, through founding secular power on the firmest basis – a science of politics. Hobbes's reasoning about the absolute nature of the sovereign grounded in a social contract was motivated in part as a response to the anarchical tendencies brought about by an aroused (misled) population, but one whose will must be acknowledged.

We can see here the potential positive outcomes of this political development, both historically (the growth of political experience of a broad population) and conceptually (Hobbes's formulation of a social contract). Religious competition never ceased in England, given the conditions of religious diversity there. Repressive regimes such as France cut short the growth of democratic experience making religious competition much less fluid, but not before a flourishing Huguenot movement elaborated a proto-democratic argument, and not officially before the Revocation of the Edict of Nantes in 1685 truncated the experiments of living among a plurality of religious believers for most of the seventeenth century. In addition to mobilisation, religious activism served as a foundation for democracy in so far as the demands of groups required political power or at least *political protection* to attain their objectives. In situations of religious plurality, one's religious objectives remained insecure without some guarantee by political rulers who were themselves subject to competing demands from other groups. This situation of competition demanded the involvement of the people in *judging* the ruler's trustworthiness to protect them. Thus, democratic mobilisation – not yet a full-fledged ideal of people's rights to govern – engendered practices and then habits of people directly responding to their rulers through protest, critique and judgement.

---

[19] *Ibid.*, p. 159.   [20] *Ibid.*, p. 16.

The contribution of religious activism to the foundation of the independent value of the political sphere also emerges in the ideological, philosophical works written in response to these political–religious debates. In 1573 the Frenchman François Hotman produced one of the first texts of the monarchomachs, *Franco-Gallia*, arguing the cause of representative government. Hobbes's own work, while certainly not in this vein, nevertheless established the fundamental discourse within which the nature and power of 'the people' must be argued; furthermore, his work is dedicated in all respects to what we might call the 'dignity' of the political realm as an independent authority. Locke and others were clearly integral to this project as well. We would not call any of these writers democrats in the modern sense of the term, yet they all recognised and helped to foster the change in the status of politics and government in relation to religious authority and doctrine, which emerged from popular mobilisation.

National identity

Religious activism during the early modern era produced extended periods of war, ungovernability and mayhem, which led to the disintegration of fixed identities and membership. The crisp observations of Michel de L'Hôpital captured this confusion in 1560: 'We … see that a Frenchman and an Englishman of the same religion are more friendly towards each other than two citizens of one town, but of different religions, so far does the relationship of religion surpass that of nationality.'[21] Where did primary allegiance belong? One of the major modern innovations to come out of early modern conflict was the consolidation not only of nation states and the system of sovereignty but also the idea of the nation. Religious conflict directly provoked leaders to find alternative bases of political belonging, and consolidation of national identity could be enhanced for this purpose. That conflict also forced subjects to rethink the basis of the collective 'we'.

Defining and timing nationalism remains a vigorous source of controversy.[22] An important distinction between *national identity* as a sense of available identification among a particular people and *nationalism* as a self-conscious, formally demanding political movement should be kept

---

[21] Quoted in Joseph Lecler, *Toleration and the Reformation*, vol. II, trans. T. L. Westow (London: Longmans, 1960), p. 45.

[22] For one recent argument that ideas of national identity can be found in ancient Greece and ancient Israel, see Aviel Roshwald, *The endurance of nationalism: ancient roots and modern dilemmas* (Cambridge: Cambridge University Press, 2006).

in mind for thinking through origins. Conflict within and between countries exerted a tremendous catalysing effect on public formulations of being a 'unique people'. As Greenfeld remarks in regard to England: 'The great importance of Henry's break from Rome consisted in that it opened the doors to Protestantism, perhaps the most significant among the factors that furthered the development of the English national consciousness.'[23] The intensification of national identity via religious differentiation would not seem to be fertile ground for secularisation, indeed quite the opposite. How then is national identity an innovation conducive to secularisation if it initially underscored embattled religions?

Two divergent models result from the interplay between religious and national identity. One holds that religion (as a particular confession) anchors national unity. Anthony Marx, in his book *Faith in nation*,[24] argues that rulers consciously used exclusionary bases for nationalist state-building policies to achieve consolidation: 'the more pervasive pattern of intolerance' against internal and external others was used 'as a tool for managing discord; religious antagonism again reemerged as more cohering, overwhelming efforts at more "civic" nationalism'.[25] Marx's concern is to call into question the timing of nationalism (stressing the sixteenth and seventeenth centuries) and the Whig depiction of national cohesion based upon liberal inclusiveness. In his alternative interpretation, the project of early modern state-building used animosity directed outwardly (and against potential 'outsiders' hiding internally) to build unity based on passions of hostility and fear of an enemy. This model of belonging through a communalist ethic tied to transcendent meaning/truth, and sameness vs otherness, has generated a tradition with a long lineage. The model may be found in secularised form: ethnic communalism could be viewed as a similar type even if not predominantly based on religious confession. But if our definition of secularisation has stressed the reinterpretation of the political sphere as a realm of conflict resolution, can this model contribute to that project? Protection against the threat of other nations, in and of itself, does provide intrinsic value to the state and enhances its legitimacy. Nevertheless, it is not enough. National identity as particularist and exclusionary and tending towards suspicion of others does not inherently contribute to the process

---

[23] Liah Greenfeld, *Nationalism: five roads to modernity* (Cambridge, MA: Harvard University Press, 1992), p. 51. For a powerful argument detailing the importance of religious ideology to national identity and foreign policy, see Steven Pincus, *Protestantism and patriotism: ideologies and the making of English foreign policy 1650–68.* (Cambridge: Cambridge University Press, 1996).

[24] New York: Oxford University Press, 2003.

[25] Marx, *Faith*, p. 116.

of secularisation. When the state accentuates hostility towards outsiders as core to its identity, it intensifies a feature of political emotion that submerges diversity and undercuts the political experience and habits of resolving conflict through processes of compromise and law.

But religion interacted with national identity in another mode as well, which we can interpret as facilitating the classic notion of civic national-ism. Domestic religious conflict spurred leaders to search for alternative bases of political belonging. The wounds of internal civil strife might be used as an emotional glue – by leaders persuasive, eloquent and powerful enough – to establish other grounds of unification. While religion is initially a component of national identity, the corresponding activation of tolerationist policies and democratising movements based on religious identity *within* each country required a reformulation of a different national image. National identity came to be defined as the conscious attachment between those sharing the land, history, language and cul-ture of a specified people. But whatever the vivid substance one shared, the aim to find a common level tying together diverse religious believers created the basis for civic nationhood. National identification of a 'civic' form assisted in secularisation insofar as it transferred communal emo-tion from religion to a national body as protective. Secularisation may be seen as tied to this process of social transformation, as people found a way to reconceive what bound them together. My point here would be to insist upon the necessary reflection, at the political level, of this shift in a concept of social unity through the enhancement of a distinct political sphere to maintain allegiance based on the capacity of the state to resolve deep conflicts in a changing society. This new conception of national identity, forged nonetheless out of religious animosity and through a conscious will to find connections across religious faiths, did move secularisation forward.

Conclusion

I have examined some aspects of political innovation from the late sixteenth through to the eighteenth century which contributed to recre-ating the political sphere as a locus of allegiance and normative justifica-tion. These struggles over toleration, democratising movements and national identity invested politics with powerful interests and moral attachments among a broader public. These three processes created the bases of modern state legitimacy, as an idea and as a felt commit-ment. Religion became less abstractly authoritative but remained a powerful element in public life, and how it is handled conveys authority to political leaders and institutions.

Today, religiously mobilised groups have again put intense and vocal pressure on politics, leading many to question religion's role in social and political order. Existentially, religion may never have waned to the extent secularisation theorists predicted but it did become manageable within an economy of political legitimacy and value. How do we explain the current resurgence of religious claims on politics? This is a question for another study. But we might say this much: large-scale and distinctly political factors play a role in the resurgence of religious activism. The political sphere within states is under pressure (even attack) from forces of globalisation, which have weakened the domestic polity's ability to be responsive to citizens' needs for justice, resource distribution, resolution of collective problems, security issues, and so forth. Thus on one level, the state appears weakened in its capacity to fulfil its basic functions and the status of the state itself is therefore gradually called into question. Forces of globalisation not only put difficult pressures on states vis-à-vis their responsiveness to citizens, they also directly affect citizens' views of membership, connectedness and the relevant context of comparison when attempting to make sense of the conditions of their lives. Furthermore, global communications technologies link persons together across national boundaries. But domestic factors as well serve to undermine citizens' trust in government and in political leadership, perhaps pushing citizens to search for public authority in ready-made or reinvented religious channels. Finally, the challenges of pluralism always remain to be continually negotiated. Demands for legal enactments of values that persons find alien and 'immoral' (a 'right to privacy' as justifying abortion, for instance) continue to mobilise religious believers.

All of these considerations make some sense of religious activism and also underscore the necessity of working to rebuild a new understanding of the basis of distinctly political institutions and allegiance in the contemporary context of shifting political demands and boundaries. The domain of the political sphere represents the struggle by humans to construct a collective existence that maintains a fundamental commitment to ethical connection beyond symbolic differences, no matter how much we may cherish these. This aspect of politics must constantly be kept in view if the benefits of political secularisation as well as the value of religion to masses of people are to be protected.

2 Regarding toleration and liberalism: considerations from the Anglo-Jewish experience

Ira Katznelson

'Toleration is of course an essential and inseparable part of the great tradition of liberalism.'[1] With this ringing affirmation, Friedrich Hayek identified with Thomas Babington Macaulay, W. E. H. Lecky, Lord Acton, A. A. Seaton, and other nineteenth- and early twentieth-century predecessors who chronicled the welcome rise of toleration in England as a history of ideas and practices that were constitutively embedded

This chapter elaborates on themes I first presented at a keynote lecture at the conference on 'Anti-Semitism and English Culture', held at Birkbeck College, London, in July 2007. I thank Anthony Bale and David Feldman, who organised the event, for the chance to test my ideas in a preliminary way, and for their thoughtful comments. I also am indebted to Karen Barkey, with whom I have been working on the situations of Jews in medieval England and France, and to Miri Rubin, with whom I have organised a series of workshops at the Centre for History and Economics in Cambridge on Jewish–Christian relations in medieval and early modern Europe. I also thank Charles Clavey and Simon Taylor for research assistance.

[1] F. A. Hayek, 'Individual and collective aims', in Susan Mendus and David Edwards (eds.), *On toleration* (Oxford: Clarendon Press, 1987), p. 46. This view is widespread. That Walter Bagehot 'defended toleration ... is the clearest mark of his liberalism'. James B. Halsted, 'Walter Bagehot on toleration', *Journal of the History of Ideas* 19 (1958), 120. 'Toleration ... is the substantive heart of liberalism ... the keystone of a non-Hobbesian way of pursuing stability'. Jean Hampton, 'Should political philosophy be done without metaphysics?' *Ethics* 99 (1989), 802. 'The phenomenon of tolerance is almost universally recognised by both critics and supporters as central to the liberal tradition, a virtue tied closely to respect for individuals and moral personhood.' Andrew R. Murphy, 'Tolerance, toleration, and the Liberal tradition' *Polity* 29 (1997), 593–4. 'Tolerance is a liberal virtue. It is among the most honourable of the respectable habits of liberal citizens ... Liberals are tolerant.' Stephen Kautz, 'Liberalism and the idea of toleration', *American Journal of Political Science* 37 (1993), 610, 618. 'Toleration stands as a value at the core of the liberal democratic political tradition.' Ingrid Creppell, Russell Hardin and Stephen Macedo, 'Introduction', in Creppell, Hardin and Macedo (eds.), *Toleration on trial* (Lanham, MD: Lexington Books, 2008), p. 1. Likewise, Steven Lukes writes of 'a range of typically liberal practices and institutions – such as constitutions, separation of powers, citizenship, toleration, rights of free speech...'; Steven Lukes, 'Liberalism for the Liberals, cannibalism for the cannibals', in Lukes, *Liberals & cannibals: the implications of diversity* (London: Verso, 2003), p. 31; and Frank Lovett distinguishes 'non-liberal theories that do not officially recognise toleration as a central value' from 'liberal theories that do' in his 2008 unpublished paper, 'Cultural accommodation and domination'.

within broader liberal and secular trends. Like these scholars, Hayek surely bore in mind how figures central to the development of liberal ideas and institutions, including John Locke, James Madison, John Stuart Mill and John Rawls, strongly advanced complementary arguments and designs for toleration, and how toleration widened and deepened as liberal political regimes matured.

This chapter guardedly probes the 'of course' in Hayek's confident statement. It considers the contingent rather than the 'essential and inseparable' status of toleration as a valued feature within the liberal tradition. Did toleration arise in tandem with liberalism? Were its timing, content and scope established by how liberal political ideas and institutions developed? Is toleration indeed part of the core configuration of liberal values and arrangements, a member in full standing among basic commitments geared to protect citizens from predatory regimes, including government by consent, the rule of law, rights for individuals, the free circulation of opinion and political representation? Toleration, I argue, is best understood not as a first-order liberal value but as a constellation of ideas, institutions and practices that came to be linked to a developing set of liberal ideas, institutions and practices by way of a 'curious patchwork of compromise, illogicality and political good sense', which is how Trevelyan put things when commenting on the Toleration Act of 1689.[2]

I probe these matters by reflecting on two eras of Anglo-Jewish history. The first spans the arrival in 1096 of Jews fleeing Crusader violence in Rouen to the community's expulsion in 1290. The second began with the return of small numbers in the mid 1650s and concluded with the seating, in 1858, of the first confessing Jewish Member of Parliament. Located at one of the most important borderlands for religious groups during the past millennium in Europe (the others being the intersections of Christianity and Islam, and of Christian churches with each other after the loss of Rome's monopoly), these trajectories afford a look at the character and fate of toleration during moments of crisis and political innovation that advanced the development of liberal institutions and ideas.[3] Even a cursory examination of Anglo-Jewish

---

[2] George Macaulay Trevelyan, *History of England* (London: Longmans, Green and Co., 1926), p. 476.

[3] Like David Feldman, I am convinced that central issues in English history 'can be seen in a new light by closely examining their relation to the Jewish minority', and Jewish history, in turn, only can be apprehended 'in dynamic interaction with the English context'. David Feldman, *Englishmen and Jews: social relations and political culture, 1840–1914* (New Haven: Yale University Press, 1994), pp. 387–8. This orientation is at odds with the view that Anglo-Jewish history is uninteresting, relatively uneventful and thus marginal. For a discussion, see Todd M. Endelman, 'Writing English Jewish history', *Albion* 27 (1995), 623–36.

history – including the consequences of Magna Carta and the expulsion during the Long Parliament of 1290, the ups and downs of the 1753 Act for the Naturalisation of the Jews when popular pressure produced a swift reversal, and the rocky path to the removal of Jewish political disabilities – reveals how toleration was not a direct or certain product of the growth of liberal rights or the progression of parliament as a central political institution. These occurrences invite us to ask why toleration for England's Jews took forms that were uneven, ambiguous and marked by precarious instability, but also why toleration eventually did come to coexist with liberal principles, so much so that for Hayek and a good many others it always seemed to have played an intrinsic role.

I

Toleration addresses some of the most difficult and persistent features of human social relations. When hatred combines with hierarchy, individuals and groups are exposed to zealotry and danger. Toleration is an act of bearing and allowing. It is a choice of not doing despite the ability to act. A condition of toleration is the existence of persons with ways of thinking and behaving that elicit more than mild discomfort, but scales of antipathy.

Toleration is grudging. The central 'problem of toleration', as Susan Mendus puts the point, is 'explaining how it can be right to permit what is wrong'.[4] Such forbearance entails a self-conscious decision to endure that which is deeply disliked. To tolerate something or someone, Steven Lukes thus notes, 'is to abstain from acting against what one finds unacceptable'.[5] Unlike tolerance, which need not be self-conscious and is a descriptive term for comparatively sociable patterns of human relationships, toleration is more than just not doing. Toleration is a reflective not doing. Authorities who possess means of repression and exclusion decide, for various reasons, to bind themselves by convention or by law.

Toleration is controversial. It rarely is anyone's first choice. For some, it is too permissive; a silencing of belief, an abdication of judgment, an unhappy compromise with ways of life that might contradict or even threaten society's most cherished standards and ideals. This is a view articulated by the moral and political philosopher Leszek Kolakowski,

---

[4] Susan Mendus, 'Review of John Christian Laursen, *Religious toleration: 'The variety of rites' from Cyrus to Defoe*', *American Political Science Review* 54 (2000), 176.

[5] Steven Lukes, *Moral relativism* (New York: Picador, 2008), p. 40.

who worried that toleration forces a suspension of judgment.[6] Even more common today is the claim that toleration is inadequate. Stopping short of warm cultural recognition, it can function as a partner of domination.[7] From these perspectives, toleration either asks too much or delivers too little.

It would be glib to simply dismiss these objections. But however flawed and inadequate, decent human life cannot do without toleration. A world without toleration is a stark world of unbridled conflict and coercion. It is a world of winners and losers, for whom costs can be very high, even ultimate. Toleration becomes necessary, the philosopher Bernard Williams observed, 'when different groups – moral, political, or religious – realise that there is no alternative to living together, that is to say, no alternative except armed conflict, which will not resolve their disagreements and will impose continuous suffering'.[8] As an alternative to suffering and violence, toleration is most needed in circumstances that make respect, cooperation and social peace difficult to obtain. 'We need to tolerate other people and their ways of life', Williams ruefully noted, 'only in situations that make it very difficult to do so'.[9] Toleration thus is motivated and should be judged by its capacity to manage deeply felt commitments in inconvenient conditions.

As a formula to manage circumstances marked by aversion, passion, and danger, toleration combines features that allow minorities to reproduce their own distinct identity, with varying degrees of particularity. Toleration permits their physical presence, abiding those who are disliked to share a geographic area with those who find them objectionable. Toleration supplies policing to provide members of the minority with physical security, protecting them from public or private violence. Toleration also makes it possible for the group to sustain material life, offering access to means of earning. By contrast, disliked groups whose members do not experience toleration may not be admitted or, if present, risk being extruded. They often live on a plateau of anxiety, fearful for their persons, and frequently are subjected to economic restrictions,

---

[6] Leszek Kolakowski, 'On toleration', in *Freedom, fame, lying and betrayal: essays on everyday life* (London: Penguin, 1999), pp. 36–7.

[7] Postmodern critics of toleration have seen it as a mask for power, as not validating multiculturalism, and as not genuinely neutral in choice among alternative possibilities. For a thoughtful example, see Wendy Brown, *Regulating aversion: tolerance in an age of identity and empire* (Princeton: Princeton University Press, 2006).

[8] Bernard Williams, 'Toleration: an impossible virtue?', in David Heyd (ed.), *Toleration: an elusive virtue* (Princeton: Princeton University Press, 1996), p. 18.

[9] Bernard Williams, 'Tolerating the intolerable', in Susan Mendus (ed.), *The Politics of toleration in modern life* (Edinburgh: Edinburgh University Press), especially pp. 65–7.

limited to particular occupational niches and subordinate roles. The not tolerated are especially vulnerable to hierarchies of humiliation.

Toleration becomes stronger and more assertive when it is embedded within liberalism. Liberal values and institutions can offer sanctuary to toleration, and make it more likely to endure. Liberal views about the autonomous person, equal citizenship and the impartiality of the state can provide justifications that show why other people's beliefs and conduct, even if grievously mistaken, should be protected and placed beyond the reach of public sanction. Unconnected to liberalism, by contrast, toleration risks being entirely instrumental, subject to the whims of political and religious authorities. Without liberalism – that is, without an affiliation with individual rights and civic membership – toleration's essential features of admission, protection and earning become provisional and structurally uncertain. In such circumstances, it becomes difficult for disliked minorities to maintain a comfortable zone within which to create and recreate cultural identity, or sustain what Tocqueville called bonds of memory.

Although the liberal tradition provides toleration with its strongest available foundation, central liberal designs regarding rights, representation and opinion nonetheless can come to be at odds with toleration.

We cannot imagine liberalism without individual rights. Liberalism is impossible without mechanisms of political representation that transmit what citizens believe and desire into the domain of the state and that adjudicate among them in a legislature whose members simultaneously represent particular and general interests, the '*Form of government*', Locke announced in the *Second treatise*, '*depending upon the placing* the Supreme Power, which is the *Legislative*'.[10] Liberalism also requires that decisions taken about public affairs be adjudicated within a climate of public discussion, debate and deliberation in the press, in civil society associations that galvanise interest and involvement, and in political parties that organise political participation and order policy choices into bundles of alternatives.

Each of these central liberal features raises difficult questions that affect disliked persons and their prospects for toleration. Questions of physical presence, personal security, economic access and group identity are bound up with rights, representation and debate. Who gets to live where liberal rights exist? How are these persons made secure? On what terms can they enter into the economy? How much adjustment are they asked to make to their cultural commitments in order to gain entry,

---

[10] John Locke, *Two treatises of government*, ed. John Laslett (Cambridge: Cambridge University Press, 1960), p. 354.

security and life's provisions? Most important, when disliked persons are admitted to a country's territory, what is their civic standing? Are they rights-bearing persons? What criteria should distinguish those who are given leave to enter inside from those who are kept outside? There is no 'of course' to guide answers to these questions.

II

Toleration first was fashioned as a self-conscious doctrine of forbearance within the medieval church to deal with Christian heresy and to manage ties with non-Christians, especially the Jews, about whom the church was deeply ambivalent. Jews, of course, were not insiders capable of heresy; but they also were not outsiders in the usual sense, for they were embedded inside the grand narrative of Christianity. Should they be considered elder brothers whose company testified to the truth of the Gospels, or as stubborn and primitive persons whose example of resistance to the truth threatens the reach and legitimacy of the Gospels? How should the boundary between 'us' and 'them' be managed?

One answer, though by no means the only answer, was toleration. It was advanced as a form of self-restraint, 'a moral triumph of truth showing charity to error'. The two primary compilations of canon law, the *Decretum gratiani* of *c.*1140 and the 1234 *Decretals* of Pope Gregory IX, a skilled lawyer, 'contain several statements on circumstances under which evil practices may be left unpunished. The verb *tolerare* is frequently used in this context', to indicate how, within the church, 'evil which cannot be corrected without disturbing the peace in the Church, should rather be tolerated', and to identify 'Jewish rites as practices that are rightfully not to be interfered with'.[11] Pope Calixtus II (1119–24) affirmed the right of Jews to keep their property and their faith, a status endorsed by later popes, some of whom, including Innocent IV in 1247 and 1253, also condemned ritual murder accusations.[12] 'The concept of *tolerantia*', Istvan Bejczy observed,[13]

was chiefly developed as an answer to how ecclesiastical authorities should deal with the practices of Jewish religion. Jewish rites were considered an evil that had to be tolerated; the major evil that was thus prevented was the forced conversion

[11] Istvan Bejczy, '*Tolerantia*: a medieval concept', *Journal of the History of Ideas* 58 (1997), 368–9. For a discussion of whether anti-Judaism is an inherent feature of Christianity, see Paula Fredriksen and Oded Irshai, 'Christian Anti-Judaism: polemics and policies', in Steven T. Katz (ed.), *The Cambridge history of Judaism*, vol. IV: *The late Roman-Rabbinic period* (Cambridge: Cambridge University Press, 2006), pp. 977–1027.
[12] John H. Mundy, *Europe in the high middle ages* (New York: Basic Books, 1973), p. 98.
[13] Bejczy, '*Tolerantia*', 371.

of the Jews, for conversion to Christianity had to be a matter of free will. Moreover, the Jews would be more willing to embrace the Christian faith, the canonists argued, when they were treated with benevolence ... The Church should not only leave the rites unpunished but should also prevent others from disturbing them.

Toleration of this kind was endorsed within medieval scholasticism. Saint Thomas Aquinas, as a leading example, made a case for toleration of Jews in *Summa theologica* and in a brief treatise on governing Jews he wrote for the Duchess of Brabant, notwithstanding his elaboration of Augustine's Catholic theory of persecution.[14] Though he designated Jews as 'enemies', as outsiders fated to live in perpetual sin because of their role in the Crucifixion, their rites, he argued, should be tolerated as harbingers of Christian belief, and because Jews provided living testimony of the lineage of Christian belief. Rulers thus should permit Jews to live their lives securely within Christian society. 'His argument', Bejczy comments, 'shows that one does not have to like the Jews to be tolerant; to the contrary, one had to dislike them to be tolerant, for tolerance only applied to evil. Tolerance was not an imperative of love but a restraint on one's hatred.'[15]

With the arrival of Jews who crossed the Channel during the depredations of the First Crusade to the forced exit some two centuries later, their physical safety and ability to reside in particular places were challenged intermittently, but not their liberty to worship or live in a manner consistent with Jewish traditions and stipulations. Though often reviled

---

[14] Thomas Aquinas, *Summa Theologica*, 5 vols. (Westminster, MD: Christian Classics, 1981); http://thomistica.net/thomas-aquinass-letter-to-marg/; translation from the Leonine edition of the works of Aquinas.

[15] Bejczy, '*Tolerantia*', 372. But beyond this basis for sufferance, toleration was absent. The restraint advocated by theologians was not conditioned on wider public and political understandings of limits and self-control. The results proved costly. During the quarter-millennium after Jews were evicted in England, such a confined sense of toleration proved insufficient as a barrier to prevent the virtually complete expulsion of Jews from France in the fourteenth century, then from much of German-speaking Europe including Vienna, Linz, Cologne, Augsburg, Bavaria, the crown cities of Moravia, and Perugia, Vicenza, Parma, Milan, Lucca, Florence and other Tuscan towns, These forced movements were followed by massive evictions from Spain, Portugal, Sicily and Sardinia as well as Lower Austria, Salzburg, Nuremberg and Ulm during the fifteenth century's last decade, and from Colmar, Mulhouse, Obernai, Brandenburg and Italy south of Rome in the early part of the sixteenth century. For an overview, see 'Exodus from the West', the first chapter in Jonathan I. Israel, *European Jewry in the age of mercantilism 1550–1750* (Oxford: Clarendon Press, 1989), pp. 5–34. A powerful consideration of medieval Jewish expulsions, arguing that the regimes that banished their Jews were both modernising and mobilising, thus insecure and in need of finding a means to reinforce loyalty and build resources, is Maurice Kriegel, 'Mobilisation politique et modernisation organique: les expulsions de Juifs au bas moyen age', *Archives de Sciences Sociales des Religions* 46 (1978), 5–20.

as obstinate and feared as menacing, in this sense they were tolerated. The result was a paradox. Even moderate Christian diversity, far less advanced than later Reformation-era heterogeneity, was anathema; yet theological considerations could instruct that Jews should live undisturbed, worship openly and maintain a right of self-governing autonomy in communal affairs not very different from that possessed by guilds.[16]

But such toleration proved conditional on how the more fundamental question of their right to live in specific locations and, ultimately in England itself, would be answered. As it turned out, Christian toleration found a place for a people it considered primitive and stubborn, but the era's nascent political liberalism, a liberalism without toleration, helped conduce their eviction.

In 1290, toleration's restraint was lifted not by the church, but by the king, Edward I, in the context of a parliamentary negotiation for changes to the fiscal basis of the English state. Edward promulgated an expulsion order on 18 July. A Jewish exodus, originating in more than eighty locations, began on 12 October, and was completed, as the king ordered, by the end of the month. Disturbed only by minor violence, the Jews set out from England's southern ports for Spain, France, Germany and the east of Europe, Sicily and North Africa. By best estimate, they numbered no more than 5,000 persons, in a population variously estimated in the range of two to three million.

As sources of capital, Jews had helped propel the growth of markets, towns and networks of trade. As sources of revenue for the king and state, they had helped fund military ventures that enhanced English power. By the late twelfth century, their taxes were sufficiently important to be separately collected and recorded. The Jews were tolerated by the church, moreover, for the reasons specified in canon law and by Aquinas. They were tolerated by kings because of their assets, but they were expelled by one of England's most effective kings despite these instrumental contributions. Any persuasive answer to why Edward banished the Jews, I argue, must assess how their circumstances were affected by Magna Carta and Parliament.

What Magna Carta established, François Guizot wrote, is the principle that 'liberties are nothing until they have become rights'.[17] Commenting on this anti-absolutist constitutional document that placed

---

[16] A millennium earlier, Augustine had endorsed coercion within Christianity, though stopping short of the death penalty in cases of heresy, while sanctioning Jewish residence in Christian settings, Saint Augustine, *City of God* (New York: Modern Library, 1950), book XVIII, chapter 46.

[17] François Guizot, *The history of the origins of representative government in Europe* (Indianapolis: Liberty Fund, 2002), p. 258.

kings under the rule of law, the American jurist Roscoe Pound celebrated Magna Carta as the 'foundation of our public law' for nearly eight
centuries, whose 'guarantees to the individual man ... are the proudest
possession of Englishmen and their descendants everywhere'.[18]

Magna Carta famously stipulated that 'all these customs and liberties
that we have granted shall be observed in our kingdom in so far as
concerns our own relations with our subjects'. The phrase 'concerns
relations with our own subjects', however, manifestly did not include the
Jews, who were the property of the crown, not rights-bearing subjects.
Indeed, the tenth and eleventh clauses of this great charter of liberty
adjust debts to Jews following the death of the debtor. These provisions
signalled that the status of Jews and their economic affairs was an
appropriate subject of negotiation between the king and a rights-bearing
civil society that Jews had not the slightest chance of entering. Soon
enough, demands for Jewish expulsion from various places within
the kingdom became regular features of thirteenth-century baronial
rebellions, especially during the upheavals of the late 1250s and 1260s,
peaking in the temporarily successful revolt led by Simon de Montfort.
Further, Jewish physical insecurity vastly increased when towns
exercised the rights offered by Magna Carta – which promised London
and 'all other cities, boroughs, towns, and ports ... all their liberties and
free customs'.

After Magna Carta, towns were given scope to expel their Jews.
De Montfort oversaw the expulsion of Leicester's Jews in 1231. Other
towns soon took the same course of action. In the decade spanning 1234
to 1244, these included Newcastle, Warwick, High Wycombe,
Southampton, Berkhamsted, Newbury and Speenhamland. The turbu-
lent transition to a parliamentary kingship at mid-century further placed
Jews in a situation of considerable hazard. The Jewish quarter of
Canterbury was burned in 1261. London's Jewry was sacked in 1262.
In a great massacre, hundreds were killed there two years later. Deadly
rioting also was directed against the Jews in 1264, during de Montfort's
ascendancy, in Canterbury, once again, and in Worcester, Bristol,
Bedford, Winchester, Lincoln and Nottingham.

The most enduring result of the Barons' War was the second most
profound feature of liberalism, the invention of a national legislature
with representatives drawn from every shire and from three different
stations in life – large landowning barons, lesser landholder knights and

---

[18] Roscoe Pound, 'Law and the state: jurisdiction and politics', *Harvard Law Review* 57
(1944), 1195.

town burgesses. Edward's first Parliament met in April 1275, when, responding to popular demand, it curbed Jewish money lending, the central permitted occupation for a group that was forbidden to own land and was excluded from urban craft guilds. The Statute of Jewry that Parliament enacted opens with the avowal that 'the king though he and his ancestors have always received great benefit from the Jewish people in the past has nevertheless for the honour of God and the common benefit of the people ordained and established that from now on no Jew shall lend anything at usury'. Jews clearly were not included in any definition of the people for whom the common good was sought. This first truly modern parliament also prescribed 'that each Jew after he is seven years old shall wear a distinguishing mark on his outer garment, that is to say in the form of two tables joined, of yellow felt the length of six inches and of the breadth of three inches. And that each one after he is twelve years old shall yearly at Easter pay to the king, whose serf he is, a tax of three pence, and this to hold as well for a woman as for a man.'[19]

Edward is remembered for being an immensely capable king who pursued war making to unify Britain, who possessed a modern sense of international relations as a balance of power, and who strengthened the crown by institutionalising a new institutional order that associated royal rule with parliamentary consent, inducing parliament to legislate effectively across a wide range, including fiscal affairs.[20] With Edward's reign, Guizot observed, 'the rights for which [Parliament] had tended to consecrate' to guarantee liberty 'were for ever recognised and tolerably respected'.[21]

Guaranteeing liberty, but for whom? Surely not the Jews who were expelled by Edward during the summer of 1290 when Parliament gathered in London at Westminster. On 15 July, the knights were summoned to join the barons to deliberate about revenues. They endorsed what today's leading student of the subject, Robert Stacey, calls 'the largest single grant of taxation conceded by parliaments to any medieval English king'. It replaced less reliable forms of traditional feudal taxation with a more modern tax on moveable wealth. The knights, who had been most vulnerable to losing their holdings to Jewish

---

[19] For an overview, see Paul Brand, 'Jews and the law in England, 1275–1290', *The English Historical Review* 115 (2000), 1138–58. Also, C. Hilary Jenkinson, 'The First Parliament of Edward I', *The English Historical Review* 25 (1910), 231–42.

[20] See G. Templeman, 'Edward I and the historians', *Cambridge Historical Journal* 10 (1950/1952), 16–35.

[21] Guizot, *Representative government*, p. 277.

moneylenders, Stacey argues, exacted expulsion as their price. 'Edward got his tax, and in return [Parliament] got the expulsion.'[22]

III

The second period of Jewish life in England was initiated by the Amsterdam Rabbi Menasseh Ben Israel's famous petition to Oliver Cromwell. Cromwell convened the Whitehall Conference of theologians, merchants and lawyers to debate the question. A massive pamphlet war ensued, a great modern expression of free speech to influence its five sessions, held between 4 and 18 December 1655. The advocates of readmission offered millenarian and mercantile reasons. The opponents argued that Jewish worship constituted blasphemy, that Jews favoured ritual murder and would induce Christians to convert, that Jewish economic competition would be unfair, that Jews would overrun an overpopulated island.[23] In *Demurrer in the Jewes: long discontinued remitter into England*,[24] one of the most forceful anti-immigrant documents ever written, the leading legal figure William Prynne, who led the opposition, insisted that Parliament, not Cromwell, make the decision about Jewish admission.[25]

That did not happen. There was no formal authorisation to open the country's borders for the Jews. No decision was announced by Cromwell. But with an apparent judgment to look the other way, some Jews did begin to return. Their security depended on the willingness, first of Cromwell, then of the crown, to abide their presence. They were tolerated, in the sense of being permitted to worship, just as they had before the 1290 expulsion. After the Restoration, their protection depended,

[22] Robert C. Stacey, 'Parliamentary negotiation and the expulsion of Jews from England', in Michael Prestwich, R. H. Britnell and Robin Frame (eds.), *Thirteenth century England*, vol. VI: *Proceedings of the Durham conference 1995* (Woodbridge: Boydell Press, 1997), pp. 78, 92, 94, 101. For a consideration of Parliament and fiscal affairs, see G. L. Harriss, *King, Parliament, and public finance in medieval England to 1369* (Oxford: Clarendon Press, 1975).

[23] Todd M. Endelman, *Jews of modern Britain, 1656–2000* (Berkeley: University of California Press, 2000), p. 25. For an overview of the Whitehall Conference and readmission more generally, see David S. Katz, *Jews in the history of England* (Oxford: Clarendon Press, 1994), pp. 107–45.

[24] London: Edward Thomas, 1656. An astute treatment of English anti-Jewish symbols and sensibilities in the period when Jews were absent is provided by Anthony Bale, *The Jew in the medieval book: English antisemitisms, 1350–1500* (Cambridge: Cambridge University Press, 2006).

[25] H. S. Q. Henriques, *The return of the Jews to England: being a chapter in the history of English law* (London: Macmillan & Co., 1905); David Katz, *Philo-Semitism and the readmission of the Jews to England, 1603–1655* (Oxford: Oxford University Press, 1982); and Eliane Glaser, *Judaism without Jews: philosemitism and Christian polemic in early modern England* (London: Palgrave, 2007).

as it had in medieval times, on royal power.[26] After the Test Act of 1673, their disabilities, moreover, were consistent with those that were imposed on Catholics and Protestant Dissenters. These demanded, as a condition of public office, a willingness to renounce transubstantiation, pledge oaths of allegiance and supremacy, and receive the sacrament as prescribed by the Church of England. A year after the Glorious Revolution of 1688, an Act of Toleration offered freedom to worship for Trinitarian nonconformists who rejected transubstantiation and took the Oaths, and thus signalled the end of Anglicanism's attempt to reintegrate Dissenters, but the law did not remove existing impediments to public office.[27] The Jews, in short, were shielded by political decisions consistent with medieval-style toleration that permitted their residence and free worship.

This, then, was no liberal toleration. Classified as alien infidels, the Jews neither asked for, nor had they any chance to obtain, admission into the political realm.

Following the model of early eighteenth-century legislation permitting the naturalisation of alien Protestants, the government of Whig prime minister Henry Pelham proposed in 1753 to do the same for the Jews. He, and other advocates, stressed how this group brought important assets to a growing English economy of global reach. At first, what was widely known as the 'Jew Bill' faced little resistance, but by the time it passed in May opponents were mobilising popular anti-Jewish sentiment. 'Petitions were gathered, pamphlets written, meetings convened, sermons delivered. Their language was intemperate and their tone alarmist, even hysterical', as they revived 'crude medieval libels'. There were instances of physical harassment.[28] A pamphlet war and a press campaign led by the *London English Post* erupted, not just about this legislation, but questioning the very presence of Jews in England.

Once passed, the bill became a principal public issue. Jews were widely represented as speculators and plundering usurers, as concerned to

---

[26] 'Both Charles II and James II stopped prosecutions brought against the Jews under the provisions of the Coventicle Acts.' Thomas W. Perry, *Public opinion, propaganda, and politics in eighteenth-century England: a study of the Jew Bill of 1753* (Cambridge, MA: Harvard University Press, 1965), p. 12.

[27] On the linkage of this law to the failure of 'comprehension', see C. F. Mullett, 'Toleration and persecution in England 1660–89', *Church History* 18 (1949), 18–43; and John Spur, 'The Church of England, comprehension and the Toleration Act of 1689', *The English Historical Review* 413 (1989), 927–46. With the failure to secure comprehension, 'a toleration of differences within the church', the legislative field shifted to indulgences, 'a toleration of differences outside the church'. H. F. Russell Smith, *The political origins of religious liberty* (Cambridge: Cambridge University Press, 1911), p. 5.

[28] Endelman, *Jews*, p. 75.

gather influence and power, as receivers of stolen property, as non-deferential, cohesive, indeed clannish interlopers, as underhanded competitors, as a menacing race of crucifiers and child killers, as desirous of converting Christians, as a danger to the integrity of the nation. Naturalisation, it was said, 'threatened the British nation in religious, legal, and economic terms. It would ... undermine Christianity, destabilise the English Constitution, and increase poverty.'[29] Generating great passion, the campaign succeeded. The Act was repealed in late November before any individual had utilised its provisions.[30] Notwithstanding the demand of William Pryne and other opponents of Jewish entry a century earlier, they had been allowed back without parliamentary deliberation and sanction. In providing 'the first opportunity for public debate in England on the status of the Jews since the Readmission under Cromwell', the arc of the 'Jew Bill' indicated that Parliament was more than a closed oligarchy or a site for elite trusteeship, but an assembly responsive to intolerant popular views and pressures.[31]

As a casualty of the permeability of the state to the preferences of members of civil society, a central tenet of liberal politics, the events of 1753 are at odds with Hayek's 'essential and inseparable' claim about liberalism and toleration. Even more, this history shows how the early spread of a print culture and proto-democratic political participation and mass mobilisation, conjoined with parliamentary representation, outran toleration as an ethical, legal and institutional value. For the Jews as for other religious minorities, toleration by the mid eighteenth century had yet to join the penumbra of liberal rights.

IV

In 1858, Lionel Rothschild entered Parliament. This was an important parliament, the one in which the government of India was transferred from the East India Company to the crown. With Rothschild's seating, a threshold of civic membership was crossed – the capacity to hold office without conversion.

---

[29] Dana Rabin, 'The Jew Bill of 1753: masculinity, virility, and the nation', *Eighteenth-Century Studies* 39 (2006), 160. For overviews, see Perry, *Public opinion*; Katz, *Jews in the history of England*, chapter 6; and Frank Felsenstein, *Anti-Semitic stereotypes: a paradigm of otherness in English popular culture, 1660–1838* (Baltimore: Johns Hopkins University Press, 1995), chapter 8.

[30] The fullest discussion is Perry, *Public opinion*.

[31] Robert Liberlis, 'From toleration to *Verbesserung*: German and English debates on the Jews in the eighteenth century', *Central European History* 22 (1989), 23. Also Todd Endelman, *The Jews of Georgian England, 1714–1830* (Ann Arbor: University of Michigan Press, 1999); and Rabin, 'The Jew Bill', 157–61, 168–9.

But this hardly was a smooth or seamless passage. Rothschild first had been elected to the Commons from the City in 1847, but had been unable to take his seat because of the nature of the required Christian oath. Elected again in 1850, he presented himself to take an oath, but on the Old Testament. The House of Commons voted to permit this innovation on 29 July. The next day, swearing on that Bible, Rothschild recited the traditional oath, absent the 'true faith of a Christian' affirmation, stating 'I omit these words as not binding on my conscience.' Before he could sign the parliamentary roll, the House resolved that, lacking the full oath, he could not be admitted. The next year, David Salomons, who had served as president of the Jewish Board of Deputies and was a leading advocate of a more confrontational movement for political emancipation, was elected as the member for Greenwich. He also refused the oath's Christian portion, and mounted a protest at his exclusion by sitting with his fellow Whigs, and actually voting three times on the status of his own case, before being removed by the sergeant-at-arms. Only when the House of Lords joined the Commons in altering the oath in 1858 did Rothschild finally become an MP.

Over the course of the three decades before Rothschild took his seat, debate in Parliament, in the press and in many public forums was intense. At stake were characterisations of the standing and character of the Jews, and the meaning of civic inclusion. As the House of Commons debated a bill to extend civic membership to Jews in 1830, a year after Catholics had secured the right to enter political office, Robert Peel, four years before he became prime minister, noted that when 'his Majesty's Ministers were asked for their votes in favour ... of Roman Catholics, it was never hinted that those who rejected Christianity should be admitted to the Legislature ... The exclusion or separation of the Jews', he continued, 'did not arise from any incapacitating laws, but from the peculiar manners and habits of the people themselves'.[32]

This and similar objections ultimately failed. This, then, was the first moment when claims about the inherent ties of liberalism and toleration resonated beyond Christians. Jewish admission to civic life did not come from the exercise of the personal prerogative of the executive, as it had in the case of readmission by Cromwell, but from within the liberal polity, following massive partisan and press campaigns. Like the 'Jew Bill' of 1753, the end of restrictions on Jewish parliamentary participation was an occasion for free public debate and parliamentary decision about which persons should have access to the status of rights-bearing citizenship.

---

[32] *Hansard*, House of Commons, vol. 24, 17 May 1830, cc784–814.

Rothschild's accession thus closed out both a condensed three decades of constitutional adjustment to relations of church and state, and three centuries of intense contestation about the meaning, status and scope of toleration, reminding us that 'toleration is a historical practice as much as it is a philosophical ideal'.[33] Heresy stopped being treason.[34] The Test and Corporation Act of 1828 repealed laws that parliament had passed in 1661 and 1673 to demand adherence to the doctrine of passive obedience, and to make a denunciation of transubstantiation and the participation in Anglican Holy Communion at least once a year a condition of holding public office. Sacramental tests thus were abolished for all Protestants (though the repeal still left standing exclusion of children of Dissenters from grammar schools and from Oxford and Cambridge, as well as restrictions on marriage and burial rites, some of which lasted until 1880). Catholic Emancipation followed a year later.[35] Once elected, a Catholic could now take his parliamentary seat without having to denounce his faith, though he still had to swear that he would make no effort at the behest of the Pope to subvert the state.[36]

Both in practice and political theory, Parliament became 'a body of mixed religious membership – it no longer consisted solely of the laity of the Establishment'.[37] Not only did the state in the main lose its confessional character, it recused itself from efforts to distinguish religious truth from religious error. But the line of inclusion continued to be drawn for the Jews. The advance of legislated toleration for Christians

---

[33] Pratap Bhanu Mehta, 'Reason, tradition, and authority: religion and the Indian State', in Creppell, Hardin and Macedo (eds.), *Toleration*, p. 193.

[34] This is a formulation offered by Geoffrey Alderman, 'English Jews or Jews of the English persuasion? Reflections on the emancipation of Anglo-Jewry', in Pierre Birnbaum and Ira Katznelson (eds.), *Paths of emancipation: Jews, states, and citizenship* (Princeton: Princeton University Press, 1995), p. 129. Memorable overviews are provided in H. S. Q. Henriques, 'The civil rights of English Jews', *The Jewish Quarterly Review* 18 (1905), 40–83; 'The political rights of English Jews', *The Jewish Quarterly Review* 19 (1907), 298–341; and 'The political rights of English Jews, II', *The Jewish Quarterly Review* 19 (1907), 751–99.

[35] A summary is offered in Michael A. Mullett, *Catholics in Britain and Ireland, 1558–1829* (New York: St Martin's Press, 1998). For the post-emancipation period, see Walter L. Arnstein, *Protestant versus Catholic in mid-Victorian England: Mr Newdegate and the Nuns* (Columbia: University of Missouri Press, 1982); and Edward Norman, *The English Catholic Church in the nineteenth century* (Oxford: Clarendon Press, 1984).

[36] A short overview of these constitutional changes can be found in L. E. Elliott-Binns, *Religion in the Victorian era* (London: Lutterworth Press, 1936). Catholic clergy continued to be prohibited from publicly appearing in ecclesiastical dress. Catholics also were precluded from holding the offices of lord chancellor and lord lieutenant of Ireland, among others.

[37] E. R. Norman, *Church and society in England, 1770–1970* (Oxford: Clarendon Press, 1976), p. 78.

'left the Jews worse off than before. They were now the only religious minority (apart from atheists) subject to serious disabilities.'[38] A bill comparable to Catholic Emancipation failed in the House in 1830 by a vote of 228 to 165. Jews continued to be ruled out for membership in Parliament, from crown offices more broadly and from corporations, though the Test and Corporation Act of 1828 benefited them indirectly by ending formal barriers to the professions (the first Jewish barrister dates from 1833). Officers supervising elections still could insist that Jews swear a Christian oath in order to vote; the vast majority, in any event, did not qualify within the ten-pound householder requirement established in 1832 by the Reform Act.

Jews ceased being one section of a much larger nonconformist population. But they were not without rights. Their condition already had altered from a population with no entitlement to enter the country, then to a community with precarious residential rights (who might still be subject to a statute passed during the reign of Edward I proscribing Jewish landholding), and then to persons who could worship openly, govern their own religious affairs, gain access to the courts, and, short of political participation, enjoy constitutional rights.

The quest for a fuller toleration that also would encompass Jewish political inclusion was led by the best-off and, in matters of religion, the non-orthodox reform-minded members of the group. They mounted claims for equal citizenship in liberal terms during the period when bills for Jewish emancipation failed either in the House or in the Lords.[39] With the return of the Whigs to power in 1847, the push accelerated. Five Jews stood as Liberals that year, but only Lionel Rothschild was elected. During the next decade, the House recurrently passed emancipation legislation, only to be refused, until 1858, by the Lords, with opponents in both houses citing the dubious moral character, economic rapacity, deformed religion and suspect nationality of the Jews ('a distinct and peculiar people', Lord Winchelsea informed his colleagues in 1858, 'bearing their nationality of character in whatever part of the world they were dispersed').[40]

As Hayek might have predicted, the position favouring toleration was closely tied to liberal arguments about the private character of belief, the importance of a voluntary sphere in civil society and the right of members of the nation, itself defined in trans-religious terms, to be

---

[38] U. R. Q. Henriques, 'The Jewish emancipation controversy in nineteenth-century Britain', *Past and Present* 40 (1968), 126.
[39] In 1846, the Religious Opinions Relief Act did extend protection for nonconformist worship and religious property to the Jews.
[40] 5 May 1858; cited in Henriques, 'Emancipation', 133.

represented in Parliament irrespective of religious conviction and standing. Liberal values concerning consent, representation and rights now provided the terms for an increasingly confident campaign that demanded full inclusion, offering the high ground of political principle in the face of traditional objections:[41]

The liberal tide which had emancipated the dissenters and the Catholics was still waxing. The electorate created by the Reform Act of 1832 ensured an almost permanent Whig majority in the House of Commons. While the century-long struggle between Whig and Liberal governments backed by a majority in the Commons, and the Conservatives entrenched in the Lords delayed Jewish emancipation for a generation, it also, eventually, induced a Whig cabinet to force it through.

What not long before had been offensive and unacceptable – the decisive removal of religious disabilities that had denied political rights to citizens – happened. This triumph over restrictive traditions had advanced by liberal assertion to fundamentally alter the religious character of Parliament, with rights to be represented and to serve as representatives having moved first from an Anglican to a more broadly Protestant frame, then from a Protestant to a Christian one, and finally, with Jewish rights, to become a trans-Christian legislature.

V

How might we best understand the shift from the quick reversal of Jewish naturalisation in 1753 to the admission of a Jewish Member of Parliament a century later? Is the development of liberal toleration best traced by a history of ideas focusing on such great texts as John Locke's *Letter concerning toleration*, composed in Amsterdam in 1685 and published anonymously in England four years later, and the even more remarkable response to the challenges and dangers of confessional pluralism within Christendom, John Toland's heterodox polemic detailing *Reasons for naturalising the Jews in Great Britain & Ireland, etc.*, a 1714 pamphlet that first used the phrase 'the emancipation of the Jews'? Or would it be better to deploy currently more fashionable instruments of historical realism that show how changes to toleration and its bonding with liberalism were matters of strategy, partisanship, instrumental reason and power?

The scholarly literature on toleration and religious liberty tends to fall into opposing evolutionary and realist camps. The first offers a chronicle

[41] Henriques, 'Emancipation', 144.

of steady success and ethical achievement. It records the advance of ever broader and appealing ideas to transcend civil disabilities for religious minorities. This record demonstrates toleration's dramatic evolution from the seventeenth century, when almost no one considered it to be a good thing, to the nineteenth century, when toleration was integrated with liberalism and achieved a positive valence, a line of development, as one 'sketch of the struggle for religious liberty of the last four hundred years' put things, that brought about a 'complete emancipation' by the mid nineteenth century.[42]

Such narratives of an ever more secular, more reasoned and more warm-hearted appreciation of religious pluralism that portray the history of toleration as a stirring line of progress in lockstep with English liberty long dominated the historiography of toleration and treatments of Jewish history in England. Now classic texts written in the first half of the twentieth century by H. F. Russell Smith, A. A. Seaton, T. Lyon and especially W. K. Jordan, and a recent assertive revival of such work in the history of ideas,[43] appreciatively detail transformations to theories of religious toleration in the early modern period after the break with Rome in 1534 was followed by the Act of Supremacy making the Queen the head of the church. Jordan's still unsurpassed four-volume survey chronicles these years as an era of 'one of the most momentous changes in the history of English thought', a shift from medieval conceptions of toleration inside 'an organic conception of Christian life' to 'the legal guarantee of free belief and the free exercise of that belief'. By 1660, he claimed, 'the conviction had gained strength in English thought that the ends of national life in the modern world could not be attained until the divisive and destructive energies of religious conflict had been tamed by toleration'. After a period of religious extremism, Anglican thought grew more moderate, the dissenting sects started to embrace religious liberty, and 'the secular forces' of political necessity, rationalism and scepticism became more prominent. On this influential view, early

---

[42] Roland H. Bainton, 'The struggle for religious liberty', *Church History* 10 (1941), 95, 119.

[43] Russell Smith, *Religious liberty*; A. A. Seaton, *The theory of toleration under the later Stuarts* (Cambridge: Cambridge University Press, 1911); T. Lyon, *The theory of religious liberty in England, 1603–39* (Cambridge: Cambridge University Press, 1937); W. K. Jordan, *The development of religious toleration in England*, 4 vols. (London: George Allen & Unwin, 1932–40); Jonathan Israel, 'Toleration in seventeenth-century Dutch and English thought', in Simon Groenveld and Michael J. Wintle (eds.), *The exchange of ideas: religion, scholarship, and art in Anglo-Dutch relations in the seventeenth century* (Zutphen: Walburg Insitut, 1994); Perez Zagorin, *How the idea of religious toleration came to the west* (Princeton: Princeton University Press, 2003); and John Coffey, *Persecution and toleration in Protestant England, 1558–1689* (Harlow: Pearson Education, 2000).

modern toleration in England thus was 'one of the most significant advances the human race has ever achieved'.[44]

An alternative history is provided by accounts that stress the expedience and expose the limits of toleration in a world marked by might and command. They offer numerous case studies that reveal the persistence of bias and bullying even in such relatively tolerant locations as Strasbourg or the Dutch Republic. On this view, when the opportunity costs of religious persecution grow too great, toleration ensues; but where the political, economic and social goals of rulers can be secured by restricting religious liberty, they will.[45] Such realism resists free-standing, progressive histories of thought, and tends to dismiss talk of toleration that is more than situationally advantageous. It rejects any suggestion that 'liberalism and religious freedom', separately or together, 'are ... predestined goals in the progress of mankind'.[46] On this critical view, toleration after the Reformation was a political concession, a pragmatic accommodation to the balance of forces, 'a function of *raison d'état* rather than a matter of principle'.[47] Toleration restricted the traditional insistence 'on an absolute unanimity in faith and practice', Herbert Butterfield famously observed, only as 'a last resort for those who often still hated one another, but found it impossible to go on fighting any more'.[48] Rejecting the 'story of the crowning triumph of liberalism and "civilised" behaviour over blind prejudice and barbarous persecution', this orientation treats toleration less as a matter of ethics or ideas, but of power. Underlining the persistence of bias and bullying under liberal and enlightened conditions, it emphasises how toleration most often has been a doctrine advanced by the weak and an idea only rarely put into practice by the strong. 'We should abandon the attempt to chart the demise of a "persecuting society" and the progress of the ideal of "toleration"' in favour of an emphasis on fear, resistance and persistent tension.[49]

[44] Jordan, *Religious toleration*, vol. I, p. 17.
[45] Anthony Gill, *The political origins of religious liberty* (Cambridge: Cambridge University Press, 2007), p. 7.
[46] Richard Helmstadter, 'Introduction', in Helmstadter (ed.), *Freedom and religion in the nineteenth century* (Stanford: Stanford University Press, 1997), p. 7.
[47] Ole Peter Grell, Jonathan I. Israel and Nicholas Tyacke, 'Introduction', in Grell, Israel and Tyacke (eds.), *From persecution to toleration: the glorious revolution and religion in England* (Oxford: Oxford University Press, 1991), p. 1.
[48] Herbert Butterfield, 'Toleration in early modern times', *Journal of the History of Ideas* 38 (1977), 573.
[49] Alexandra Walsham, *Charitable hatred: tolerance and intolerance in England, 1500–1700* (Manchester: Manchester University Press, 2006), pp. 322, 7. Other examples include three influential conference volumes: Grell, Israel and Tyacke (eds.), *Persecution to toleration*; Ole Peter Grell and Bob Scribner (eds.), *Tolerance and intolerance in the European reformation* (Cambridge: Cambridge University Press, 1996); and Ole Peter

Each viewpoint sees itself as an antagonist of the other. From the perspective of the first, what is most striking is how the zone of toleration expanded notwithstanding the pressures of bigotry, fanaticism and persecution. From the perspective of the second, the history of ideas substitutes teleology for an awareness of just how unusual, situational and evanescent toleration has been, and how often it has entwined with intolerant refusals to grant full membership even in liberal polities.

We would do well to refuse this choice, for each, to be persuasive, requires the other. Realist history and social science reminds us that there was nothing automatic or teleological about how toleration unfolded. Reciprocally, a free-standing and progressive history of ideas is radically insufficient. In law and in practice, toleration never was an uncomplicated extension of freedom, and liberalism did not necessarily fashion or link up with toleration. Nor did exclusions and patterns of persecution melt away when leading thinkers such as Locke and Toland shifted toleration from a site for theological debate about heresy and religious difference to become a political and legislative question under conditions of religious pluralism. Still, their texts, and the vast array of reflections and arguments that circulated and were debated in early modern England, did powerfully widen the available intellectual and political space for toleration. Without appreciating such ideas, and without acknowledging their engagement with broader liberal themes, the relationship between liberalism and toleration is impossible to comprehend.

Anglo-Jewish history, we have seen, clearly resists compartmentalisation in one or the other of these two contending options. English Jews, like other vulnerable groups, came to be protected from persecution and cruelty not by ideas alone, but by a combination of animating thought and reluctant expediency. If the medieval Jewish experience in England underscores how toleration once was absent from the kit-bag of liberal values and institutions, and helps us see how toleration has not been endogenous to liberal development, the second period from readmission to parliamentary inclusion teaches that only a highly particular interplay of situations and reflections on those circumstances actually advanced toleration's cause. There was nothing automatic about the innovations and adjustments that brought toleration inside liberalism's permeable circle.

The conditional quality of the Anglo-Jewish record should thus draw us to think harder about the impact of the widening latitude of ideas

Grell and Roy Porter (eds.), *Toleration in enlightenment Europe* (Cambridge: Cambridge University Press, 2000).

about toleration on practices sanctioned by Parliament, thus about how the enlargement of toleration's scope and scale in the realm of political ideas affected how political representation and lawmaking actually proceeded. From this vantage point, the key question is why there was a shift in parliamentary dispositions and behaviour from the repeal of the Jewish Naturalisation Bill in 1753 to the elimination of the group's parliamentary disabilities in 1858.

The switchboard qualities of representation that were present with such intensity to resist toleration in the revocation of the Jew Bill had played a profoundly important if paradoxical role earlier in advancing a moderate and peaceful provisional religious settlement by blocking Anglican comprehension and a place for nonconformity within limits inside the established church. After 1660, in circumstances where 'the royal person was restored but not the royal power', attempts by Charles II in tandem with sympathetic ecclesiastical authorities to implement toleration and produce religious concord by royal decree were thwarted by Parliament. Instead, between 1661 and 1664, the legislature passed statutes establishing the Clarendon Code that deepened Anglican supremacy, then the Test Act of 1672, which was extended in 1675 and 1678, that reinforced the civil disabilities of Catholics and Dissenters. Parliament also regularly failed to act on bills that reflected a moderate desire to mitigate differences among Christians and offer relief from the period's slew of indictments to nonconformists.

Parliament further insisted on its prerogatives in the face of royal efforts in the direction of toleration. When Charles issued a Declaration of Indulgence in 1672 to relieve Dissenters from particular incapacities after the 'sad experience of twelve years', as it said, had revealed the failures of religious coercion, the Commons rejoined by claiming that this involved an illegitimate usurpation of parliamentary privilege because 'penal laws could be suspended only by parliamentary enactment. In reply, the King regretted that his desire for peace had not been appreciated', and called in its place for a parliamentary indulgence, which was not forthcoming. In response, 'the Commons requested from Charles a clearer admission that he had no suspending power'.[50] This constitutional tug of war continued during the kingship of James II, who prorogued Parliament in 1687, never to meet again during his brief reign, when it challenged his decision to keep Catholic soldiers in service who, in the language of the protest sent by the Commons, were 'not qualified for their employments according to an Act of Parliament

---

[50] Mullett, 'Toleration and persecution', 20, 27.

made in the twenty-fifth year of the reign of your majesty's Royal Brother of blessed memory', and thus 'humbly represent unto your Majesty, that these officers cannot by law be capable of their employments; and that the incapacities they bring upon themselves thereby can no ways be taken off but by an Act of Parliament'.[51]

With the crucial role nonconformists had played to advance the parliamentary and Protestant cause in the Revolution of 1688, William urged Parliament in February, just before the passage of the Toleration Act, to find 'some course to beget a better union and composure in the minds of my Protestant subjects in matters of Religion'.[52] In opting for this limited relief, the Commons rejected William's call for Protestant reunification the month after the Act's passage as a means, in his words, 'to provide against the papists ... to the disappointment of our enemies'.[53] Though a comprehension bill of this kind did pass the Lords, the Commons refused to bring the majority of nonconformists inside the Anglican Church at the very moment when it was passing the Declaration of Rights to restrict royal power and strengthen parliamentary representation.

With these moves, Parliament shifted toleration from being a matter of religious governance and the supervision of doctrine and liturgy to a concern to manage the array of minority religion disabilities in a situation where a pluralism of faiths clearly would persist. Toleration took flight as the means with which to reconcile irreducible and clashing religious differences with the quest to secure peace and stability alongside parliamentary liberalism. In this particular context, toleration emerged as a complex set of layered possibilities for governmental decisions about the positive and negative regulation of religious freedom. Hovering between an expedient and a right, toleration, provisionally conjoined with liberalism, presented a series of choices. Who, or what, might be tolerated even if disliked? How great is the permissible cultural and spatial distance between those who tolerate and those who are tolerated? Which, and how many, aspects of life should fall within toleration's ambit? Are formulas for toleration impermanent and specific to particular situations of conflict and power, or must they be lasting features of a decent society? By what mechanisms should toleration be policed, from outside civil society through actions of the state or by the self-policing of communities within civil society?

---

[51] *Journal of the House of Commons*, vol. 9, 758, 759; cited in Henriques, *Return*, pp. 107–8.
[52] Cited in John Spurr, 'The Church of England, comprehension, and the Toleration Act of 1689', *The English Historical Review* 104 (1989), 934.
[53] Cited in Mullett, 'Toleration and persecution', 39.

Realists are right to stress that both in law and practice toleration never was an uncomplicated extension of freedom. They persuasively note that questions about religious regulation and deregulation were answered not by theorists of politics who articulated principles of conduct, but by political actors, pursuing interests, who would have preferred religious uniformity and ideological compliance if these could have been achieved. Patterns of exclusion and persecution, moreover, did not quickly melt away when leading thinkers shifted toleration from a site for debate about heresy and religious difference to a political and legislative question under conditions of religious pluralism. But the absence of systematic ideas and normative appraisals in such historical accounts makes it difficult to come to understand shifts in the formation and character of preferences about toleration by key actors in determinate situations. Our understanding of the formation and articulation of interests can only be curtailed and deficient without careful assessments of how key texts and the array of reflections and arguments that circulated in early modern England reshaped not just the intellectual but the political space for toleration. We know, as a non-trivial instance, that Thomas Jefferson read Locke's *Letter concerning toleration*, as well as John Milton's *Of reformation* and *The reason of church government*, and Philip Furneaux's *Essay on toleration*, as he set out in 1776 to campaign for toleration and religious liberty against the Anglican establishment in Virginia.[54] Without appreciating such ideas, and without acknowledging their engagement with broader liberal themes, the history of toleration and its relationship with liberalism are impossible to comprehend.

The hundreds, perhaps thousands, of tracts, essays and books, ranging from the ephemeral to the enduring, that sought to advance visions of toleration, whether separately or in harness with liberalism, possessed two vital features. Written to enlarge the range of possibilities, these texts offered what John Rawls has called 'realistic utopias', designs close to social reality yet still distant from immediate realisation.[55] In insisting on the worth of toleration in difficult historical circumstances, such writings pushed out the boundaries of what could be supposed and conceived, and suggested constellations of means with which to contend with coercion and bloodshed just outside and beyond existing conventional wisdom. In that way, they linked advocacy,

[54] Richard L. Greaves, 'Radicals, rights, and revolutions: British nonconformity and roots of the American experience', *Church History* 61 (1992), 151–68; and Coffey, *Persecution*, p. 208.
[55] John Rawls, *Law of Peoples* (Cambridge, MA: Harvard University Press, 1999). Useful discussions can be found in Rex Martin and David Reidy (eds.), *Rawls' law of peoples: a realistic utopia* (Oxford: Blackwell, 2006).

showing why toleration is desirable, to potentially feasible institutions and policies. Such proposals of the kind found in Locke's *Letter concerning toleration* connected abstract norms to particular historical circumstances. Such writings also grappled with how to distinguish two kinds of wrongs – those that can or should be tolerated in order to secure a good or prevent something worse, and those that should not because toleration would either protect something too awful, or bring about a dangerous or otherwise unbearable outcome within a matrix of universal moral obligation and reasoning specific to particular historical contexts and situations.

The debates and decisions about Jewish inclusion thus offer an extended occasion to discover how the relationship between toleration and liberalism was not fixed or inherent, but contested and contingent. But they also invite a consideration of how Hayek's 'of course' describes a process of engagement and enlargement – both for liberalism and toleration. When Lionel Rothschild took up his mandate, it became possible to more confidently envision toleration as essential to political liberalism, notwithstanding inherent strains and persistent perils of recidivism. The more we recognise the jagged genealogy of this achievement, and the more we acknowledge its uncertain and precarious crosscurrents, the more we can appreciate the value of liberal toleration.

3   The Enlightenment, the late eighteenth-century revolutions and their aftermath: the 'secularising' implications of Protestantism?

David M. Thompson

The word 'secular' originally distinguished parochial clergy from those in religious orders; more generally it distinguished civil political power from that of the church. 'Secularisation' was used to describe the appropriation of church property by the (secular) state, for example, Henry VIII's dissolution of the monasteries in England. The word therefore presumes opposition. As scientific methods of inquiry became more sophisticated from the seventeenth to the nineteenth century, thinkers began to wonder whether such methods were applicable to human beings themselves; several of the founding fathers of sociology and social anthropology posited their theories in deliberate opposition to religion. Just as Christians had in earlier centuries treated pagan beliefs as superstitions, so from the Enlightenment Christian beliefs in their turn were regarded as superstitious. The scientific study of humanity was thus originally a deliberately anti-religious, or more precisely anti-Christian, programme. Karl Marx is but one example. To the extent that Protestant approaches to Christianity had dismissed aspects of Catholicism as superstition and also sought to adjust Christian belief to new scientific discoveries, Protestants may be regarded as 'covert' secularisers.

It is not necessary here to enter into the debate about the relationship between the rise of modern science and the development of industrial capitalism in western Europe.[1] But at least since Max Weber sociologists have linked Protestantism and the rise of capitalism.[2] The replacement of churches, to which everyone belonged, by sects, which were voluntary associations of committed believers, was itself seen as a secularising

---

[1] R. K. Merton, *Science, technology and society in seventeenth-century England* (New York: Harper Torchbooks, 1970); 'Puritanism, pietism and science', in *Social theory and social structure* (New York: Free Press, 1968), pp. 628–58.

[2] M. Weber, 'The Protestant Sects and the spirit of capitalism', in H. H. Gerth and C. Wright Mills (trans. and eds.) *From Max Weber: essays in sociology*, (London: Routledge, 1948), pp. 302–22; cf. M. Weber, *The Protestant ethic and the spirit of capitalism*, trans. Talcott Parsons (New York: Dover, 1958).

process, because of the laity's dominance in sectarian organisation. Ernst Troeltsch, a close friend of Weber, regarded Protestantism as characteristic of 'the modern world'.[3] Industrialisation was also regarded as one of the main solvents of traditional structures of Christianity by contemporaries and subsequent historians. The link between modernisation and secularisation thus seemed obvious. According to Steve Bruce, 'the decline of religion in the modern West is not an accident but is an unintended consequence of a variety of complex social changes that for brevity we call modernisation'.[4] Although not inevitable, Bruce does believe the process is irreversible, because he sees 'the increasing cultural autonomy of the individual' as a permanent change. Individualism is also often regarded as a characteristic of Protestantism, both because of Luther's emphasis on justification by faith and the importance attached to the right of private judgement.

Bruce's essay is useful because of the clarity with which (following Weber) he locates the phenomenon in 'the West', without regarding it as inevitable elsewhere. He implicitly acknowledges that 'religion' in this case means Christianity, and thus there are no necessary implications for the fate of non-western religions. Furthermore he recognises that 'the Judeo-Christian tradition involved a considerable rationalization of religion', largely because of its monotheism. The re-mythologisation of the cosmos in early Christianity was reversed 'as the Protestant Reformation demythologized the world, eliminated the ritual manipulation of God, and restored the process of ethical rationalization'.[5] Again the role of Protestantism is highlighted. Although he affirms that the secularisation thesis 'explains the *past* of a particular part of the world',[6] this explanatory emphasis fits uneasily with his conclusion that it is 'an unintended consequence of a variety of complex social changes'. That sounds more like a description of a historical process; but descriptions are not explanations.

Even Bryan Wilson's definition of secularisation – 'the process whereby religious thinking, practice and institutions lose social significance'[7] – begs the important questions of which religion had social significance, when and for whom. Bruce is in no doubt:

[3] E. Troeltsch, *Protestantism and progress*, trans. W. Montgomery (London: Williams & Norgate, 1912), pp. 9–42. The works of both Troeltsch and Weber have tended to be treated as essentially descriptive by sociologists and historians, notwithstanding the former's firm identification with the *Religionsgeschichtliche* school and the latter's rejection of religion.

[4] S. Bruce, 'The social process of secularisation', in R. K. Fenn (ed.), *The Blackwell companion to sociology of religion* (Oxford: Blackwell, 2003), p. 262.

[5] *Ibid.*, p. 253.   [6] *Ibid.*, p. 250.

[7] B. R. Wilson, *Religion in secular society* (London: C. A. Watts, 1966), p. xiv.

The peoples of preindustrial Europe were thoroughly religious . . . Most knew by heart the Lord's Prayer and the Hail Mary, and could make the sign of the cross. They knew the Ten Commandments, the four cardinal virtues, the seven deadly sins, and the seven works of mercy. They paid their tithes, brought their babies for baptism, and married in church. They believed sufficiently in hell, the power of the church, and the unique status of Holy Writ for the swearing of oaths on the Bible to be an effective means of social control . . .[8]

The basis for this is his more nuanced article of 1997,[9] describing the historical discussion since the 1960s, when, in his words, social scientists might be expected to have a greater familiarity with history. In it he attacked the 'straw man' theory that secularisation depends on the demonstration of an earlier 'golden age', when it was normal to be religious.[10] Bruce cites both Keith Thomas and Margaret Spufford concerning the relative extent of belief in magic and religious belief in the seventeenth century, acknowledging Spufford's methodological agnosticism about the possibility of recovering quantifiable evidence for 'genuine religious conviction'. But he cites Bernard Hamilton's *Religion in the medieval west* (1986) as the basis for his generalisations.[11] Unfortunately for Bruce, in the second edition of his book Hamilton moderated some of his earlier statements, though even then he cited scarcely any evidence, other than church decrees, and he noted in his preface that

Anyone who wishes to understand the Middle Ages must come to terms with the paradox of a society in which belief was almost universal, but religious observance much of the time was fairly minimal except among a devout minority, while at the same time almost everybody was capable of responding to religious stimuli on some occasions in their lives.[12]

At the end of his 1997 article Bruce made a tactical retreat, by saying that the secularisation thesis is not actually about the decline of religion, but of belief in the supernatural:

---

[8] Bruce, *Blackwell companion*, p. 249.
[9] S. Bruce, 'The pervasive world-view: religion in pre-modern Britain', *British Journal of Sociology* 48/4 (1997), 667–80.
[10] Typified by N. Abercrombie, S. Hill and B. S. Turner, *The dominant ideology thesis* (London: Allen & Unwin, 1980).
[11] Bruce, 'The pervasive world-view', 677. Most of the references from Hamilton on this page are inaccurate.
[12] B. Hamilton, *Religion in the medieval west*, 2nd edition (London: Arnold, 2003), p. viii. Even in his first edition (London: Arnold, 1986), p. 1, Hamilton warned readers against thinking of the Middle Ages in terms of the 'well-instructed religious fervour, which was a product of the Counter-Reformation' suggesting that a more accurate analogy would be with some modern South American countries 'where the population is almost entirely Catholic, but the general degree of instruction, practice and commitment is low'.

What is required ... is that there be an identifiable difference ... in the popularity and salience of *beliefs, actions and institutions which assume the existence of supernatural entities with power of action, or impersonal powers or processes possessed of moral purpose.* (emphasis original)[13]

However, Bruce's clinching argument in 2003 was the change in the levels of popular religious practice between 1851 and 1990. What do such statistics actually show? Although Bishops' Visitation Queries in the Church of England after the Restoration began to ask questions about the numbers baptised, communicants at festivals of obligation and the size of weekly congregations, these were never totalled. Neither the Church of England nor the Catholic Church understood church membership in the same way as the Presbyterian, Independent, Baptist or Quaker dissenters. John Wesley began the modern interest in numbers by introducing class tickets, renewable each quarter, and publishing the number of class members in each circuit in the *Minutes of the Wesleyan Conference*. When the Baptist and Congregational Home Missionary Societies were formed in the early nineteenth century – the precursors of the later Baptist and Congregational Unions – they also collected statistics to encourage and justify their evangelical efforts, and this became normal in English nonconformity. But the Church of England and the Catholic Church have never produced parallel statistics; and continental Europe has not had the same interest in numbers. So, although we know that there was a significant decline in membership in the twentieth century, we do not know whether this signals a return to the pre-eighteenth-century situation (just as there are more multiple parish benefices in the Church of England because of the shortage of clergy) or a completely new situation. And the whole discussion raises the question of whether church attendance is the best measure of religiosity. For example, the increasingly widespread use of such figures in the later twentieth century as a basis for assessing the financial liability of parishes and congregations to support the payment of ministers has encouraged them to eliminate any doubtful cases.

What is not in doubt is the declining use of religious rites of passage, largely made possible by secular alternatives. Great Britain is one of the few European countries where civil marriage was not made compulsory in the nineteenth century. Perhaps more important, however, are the consequences of twentieth-century welfare systems that enabled unmarried women with children to survive financially. Civil registration of births also rendered baptism unnecessary as proof of legal identity.

---

[13] Bruce, 'The pervasive world-view', 679.

The decline in levels of religious practice as measured by the rites of passage is significant; but where religious monopoly of such rites is broken, it is difficult to be sure whether one is measuring a change in religiosity or the exposure of a potential pluralism which has been concealed.

Another question begged by the emphasis on religious practice is how far such practice in any form and at any time is exclusively the product of religious beliefs. Since the kinds of religious practice discussed – church attendance, church membership and rites of passage – are intrinsically social in character, it is impossible to avoid asking about the social pressures to behave in particular ways. However reluctantly, historians have to accept that they cannot discover in any other than a fragmentary way the extent to which religious practice was 'religiously' motivated, before questionnaire-type methods of social investigation were developed. All the religious practices mentioned should be regarded as constituting ritual in the way that Emile Durkheim used the term; such rituals need not be sacerdotal in character. This approach is different from that exemplified by Weber, which places more emphasis on belief, particularly ethical beliefs. Durkheim's emphasis that religion is essentially social led him to assert that 'radical individualism' misconceived 'the fundamental conditions of religious life'.[14] From this perspective the question is not whether a particular society is religious, but what the 'religion' of a particular society is.

This does not mean that the concept of secularisation is historically useless. Its utility lies in the history of ideas, particularly in the relation of religion and politics.[15] It has usually been linked to, but is not identical with, anti-clericalism or hostility to the hierarchical authority of the clergy.[16] That is certainly what makes the Enlightenment, the late eighteenth-century revolutions and their aftermath a particularly important period. My thesis is that secularisation happened primarily in people's minds, but not in the mind of everyone.[17] One can go back as far as Hobbes, or even Marsilius of Padua; but a commonly accepted secular understanding of European history began to emerge in the eighteenth

---

[14] E. Durkheim, *The elementary forms of the religious life,* trans. K. E. Fields (New York: Free Press, 1995), p. 427.

[15] This is another way of expressing the distinction between 'existential' and 'political' secularisation developed by Ingrid Creppell in this volume.

[16] See E. Troeltsch, *The social teaching of the Christian churches,* trans. O. Wyon (London: Allen & Unwin, 1931), pp. ii, 470–1, 591–2.

[17] See Owen Chadwick, *The secularisation of the European mind in the nineteenth century* (Cambridge: Cambridge University Press, 1975); and Nicholas Boyle's review in *The Cambridge Review,* 7 May 1976, pp. 149–52.

century. In Paul Hazard's words, 'What the critics were determined to destroy was the religious interpretation of life.'[18] As noted by Bruce earlier, the Judaeo-Christian tradition had always had a strong rationalising character: the Greek or Roman pantheons were replaced by monotheism, which was closer to a philosophical first cause. An understanding of God as creator meant that discovery of the 'laws of nature' was tantamount to discovering the laws, or even the mind, of the creator. By the time of Francis Bacon the distinction between primary and secondary causes was well established, giving in effect a licence to explore the world of secondary causes without limit. The last stage was to ask whether the first cause was still necessary to the explanation. More sharply, did it make sense for God to intervene in the world? If not, did this reduce God to the 'absentee watchmaker', as Leslie Stephen (unfairly) criticised Paley for doing?[19]

The issue was the role of providence. Here a significant divide opened up between elite and popular culture. In the writing of history, God was quickly banished as an irrelevance. B. G. Niebuhr's *History of Rome* (first German edition, 1812, E. T. vols. I and II 1828) was significant because it went behind myths of origins to create a historical narrative based on recoverable evidence, linguistic and archaeological. Its first English translators, Julius Hare and Connop Thirlwall, both became distinguished Victorian clergymen after their time as Fellows of Trinity College, Cambridge. They were keenly aware of the significance of this work for the appraisal of the early books of the Old Testament, but were completely untroubled by the implications of this for Christian faith.[20] Similarly, even German biblical critics like David Strauss, whose *Life of Jesus critically examined* (1835–6) eventually cost him his job at Zurich, believed they were offering a believable Christianity for the nineteenth century. Most twentieth-century Christian theologians doubted the historicity of Genesis. But the extent to which any of these views penetrated the mass of the population was limited. Tom Paine's *Age of reason* (1795) appalled many, as much because it was spreading such views among the people, as because it was untrue. In fact many of the problems in biblical criticism, which exercised the minds of middle-class professors in Germany and Britain in the 1830s and 1840s, had already been the stuff

---

[18] P. Hazard, *European thought in the eighteenth century* (London: Hollis & Carter, 1954), p. xviii.

[19] 'The contrivance once put together, and the religion once revealed, God interferes no more.' L. Stephen, *English thought in the eighteenth century*, 2nd edition (London: Smith, Elder, 1881), pp. i, 415.

[20] D. M. Thompson, *Cambridge theology in the nineteenth century* (Aldershot: Ashgate, 2008), pp. 78–81.

of popular knockabout anti-religious rhetoric for thirty years or more.[21] The so-called mid-nineteenth-century 'crisis of faith' was very much a problem for the intellectual classes, and had strikingly little impact on working-class evangelical religion. Although some working-class autodidacts became enthusiastic secularists, others became increasingly critical of middle-class evangelical (or Catholic) clergy, who continued to espouse incredible views. Much work on popular culture has shown that a belief in providence remains a mainstay of working-class attitudes to life, though it can also be seen in terms of luck, or chance or fate. So any generalisation about secularisation, which implies a shift in the significance of providence, needs qualification.

Some Enlightenment scholars set out to write (or rewrite) history from an anti-clerical point of view. The principal place in England is occupied by Edward Gibbon's *Decline and fall of the Roman Empire* (1776–88), with his deliberate reversal of the view that Christianity was the crowning glory of the Roman Empire. His famous fifteenth chapter virtually set the programme of Christian apologetic for the century following, and his reference to 'the indissoluble connexion of civil and ecclesiastical affairs' as he paused to reflect on the situation at the end of the fifth century implicitly raised the question of whether such a connection was necessary, desirable or permanent.[22] By contrast Edmund Burke, in reflecting on the French Revolution, began his counter-argument about the English constitution by affirming that the 'consecration of the state, by a state religious establishment, is necessary ... to operate with a wholesome awe upon free citizens'.[23]

The Enlightenment, whenever and wherever it is located, was a movement of thought based on reason. Reason was regarded as a universal human possession – hence the inherently universalising tendencies of Enlightenment thinkers – and also accessible to all in a way in which revelation-based religions were not. It is another of the ironies of history that the recovery of a reason-based discourse in twelfth- and thirteenth-century Europe was related to the need to find a basis on which adherents of the three revelation-based faiths in Europe at that

---

[21] T. Larsen, *Contested Christianity: the political and social contexts of Victorian theology* (Waco: Baylor University Press, 2004), pp. 43–58, 79–95.

[22] 'The indissoluble connection of civil and ecclesiastical affairs has compelled and encouraged me to relate the progress, the persecutions, the establishment, the divisions, the final triumph, and the gradual corruption of Christianity.' E. Gibbon, *The history of the decline and fall of the Roman Empire*, ed. D. Milman, F. Guizot and W. Smith (London: Murray, 1908), vol. IV, p. 305. Chapter 15 is in volume II, pp. 151–219.

[23] Edmund Burke, *Reflections on the revolution in France*, ed. J. C. D. Clark, (Stanford: Stanford University Press, 2001), p. 257.

time – Christianity, Judaism and Islam – could talk to one another. Similarly the religious wars of the seventeenth century led to a new hope that reason could resolve religious differences, arguably laying the foundations for the Enlightenment itself. In Catholic countries the Enlightenment generally took a straight anti-clerical form, whereas Protestant countries were more sympathetic to the Enlightenment. What was more problematic was where to draw the line: just how far could reason go?

Burke's *Reflections on the revolution in France* were prompted by Dr Richard Price's sermon, later published as *A discourse on the love of our country*, at his chapel in the Old Jewry on 4 November 1789, which he compared with the more radical sermons of the Civil War period. Burke denied that politics had any place in the pulpit, and also Price's claim that the king of Great Britain was the only monarch who owed his throne to the choice of his people. So his later argument for a religious establishment depended on a careful separation of the roles of church and state. In this respect it was in perfect continuity with the principles of the Protestant Reformation, when secular political power asserted its pre-eminence over the church. Burke's position differs from medieval Christendom but is more reminiscent of Justinian or Theodosius.

A brief excursus on the Roman Empire is illuminating. The *Ara Pacis*, the altar erected for the imperial cult by Augustus in 13 BC, has now been repaired and housed in a new museum in Rome, with a detailed explanation of its relationship to the Pantheon and the Campus Martius. It is a reminder of the significance of the imperial cult, to which ancient historians are now paying more attention. A. H. M. Jones asserted confidently 'that the later Roman empire was intensely religious'.[24] Nearly seventy years earlier Samuel Dill used 'the tenacity of paganism' to describe the same period. Unlike Jones, Dill referred directly to the imperial cult, describing religious conservatism as the most difficult form of attachment to the past to overcome:

this form of attachment is peculiarly obstinate when it is identified, as religion has so often been, with patriotic reverence for the glory of an ancient state ... Superstitious fancy, or the seductive charm of ancient festivals, may keep the vulgar constant to the old faith; but the class which in high office has been specially charged with the safety of the State, and which, by a chain of real or imagined ancestry, is more closely identified with its career, is penetrated with a deeper conservatism than that of the common herd.[25]

[24] A. H. M. Jones, *The later Roman Empire, 284–602* (Oxford: Blackwell, 1964), pp. ii, 938, 957.
[25] S. Dill, *Roman society in the last century of the western Empire*, 2nd edition (London: Macmillan, 1899), p. 3.

The recent volumes of the *Cambridge ancient history* offer a new appraisal of the imperial cult. Simon Price argues that in the Augustan period Roman religion was restructured around Augustus, seen as a new Romulus. Moreover the traditional religion of place was reinforced by the new ruler cult, expressed in the fact that the office of *pontifex maximus* became, from the time Augustus acquired it in 12 BC, 'the keystone of the religious system'.[26]

This is why the imperial cult caused Jews and Christians such concern in the first three centuries of the Christian era. The twentieth century demonstrated in a new way the significance of ritual ceremonies glorifying secular rulers, and the dire political consequences of ignoring them. When Damasus I as bishop of Rome assumed the title of *pontifex maximus* towards the end of the fourth century, this was not just a secular tail wagging a religious dog: the assumptions of one religious system were transferred to another. The Christian emperors, Theodosius and Justinian, made no such claim, whereas the bishops of Rome did. Which was the more authentic Christian position, or was neither in the spirit of the New Testament?

Historical context is relevant for two reasons: first, it is not self-evident that either the Enlightenment or the Protestant Reformation are the obvious points at which to begin any discussion of secularisation, though each is distinctively important; and secondly, a broader historical view relativises the significance of both those and other significant events, such as the fifteenth-century Renaissance. The emphasis on classical civilisation characteristic of both the Renaissance and the Enlightenment makes the place of religion in the Roman Empire worth pondering. In so far as the imperial cult was a religious ratification of the political order, it raises questions about the 'secular' interpretation of classical civilisation presented by its eighteenth-century champions. More specifically it provokes the question of whether the political developments of the last few centuries simply mark the abandonment by the European political orders of the Christian buttressing which they acquired as a result of the 'secularisation' of Christianity in the fourth century.

What is fascinating about the revolutionary or secularist schemes of the late eighteenth and early nineteenth century is the way in which new rituals replaced Christian ones. Those of revolutionary France have faded somewhat; but the inauguration ceremony for a new president of the USA continued to appropriate ostensibly Christian overtones during

[26] A. K. Bowman, E. Champlin and A. Lintott, *The Cambridge ancient history*, vol. X: *The Augustan Empire, 43 BC–AD 69*, 2nd edition (Cambridge: Cambridge University Press, 1996), pp. 812–47 (quotation p. 827).

the 1950s.[27] From the point of view of civil government the whole direction of the secularisation hypothesis may have been misconceived. Instead of looking at how the churches have been marginalised according to a narrow understanding of religion, historians should have examined how 'secular' government has assumed quasi-religious roles and functions vis-à-vis the governed.

However complete secularisation may have been in religious practice or historical ideas, there is no doubt about the radical change in the institutional relations between churches and the state following the American and French Revolutions. In earlier times the church, as the only institution of social mobility in an aristocratic society, had supplied the stipends for those of relatively lowly social status, who rose to positions of political influence. As that became less necessary, the churches in different countries sought appropriate internal autonomy, albeit at different paces. As a result the notion of the state itself was changed, and the basis for legitimacy was found less in religion and more on exclusively political grounds, whether prescription or popular consent. With this religious autonomy in the USA and Great Britain there was a growing religious pluralism.[28] Pluralism was a more positive position than toleration; and the 'strong' theological argument for toleration – that it was inappropriate to make human formulations as binding as revelation – can be distinguished from a 'weak' political argument – that religious agreement between different groups is difficult or impossible to attain. These positions were more characteristically Protestant than Catholic. The emergence of religious autonomy or pluralism was therefore an important shift. The largest Protestant churches – the state churches of England, Scotland, Germany and Scandinavia – had already legitimated a new place for the political ruler in the governance of the church.[29]

In continental Europe the recovery of autonomy in Protestant churches began after the Congress of Vienna.[30] The lead was taken by

[27] In 1903–4 Weber was annoyed to find that the US Supreme Court and the Party Conventions opened with prayer: Gerth and Mills, *From Max Weber*, p. 303.

[28] See S. E. Mead, *The old religion in the brave new world* (Berkeley: University of California Press, 1977); N. O. Hatch, *The democratization of American Christianity* (New Haven: Yale University Press, 1989).

[29] H. Lehmann, 'Continental Protestant Europe,' in S. J. Brown and T. Tackett (eds.), *The Cambridge history of Christianity*, vol. VIII *Enlightenment, reawakening and revolution, 1660–1815* (Cambridge: Cambridge University Press, 2006), pp. 33–53, especially pp. 52–3. Gallicanism in France and Josephism in Austria were Catholic examples of the same tendency.

[30] N. Hope, *German and Scandinavian Protestantism, 1700 to 1918* (Oxford: Clarendon Press, 1995), pp. 316–53, 456–96.

the Reformed (as distinct from Lutheran) churches in some of the German states, Holland, Switzerland and Scotland. Reformed church polity, following Calvin, was always less comfortable with an ecclesiastical role for the civil ruler: a *summus episcopus* did not sit easily within their structures, and not only because they generally did not have bishops. The Disruption of the Church of Scotland in 1843 was the most spectacular example of the schism such claims for autonomy could cause, when 400 ministers of the Church of Scotland left the establishment and set up the Free Church of Scotland as a rival to it through the length and breadth of the country. The result was a curious combination of anti-landlord sentiment in the Highlands and emerging middle-class industrialists in the Lowlands, but the popular rallying cry was an appeal to surviving Covenanting sentiments from the seventeenth century.[31] In some of the Rhineland states in Germany, where Reformed outnumbered Lutherans, it was possible after the end of the Holy Roman Empire in 1806 to create autonomous churches, which were still *Landeskirchen*. The Protestant cantons of Switzerland were different again, with a clash between the 'enlightened' approach to doctrine of the older generation of pastors, and a new movement of revival, comparable to (and linked with) the evangelical revival in Britain and the USA.

In the United Kingdom the Protestant Churches of England and Scotland defended the established political order firmly, notwithstanding their limited internal autonomy. The Church of England feared the loss of its rights and privileges in the radical climate created by the French Revolution in the 1790s, and also after 1815. The grounds for this position were essentially Protestant, with high churchmen defending the Reformation settlement as much as evangelicals. Such Protestant sentiment was affronted by Catholic Emancipation in 1829, which was why Peel lost his seat as MP for Oxford University.[32] Nor did it die then.[33] Protestant/Catholic differences remained fundamental to Irish politics throughout the nineteenth century and into the twentieth, and there were echoes of what are more often regarded as the problems of

---

[31] T. Brown, *Annals of the disruption* (Edinburgh: Macniven & Wallace, 1890) shows how Free Churchmen saw the conflict. The phrase 'the crown rights of the Redeemer', which seems to have been coined by Robert Candlish, was represented as the essence of the Covenanters' position, though that usage of 'rights' was uncharacteristic of mid-seventeenth-century political discourse.

[32] R. Hole, *Pulpits, politics and public order in England, 1760–1832* (Cambridge: Cambridge University Press, 1989), pp. 238–44; R. Brent, *Liberal Anglican politics* (Oxford: Clarendon Press, 1987), p. 23.

[33] See J. Wolffe, *The Protestant crusade in Great Britain, 1829–1860* (Oxford: Clarendon Press, 1989).

Belfast in Liverpool and Glasgow until the late twentieth century. Although John Henry Newman linked the beginning of the Oxford Movement with John Keble's Assize Sermon in 1833 attacking the government's proposals to reorganise the Irish Church – timid proposals by comparison with the reorganisation of diocesan boundaries in France and Germany as a result of the Revolution – the political dimension of the movement was forgotten almost immediately; and the *Tracts for the Times* were concerned with pastoral, liturgical and theological topics. The movement's re-presentation of the Church of England by minimising the significance of the Reformation was an innovation, recognised as such at the time, though it is now the norm for the church's self-understanding.

What is striking about church reform in Britain is the extent to which the churches embraced secular agendas. The utilitarian justification offered for the establishment of the Church of England goes back beyond Paley to Bishop William Warburton's *Alliance between Church and State* (1736).[34] In this respect there was little difference between Whig and Tory approaches to church reform, and what they had in common is more significant. Sir James Graham, a Tory, told the House of Commons in the debate on the final petition from the General Assembly of the Church of Scotland that 'It is true ... that the Church is not the creature of the State, but still the state employs the Church on certain terms, as the religious instructor of the people of Scotland.'[35] The trio of Anglican bishops who ran the Ecclesiastical Commission, which initiated the reforms in the Church of England of the 1830s, Blomfield, Kaye and Monk, were all educated at Cambridge and accepted a general utilitarian understanding of the church as an agency of religious education, modelled more on William Paley than Jeremy Bentham. It is usually forgotten that the 1851 census of religious worship was half of a dual exercise, the other half being the census of provision for education; which is why church accommodation, rather

---

[34] 'If truth and public utility coincide, the nearer any Religion approaches to the Truth of Things, the fitter that Religion is for the Service of the State.' W. Warburton, *The alliance between Church and State*, 4th edition (London, 1766), p. 89. Warburton argued that religion in its 'natural independent state' would cause mischief to civil society.

[35] *Parliamentary Debates*, 3rd series, lxvii, p. 385 (7 March 1843); cited, in part, by H. Laski, *Studies in the problem of sovereignty* (reprinted London: Allen & Unwin, 1968), p. 59. No historian, who defends the established Church of Scotland, ever quotes these words. Even Graham's biographers disagree on his later thoughts: T. M. Torrens, *The life and times of the Right Honourable Sir James R. G. Graham* (London: Saunders & Otley, 1863), pp. ii, 233, said that he 'looked back with deep regret' on his policy, but his daughter insisted that he never changed his mind (J. T. Ward, *Sir James Graham*, London: Macmillan, 1967, p. 202).

than church attendance, was the original focus of attention, and also why Sunday school attendances were collected as carefully as attendances at public worship. The census was a practical demonstration of this educational understanding of religion, quite apart from what it suggests about the churches' function as agents of social control.[36]

Continental Lutheran churches also backed the new political order after Vienna. Denmark is now alone in Europe in having a Protestant church, which is totally subordinate to parliament.[37] The contrast between the Free Church of Scotland's claims for independence of the state in matters spiritual and the Danish Church's lack of any power of independent action is remarkable. In Sweden it remained illegal to be a Roman Catholic until the twentieth century; and the evangelical movement, which became the Swedish Covenant Church, was kept technically within the established Lutheran Church. In the German states the Lutheran churches generally acquired some internal autonomy, because of the necessity to make legal provision for Catholics as well as Protestants. The most striking ecclesiastical development of the nineteenth century was Frederick William III's creation by royal fiat of the Old Prussian Union of 1817 – a union of Lutheran and Reformed, which so offended some of the high Lutherans that they emigrated to the USA in the 1830s. Even the liturgical reforms longed for by the Oxford Movement in England were actually brought about in parts of Germany and Scandinavia in the early nineteenth century, demonstrating a Romantic as much as a Catholic tendency in such liturgical reform, which also shows that the Catholic Church of England imagined by the Oxford Movement could be found elsewhere in Europe with an even stronger Reformation pedigree.[38]

How does the most creative (or poisonous) piece of imagination in the nineteenth century – nationalism – relate to religion? Nationalism sacralises the state, and thus has strong religious, or quasi-religious, overtones, which are a reminder of the broader sociological or

---

[36] See the chapters by J. M. Goldstrom & D. M. Thompson on the educational and religious censuses in R. Lawton (ed.), *The census and social structure* (London: Cass, 1978).
[37] A church council was intended in the Danish constitution of 1849, but it was never set up because of disagreement over its composition. Between 1901 and 1922 it was agreed to establish congregational councils, but parliament retained effective control. 'The people's church has no single-highest ecclesiastical organ, such as a synod of priests and laity, an Archbishop, or a bishops' assembly, which is empowered to speak on behalf of the Danish people's church. In this sense there really is no one who can set the agenda.' M. S. Lausten, *A church history of Denmark* (Aldershot: Ashgate, 2002), p. 283, cf. pp. 229–33, 278–84.
[38] Hope, *German and Scandinavian Protestantism*, pp. 471–81, 447, 281–300.

anthropological understandings of religion, so effectively utilised in late twentieth-century historical studies. A discussion of nationalism in exclusively Romantic terms conceals the significance of earlier biblical antecedents. Aspects of nineteenth-century nationalism have a Protestant pre-history. The translation of the Bible into the vernacular, typical of Protestantism, enabled people to read whole books rather than simply the lectionary readings or extracts in Books of Hours.[39] One principal consequence was a new emphasis on the Old Testament. The New Testament offered little helpful political guidance on the exercise of power. The Old Testament, however, was full of stories of good, and bad, kings, with the consequences of bad rule clearly spelt out. From the Old Testament Protestants drew their principal arguments against the idolatry they found in the Roman Church. The most potent emphases in nationalism – on a promised land and a people of pure race – also came from the Old Testament. The concept of the 'elect nation' is almost a defining characteristic of any form of nationalism. New Testament Christianity abandoned the idea of one particular chosen nation – Jesus and the apostles failed to pick up the motif of 'the promised land' – but when Protestant Reformers read the Old Testament literally rather than typologically, the way was open for the reintroduction of those themes into Christian teaching.

The Calvinist appeal to the elect nation in Holland, England and New England in the seventeenth century has often been noticed; but the idea did not die then.[40] The association of the idea with Puritan government in the Commonwealth period is a reminder that nationalism can go hand in hand with constitutionalism. Indeed for Great Britain Protestant constitutionalism was the defining form of nationalism; hence the significance of the Glorious Revolution, and the slightly puzzled sense Orangemen have that the rest of the British Isles no longer thinks like them.[41] Commentators today, who draw attention to what they regard as anachronistic survivals of the Revolution such as the Act of Settlement of 1701, are like so many Rip Van Winkles, who have awakened after a deep sleep to discover what the English constitution really is.[42]

[39] E. Duffy, *Marking the hours: English people and their prayers, 1240–1570* (New Haven: Yale University Press, 2006).

[40] The concept was also common in Catholic Spain and France.

[41] The implications of this for foreign policy in the early eighteenth century are discussed in A. C. Thompson, *Britain, Hanover and the Protestant interest, 1688–1756* (Woodbridge: Boydell, 2006).

[42] I am not defending the Act of Settlement, but pointing out the intrinsic link between religion and the constitution.

Even the restored monarchy retained certain religious practices, which celebrated the state as much as Christianity. The proclamation of fast days, for public penance and prayer – a key dimension of the liturgical calendar of the Reformed Church of England – was last used in the reign of William IV for the cholera epidemic of 1832. The state services – commemorating the accession of the monarch, the gunpowder plot, the execution of Charles I, the Restoration of Charles II – were abolished in 1859, apart from the accession service; although King Charles, now seen as a martyr, is commemorated in the new Church of England Calendar.[43] This is 'the imperial cult' dimension of Anglicanism. It might be evidence of secularisation, or a broader Christian Calendar, no longer confined to the earliest times. But the latter interpretation (intended by the liturgical revisers) implies that the New Testament political situation of the church as a minority movement, both in relation to Judaism and the Roman Empire, is now taken more seriously theologically than Old Testament analogies linking religion and political power. In such a view Ezra and Nehemiah, instead of being heroes of a restored exiled community, might be seen as those who betrayed the wider vision of Deutero-Isaiah through their emphasis on ethnic purity, which created problems between Jews and Samaritans in Jesus' day, and an ambiguous legacy for the modern world.

Furthermore a common Protestantism could hold together otherwise incompatible ecclesiastical settlements in England and Scotland in a single nation.[44] In Germany Protestantism was a more problematic defining national characteristic, because of the larger proportion of Catholics. Nowhere in Germany, even in Prussia, which had the highest proportion of Protestants, could Catholics be ignored. This was one permanent legacy of the Peace of Westphalia. Nevertheless German history has often been treated as Prussian history writ large, which is regrettable, not only because of a tendency to marginalise Bavaria and Württemberg (to name but two), but because it prioritises one stream of German history.

The University of Berlin was a nineteenth-century foundation – one of the 'new' universities of Europe. Two of its professors, Hegel and Schleiermacher, are particularly associated with the relationship between religion in general (and Protestantism in particular) and

---

[43] The Calendar in *Common worship* (London: Church House, 2000) commemorates many from the Reformation to the twentieth century, including non-Anglicans such as John Bunyan, Isaac Watts, the Wesley brothers and William Booth.

[44] L. Colley, *Britons: forging the nation, 1707–1837* (New Haven: Yale University Press, 1992) offers one interpretation of this.

nationalism.[45] Hegel's argument that the nation is a necessary element in political society and that certain 'world-historical' nations each have their moment in world history comes so near the end of *The philosophy of right* that many readers have given up by then and miss its significance; but he uses a similar argument in his lectures on *The philosophy of religion* in relation to particular faith traditions. Thus, just as the Germanic realm 'grasps the principle of the unity of the divine nature and the human', so the consummate religion is specified as that in which 'the unity of divine and human nature ... appear in *just one human being*'.[46] For Hegel Christianity (i.e. Protestant Christianity) is the final development in religion, such that Christianity and religion can be equated. Schleiermacher, from a very different, pietist background, also saw Protestant Christianity as the binding force of the new German state. He criticised the King's decision to create the Old Prussian Union, and had reservations about aspects of the King's ecclesiastical legislation; but he retained the favour of the court.[47] More could be written in English about the views of other German university professors, for example at Göttingen, Tübingen and Heidelberg. Some theology professors at Göttingen protested at the abolition of the 1833 Hanoverian constitution in 1837, as did the brothers Grimm, who certainly had strong nationalist views. Many of those professors became members of the Frankfurt Parliament in 1848, illustrating the German links between liberalism and nationalism.[48]

Across the Atlantic in the last thirty years American historians, such as Sidney Mead, Nathan Hatch and Mark Noll, have drawn attention to the crucial significance of the evangelical revival in eighteenth- and nineteenth-century North America. The chief beneficiaries of those revivals were Methodists and Baptists, rather than the Congregationalists, Presbyterians and Anglicans – the established churches socially, if not always politically, of the Thirteen Colonies. The reason they give is important. Revivals were dominated by the laity, and embodied the right of people to make up their own minds in religion. They were religiously 'democratic'. Although Methodists, more than the Baptists,

---

[45] T. H. Howard, *Protestant theology and the making of the modern German university* (Oxford: Oxford University Press, 2006), especially pp. 212–66.

[46] G. W. F. Hegel, *The philosophy of right*, trans. T. M. Knox (Oxford: Clarendon Press, 1942), §358, p. 222; G. W. F. Hegel, *Lectures on the philosophy of religion (The lectures of 1827)*, ed. P.C. Hodgson (Berkeley: University of California Press, 1988), p. 455.

[47] Hope, *German and Scandinavian Protestantism*, p. 322.

[48] C. D. Thompson, 'Politics and state-building in *Vormärz* Hanover: the role of King Ernst August, 1837–51', unpublished PhD dissertation, University of Cambridge, 2007, pp. 65, 81–96.

struggled to affirm the role of the clergy, in the revival days there were not enough ministers to serve all the new churches. Thus, as in Africa today, Christianity expanded as a lay rather than a clerical movement. Although Tom Paine's *Age of reason* was banned in Britain because it publicised biblical discrepancies, which were particularly threatening to Protestantism in the absence of an ecclesiastical teaching authority, this did not seem to hinder the growth of evangelical Christianity in the USA. Lay dominance in the expansion of North American Protestantism after the First and Second Great Awakenings reinforced the separation of church and state. None of the fastest growing denominations in that period were established churches. However, within two generations the institutionalisation of the North American denominations had created their own clergy and the colleges to train them, even if their curricula were initially different from those of classical theological seminaries. What Max Weber and Ernst Troeltsch saw in the United States in 1904 convinced them of the vitality of what they called 'sects', i.e. voluntary, rather than established, churches. Weber saw even in this development signs of secularisation.[49]

The interchange between the North American and British Free Churches in the nineteenth century explains why the North American model is also relevant in Britain. The American separation of church and state remained an aspiration for the British Free Churches until well into the twentieth century, even though the disestablishment of the Church of Ireland, and later the Welsh dioceses of the Church of England weakened the general cause. If disestablishment is a secularising solution to church–state relations, then the decline of Protestant nonconformity in the twentieth century might be evidence for the waning of secularisation. Relatively few modern British historians are Protestant nonconformists today by comparison with a century ago. The writing of history has increasingly been dominated by those who have not appreciated the significance of religious diversity. This is one reason why many are surprised to discover that more of the population are religious – in some sense – than they had supposed.

A similar prioritisation of the historical concerns of one section of the political classes is found in both France and Germany in the nineteenth century. For many years the political history of nineteenth-century France was written as though the Revolution had eliminated religion. But the rate of recruitment to religious orders, particularly for women,

---

[49] Weber, 'The Protestant sects', *From Max Weber*, pp. 304–8; W. Pauck, *Harnack and Troeltsch: two historical theologians* (New York: Oxford University Press, 1968), pp. 71–3. (Pauck mistakes the date of their visit.)

shows that even amid the anti-clericalism of the Third Republic numbers continued to grow steadily. One curious effect of the 'revolutionary' view was that the popularity of right-wing, anti-Semitic religious support for the anti-Dreyfusard party became inexplicable. What really tested the position of the Catholic Church was the withdrawal of state funding after 1905. Nor should the significance of French Protestant support for the Republicans be ignored. Protestant support for secular solutions was probably greater in France than Free Church support for similar secular solutions to problems such as education in England. In imperial Germany after 1870 the *Kulturkampf* exposed how easily religious issues could become a political driving force. If the 'enemy' is simply identified as ultramontanism, the analysis can be presented as a traditional Catholic/Protestant or conservative/liberal divide; but if the issue is independence of the church from political control, the groupings change, so that in England, for example, Catholics and nonconformists are together against Anglicans. And it only takes a surge of immigration, whether of eastern European Jews in the late nineteenth century or of Pakistani Muslims and Indian Hindus in the mid twentieth century to raise another set of questions: is the apparent hostility the result of competition for jobs, xenophobia or perceived religious difference?

Finally, it is interesting to reflect that in Max Weber's *Sociology of religion* there are only two direct references to secularisation. Both come in the chapter on 'Asceticism, mysticism and salvation religion'. The first notes that ancient Buddhism recommended inaction as the precondition for maintaining the state of grace, because 'rational, purposive activity' was 'regarded as the most dangerous form of secularization'.[50] Secondly, Weber suggests that in so far as an inner-worldly religion of salvation was determined by contemplative features, 'the usual result is the acceptance of the secular social structure which happens to be at hand'.[51] Such people would not be in a rush to change the world. Weber's point that inner-worldly asceticism can lead to an unquestioning acceptance of the social and political status quo indicates his concern about the political implications of religion; and his argument elsewhere that a this-worldly asceticism, combined with a sense of personal calling, might explain the rise of capitalism, is an alternative analysis of the implications of religious commitment. Troeltsch, from a liberal Protestant perspective, despite a residual belief in the superiority of the church form of Christianity, felt that

[50] M. Weber, *The sociology of religion* (London: Methuen, 1965), p. 171.
[51] *Ibid.*, pp. 175–6.

sects better preserved the vitality of religion. But he also feared that all religious movements were losing influence.[52]

Weber's view was milder than the biting words of Søren Kierkegaard in Denmark, who wrote that 'If we are all Christians, *eo ipso* Christianity does not exist', adding:

> The human race ... sagacious as it is, perceived that Christianity could not be thrown out by power – so let us do it by slyness: we are all Christians; then Christianity *eo ipso* is abolished. And that is where we are now. The whole thing is skulduggery ... we reassure ourselves with 'We will all be saved' or 'I will be saved just like the others', since with that label one is not received into heaven; one arrives there no more than one reaches Australia by land.[53]

Kierkegaard is the nineteenth-century critic of Christendom who most clearly regarded the establishment of Christianity as a betrayal of its underlying spirit. (Does this have anything to do with the Danish constitution described earlier?) Both Weber and Kierkegaard therefore regarded accommodation to worldly structures as a betrayal of the original religious ideal; but readiness to suffer persecution remains a puzzle for the rationalist worldview.

That raises sharply the question of how secularisation is understood, and particularly whether it is seen as a political or a religious question. One view might be that the key is political power: that government, initially the Roman Empire, but subsequently repeated elsewhere, exploited Christianity to support the political order (and the same might be true of other faiths in countries outside Europe). In such situations those of other faiths either have to subordinate their own faith to that of the state or remain outside the political system. The development of political democracy makes the latter option problematic, both for the ruled and the rulers. Hence the idea of separation of church and state, or the privatisation of religion, developed. Marx's *Essay on the Jewish Question* (or Bruno Bauer's essay to which it was a response) is the *locus classicus* for the idea of the privatisation of religion, and reflects one form of secularisation in nineteenth-century Europe.[54] An alternative view might emphasise the wish of religious traditions to mould the state in their own image – whether the medieval Catholic Church, seventeenth-century Puritans or nineteenth-century nonconformists and social

[52] Troeltsch, *Social teaching*, pp. ii, 1006–13. (Written in 1911.)
[53] S. Kierkegaard, 'The moment, no. 5, 27 July 1855,' in H. V. Hong and E. H. Hong (eds.), *Kierkegaard's writings, XXIII: 'The moment' and late writings* (Princeton: Princeton University Press, 1998), pp. 187–8.
[54] J. O'Malley (ed.), *Marx: early political writings* (Cambridge: Cambridge University Press, 1994), pp. 31, 36, 38.

gospellers. The success of such efforts has varied from time to time and place to place. But there is no obvious reciprocal relationship between these two kinds of development; and it is essential not to confuse them in the analysis of political society. The separation of church and state frees the churches to become political actors in the same way as any other political pressure group. Nineteenth-century English nonconformity is an early example. It is not therefore surprising if religious groups are more politically active in a 'secular' society than in one with an established religion: the political campaign is the only avenue left open, once privileged access to government is cut off. Furthermore, non-Christian faith groups, which have never enjoyed any kind of 'establishment' status, are quite likely to become politically active sooner than those with lingering establishment aspirations. This was exactly what Bishop Warburton sought to avoid in the eighteenth century, by pointing out that if religion was independent it was likely to cause 'civil mischief'. A secular state works well if everyone agrees that religion is unimportant: even if only a minority do not believe that, there are problems. The failure of 'rational critics' to acknowledge such minorities is simply obfuscation.

Serious confusion arises if 'secularisation' is used to describe both the failure of religious groups to impose their values on the society in which they live and also the process by which political societies abandon their historic support of particular religious traditions in favour of their own quasi-religious substitutes. In modern times the most popular substitute has been some kind of nationalism. The critical questions for reflection do not concern the strength or otherwise of what are conventionally called 'religious' systems of belief and practice, but the relative significance of the systems of belief and practice, which either support or challenge political power.

4 In the lands of the Ottomans: religion and politics

Karen Barkey

Introduction

While the relationship between religion and politics has always been interesting to scholars, its study has acquired a special urgency in the last decade. This urgency is associated with the rise of fundamentalism within different religions, the increasing use of the religious idiom in politics and the apparent reversal of the long-standing secularisation thesis. While the belief that secularisation had become the way of the world has been strong since the late nineteenth century, careful study of the relationship between religion and politics actually shows that religion remained in the social and political realm and that secularisation did not destroy but instead based itself on particular state–church arrangements. Today, as we experience a resurgence of the religious idiom, the relationship between religion and politics has become as controversial as it is urgent, requiring scrutiny in a variety of contexts, time periods and political formations. As we move towards more in-depth analytic studies of how religion and politics perform, we need to treat them as separate institutional frames, paying attention to the different relations engendered at different times and in different contexts while remaining faithful to the idea that processes of institutional continuity and change are both equally possible.

The changing position of religion in modern Turkey and its predecessor, the Ottoman Empire, presents an excellent case study of a negotiated and contested relationship between religion and politics. Turkey's current post-Islamist government remains an important example of a relatively successful negotiated outcome between state and religion, demonstrating that Islam, modernity and democracy can coexist and that Islam can be a force for moderate rather than necessarily fundamentalist politics. The recent accommodation between Islam and politics has been associated with a response to the intense secularisation of late Ottoman, early Republican states. Atatürk's reforms have become the easy trope upon which an explanation of Islamism is all too easily built.

Instead, I present an alternative, more historicised and analytic perspective on the relationship between religion and politics in Turkey. I believe that it is more fruitful to study a longer time span of the relationship between politics and religion, looking at varying arrangements through time to explore the underlying logic of structures and decision-making for each. Such a perspective leads me to explore the Ottoman antecedents of the particular relation between state and Islam today. This chapter deliberately pursues a historical approach to the institutional continuities and discontinuities between the past and the present as well as the path-dependent manner in which social actors innovate. In three main sections, an analytic overview of Ottoman Islam, a transitional moment between empire and nation state and the modern re-embodiment of a reformulated Turkish Islam, I show that with regard to the role of Islam, it is possible for such seemingly contradictory processes of institutional continuity and change to happen together. In explaining those institutions that both experience change and keep many important features of their past, I try to clarify the varying relations between religion and politics in time.

The three periods that demonstrate marked differences in particular arrangements between religion and the state are not well delineated. An imperial style mostly dominated until the late eighteenth century, a transitional style until the early Republic, and the modern nation state emerged out of the transformation of empire. Empire was defined by negotiated state–society agreements, a flexible and integrationist state, an insistence on multiple religious arrangements, and the expectation of competing and dual arrangements as well as multi-vocality of projects. The transitional period is recognisable by the questioning of the imperial dualities and identities and defined by claim-making along new identities. It is also familiar in the application of a tight reform agenda that closely associated modernisation with secularisation, as interpreted by western-educated elites. Finally, the nation state is the crystallisation of a predominant identity vessel to represent the new Turkey, based on the clear rejection of alternatives, the move away from flexible and multiple negotiations to one clean compact between state and society and state and religion. This new compact is western, secular and modern and, based on a Turkish national identity, constructed and secured by the state.

The conclusions are clear: first, the variations in the relationship between religion and politics show that there is no single role for Islam in politics and that just as there is no single Islam, there are also within Islamic traditions multiple paths to modernisation. Second, there has been tremendous continuity in Ottoman and modern Turkish history on the leading significance of the state. The principal role of the state was reproduced throughout the centuries of imperial and national rule. This continued significance of the state has lead to distortions of the manner in which the state is viewed and reified in everyday practice. Third, what modern Turkey lost in the particularities of Ottoman religion was its nature as glue for communities of faith and it might very well be that this characteristic re-emerged nearly intact in the contemporary Islamist discourse. During the period of reform and republican politics, the state and the cult of Atatürk had come to replace 'religion' as the unifying force in the country. Islam as it re-emerged embodies Ottoman Islam: it remains an institutional framework for governance that is tied to the state and reinstitutes its strength as a source of Durkheimian solidarity and of a Geertzian understanding of religion as a system of meaning.

To preview then, the Ottoman solution to challenges of religious heterogeneity in an overwhelmingly Muslim society was both an early domination of religion by the state and a capacious administration of diversity that broadly relied on an understanding of difference without the compulsion to transform difference into sameness. Imperial flexibility, negotiated arrangements, the openness to varieties of worship, and dualities of practice in law and religion made the Ottoman system relatively tolerant and open to diversity. In the transitional reformist era, westernisation was in part implemented as a panacea to macrostructural strains experienced by war, and commercial and demographic shifts. The westernisation of the Ottoman state and society generated uncertainty about most Ottoman identities and practices, prompting reorganisation, reform and adaptation to the West. Modernisation was strongly associated with the notion of science and progress, away from religious obscurantism shaping a bond between modernity and secularism. In the transitional road out of empire the Ottomans traded their pluralism and toleration with liberal notions of citizenship and nationhood. They applied models of homogeneous nation building that spelled disaster for non-Muslims, especially Armenians. For the Muslim population, the dramatic process by which the empire transitioned into a secular republic created havoc with Islamic institutions and practice. The nation state settled on a simple vessel of Turkish nationalist identity, in the process eliminating Ottoman ideals, Islamist belief and practice, and the complexity of empire as its negotiated practice became standardised. Post-Islamic politics in Turkey must be seen as a renewed resourceful balance, between the state, social and religious actors and Islam. We therefore must look back at some creative moments of the Ottoman past to understand the re-emergence of a new politics of Islam.

The nature of Ottoman Islam

The relationship between religion and politics in the Ottoman Empire resembled other empires where religion played an important role in the legitimisation of rule and where diversity was the standard. Despite the Islamic origins of the Ottomans, their subjects were overwhelmingly Christian until the early sixteenth century forcing a different style of early politics. Many characteristics of the relation between politics and religion and church and state made the Ottoman Empire a relatively forward-looking polity where both secularity and fundamentalism flourished. The state's supreme influence in demanding absolute obedience in matters of religion, the administrative function of the religious establishment, the separation between religious and sultanic law, between orthodox and heterodox Islam, between state and folk religion and culture led to creative and open-minded arrangements.

The nature of the relationship between politics and religion was partly determined by imperial characteristics. Empire is a large composite multi-ethnic and multi-religious political formation, where imperial legitimacy, diversity and a network structure of segmentation and integration are significant dimensions. Empires conquered and ruled by maintaining a structure resembling a hub-and-spoke network, where each spoke was attached to the centre but was less directly related to the others. Given their tremendous size, expanse and diversity, empires worked well as 'negotiated enterprises' where each segment made different bargains with the centre, communicating directly with the centre, rather than peripheries. Consequently, empires had to be flexible, adaptable to circumstances, political bargains, various groups and shifting boundaries while remaining multi-vocal, appealing to different constituencies with the same discourse.[1]

For centuries the Ottomans were a strong imperial polity that claimed Islam as their main source of legitimacy, and interpreted and practised religion as an important political means of the empire. The rulers understood themselves as the rulers of the empire, but also as the caliphs, that is the leaders of the Sunni Islamic community. Vis-à-vis the world this claim remained a potent source of Islamic unity and strength, though within the empire, an 'Ottoman Islam' represented a particular relationship between Islam and the state, where the state was dominant and religion was compliant and constrained. The particular construction of the Ottoman state was such that it maintained and nurtured an important separation between religion as an institution and religion as a system of

---

[1] Karen Barkey, *Empire of difference: the Ottomans in comparative perspective* (Cambridge: Cambridge University Press, 2008).

meanings and relations that connected a community of faith. Religion as an institution would help administer the empire. Religion as a system of beliefs would provide the tools for everyday practice and the answers to the practitioners' existential issues.[2] The institutional and meaning-generating aspects of religion were not entirely separate as they were connected in the person of the judge.[3]

The Ottoman state was not a theocracy, in that neither the sharia (religious law) nor the *ulama* (religious scholars) were at the helm of the state. On the other hand, the Ottoman state was not a 'secular' state as part of its legitimacy was obtained through Islam. In the words of Ocak: 'Ottoman Islam bestowed sacredness on the concept of sovereignty and, at the same time, performed an active function by providing a means of governing.'[4] Ottoman Islam was primarily a political Islam, subordinated to the state, used to develop the institutions of the state and administer the various functions of the state. At a historical moment when religion and politics were entangled in Christian Europe and when the church often dominated, the Ottoman state stood out by its peculiar appropriation of Islam.

To explain the early state domination of religion we have to study the particular conditions of Ottoman emergence, which forced patterns and institutional behaviour, and generated the legal framework and the multiple dualities that helped the state control religion. Immediate historical conditions were such that because of rapid expansion and lack of adequate manpower, the Ottoman state was constructed as a hybrid one where Christians were as necessary and welcome as Muslims, and where Islam was one among many other forces of imperial emergence and engagement. Islam gained prominence in the empire only after traditionally Islamic territories were appropriated in the sixteenth century. However, by then, it was easily subordinated to a strong, yet flexible and integrationist state.

The sultanate in the empire wielded supreme sway since absolute obedience to the sovereign meant that even religious law was subordinated to the state. In fact, Ottomans did not start with the strict

[2] Şerif Mardin, 'Power, civil society and culture in the Ottoman Empire', *Comparative Studies in Society and History* 11 (1969), 258–81; 'Religion and secularism in Turkey', in Ali Kazancıgil and Ergün Ozbudun (eds.), *Atatürk: founder of a modern state* (Hamden, CT: Archon Books, 2000), pp. 191–219; 'The Nakşıbendi order in Turkish history', in R. Tapper (ed.), *Islam in modern Turkey: religion, politics and literature in a secular state* (New York: I. B. Taurus, 1991); 'The just and the unjust', *Daedalus* 120 (1994), 113–28.
[3] Barkey, *Empire*.
[4] Ahmet Yaşar Ocak, 'Islam in the Ottoman Empire: a sociological framework for a new interpretation', *International Journal of Turkish Studies* 9 (2003), 188.

establishment of a formal body of Islamic law. Rather, decision-making was based on the sultan and his immediate associates, the Turkish traditions of Central Asia, the *legal code* and customary law, as a repertoire of local knowledge about everyday dealings. Mehmed II (1451–81), the Conqueror, initiated and Süleyman the Magnificent (1520–66) ensured that customary laws were codified and strengthened into the *kanun* – the dynastic laws of the realm dealing with the relations between subjects, officials and the state. Every sultan re-enacted these laws as sultanic laws to be enforced by the sultan for the sultan. Therefore, though according to Islam there can be no other law than religious (sharia) law, the Ottomans contradicted such a dictate by opening up the way for the legislative power of the sultan to promulgate *kanun*. Tursun Bey in the fifteenth century discussed this duality in the following manner:

> Government based on reason alone is called sultanic yasak; government based on principles which ensure felicity in this world and the next is called divine policy, or şeriat. The prophet preached şeriat. But only the authority of a sovereign can institute these policies. Without a sovereign, men cannot live in harmony and may perish altogether. God has granted this authority to one person only, and that person, for the perpetuation of good order, requires absolute obedience.[5]

It is in this fashion that Ottomans early on established the authority of the sovereign ruler and his customary and sultanic law over religious law. That is, a sovereign and just ruler was indispensable to the application of religious law.

The religious and administrative authorities implemented Ottoman justice based on dynastic and Islamic law.[6] Sharia, which Ottomans understood as it was perceived at this time, that is more as a path, a way to apply God's will as interpreted by different schools of Islamic learning, was mainly used in controlled fields such as family and personal law.[7] It is not clear that sharia was meant to be an all encompassing and defining part of the state. The sometimes uneasy balance between dynastic and Islamic law would tend to rupture under a weak ruler. In Cornell Fleischer's words:

> Şeri'at was universal, immutable, divinely revealed, and hence spiritually supreme, while kanun was regional, amendable, and created by human reason, and for that very reason was often of greater immediate relevance to the life of

---

[5] Halil Inalcık, *The Ottoman Empire: the classical age 1300–1600*, trans. Norman Itzkowitz and Colin Imber (New York: Praeger, 1973), p. 68.
[6] Haim Gerber, *Islamic law and culture 1600–1840*, vol. IX (Leiden: Brill, 1999).
[7] Ocak, 'Islam in the Ottoman Empire', 189.

the Ottoman polity than the şeri'at. Only the wisdom of the ruler, whose duty it was to protect both religion and state could keep the one from overshadowing the other.[8]

In everyday practice, the workings of the sharia courts show clearly that magistrates (*kadı*) were equally adept at interpreting both religious and sultanic law, pressed for local custom and precedent when necessary and allowed each source of legal wisdom to function independently from the other.[9] I stress this conclusion since it demonstrates the degree to which the relationship between state and religion was mediated by local knowledge and circumstances, and particular social and economic processes that operated locally.

The dual function of religion both as an administrative and a belief system subordinated religion to the state, while keeping it meaningful in the life of the faithful, providing them with a sense of belonging and a set of practices. The magistrate was the embodiment of this duality, being the administrative official entrusted with popularly resented practices such as tax collection, but also remaining an important religious figure at the local level. Appointed to positions over the vast expanse of the empire, the magistrate remained the key interlocutor between the state and the people and between religious administration and the local interpretation of religious meanings. Madrasa-educated, trained in secular and regional law, magistrates went out into the provinces and cities as men of the empire; they applied Islamic law; adjudicated according to the sharia and sultanic law. In their role as administrators, and religious scholars, they tied the state to the people; they were the source of a state-driven unity between centre and periphery. Thus, they could not just be religious men; they had to be religious men of the centre.

In the routines of daily court practice, the *kadıs* reproduced the demands of the sharia, that is, they watched over those who were of Islamic faith. They both watched for transgression from Islamic life and helped define the parameters of Islamic practice. That is, they performed Islamic practice, and even though they ruled in religious and customary local terms, they still represented Islam and connected people to the religion and its forms of thinking, richly conveying a sense of Islamic identity to the people. When common folk came to court to ask for justice, asking for adjudication between adversaries, and the *kadı* ruled as the representative of the sultan, all members of the community were re-enacting a very old traditional Islamic concept of the just ruler.[10]

---

[8] Cornell H. Fleischer, *Bureaucrat and intellectual in the Ottoman Empire: the historian Mustafa Ali (1541–1600)* (Princeton: Princeton University Press, 1986), pp. 290–1.
[9] Gerber, *Islamic law.*   [10] Fleisher, *Bureaucrat.*

Beyond the performance side of this relationship, the fact that the religious official and the religious court offered the locals resolution, clarification, support and relief focused them on religion and its day-to-day signs and symbols. Together with the mosque and the dervish lodges (*tekke*), the court became an important centre of Islamic life, but also *the* source of linkage between the state and religion.[11] A rich local spiritual life was then allowed to flourish as it remained connected to the state and its officials.

Ottoman Islam included a vast array of beliefs and practices ranging from orthodox and Sufi heterodox Islam, both included and adopted by the state. While saintly heterodox Sufi dervish leaders had taken the lead in the early establishment of the Ottoman state and had been the trusted companions of the early sultans, helping shape popular Sufi Islam into the backbone of Ottoman cultural life, the turn towards an ordered Sunni orthodoxy presented tensions and opportunities for action.[12] The divisions between orthodox and heterodox forms of Islam were important to maintaining state autonomy from religious institutions, with Sufi forms of Islam becoming vehicles for folk contention as well as the source of behaviour and imaginings outside the realm of the mainstream. Therefore, even at the height of Sunni Islamic zealotry, rulers who condoned such orthodoxy still maintained Sufi sheiks in the palace and in the major Istanbul mosques.[13]

Religion – understood in Geertzian terms as a socially accepted system of significance – was for centuries under Ottoman rule mediated by institutions with strong state intervention. More important than belief, religious practice was reproduced in the everyday actions of magistrates and the court.[14] Islam in that way permeated social relations and gave meaning to the social action of its practitioners.

Ottoman toleration: character and limits

Another aspect of the transactions between religion and politics can be displayed in the relations between the politically dominant religious group and others. Ottoman Islam watched over the administration and lives of the Muslim masses while also only partially shaping the lives of

[11] Barkey, *Empire.*   [12] Mardin, 'The Nakşibendi order', 128.
[13] Madeline C. Zilfi, *The politics of piety: the Ottoman ulema in the postclassical age (1600–1800)* (Minneapolis: Bibliotheca Islamica, 1988), pp. 137–43.
[14] This is not to say that everyone lived within moderate and state-controlled Islam. The countryside was strewn with heterodox movements of Sufi, even Shi'a persuasion. However, between the forces of dissent and the state the court remained a stable local institution.

the non-Muslim populations of the empire. That Islam was not the main source of authority on how to rule diversity, but acted only as a partial blueprint for the administration of non-Muslims, is significant. The basis of state diversity politics was to be found in the establishment of a strong state with a relatively modest Islamic identity, and a pattern of flexible, multi-vocal politics that was meant to appeal to all groups. The state ruled diverse religious groups as it did its Muslim populations; it organised them into administrative categories and enlisted their religious leaders as state officials. Ottoman toleration therefore was an administrative process, a pragmatic solution to imperial diversity. As such it was robust as long as the key actors at the helm of these institutions remained strong and committed to diversity. It was to disintegrate under conditions of weak leadership and increased economic competition that led to ever more closed communities.

The Ottoman state organised and administered a system of religious and communal rule that instituted religious boundaries, marking difference, yet allowing space, movement and parallel administrative structures to maintain a divided, but also cohesive and tolerant imperial society. Ottoman indirect rule vis-à-vis religious communities produced the *millet* system: a loose administrative set of central–local arrangements for each community used as a script for multi-religious rule. *Millet* allowed for the simultaneous division and integration of communities into the state and, similar to other indirect forms of rule, permitted intermediaries with a real stake in the maintenance of the status quo to administer internally autonomous self-regulatory religious communities. Such top-down pressure from the state authorities and bottom-up enthusiasm for peace and order from the intermediaries was the key to many centuries of Ottoman pluralism.

Initially, a need for 'legibility'[15] determined how to administer newly conquered communities, where to settle various populations and what their contribution to the empire would be. In the aftermath of the conquest of Constantinople, state community relations were established, developing into organisational forms that grew into three large-scale identity vessels that organised diversity for the empire. The Orthodox *millet* was recognised in 1454, the Armenian in 1461 while the Jewish *millet* was unofficially recognised around the same time as the other two. In 1477, there were 3,151 Greek Orthodox, 3,095 Armenian, Latin and

---

[15] Legibility refers to the need of a state to map its terrain and the people, to arrange the population of a country in ways that simplify important state functions such as taxation, conscription, administration and prevention of rebellion. See James Scott, *Seeing like a state* (New Haven: Yale University Press, 1998).

Gypsy combined and 1,647 Jewish households in Istanbul. The number of the Muslim households had reached 8,951.[16] The puzzle of rule was solved in the following way.

First, Islam provided the normative guidelines by which Muslim and non-Muslim communities would be incorporated into Ottoman society and state. Islamic law and its practice dictated a relationship between a Muslim state and non-Muslim 'Peoples of the Book', that is, Jews and Christians. According to this pact, non-Muslims would be protected, could practise their own religion, preserve their own places of worship and to a large extent run their own affairs provided they recognised the superiority of Islam. As such, Islam was pervasive and the primary marker of inclusion in the political community.[17] Three words described relations between Muslims and non-Muslims: *separate*, *unequal* and *protected*. The immediate public markers of a boundary between Muslims, Jews and Christians were codes of conduct, rules and regulations around dress, housing and transportation. Despite frequent references to physical markers of difference such as clothing, colours, height of residence and ownership of slaves, the sultanate did not fully enforce such regulations. Often by citing ancient practice and previously allowed local custom, various Ottoman communities interpreted and gave meaning to this Islamic framework as their repertoires of lived and shared experience helped them develop common strategies of action. Negotiations were common practice in every community, making imperial rule eminently flexible.

Second, beyond the role of Islam in establishing the simple rules of multi-religious living, the *millet* arrangement was forged by the sultans, Mehmed II in particular, who shaped the early arrangements periodically renewed by the communities. These arrangements did not entail much innovation since they folded into their practice the existing authority structures of each community and, thereby, provided them with significant legal autonomy and authority. Institutional adaptation and continuity required that where there was strong community organisation and/or strong ecclesiastical hierarchy, the central state adopted these

---

[16] Halil Inalcık, 'The policy of Mehmed II toward the Greek population of Istanbul and the Byzantine buildings of the city', *Dumbarton Oaks Papers* 23 and 24 (1969/70), 247; Halil Inalcık, 'Foundations of Ottoman–Jewish cooperation', in Avigdor Levy (ed.), *Jews, Turks, Ottomans: a shared history, fifteenth through the twentieth century* (Syracuse: Syracuse University Press, 2002), p. 5.

[17] C. E. Bosworth, 'The concept of Dhimma in early Islam', in Benjamin Braude and Bernard Lewis (eds.), *Christians and Jews in the Ottoman Empire: the functioning of a plural society* (New York and London: Holmes & Meier Publishers, 1982), pp. 1–34, 37–51; Bruce Masters, *Christians and Jews in the Ottoman Arab world: the roots of sectarianism* (Cambridge: Cambridge University Press, 2001), pp. 17–40.

institutions as the representative structures of the community. As the Conqueror recognised the power of the Greek Orthodox patriarchate he entrusted the church with the administration of ethnically and linguistic-ally diverse populations that followed Orthodox practice. The Jewish communities were of much smaller size, urban and scattered across the empire, with no overarching rabbinical authority, but an assembly of religious and lay leaders. An attempt to appoint a Chief Rabbi to oversee the relations between the state and Jews failed and Ottomans went back to recognising Jews as a series of communities with their own leaders, adapting to the facts on the ground. The Armenians were in an inter-mediate position with regionally complex configuration of communities as well as few patriarchs claiming jurisdiction over them. In each of these encounters, the facts on the ground, the relations between state and religious communities and the interests of each leader helped shape the rules of governance.

Once *millet* arrangements were agreed upon, they were maintained by religious or secular intermediaries from each community, enforced by incentives and punishments. As the key brokers between the state and the *millets*, these men strategically behaved as boundary managers, maintaining peace and order through the active and efficient monitoring of relations across religious and community lines. Fearon and Laitin, who discuss such issues of interethnic peace, call such attempts 'institutionalized in-group policing', where leaders successfully police their own members within the community and in transaction across communities.[18] For such incidents not to blow up into large-scale ethnic conflict, the intermediaries, be they religious or secular leaders, were empowered by the state to monitor their internal affairs in return for continued benefits and autonomy. Community leaders who maintained peace and paid their dues on time would be rewarded with continued appointment and increased opportunity for wealth. Community leaders who were embroiled in violence or were unable to collect taxes lost their livelihood and, more often, their head. This intense monitoring was also successful because especially the ecclesiastical leadership was interested in maintaining boundaries for religious reasons as much as political ones, and also because they invested much time learning the legal and religious systems of the others, especially the ruling Islamic ones, in order to predict, prevent and manage possibly detrimental breaches of intercommunal relational space.

---

[18] James D. Fearon and David D. Laitin, 'Explaining interethnic co-operation', *American Political Science Review* 90 (1996), 715–35.

The character of Ottoman toleration, was therefore not entirely a political and administrative product of state policy, nor was it the result of an internal organic ideological germination by Ottoman humanists who thought that toleration should be normative in society. It was rather an organisational by-product of top-down interests in legibility and inter-religious peace and order and bottom-up concern for maintaining an interference- and coercion-free imperial space. The upside of such an arrangement was that once it was perceived as successful, it acquired momentum as it was reproduced and applied more widely. The downside of such an arrangement was that it could be maintained as long as boundaries were prevalent, and state and social actors were powerful enough to define and preserve the rules of inter- and intra-boundary relations.

In conclusion, the main Ottoman style of relations between politics and religion and church and state was derived from an imperial feature of rule that emphasised strong central authority combined with the inherent flexibility of a brokered state, and a historical tradition of diversity with subordination and integration into the state. The result was a form of toleration that loosely lasted from the early fourteenth to the beginning of the nineteenth century.

Road out of empire: ideologies and strategies

The relations between religion and politics were negotiated many times over the course of Ottoman centuries, but were effectively transformed during the transition from empire to nation state. In the late eighteenth and early nineteenth centuries, the Ottomans entered a period of transition from empire to multiple nation states, as territories were claimed as independent states. The transition culminated in the establishment of a modern Turkish Republic in 1923. It is during this period that – as a consequence of many internal and external changes – the relations between politics and religion were profoundly altered. Yet the continuity in the institutional makeup of the state was remarkable: the transitional Ottoman and later the Republican states remained omnipotent and critical to the restructuring of the new national entity, and the state elites actively forged a new set of relations between politics and religion. That elites kept religion subordinate to state interests was entirely in keeping with Ottoman practice. However, that they struggled to extrude religion from the public realm was quite new. The transformation entailed then an entirely different and new secular politics, accompanied by a less tolerant state and society. We can only understand these outcomes when we look at how religion was viewed by elites and understood by the masses, and how relations between the various religious groups unfolded during the transition.

Macro-level historical changes during the eighteenth and nineteenth centuries initiated a lot of the shifting relations between politics and religion. Here, I briefly concentrate on the historical causes of imperial change and discuss the actors and institutions that adapted to and reflected these changes. Imperial change was the result of the subordination of the Ottoman Empire to the world economic order dominated by European powers, international warfare with its growing financial demands, and the shifting demographic balance of the empire. The long-term experience of economic and political disability which rendered the Ottoman state insecure and the local populations discordant along religious, ethnic and sectarian dimensions was a prelude to the Tanzimat reforms of the nineteenth century, during which a reformulation of the state–society compact was attempted. The reorganisation only fuelled further the emerging tensions along lines of religion and toleration.

Starting in the eighteenth century the commercial development of the empire forced a reorganisation of community networks in ways that accentuated religious and ethnic rivalries and therefore prejudice and antagonism across boundaries. The growing commercialisation of the empire under western incorporation increased the density and intensity of trade networks, engaging many more individuals and intensifying competition and friction. In the rivalry that ensued the administrative boundaries ruptured and conflicts between Muslims and non-Muslims, as well as among non-Muslim populations, could not be contained any longer, making local instances of violence possible. European merchants, consulate personnel and other western officials favoured Christian traders, and redefined boundaries, creating confusion within the units of the old traditional order maintained by the Ottomans. As foreign powers entered the Ottoman social and economic space, they projected their definitions of groups and insisted on change based upon new ideals. Even though westerners often formulated constructive ideals, hierarchies and inequalities developed in the treatment of Ottoman subjects by foreign traders, leading to advantages for non-Muslim groups over others.

Changing economic relations over time damaged the finances of the empire. The Ottomans early on recognised the British and the French by giving them capitulations, rights to trade freely in the empire and open numerous trading houses in port cities, and financial incentives to use the empire for their own benefit. Starting in 1838 with Britain, the Ottomans signed many free-trade treaties, and in the 1840s started to borrow from abroad for the first time in their long history. Furthermore, the Ottomans had lost many lucrative provinces; Greece had become independent, and Algeria, Syria and Egypt had entered French and/or British zones of influence. The increasing contact with the world economy more often exploited the remaining Ottoman provinces than regenerated their wealth. Local industries were unable to compete with the influx of cheaper European goods flowing into the empire.[19]

Warfare during the eighteenth and nineteenth centuries was similarly destructive. From 1736 to 1739, Austria and Russia had inflicted some losses on the Ottomans, who had to recognise Russian military organisation and strength. Warfare resumed after Catherine of Russia attacked the Ottomans on multiple fronts from 1768 to 1774, resulting in the loss of the Danubian Principalities and the Crimea. After the Treaty of Küçük Kaynarca in 1774, where the Russians asserted their claims over the Orthodox population of the empire, a third round of warfare between 1787 and 1792 ended with the Treaty of Jassy, when European powers finally shielded the empire from further territorial losses as well as more humiliating agreements with the Russians. In the nineteenth-century Balkans, nationalism became the ideology to articulate discontent with a centralising imperial state, local commercial development, inadequate rule and the effect of disastrous wars. Nationalism was a new world system of ideas that peripheral regions of large-scale polities could adopt to accelerate their autonomy and independence.[20] The Serbs, starting with the uprising of 1804, opened up the doors to a process of imperial exit, followed by the Greeks in 1821 and the Romanians in 1848 and by other contentious Balkan nations.[21] These growing appeals to independence in the periphery were a wake-up call for Ottomans who had not envisioned such a disintegration of their territory.

International warfare against increasingly better-organised adversaries, the nationalism of non-Muslim communities and the perceived deterioration of its international standing pushed the Ottoman state towards a modernisation programme, especially in military and administrative functions. Reform was initiated by Selim III (1789–1807) and Mahmud II (1808–39), then significantly pursued during the era of the

---

[19] Manfred Pittioni, 'Economic decline of the Ottoman Empire', in Emil Brix, Klaus Koch and Elisabeth Vyslonzil (eds.), *The decline of empires* (Vienna: Verlag für Geschichte und Politik; Munich: Oldenburg, 2001), pp. 21–44.

[20] Daniel Chirot and Karen Barkey, 'States in search of legitimacy: was there nationalism in the Balkans of the early nineteenth century?', *International Journal of Comparative Sociology* 24 (1983), 30–46.

[21] Georges Castellan, *Histoire des Balkans XIVe–XXe siècle* (Paris: Fayard, 1999); Richard Clogg (ed.), *Balkan society in the age of Greek independence* (London: Macmillan, 1981).

Tanzimat (1839–76) and finally reformulated during the reign of Abdülhamid II (1876–1909). These reforms culminated in the Young Turk Revolution (1908) setting up the government that would oversee World War I.[22]

It is important to understand the contradictory role of these reforms since on the one hand they pushed for western values of equality, but on the other hand they increased tensions between Muslims and non-Muslims, reinforcing each groups' identity. With the Tanzimat of 1839 reformers pledged to guarantee the life, honour and property of all subjects of the sultan, as well as their equality under the law, and to establish a military system of conscription, while also restructuring the antiquated tax-farming system by switching to a state-controlled, direct system of taxation. Provincial representative assemblies were established, together with state courts that ruled independently of the *ulama*.[23] Local administrative councils and new codes of commercial and criminal law were introduced. A conscription system based on Prussian patterns signalled the end of traditional privileges for both Muslim and non-Muslim communities. Muslims, the warrior class of the empire with special dispensation and attached to their superior status, were disappointed by the inclusion of others. Non-Muslims, who had been content in their non-combatant role, were distressed. Direct taxation and equality for all affected Muslims since non-Muslims were already paying direct taxes, but Muslims had never paid such taxes.

While the achievements of the Tanzimat are generally accepted, the impact of such reform on the role of Islam in the empire and on the relations between religious communities was more mixed. Many among the Muslim population saw the Tanzimat as robbing Muslims of their religious institutions; secular courts and personnel replaced the sharia courts and the *kadıs*. Islam as an administrative instrument would start to disappear. Likewise the meaning of being Muslim was also changing since equality before the law would deprive Muslims of their superiority.

[22] Carter V. Findley, *Bureaucratic reform in the Ottoman Empire: the sublime porte* (Princeton: Princeton University Press, 1980); Erik Zürcher, *Turkey: a modern history* (London: I. B. Tauris, 1993); Bernard Lewis, *The emergence of modern Turkey*, 2nd edition (Oxford: Oxford University Press, 1961); Stanford J. Shaw and Ezel Kural Shaw, *History of the Ottoman Empire and modern Turkey*, 2 vols. (Cambridge: Cambridge University Press, 1977); Roderic H. Davison, *Reform in the Ottoman Empire, 1856–1876* (Princeton: Princeton University Press, 1963).
[23] This was inevitable since the Ottomans were unable to prevent the growth of *ulama* dynasties and privileges. By the late eighteenth century, the empire had developed a powerful aristocratic *ulama* class that reproduced itself successfully, holding on to the main positions of power and interpreting any form of change, whether political or technological, to be against the laws of Islam. Zilfi, *The politics of piety.*

Educational reforms intending change for all religious *millets* in the empire became detrimental to the Muslim population. Even though the reforms promoted Muslim schools, they also increased internal competition between groups, as well as encouraging more missionary and western involvement in separate Christian and Jewish schooling, with non-Muslim school students obtaining a superior education.[24] The consequences of this separation and competition were dire for interethnic relations in the empire, forcing closure in communities rather than interaction, teaching young students separation, difference and competition. The reform of education, which during the Tanzimat lead to increased differentiation among communities and produced a sense of Muslim inferiority, pushed Sultan Abdülhamid II to put enormous energy and resources into Muslim education, creating the basis of a distinct religious and national identity for the Muslim population of the empire.[25]

Religion and religious differences had become a demanding political issue to which every group and actor wanted to contribute. In the third era of reforms, the new Ottoman elites were ready and intent on transforming religion. The Young Turks fought Abdülhamid II, and their victory culminated in the establishment of a constitutional government. The Young Turks and their Committee on Union and Progress were key actors from 1908 to 1918, transforming the empire into a national state, while framing the political ideology of the new state. They remained central as they provided the initial leadership of the Turkish Republic and their influence was long lasting in modern politics. Raring to go, the Young Turks centralised their power swiftly, introduced a serious programme of modernisation of the empire, ushering an era of modern nationalism. While they succeeded at many internal reforms, it was also under their stewardship that the empire fell into disarray and committed terrible atrocities against its Armenian population.

In their modern, positivist, statist and elitist vision, the Young Turks saw the 'state' to be in danger, needing protection and consolidation. Different groups presented diverse ideologies and solutions that were neither clearly delineated nor fully espoused. Rather, the three ideologies, Ottomanism, Islamism and Turkism, were three complex paths of

---

[24] Benjamin C. Fortna, *Imperial classroom: Islam, the state, and education in the late Ottoman Empire* (Oxford: Oxford University Press, 2002).

[25] Kemal H. Karpat, *The politicisation of Islam: reconstructing identity, state, faith, and community in the late Ottoman state* (Oxford: Oxford University Press, 2001), pp. 98–100.

identity that defined the political culture of the empire in transition, used for claim making in the political arena. Ottomanism, which at the height of empire meant tolerance and accommodation, acquired during the Tanzimat a different neutrality based on the equality of rights and obligations provided by the new laws of the empire. Islamists focused on Ottoman rights to the caliphate and Muslim unity represented by a pan-Islamist revival, with Abdülhamid II acting on their behalf. Finally, Turkism emphasised the linguistic and cultural characteristics of the Turks, who, according to the prevalent arguments, had been the dominant nation of the empire all along. Turkism became the origin of a broader nationalist platform, one formulated by the Young Turks and fully realised during the early Republic.

These identity debates coexisted within the larger framework of accelerated modernisation. Modernisation, an umbrella concept for the empire, moved from being an administrative and technological tool to a social and political project, with strong Jacobin tendencies to exchange religion with science. The pairing of modernity and secularism had been part of the Ottoman understanding since the eighteenth century when the development of trade and commerce, the port cities and their immediate hinterland displayed a local indigenous 'modernity' associated with local actors changing society from within. Commerce and development necessitated modern concepts of exchange, contracts and trust, but also pushed in the direction of secular practices. By the mid nineteenth century the western influence had pushed the Tanzimat reforms under the watchful eyes of European powers, but these were large-scale, aimed at reforming the imperial social structure. Simultaneously, the secularism of many young reformers was an earnest response to the perceived obscurantism of the religious men of the empire. Many of the best early Young Turk thinkers wrote that the social ills of the empire were caused by increased power of the *ulama*, but urged maintaining a Durkeimian vision of religion as the source of social cohesion.[26]

The Young Turks, however, brought a scientific and materialist outlook to modernisation. Their experience with European materialist thinkers helped shape their ideology and political platform. Influenced by French members of the Royal Medical Academy, by the École Libre des Sciences Politiques in Paris, by the German thinker Ludwig Büchner and the French Gustave LeBon, they formulated a Social Darwinist, elitist, scientific materialist world view that was vehemently

---

[26] Şerif Mardin, *The genesis of Young Ottoman thought: a study in the modernization of Turkish political ideas* (Princeton: Princeton University Press, 1962).

anti-religious.[27] The transfer of these ideas into the Ottoman context of the Military Academy, the Schools of Medicine and the School of Political Science ensured the application of positivism, but as Şerif Mardin perceptively argues, in a manner that was mostly intolerant of 'the stock of knowledge of those who had retained their traditional worldview constructed with elements of the religio-mystical tradition'.[28] Political activists and writers such as Abdullah Cevdet or Ziya Gökalp advocated the complete separation of church and state, but they also believed that religion had to be squeezed out of the people's social and cultural perspectives to leave only a scientific rational outlook to life.[29] They argued for the abolition of the institutions of the Şeyh-ül-Islam and madrasas, contested the role of the dervish orders and religious institutions that had been an integral part of the Ottoman system of public welfare. In the process, they wanted not only to extrude religious institutions from state and society, but more importantly, wean people from their belief system and transform them into modern secular and scientific human beings.[30]

The Young Turk struggle with religion was, however, much more complex. As Ottomanism and Islamism were weakening in the minds of the Young Turks, Islam was being reinforced especially at the popular level by the new inequities in commerce, the increased advantages of non-Muslims who with the help of Europeans had become the main interlocutors of the trade between the Ottomans and the West. Muslims interpreted their plight in religious terms, fashioning a stronger Islamic identity. Such ill feelings were only strengthened by the arrival of Muslim refugees from the Balkans, the Caucasus and the Crimea. The Ottoman government settled between five and seven million disgruntled Muslim refugees in Anatolia through the nineteenth century. This immigration originating in the nationalist movements and independence politics of the Balkans, the Russian Wars and Ottoman defeats introduced another element of Muslim discontent. These immigrants came with some ethnic and nationalist feelings, but in the Anatolian context they quickly espoused their Muslim identity, finding it to be a source of commonality with the local population. As mentioned earlier, Abdülhamid II had

---

[27] Şükrü Hanioğlu, *The Young Turks in opposition* (Oxford: Oxford University Press, 1995); *Preparation for a revolution: the Young Turks 1902–1908* (Oxford: Oxford University Press, 2001).

[28] Mardin, 'The just and the unjust', 123.

[29] Şerif Mardin, *Jön Türklerin siyasi fikirleri 1898–1908* (Ankara: İş Bankası Yayınları, 1964).

[30] Erik-Jan Zürcher, 'Kemalist düşüncenin Osmanlı kaynakları', in T. Bora (ed.), *Modern Türkiyede siyasal düşünce* (Istanbul: İletişim Yayınevi, 2002), pp. 44–55.

previously emphasised Muslim unity as an essential tool for maintaining the integrity of the empire. As Young Turk elites became secular, the Anatolian population became more faithful to their Islamic origins.

It is in this contradiction that we can find the solutions to our puzzle of change and continuity. Young Turk elites were pushing for secular, state-centred national policies of development while the Anatolian populations felt threatened as Muslims. With the advent of World War I, elite and mass fears of dismemberment culminated in the vicious end of toleration as state policy. Ironically, the rebuilding of the state required modernity and this latter was associated with secularism. Secularisation was imperative to positivist scientific thinking, but also absolutely necessary in the struggle against an obscurantist clergy and a growing politicised Islamic population, resulting from the demographic shift of the empire.

After the Ottomans: secular and Islamic politics

The Young Turk ideology and political strategy became the centre of the new Republican understanding of state making. As Şükrü Hanioğlu argues in many of his volumes on the Young Turks, it is at this particular moment of the transition that the official ideology of the modern Republican state was shaped, with all of its elements: secularism, positivism, faith in the role of science, elitism, racialism and nationalism. As Zürcher maintains:

> Clearly, Kemalist secularism was anchored in the mainstream of Young Turk ideas on the subject. The Kemalist reforms of 1924 (abolition of the caliphate and Şeyhulislamate, closing of religious courts, the unification of education under a secular ministry and the institution of directorates for religious affairs and for charitable foundations) can all be seen as the logical conclusions to the Ottoman secularisation process.[31]

Moreover, Republican state makers completed the task as they abolished religious courts, dissolved the dervish orders and closed the local shrines. They instituted European family law, romanised the alphabet, reformed the calendar and 'turkified' the call to prayer as they closed religious schools, centralising educational institutions under one Ministry of Education. In making all these changes, 'the secularizers saw themselves as bringing into Turkish society the principles of toleration and religious freedom which prevailed in the West'.[32]

[31] Zürcher, 'Kemalist düşüncenin Osmanlı kaynakları'.
[32] Mardin, 'The just and the unjust,' p. 127.

Yet the new Republican secularism entailed other attributes. Early in the transition secularism and nationalism became tightly intertwined. Atatürk referred to the post-imperial territory as a Turkish state, delineating it clearly from the empire, but also implying a territory where Turks lived. Yet the Young Turk struggle for the mobilisation of the masses was to reproduce itself. Nationalism was not enough; religion was still a necessary ingredient, demonstrating the weakness of the grasp of nationalism. Therefore, Atatürk consistently used religious imagery, references to a Muslim nation and an appeal to Muslim values in his speeches. That religion was used to mobilise the masses became apparent soon enough, but state makers believed nationalism would succeed only if religion was eliminated.[33] How would religion be eliminated? By controlling its institutional manifestation as well as withholding its cultural meaning in everyday life.

We thus return to the institutional continuity with the Ottoman format. That is, in the establishment of the Department of Affairs of Piety (Diyanet) subordinated to the office of the prime minister, the new Republic emulated the institutional control of religion that the Ottomans had always maintained. The control of religious institutions was re-enacted, yet since religion was to become a private matter, the Diyanet was instructed to issue religious thoughts on private matters. The counterpart Ottoman institution, on the other hand, had maintained its discourse on issues of state and law.[34] Moreover, beyond the private, the role of the Diyanet, as an institution closely associated with and controlled by an authoritarian state, became one of promoting national Turkish identity and unity, representing the state and its accomplishments in a positive light. The weekly Friday sermon, prepared by the Diyanet and circulated all over the country, became the main articulation of the relationship between state and community. In many ways, the duty of the magistrate was replaced by the weekly sermon. The state controlled religion and its dissemination, and by eliminating the local, educational and orthodox as well as heterodox manifestations, state makers succeeded in eliminating the meaning people gave to its everyday expression. Religion came to them in ten- to fifteen-minute canned speeches prepared very far away, removed from local customs and concerns. The local, mystical orders were persecuted, and went underground. There remained very little that connected a state Islam and the public devotional Islam of the people.

---

[33] Haldun Gülalp, 'Enlightenment by fiat: secularization and democracy in Turkey', *Middle Eastern Studies* 41 (2005), 351–72.
[34] *Ibid.*

The new Turkish Republic had therefore discarded one form of relationship between state and religion and toleration for an entirely different one. An Ottoman imperial solution to the challenges of diversity had been abandoned for a nationalist, modernist and secularist version of a Turkish Republic that built its nation on assumptions of homogeneity and unity, Turkishness. In the euphoria of the creation of a new nation, state makers constructed a new religion based on the secular ideal of the nation and its most successful representative, Atatürk, the father of the nation.[35] Tremendous continuity with the empire remained in the relationship between the state and Islam, where a strong state dominated Islamic institutions and Islam's daily representation. The state dominated religion, but unlike the rich, textured and meaningful Islam of the Ottomans, the Islam of the modern Republic was voided of its content.

Today Turkey stands among many Middle Eastern nations as a democratic example of a fruitful relationship between religion and politics. The current governing Justice and Development Party, an Islamic party, has re-established a dialogue and a new balance between religion and politics. This balance means relations between the state and Islam, contention and negotiation between secular and religious actors on issues of the role of religion in a secular society and, especially, the role of religion in education. Further, this balance is slowly changing the role of the Diyanet, moving it from an extremely centralised state-controlled institution towards a more flexible, decentralised as well as open organisation capable of absorbing outside influence.

The challenges to understanding the unfolding of modernisation and secularism and the recent reaction to such a process in the resurgence of Islam are extraordinary. In this chapter I sought to understand the varying relations between politics and religion in a turbulent transition from an imperial political formation to a national state. I contrasted the Ottoman model with the post-Tanzimat transitional reconfiguration of Ottomanism en route to the Republic. I showed the strengths of the Ottomans, as well as the structural weakness of their imperial arrangements. The chapter also traced the transition in the outcomes of the eighteenth-century transformation and the exigencies on the ground that compelled a new generation of elites to rethink the politics of empire and innovate. That they innovated very sharply under European influence, without enough attention to those social and political arrangements and practices that worked might be understandable in the

[35] For a very interesting argument on this aspect of the cult of Atatürk, see Yael Navaro-Yashin, *Faces of the state: secularism and public life in Turkey* (Princeton: Princeton University Press, 2002).

context of the urgency of the time. Yet in order to recognise the latest post-Islamist politics of the Republic in the Justice and Development Party phase, we need to understand the degree to which modernisation and secularisation were intertwined in the Turkish context, in a sense with a continuity from Ottoman separation of state and religion, through the radicalisation of this separation in the ideology of the Young Turks and the Kemalists, finally to be forcefully ingrained in the fabric of society. That the Kemalist success at the War of Independence came enveloped in the thick new social fabric of modernisation, secularisation and nationalism made it acceptable to large segments of the population. In the post-imperial age, the new leaders of the Turkish Republic were afforded autonomy and earnest backing for their policies. That today a new interpretation of the Kemalist era questions such an interlude is a case of denying the information on the ground.

In a sense it was not that modernisation theorists misunderstood Turkey, but rather that, at one level, Turkey lived and implemented the link between modernisation and secularisation intensely. However, at another level, an Ottoman tradition of popular Islam, a belief system that –though managed by the state – clearly offered 'a socially accepted system of significance', was destroyed during the Kemalist era. The Turkish revival of an Islamist political perspective and its success is based as much on the exhaustion of the modernisation–secularisation partnership as it is on the slow regeneration of a public, folk and popular Islam, out of the ruins of empire.

5 The Russian Orthodox Church and secularisation

Geoffrey Hosking

In his study of religion in western Europe, Hugh McLeod claims that the nineteenth and twentieth centuries up to 1970 were a period not of secularisation but rather of polarisation, in which both Christianity and militant secularism were major forces in political, social and cultural life.[1] As he sees it, three tendencies were in contention: (i) radical Protestantism; (ii) ultramontane Catholicism; (iii) the secular 'religion of humanity'.[2] I will argue that the equivalent of (ii) and (iii) were clearly present in Russia, and indeed that they conducted a bitter and mutually destructive war in the twentieth century. (i) was far less conspicuous, but many of the forces that generated Protestantism elsewhere were also active in Russia, and they stimulated the appearance of quasi-Protestant forms of religiosity, though without the cultural underpinnings that sustained Protestantism elsewhere in Europe.

An alternative way to look at religious evolution in Russia in the eighteenth and especially nineteenth centuries has been mooted by Christopher Bayly. Writing about the world as a whole, he suggests that secularisation was

only one small part of the reconstruction from within of the religious sensibility and of religious organisation ... Almost everywhere in the world religions sharpened and clarified their identities, especially in the later nineteenth century. They expanded to try to absorb and discipline the variegated systems of belief, ritual and practice which had always teemed beneath the surface in the earlier ages of supposed religiosity.[3]

I am grateful to Professor Simon Dixon for his careful reading of an earlier draft of this chapter. Mistakes and misconceptions remain my own.

[1] Hugh McLeod, 'The modern world –secularised or not?', in Peter Blickle and Rudolf Schlögl (eds.), *Die Säkularisation im Prozess der Säkularisierung Europas* (Epfendorf: Bibliotheca-Academica-Verlag, 2005), pp. 533–49.

[2] Hugh McLeod, *Religion and the people of western Europe, 1789–1970* (Oxford: Oxford University Press, 1981).

[3] C. A. Bayly, *The birth of the modern world, 1780–1914* (Oxford: Blackwell, 2004), p. 330.

Both McLeod and Bayly can help us interpret Russia's religious development. Its decisive phase took place in the late nineteenth and early twentieth centuries. At that time processes common to other European countries, but more spaced out there, reached a crucial threshold simultaneously. The problems of urbanising rapidly, establishing a secure national identity, launching a democratic political system and providing a legal basis for religious toleration all came to a head together, colliding with one another in ways that ultimately fuelled the revolution of 1917. They also profoundly affected the evolution of the Orthodox Church.

Like its Ottoman counterpart, the Russian Empire was a multi-ethnic, multi-faith community of peoples living on the borderlands between Christianity and Islam. Among its subjects were adherents of various strands of Christianity, Islam, Buddhism, Judaism and a multiplicity of animist faiths. To hold the far-flung and diverse conglomerate together, the Russian state had to employ every instrument at its command, including – perhaps especially – religion, which was viewed as a means of bringing both administrative integration, civilisation and Russian political identity to non-Russian, non-Christian peoples.

From the time when Muscovy incorporated the Tatars of the Volga region in the sixteenth century, Russia's rulers tried every means to integrate and acculturate non-Christians into their state. At times they attempted campaigns of forcible conversion, with a degree of success among the pagan, animist peoples. On the whole, though, they found that such campaigns were counter-productive, since they provoked resistance, disorder and even rebellion which threatened the internal security of the empire. This was especially true when dealing with long-established religions that had their own strong internal structures, such as Islam or from the eighteenth century the Catholicism of the Poles.

Instead of mass conversion, then, the Tsars' normal policy was to co-opt religious leaders of non-Orthodox faiths, inducing them where possible to convert to Orthodoxy, but, even if they did not, integrating them into the imperial channels of command. In a few cases this practice had the paradoxical effect of enserfing Russian Christian peasants to Tatar Muslim landowners – an indication of the extent to which in the minds of Russia's rulers the imperatives of empire outdid those of religion or nationality. The practice, however, was stopped in the Law Code of 1649.[4]

---

[4] Andreas Kappeler, *Russlands erste Nationalitäten: das Zarenreich und die Völker der mittleren Wolga vom 16. bis 19. Jahrhundert* (Cologne: Böhlau, 1982), pp. 217–18.

From the eighteenth century onwards, the regime consciously aimed to 'civilise' non-Christian peoples through the peaceful spread of Orthodoxy. As the governor of Astrakhan observed in 1775, talking of local nomadic peoples, 'Nothing can tame their barbarity better and make them more docile than their conversion to Christianity. Then, through contact with our people, it will not be difficult to eradicate their language and customs.'[5] Even when not attempting conversion, the Russian state was becoming a kind of super-patron to the non-Christian peoples, offering a canopy of protection, guidance and administrative support to their local leaders. In return, those leaders had to shape their own faith structures to make them more like those of the Orthodox Church, with which the government was accustomed to deal. As Robert Crews has recently shown, Islam, which is a congregational, non-hierarchical faith, without a separate clergy, had to improvise some of the centralised, hierarchical and clerical structures characteristic of the Orthodox Church, in order to relate in an ordered way to the imperial regime.[6]

These imperial policies also affected the nature and function of the Orthodox Church itself, which had to take on itself the priorities of the 'well-ordered police state'. A multitude of 'local Orthodoxies' constituted the traditional faith of the great majority of Russian people. The church now had to discipline and co-ordinate this great variety of popular beliefs and practices. It imposed uniform service books for use in all parishes and insisted that the sacraments be performed only inside consecrated church buildings. It opened seminaries in each diocese to ensure that priests were properly trained, that they had some knowledge of the scriptures, and could conduct the liturgy consistently, give sermons expounding the faith, and provide elementary religious training – the catechism, basic prayers, the creed, the New Testament – for their parishioners, at first among elites, then among ordinary people too. The church was trying to discourage religious behaviour regarded as 'superstitious', for example, the worship of unauthorised 'wonder-working' icons or the spontaneous proclamation of admired local individuals as 'saints'. It aimed to regularise marriage and family life and where necessary divorce.[7] As a result it was pursuing what might be seen

[5] Michael Khodarkovsky, *Russia's steppe frontier: the making of a colonial empire, 1500–1800* (Bloomington and Indianapolis: Indiana University Press, 2002), p. 189.
[6] Robert D. Crews, *For prophet and Tsar: Islam and empire in Russia and Central Asia* (Cambridge, MA: Harvard University Press, 2006).
[7] Gregory L. Freeze, 'Institutionalising piety: the church and popular religion, 1750–1850', in Jane Burbank and David Ransel (eds.), *Imperial Russia: new stories for the empire* (Bloomington: Indiana University Press, 1998), pp. 210–49.

as contradictory missions, mobilising popular religious faith, yet also endeavouring to tame the spontaneity and diversity of that faith, to confine it in a rigid framework.

Throughout the state took the lead, moulding the church to the requirements of governing the empire. In the early eighteenth century Peter the Great reformed the church according to the political prescriptions of the early Enlightenment, which regarded its role as being mainly civic. He reformed the monasteries so that they could carry out properly their secular tasks as charitable, cultural and educational bodies. He abolished the church's inherited system of governance, in which the sovereign body had been an elective 'national council' (*pomestnyi sobor*) headed by an elected patriarch. Peter replaced both with a Holy Synod, an ecclesiastical governing council, whose members, mostly bishops, were described as 'individuals assembled for the general welfare by the command of the Autocrat and under his scrutiny, jointly with others'. The Tsar also sent to its meetings his own personal representative and 'eye', the 'Over-procurator', who might be and sometimes was a layman. His function was to 'sit in the Synod and make quite sure that the Synod does its duty and acts in all matters which pertain to the Synod's consideration and decision truly, fervently and honestly without time-wasting, in accordance with the regulations and decrees'. Naturally enough, it was generally assumed that the Tsar was now head of the church, even though Peter I never referred to himself as such.[8]

In many respects, then, Russia now had a Protestant ecclesiastical settlement, even though one of the essential prerequisites for Protestantism, widespread literacy, was absent. Another prerequisite, strong local congregations, was being seriously weakened. Up to the eighteenth century parish and village community had normally been one and the same body. Now, however, the church was beginning to separate its parishes from the village institutions of which they had been an integral part. Many parishes ceased to perform secular functions, such as the conduct of basic local government, and concentrated on their ecclesiastical role. Priests gradually ceased to be elected by their parishioners – or appointed by the local landlord – and instead were nominated or even directly appointed by the diocesan consistory, which was in a better position to check that they had completed their seminary education and were properly prepared for their function. In apparent contradiction to this development, however, the priest was still responsible for carrying out certain secular state functions, such as the reading out of official

[8] Lindsey Hughes, *Russia in the age of Peter the Great* (New Haven and London: Yale University Press, 1998), pp. 337–43; quotations on pp. 339–40.

edicts and the registration of births, marriages and deaths; he was also instructed to violate the secrecy of the confessional if he learned of 'ill-intentioned plots' against the imperial family, on pain of 'loss of honour, life and rank' for failing to do so.[9] As a result of these changes, the priest increasingly played the part of an emissary from above, from both church and state acting in concert. The Orthodox Church was reduced roughly to the status of a German princely *Landkirche*.

These were mostly measures that the Tridentine Catholic Church had been implementing a little earlier in various European countries. The Russian Church did not, however, have quite the Catholic Church's confidence in its own strength: on the contrary, it was troubled by a nagging feeling of inferiority towards other Christian denominations. Orthodox clergymen who had contact with their colleagues from other Christian churches were haunted by the sense that Catholicism and Protestantism were theologically more articulate and organisationally more efficient. Protestant churches in particular had more self-reliant parishes and more literate congregations. Orthodox Church people also feared the competition of Russia's own home-grown unofficial Christian movements, the Old Belief and the heretical sects, such as the Dukhobors and Molokane, whose worshippers seemed more zealous and better informed than the average Orthodox parishioner. By the late nineteenth century Protestant movements such as the Baptists were also gaining ground, especially in the fast-growing industrial towns, where the Orthodox Church was slow to establish new parishes.[10]

So worried was the church by this competition that it established a special chair at the St Petersburg Spiritual Academy to study the 'schism' (as it termed the Old Belief) and oversee the training of special missionaries to combat the 'heresies'. Bishops were instructed to keep lists of Old Believers active in their dioceses, and in those which were particularly 'infected' special committees were set up to co-ordinate the missionary effort. Churchmen remained uncertain, however, whether they were making any headway. Konstantin Pobedonostsev, over-procurator of the Holy Synod, complained as late as the 1880s that 'we print

---

[9] Gregory L. Freeze, 'The disintegration of traditional communities: the parish in eighteenth-century Russia', *Journal of Modern History* 48 (1976), 32–50; Freeze, *Russian Levites: parish clergy in the eighteenth century* (Cambridge, MA: Harvard University Press, 1977), pp. 25–9; P. Znamenskii, *Prikhodskoe dukhovenstvo v Rossii so vremeni reformy Petra* (Kazan, 1873), especially chapter 1.

[10] Freeze, 'Institutionalizing piety'; his 'The re-christianization of Russia: the church and popular religion, 1750–1850', *Studia Slavica Finlandensia* 7 (1990), 101–36; Igor Smolitsch, *Die Geschichte der russischen Kirche, 1700–1917*, vol. II in *Forschungen zur osteuropäischen Geschichte* 45 (1991), 169–94, 232–45.

books and distribute them, and then it turns out that they merely moulder in the diocesan offices'.[11]

The Orthodox Church, then, was in a kind of double bind. It had the advantages of being the established church, but also the disadvantages of not being able to order its own internal life according to its own principles. At the same time that it was becoming more formalised and distancing itself institutionally from the lives of ordinary people, it was also trying to fulfil functions delegated to it by the imperial state whose priorities were not its own.

In the late nineteenth and early twentieth centuries the problems created by these contradictory processes were coming to a head. First of all there was a broad and varied upsurge of popular religious life which reflected the tumultuous changes taking place in society. The peasants, emancipated from serfdom, were gradually acquiring primary education, picking up urban skills and being integrated into the market economy; they were working in the towns, on the railways and rivers, and many of them were serving for a few years as conscripts in the army. These changes meant a new and unsettling way of life, but also a broadening of horizons. Old social bonds were being undermined or transformed, and so the spiritual life of ordinary people had to reorient itself.

- There was increasing demand for healing and spiritual comfort through pilgrimages and visits to sacred shrines, wonder-working icons and monasteries, whether near or far: people were using modern means of communication to make their journeys.[12]
- The number of monasteries was growing, especially that of convents, whose number grew from 197 in 1890 to 283 in 1907. Women generally were playing an increasing role in voluntary associations concerned with medical and educational work; they were finding a distinctive if not always autonomous role for themselves.[13]
- Peasants were building new churches and chapels for themselves or at least petitioning the church authorities to do so; sometimes the aim of the new foundations was to shorten the distance that needed to be

---

[11] Smolitsch, *Geschichte der russischen Kirche*, vol. II, 199–200.

[12] Vera Shevzova, 'Icons, miracles and the ecclesial identity of the laity in late Imperial Russian Orthodoxy', *Church History* 69 (2000), 610–31; Chris J. Chulos, *Converging worlds: religion and community in peasant Russia, 1861–1917* (DeKalb: Northern Illinois University Press, 2003).

[13] Brenda Meehan-Waters, 'Popular piety, local initiative and the founding of women's religious communities in Russia, 1764–1907', *St Vladimir's Theological Quarterly* 30 (1986), 117–42; William Wagner, 'The transformation of female Orthodox monasticism in Nizhnii Novgorod diocese, 1764–1929, in comparative perspective', *Journal of Modern History* 78 (2006), 793–845.

covered to get to divine service, sometimes it was to commemorate some event or person. The church authorities were not always keen on these initiatives: neighbouring clergymen feared losing part of their flock and hence part of their income.[14]

- Workers, their lives in many cases disrupted by a recent move to the city, were seeking new forms of religious belief and community life, which might take the form of socialist atheism, but included new versions of semi-orthodox Christianity, such as Baptism or the temperance movement of the layman Ivan Churikov.[15]
- Sectarians such as the Molokane were becoming more active and more organised, building themselves prayer houses (which earlier they had shunned on principle), calling congresses and gradually acquiring some kind of civil status.[16]
- Intellectuals, whose ethos had long been secular, were beginning to take an interest in Orthodoxy again. In 1901 a group of them headed by the poet and novelist Dmitrii Merezhkovskii took the initiative in arranging joint seminars with clergymen under the chairmanship of Sergii Stragorodskii, Rector of the St Petersburg Spiritual Academy. They discussed matters of joint concern, such as marriage, freedom of conscience and the relationship of church to state. Most of the papers were given by the lay intellectuals, and there seems to have been little meeting of minds. After about eighteen months further meetings were vetoed by the Holy Synod.[17]

One indication of the strength of the religious revival was the popularity of John of Kronstadt, the priest of the island naval base at Kronstadt, just outside St Petersburg. Father John believed that the parish priest was the true descendant of the Apostles, directly responsible for encouraging

[14] Vera Shevzov, *Russian Orthodoxy on the eve of revolution* (Oxford: Oxford University Press, 2004).

[15] Simon Dixon, 'The Orthodox Church and the workers of St Petersburg, 1880–1914', in Hugh McLeod (ed.), *European religion in the age of great cities, 1830–1930* (London: Routledge, 1995), pp. 119–44; Page Herrlinger, 'Raising Lazarus: Orthodoxy and the factory *narod* in St Petersburg, 1905–1914', *Jahrbücher für Geschichte Osteuropas* 52 (2004), 341–54; Mark D. Steinberg, *Proletarian imagination: self, modernity and the sacred in Russia, 1910–1925* (Ithaca: Cornell University Press, 2002).

[16] Nicholas B. Breyfogle, 'Prayer and the politics of place: Molokan church building, Tsarist law and the quest for a public sphere in late imperial Russia', in Mark D. Steinberg and Heather J. Coleman (eds.), *Sacred stories: religion and spirituality in modern Russia* (Bloomington: Indiana University Press, 2007), pp. 222–52.

[17] Jutta Scherrer, *Die Petersburger religiös-philosophischen Vereinigungen: die Entwicklungen des religiösen Selbstverständnisses ihrer Intelligencia-Mitglieder, 1901–1917* (Wiesbaden: Harrassowitz, 1973); Christopher Read, *Culture and power in revolutionary Russia: the intelligentsia and Bolshevism before Stalin* (Basingstoke: Macmillan, 1990).

and strengthening the spiritual life of his flock. He did this by simplifying the requirements for ordinary parishioners to take Holy Communion, so that they could do so more frequently than was customary in the Orthodox Church, and also by explaining the various stages of divine service so that they were comprehensible even to those unaccustomed to regular attendance. In a parish which had many poverty-stricken families he devoted much of his time and effort to organising charitable work. He also gained a reputation as a spiritual healer, so that people began to come to seek his advice from all over Russia, more or less as if he were a *starets* (elder) in a monastery. Some of his supporters made extravagant claims, such as that 'God has appeared in the flesh in the Kronstadt *batiushka.*' His superiors, however, were much divided in their opinion of him, some regarding him as a heretic because he conducted divine service in an unaccustomed and flamboyant fashion and took on functions more becoming to a monk than to a priest.[18]

It might be argued that a kind of popular Reformation was taking place in the late nineteenth and early twentieth centuries, under the eyes of a church hierarchy which felt institutionally and intellectually poorly equipped to respond. Popular religious feelings, in all their vigour and variety, had long fitted uneasily into an increasingly disciplined and semi-statised church. Now those feelings burst out of ecclesiastical bounds altogether, reaching their climax with the Revolution of 1905, when political events superimposed themselves on religious turmoil and provided the impetus for projects of radical reform of the Orthodox Church and religious life in general.

It is significant that the event which is usually seen as the starting point of the revolution was a semi-religious one: the procession of workers led by the St Petersburg priest Gapon to petition the Tsar for an improvement in their rights. Gapon, like John of Kronstadt, was a priestly activist, though his political convictions were Christian socialist, at the opposite end of the spectrum from those of John. He was anxious to find a way of reconciling the unruly but deeply felt religiosity of the workers with the political order. In the demonstration he organised on 9 January 1905 thousands of workers, bearing icons and portraits of the Tsar, and dressed in their best clothes as if for a religious festival, marched from the various suburbs to converge on the city centre. There, as is well known, they encountered soldiers who had been poorly briefed, panicked and shot at the workers, killing some two hundred of them. Gapon had hoped to form a revivalist movement through which workers could

---

[18] Nadieszda Kizenko, *A prodigal saint: Father John of Kronstadt and the Russian people* (University Park: Pennsylvania State University Press, 2000), p. 200.

turn away both from drink and from atheist socialism to express their grievances directly to the Tsar. The horrifying outcome thwarted his aim, weakened the church's claim to mediate between people and rulers, and instead intensified the political polarisation and religious anarchy of Russian society.[19]

The political reforms which followed impinged directly on the Orthodox Church. Under strong pressure from his advisers, Tsar Nicholas II had reluctantly decided he had to make Russia more like the parliamentary and constitutional nation states of western Europe, notably by setting up an elected parliament, the State Duma. He proceeded, however, in an unsystematic manner. In the ecclesiastical field his initial reform was to issue in April 1905 an edict of toleration, which for the first time made it legal to quit the Orthodox Church and convert to another Christian faith. This edict gave non-Orthodox the right to proselytise and thus created a situation deeply threatening to the Orthodox Church. After all, non-Orthodox denominations governed themselves in accordance with their own principles – a right which the supposedly established Orthodox Church did not yet have. In a setting where religious movements could compete freely for adherents, it was in a uniquely vulnerable position.

This was almost certainly a reason for the flourishing condition of the Old Belief, whose adherents had for more than two centuries been attacking the official church for its servility to worldly power. They had always claimed to be the custodians of true Orthodoxy, from which the 'Nikonian' (official) Church had allegedly departed through its reforms in the seventeenth century. Now, following the toleration edict, the Old Believers were to be allowed to create their own self-governing church, with full rights of worship and proselytisation, and with a hierarchy of bishops which would rival that of the official church itself. This rivalry constituted a powerful motive for the official church to reclaim its freedom from the state and re-establish its full canonical government, headed by an elected church council and patriarch. For many Orthodox clergymen the competition of the Old Believers was the cardinal motive for urging ecclesiastical reform.[20]

As a result, when in 1905 the opinion of Orthodox bishops was sought, they virtually all criticised the subordination to the state which

[19] Walter Sablinsky, *The road to Bloody Sunday: Father Gapon and the St Petersburg massacre of 1905* (Princeton: Princeton University Press, 1976); on the significance of Gapon and John of Kronstadt, also Laura Engelstein, 'Holy Russia in modern times: an essay on Orthodoxy and cultural change', *Past & Present* 173 (2001), 151–3.

[20] Peter Waldron, 'Religious reform after 1905: old believers and the Orthodox Church', *Oxford Slavonic Papers* 20 (1987), 110–39.

their predecessors had tolerated for two centuries. Many of them considered it contrary to canon law, in that the church was not ruled by its own elected 'national council', headed by its own patriarch. One of them, the Bishop of Volynia, put it like this: 'On paper the Orthodox faith is dominant, but in reality it is the most subjugated of all denominations. The church in Russia has lost what the Latins [Catholics], Protestants, Armenians, Mohammedans and adherents of Lamaism have; it has been deprived of its legitimate leader and delivered into subjugation by secular officials.'[21] The toleration edict of 1905 threatened to make its situation even more vulnerable and anomalous. As Bishop Sergii remarked in alarm, 'After a century of peaceful existence under the protection of the law, behind the strong wall of state security, our church now ventures out, defenceless and without shelter, directly on to the field of battle, to face the enemies' attack.'[22]

National identity was also at issue. The Russian (*rossiiskii*) imperial state had always had a tense relationship with Russian (*russkii*) nationalism, since any enhancement of ethnic national identity threatened the empire with fragmentation and conflict, perhaps ultimately with disintegration. In this respect it closely resembled the Ottoman Empire, to which the national movement of its principal people, the Turks, was in the end to prove fatal.[23]

One of the main complaints of Slavophiles and Russian nationalists had long been the subordination of their national church to a secularised imperial state, many of whose leading officials were not Russian. The well-known Slavophile Ivan Aksakov, for example, had complained as long ago as 1865 of the 'confusion of Caesar's with God's' and of the 'spirit of German chancelleries' in the Holy Synod. He particularly objected to the loss of parish self-government, writing in 1868 that 'We have parishioners but no parish in the proper meaning of the word. People are registered with churches, but they do not constitute a church congregation in its true and authentic meaning.'[24] The pressure for radical ecclesiastical reform was thus gathering force and becoming associated with national identity.

---

[21] Erwin Immekus, *Die russisch-orthodoxe Landpfarrei zu Beginn des XX Jahrhunderts nach den Gutachten der Diözesanbischöfe* (Würzburg: Augustinus Verlag, 1978), p. 266.

[22] Quoted in Simon Dixon, 'The Russian Orthodox Church in Imperial Russia, 1721–1917', in Michael Angold (ed.), *The Cambridge history of Christianity*, vol. V: *Eastern Christianity* (Cambridge: Cambridge University Press, 2006), p. 346.

[23] I deploy this argument more fully in my *Russia: people and empire* (London: HarperCollins, 1997).

[24] *Sochineniia I. S. Aksakova* (Moscow: Tipografiia M. G. Volchaninova, 1886), vol. IV, pp. 35, 121–2, 144.

That reform never happened, though. The reasons for the delay and then indefinite postponement of the planned council are not fully clear from the sources. It seems though that after the suppression of the revolutionary movement by 1907, not only was the sense of urgency lost, but the Tsar and his ministers feared that a church council might stage a kind of repetition of the turbulent First Duma (1906) and actually rekindle political opposition which was beginning to die down after the upheavals of 1905–6. After all, a significant minority of priests – not just Gapon – were inspired by Christian socialist ideas, and supported, among other things, the peasants' demand for land to be compulsorily expropriated from the landowners.[25] At the same time on the right wing of Russian politics fears were growing that detaching the church from the tutelage and protection of the state would lay it helplessly open to competition both from atheist socialism and from other Christian denominations, some of which were by now better organised, theologically more articulate and spiritually more vigorous. An Orthodox missionary congress held in Kiev in 1908 voiced these fears and resolved to move into alliance with the monarchist political parties, which were urging the government to drop all ecclesiastical reform. Under this kind of pressure Prime Minister Stolypin decided to withdraw from the Duma several of the bills which were intended to give legal form to the 1905 toleration edict, including that concerning the Old Believers.[26]

Even those who favoured reform were beginning to be anxious about the convening of the council which was supposed to give effect to their ideas. Debates in the press and in the pre-conciliar consultations had shown that the church was internally split. While nearly everyone wanted change, they disagreed profoundly about what form that change should take. Some – the Christian socialists among them – wanted the centre of gravity of the new church to be in the parish congregation. They envisaged parishioners running their own affairs, including their finances, and electing their own priests. They also wished to enhance the status of secular clergy, ending the system whereby only monks (or widowed priests) could aspire to become bishops. This was, if you like, the 'Protestant' variant of church reform; some of its adherents also wished to reform the liturgy to bring it closer to the congregation by,

[25] Sergei Firsov, *Russkaia tserkov' nakanune peremen (konets 1890-kh – 1918 gg)* (St Petersburg: Kruglyi stol po religioznomu obrazovaniyu i diakonii, 2002), pp. 318–42.
[26] Heather J. Coleman, 'Defining heresy: the Fourth Missionary Congress and the problem of cultural power in Russia after 1905', *Jahrbücher für Geschichte Osteuropas* 52 (2004), 70–91.

for example, conducting it in modern Russian and moving the iconosta-sis back so that the preparation of the Eucharist took place in full view of the congregation. On the other side were the 'Catholics', the episcopal conservatives, who wished to preserve the demarcation between secular (white) and monastic (black) clergy and emphasised the re-establishment of the patriarchate as the measure which would restore to the church its full canonical status.[27] Both sides feared that, if no compromise could be found between these two approaches, then the church might actually split up in a manner reminiscent of the Reformation division of western Christianity.

In the absence of church reform and of legislative measures defining the legal procedures for guaranteeing religious freedom, the religious situation in Russia from 1905 to 1917 remained ambiguous and highly conflictual. Each party made maximum use of freedoms declared but not yet enshrined in law, and the newly emancipated newspapers ensured that the variety of opinions was reflected in vigorous and shrill debate. The precipitate introduction of party politics and something close to press freedom during 1905–6 combined here to impede the project of orderly ecclesiastical reform.

The long-awaited 'national council' *was* eventually held, but in very different circumstances from those envisaged in 1905–7. It took place in the summer and autumn of 1917, at the height of the revolution, at times with cannon literally booming within earshot of the Kremlin, where it was being held. The splits of the preceding years were reproduced within the council and led to heated debates. In the end the episcopal conserva-tives emerged victorious: they achieved their great aim, the restoration of the patriarchate.

Even that potentially momentous achievement – the reversal of two hundred years of ecclesiastical history – was however immediately and drastically diminished: the new Bolshevik regime imposed its own ver-sion of the separation of church and state, which amounted to the blatant re-subordination of the church to the state – to a state, moreover, which was not even formally Christian, but professed atheism as its official ideology. This was not merely an extreme version of, say, the French Radicals' secularism of the early twentieth century. The Bolsheviks aimed not to restrict the church to a modest social role as an unprivileged civil association, but to destroy it altogether (though they differed among themselves about how that might best be achieved). They had their own vision of humanity's salvation, one which differed

[27] J. Y. Cunningham, *A vanquished hope: the movement for church renewal in Russia, 1905–1906* (Crestwood, NY: St Vladimir's Seminary Press, 1981), pp. 133–62.

totally from that of the church, and they were determined to push it through at all costs. Theirs was a thoroughgoing 'religion of humanity': it promised a secular heaven to be built by means of science, technology, modern industry and state economic planning. The Bolsheviks had not fully worked out by 1917 how that transformation was to be achieved, but they were all confident of the general direction in which they were heading, and they all regarded ecclesiastical religion as a rival to be defeated, whether by direct and violent or by gradual and peaceful means.

The new Soviet government began its anti-religious campaign with draconian decrees. In 1918 it expropriated all ecclesiastical land and property without compensation and stripped all religious associations of their status as legal persons. Later legislation provided that congregations could lease back church buildings free of charge for worship, and they could hire a 'servant of the cult' to perform their services for them. A 'congregation' had to have twenty believers registered as such with the authorities: people who did so tacitly condemned themselves to inferior status in society. The priest now became an employee of his flock rather than a pastor, and most religious activities – charitable work, prayer meetings, Sunday schools and public processions – were forbidden.

Tikhon, the new patriarch, reacted vigorously to the regime's challenge. He pronounced anathema on atheists and on all who committed violence against the innocent. He urged only spiritual not physical resistance to the Soviet regime, but that was not true of Orthodox clergymen who lived under the Whites or had escaped into emigration: they called publicly for its overthrow. In that way the church got caught up in the civil war, and clergymen were treated as the enemy. Many of them were murdered or arrested and sent to concentration camps, while the central organisation of the church was irreparably weakened.[28]

After the end of the civil war, the regime continued its efforts to undermine the church, only now by more peaceful means, by offering what they hoped would be a more attractive atheist–humanist culture. There was a solid social basis for this alternative, particularly in the cities and particularly among young men who had consciously rejected all forms of Christianity and/or had fought in the Red Army during the civil war. During the 1920s the Bolsheviks founded the League of Militant Godless, with its own newspapers and with cells in towns and

[28] Dimitry V. Pospielovsky, *Soviet anti-religious campaigns and persecutions* (London: Macmillan, 1988), vol. II, pp. 14–16; Edward E. Roslof, *Red priests: renovationism, Russian Orthodoxy and revolution, 1905–1946* (Bloomington: Indiana University Press, 2002), pp. 18–31.

villages all over Russia. The Militant Godless organised public meetings, debates, film shows and festivals ridiculing church rituals and propagating their vision of Russia transformed by science, technology and wise Communist leadership. But their activists, with few exceptions, were poorly educated, knew too little about the church they were attacking, and did not succeed in rapidly implanting their own celebrations as replacements for Christmas and Easter. In the villages, moreover, they were isolated and surrounded by a suspicious and largely hostile population which clung the more inflexibly to its traditional way of life precisely because of the upheavals going on around them.[29]

The regime also proceeded by attempting to split the church from within. The famine in the Volga region in 1921–2 offered them a convenient opportunity. In February 1922 the regime demanded that the church should surrender all its valuables to raise money for famine relief. Patriarch Tikhon replied that the church would sell all valuables not consecrated for liturgical use to raise funds for a famine relief programme which it would conduct itself. The Communists rejected this declaration of self-reliance and began to confiscate religious objects by force. They met with fierce resistance on the part of local believers.

Some churchmen however – the Christian socialists and renovationists of 1905–7 – argued that the church should co-operate with the regime and work together with it to help the victims of famine. They coupled this with proposals for a broad programme of reform, many of whose points were familiar from the debates of nearly two decades earlier. They laid great emphasis on the reform of the liturgy to bring it closer to ordinary people and make it more comprehensible to them. In general terms they argued that if Jesus were alive today he would become a Communist, since Communism was the application of Christian principles to the twentieth century. With the help of the GPU (security police) the renovationists staged a *coup d'état* inside the church, deposed Patriarch Tikhon and took over the church administration. They dismissed many bishops and parish priests and installed their own nominees. The ousted clergymen were accused of counter-revolutionary activity and some of them were arrested and executed.[30]

Neither the regime nor the renovationists enjoyed much support among ordinary believers. When GPU activists turned up at a church

[29] Glennys Young, *Power and the sacred in Revolutionary Russia: religious activists in the village* (University Park, PA: Pennsylvania State University Press, 1997), especially chapter 3; William B. Husband, *'Godless Communists': atheism and society in Soviet Russia, 1917–1931* (DeKalb: Northern Illinois University Press, 2000), chapter 2.

[30] Roslof, *Red priests*, chapters 2–3.

to confiscate sacred vessels, they were not infrequently confronted by an indignant crowd of believers, sometimes armed with pitchforks and other primitive weapons. In one such incident, in the manufacturing town of Shuia, not far from Moscow, a violent skirmish resulted in which four or five people were killed, including a Red Army soldier. Lenin decided to use the occasion to mount another all-out assault on the church as the Bolsheviks' leading enemies in the class struggle. He told the Politburo 'The greater the number of representatives of the reactionary clergy and the reactionary bourgeoisie we manage to shoot on this basis, the better.' They took him at his word. In Petrograd, Metropolitan Veniamin was arrested for resisting confiscations in the parishes of his diocese; he was tried for counter-revolutionary activity, sentenced to death and shot.[31]

The renovationist church did not triumph for long, however. Most parishioners rejected its priests, seeing them correctly as stooges of the secret police. Furthermore, having achieved their aim of splitting the church, the Communists abandoned their support for the renovationists, and resumed a policy of combined co-optation and repression of the established church, which was thus faced with the problem of how to relate to an atheist regime determined to undermine it. In order to ensure its bare survival, in 1927, the leading metropolitan, Sergii of Moscow, publicly declared that 'We wish to be Orthodox believers, and at the same time to claim the Soviet Union as our civil motherland, whose joys and successes are our joys and successes, and whose misfortunes are our misfortunes.' Ostensibly, he was pledging loyalty not to the regime but to the motherland. However, the name of that motherland now contained a political term, 'Soviet'. In any case, he added 'We need to show not only in words but also in deeds that ... the most loyal adherents of Orthodoxy can be true citizens of the Soviet Union, loyal to the Soviet authorities [*sovetskoi vlasti*].' He also instructed clergy to pray for the regime.[32]

Sergii hoped that in making these concessions he was ensuring the survival of the church. However, the immediate result of his declaration was to provoke a further schism. A number of bishops refused further allegiance to him, on the grounds that he had pledged loyalty to an atheist regime. They were unable to set up an alternative church organisation,

---

[31] *Ibid.*, pp. 66–7; Robert Service, *Lenin: a political life* (London: Macmillan, 1995), vol. III, p. 246.

[32] *Russkaia Pravoslavnaia Tserkov' i kommunisticheskoe gosudarstvo, 1917–1941 gg: dokumenty i fotografii* (Moscow: Bibleiskii-bogoslovskii Institut, 1996), pp. 203–6.

but in the underground formed several semi-sectarian movements of their own, fragmenting and weakening Orthodoxy still further.[33]

Meanwhile, Sergii's surviving 'above-ground' church did not benefit much from his concessions. During the 1930s the regime carried out a ruthless and radical revolution from above, which included the imposition of five-year economic plans in industry, the collectivisation of agriculture and the statisation of the whole of educational and cultural life. An intrinsic part of this campaign was a determined drive to extirpate Christianity in all its forms. In the most dramatic single incident the Cathedral of Christ the Saviour in Moscow, the largest place of worship in Russia, built in the nineteenth century to commemorate victory over Napoleon, was laced with high explosives and blown up on 5 December 1931. This was a crushing symbolic blow not just against Christianity, but against Russian national pride.

On a more modest level, similar scenes were played out all over Russia. Most churches, it is true, were not destroyed but closed and turned into stores, village clubs or cinemas. The closure was sometimes accompanied by symbolic desecration: in one case icons were not only taken down, but lined up against the walls and shot, on the grounds that the saints they depicted had 'resisted kolkhoz construction'.[34] Such scenes frequently provoked the most serious crisis in the collectivisation of any village. As the Riazan OGPU reported in March 1930,

Alongside the heightened anti-Soviet agitation of the kulaks, the clergy, Orthodox believers and sectarians have stepped up their activity. Priests organise the peasantry around the church, stirring them up with calls for 'defence of the faith and the church'. The churches become headquarters of anti-Soviet and anti-kolkhoz propaganda, and believers spread all kinds of rumours, opinions and anti-kolkhoz sentiments. Like the kulaks, believers convene illegal gatherings and mobilise mass demonstrations. They vigorously resist the closure of churches when that is proposed at meetings by local officials.[35]

A leaflet from the north Caucasus illustrates the premonitions of catastrophe felt by many peasants:

In the kolkhoz there will be a special branding iron, [they] will close all the churches, not allow prayer, dead people will be cremated, the christening of children will be forbidden, invalids and the elderly will be killed, there won't be

---

[33] The largest such movement is examined in Mikhail Shkarovskii, *Iosifliane: techenie v Russkoi Pravoslavnoi Tserkvi* (Moscow: Memorial, 1999).

[34] Lynne Viola, *Peasant rebels under Stalin: collectivisation and the culture of peasant resistance* (New York: Oxford University Press, 1996), pp. 38–41.

[35] *Riazanskaia derevnia v 1929–30gg: khronika golovokruzheniia. Dokumenty i materialy* (Moscow: Rosspen, 1998), p. 405.

any husbands or wives, [all] will sleep under a 100-metre blanket ... Children will be taken from their parents, there will be wholesale incest: brothers will live with sisters, sons with mothers, fathers with daughters, etc. The kolkhoz – this means beasts in a single shed, people under a single blanket.[36]

What is striking about this document is that it combines accurate predictions of the future with wild apocalyptic nightmares. Here the clash of holy and secular Russia reached its terrible climax.

As for the incumbents of the closed churches, most were arrested, accused of counter-revolutionary activity and imprisoned or exiled. Many of them were killed. By 1939, of 163 bishops active in 1917, only four were still at liberty and able to conduct any kind of diocesan business. One of them, Metropolitan Aleksii of Leningrad, was living in a closet in the bell-tower of the cathedral, in accommodation intended for the caretaker.[37]

Then came World War II and with it the regime's attitude to the church softened. They both shared a mood of Russian imperial nationalism. Even a Communist government now needed the church to sustain the patriotism of the Russian people and to support the Soviet Union in its aspiration to create a new power bloc in central and eastern Europe after the war.[38] Stalin restored the patriarchate, and sanctioned a reduced but viable network of dioceses, parishes, and seminaries for the training of priests. The church thus did manage to survive, but in a truncated and dependent form, manipulated by the Soviet regime for its own foreign policy objectives, including the post-war domination of central and eastern Europe. Its most tangible achievement was the incorporation of the Greek Catholic Church in Ukraine, a 'success' which underlined the church's imperial role.

After the war national pride combined with grief over the huge loss of life stimulated a genuine religious revival among the Russian people. It alarmed the regime and prompted it to reinstate many of the restrictions it had briefly lifted during the war. An incident at Saratov in January 1949 illustrates what Communists feared. At Epiphany some 10,000 people took part in a cross-bearing procession round the cathedral and then went down to the banks of the Volga to commemorate Christ's baptism in the Jordan by receiving a blessing given with a crucifix dipped in the river. Several hundred of the celebrants decided

---

[36] Viola, *Peasant rebels*, pp. 57–60.

[37] Dimitry I. Pospielovsky, *The Russian Church under the Soviet regime, 1917–1982* (Crestwood, NY: St Vladimir's Seminary Press, 1984), vol. I, pp. 174–7.

[38] Steven Merritt Miner, *Stalin's holy war: religion, nationalism and alliance politics, 1941–1945* (Chapel Hill: University of North Carolina Press, 2003).

this ritual was inadequate: they broke through a police cordon and insisted on taking their blessing in the form of a full immersion in the water. The regime could not stomach this kind of spontaneous enthusiasm. *Pravda* published a satirical article on the 'Saratov bathings'. What is even more striking is that the church itself felt compelled to act as the agent of the atheist state. Patriarch Aleksii reprimanded the local clergymen for failing to foresee and prevent the disorders; he forbade any further 'pilgrimages to the River Jordan' and ordered that future Epiphany blessings must take place within the precincts of the church itself.[39]

In the interests of the church's survival, then, its leaders were actually being compelled to suppress religious enthusiasm. They probably had no choice. All clergymen were subjected to a state-run Council for Religious Affairs, and bishops were in effect members of the Communist Party nomenclature elite, their behaviour monitored for loyalty to the regime and lack of zeal in their religious tasks.[40]

Thereafter for most of the remaining Soviet period the only legal activity that the Orthodox Church could undertake was regular divine service on Sundays and special saints' days; the baptism of children was also permitted but discouraged. All other religious pursuits were forbidden. That included processions, public religious funerals, prayer meetings, Sunday schools and any kind of charitable activity. The church became identified almost exclusively with the liturgy, to the detriment of its wider social role.

As a result, since the fall of the Soviet Union it has had difficulty in re-establishing a full parish life. It feels vulnerable to the competition of other faiths, especially those that come from abroad, well financed and experienced in techniques of conversion, religious education and social work. Although a few parishes are lively and successful, the Orthodox Church has tended rather to emphasise its territorial and national role – the role in which it has always felt sure of itself – with a prior claim to the loyalty of the Russian (including Ukrainian and Belorussian) people.

Since in the USSR many places had been without a functioning church or priest for decades, lukewarm believers had abandoned the practice of their faith altogether, while more fervent ones had gone

---

[39] Tatiana A. Chumachenko, *Church and state in Soviet Russia: Russian Orthodoxy from World War II to the Khrushchev years*, trans. and ed. Edward Roslof (Armonk: M. E. Sharpe, 2002), pp. 96–9, 112–13.

[40] Jane Ellis, *The Russian Orthodox Church: a contemporary history* (London: Croom Helm, 1986); M. V. Shkarovskii, *Russkaia pravoslavnaia tserkov' pri Staline i Khrushcheve: gosudarstvenno-tserkovnye otnosheniia v SSSR v 1939–1964 godakh* (Moscow: Krutitskoe Patriarshee Podvor'e, 1999).

underground and taken up an often narrow and fundamentalist version of it. In general, the project of reforming the church for the needs of the modern world became identified with complicity in the crimes of the Communist regime. Hence the church that has survived is old-fashioned and in many ways ill-adapted to a social mission, to spreading the faith and to competition with other denominations, some of which operate in Russia with more money, better organisation, more zealous activists and/ or a more articulate theology.

Perhaps more than any other European church, then, the Russian Church became a victim of volatile political processes in which democ-ratisation, toleration/intolerance, national identity and imperial mission were all mixed in a complex and explosive form. What Christopher Bayly refers to as the sharpening and clarification of religious organisation coincided with massive social, cultural and political changes which moved both Russians and non-Russians to seek new spiritual orientations.

Figures suggest that nowadays Russians are among the most secular-ised peoples in Europe, at least as regards religious practice: according to surveys, some 6–7 per cent attend divine service at least once a month, and this figure may be as low as 2 per cent in Moscow; 18 per cent of Russians believe in a living personal God and 24 per cent in life after death – though not always in a manner that would be accepted as 'orthodox Orthodox'. At the same time, though, some 80 per cent of Russians still identify themselves in questionnaires as *pravoslavnye* (Orthodox) – which seems to confirm the church's own conception of its national role.[41] We have, then, a paradox: a secular society which nevertheless regards the church as having a crucial role to play.

Russians are anxious today to reassert their separate and distinctive national identity after the loss of the multi-national state which used to give it substance. In those circumstances, the Orthodox Church remains the most conspicuous and tenacious symbol of nationhood. That helps to explain why the church is relatively poorly attended, yet retains the external allegiance of so many Russians.

In general, McLeod's observation that we should talk of polarisation rather than secularisation for the late nineteenth and most of the twenti-eth century is amply borne out by the Russian experience, indeed in such an extreme and violent form that we should perhaps be seeking a new dimension in order to explain it. In fact, the history of the Soviet Union could well be regarded as in large measure the story of the clash of

[41] S. B. Filatov, *Religiia i obshchestvo: ocherki religioznoi zhizni sovremennoi Rossii* (Moscow: Letnii Sad, 2002), pp. 470–84.

messianic socialism with messianic Orthodoxy – a clash which proved in the end fatal to Russian socialism and severely weakening to the Orthodox Church.[42]

Secularisation in Russia came in two great waves, both of them sponsored by the state. The first was launched by the Tsarist regime from the late seventeenth century in the interests of administering a multi-ethnic, multi-confessional empire, the second by the Soviet regime with the aim of building an atheist socialist society. The first required the church to accept ultimate state hegemony in quasi-Protestant guise, and a form of 'confessionalisation' which had imperial rather than ecclesiastical priorities in mind; it created an uneasy and in the long run deteriorating relationship between the church and popular religious practices. By the late nineteenth century this state-sponsored regularisation of the church was coming up against increasingly lively movements of spiritual renewal among both clergy and laity – movements which pointed in many different directions and which an unreformed church simply could not contain. The Soviet version of secularisation went much further: it aimed to destroy the church, but, concluding eventually that this was both impractical and unadvisable, settled for a very rigid form of control from above. It interrupted, then suppressed, the many-sided spiritual searching of the Russians (and all the Soviet peoples) at the very time when they were undergoing extremely rapid social and economic changes. For many Russians, everyday religious life, where possible at all, was restricted to a weekly divine service; for the minority of extremely zealous and committed believers it was confined into tiny, hermetic, sect-like groupings bereft of any public manifestation of their faith.

The long-term result has undoubtedly been secularisation, though in a somewhat paradoxical form. The result is the contradictory situation I noted at the beginning of this chapter. The post-Soviet Russian Orthodox Church is in some ways in a very strong position: it enjoys more public esteem than any other institution, it is the only public association that has existed continuously for many centuries, and it symbolises the Russian nation. Yet its potential remains only partially realised: its role in social and economic life is modest. Two major waves of secularisation have intersected with tumultuous social and political change to produce a situation where the Orthodox Church is the most respected institution in Russia, but where it does not seem to satisfy the spiritual searchings of most Russians.

---

[42] I have expounded this view at length in my *Rulers and victims: the Russians in the Soviet Union* (Cambridge, MA: Harvard University Press, 2006).

6   The American experience
of secularisation

Michael O'Brien

There are many ways to approach the question of how far the United States is a standing reproach to the 'secularisation thesis', not least because there are many versions of that thesis. The strongest version, whose intellectual genealogy runs from Condorcet via Auguste Comte to Max Weber, suggests that religion is irrational and childlike, that modernity promotes rationality and maturity, and that in time religion will be extinguished because redundant. The weaker version argues that religion may be a continuing human need but is a private matter, confined to voluntary associations, but that public institutions (especially the state and education) are obliged to be secular. Within this latter version, one can discern two varieties, rooted in differing estimates of religion: the first mistrusts religion's moral influence as narrow, sectarian and intolerant, and hence incapable of furnishing a shared social morality for the public realm; the second thinks better of religion and acknowledges that it might promote, say, charity or altruism, but is conscious that religions are too plural and particularist to be allowed free rein, because their actions often generate social conflict and disharmony, and that, at best, religions can act in the public realm only when their idiosyncrasies are filtered out. Indispensable to these standpoints, with the exception of the last, is the presumption that, over time, there come to be a growing number of agnostics and atheists, who acquire cultural and social power, which is used either to extirpate or to quarantine the religious. Indispensable, too, is some sense that, as modernity and enlightenment advance, so religion retreats; whereas once religion dominated every thought and every institution, private and public, eventually it comes to be confined to a few thoughts, for a few people, in a few private institutions. Hence the secularisation thesis has been, habitually, a dialectical theory and a programme for struggle, for what the nineteenth century often likened to war.[1]

---

[1] A rhetoric evident most notably in the American tradition by John William Draper, *History of the conflict between religion and science* (New York: D. Appleton, 1874) and, less drastically, Andrew Dickson White, *A history of the warfare of science with theology in Christendom* (New York: D. Appleton, 1896).

It is evident that the American experience maps on to these various propositions with great irregularity. In the modern world, the ideological framework for American thinking about religion and public life was established unusually early, from the late eighteenth to the early nineteenth century, before a developed concept of secularisation was available, and this framework came to form a predicate for interpretations of the more systematic secularisation of thought, loosely associated with the development of the modern natural sciences, intimated in the late nineteenth century. The result was a version of secularisation that has been peculiarly accommodating to religion, and conversely a version of religion that became (though only eventually) surprisingly accommodating to secularisation, if on peculiar terms. That is, in American history, there has scarcely ever been outright warfare between religion and the secular realm, but a negotiation over boundaries, in which those committed to religion and secularity have often conceded the value of the other, indeed have sometimes (if not habitually) been the other, and each has been modified by the experience of negotiation.

A few facts will be helpful. The most obvious and salient fact is that the American experience since the eighteenth century has seen not the decline but the growth of religious adherence. Numbers are slippery, since they can be given for many different things – church membership, church attendance, religious belief, observance of ritual – but Finke and Stark's valuable study, *The churching of America, 1776–2005*, asserts that in 1776 only 17 per cent of Americans adhered formally to any church, that by 1850 this had risen to 34 per cent, by 1890 to 45 per cent and by 1980 to 62 per cent, where it remains.[2] These numbers, doubtless, show a more dramatic increase than is plausible, since the criteria for church membership were more strict in the eighteenth century than in the late twentieth century. Still, the overall pattern seems broadly right and, for the present day, is compatible with other data. In 2001, for example, the 'American religious identification survey' conducted by the Graduate Center of the City University of New York suggested that 77 per cent of Americans classified themselves as Christian, while another 3.7 per cent claimed to be religious but non-Christian – Jews, Muslims, native Americans, Hindus, Unitarians, Druids, and so forth. Only 0.4 per cent of Americans (about 900,000 people) described themselves as atheist, only 0.5 per cent (just under a million) as agnostic.[3]

---

[2] Roger Finke and Rodney Stark, *The churching of America, 1776–2005: winners and losers in our religious economy* (New Brunswick: Rutgers University Press, 2005), p. 23.

[3] See www.gc.cuny.edu/faculty/research_briefs/aris/aris_index.htm.

However, mildly cutting across the general pattern of religious growth, this survey, which had also been done eleven years earlier, showed a growth in the number of Americans who declined any religious identification. In 1990 there were 14.3 million of these (8 per cent), but in 2001 there were 29.4 million (14 per cent). As one might expect, the non-religious are distributed very unevenly, from highs of 25 per cent of the adult population of the state of Washington, 22 per cent of Vermont, 21 per cent of Colorado and Oregon, and 20 per cent of Wyoming, to lows of 6 per cent in Alabama and 3 per cent in North Dakota.[4] However, this category of non-religious needs interpretation; it describes those Americans who have no meaningful relationship to organised religion and its rituals – do not attend churches, do not pray, etc. – rather than those who actively disbelieve in the supernatural or are hostile to organised religion. Over the last fifty years, Gallup polls have put the percentage of those Americans who believe in God in a range between 94 per cent and 99 per cent.[5] Only a tiny minority might accept the proposition that American society would improve in proportion as religion declined. Hence that strong version of the secularisation thesis which requires a diminishing number of believers and a growing number of sceptics is profoundly inapplicable to the American experience.

On the face if it, this seems puzzlingly at odds with the fact that the United States was notable in the eighteenth century for setting limits to religion's scope, especially its involvement in government. Though the Declaration of Independence invokes, delicately, 'the laws of nature and of nature's God', appeals to 'the supreme judge of the world' and expresses 'a firm reliance on the protection of divine providence', the Constitution of 1787 is strikingly devoid of religious language. To be sure, it does end with the annotation, suggesting the equivalence of the sacred and profane, that the document was signed 'in the year of our lord one thousand and seven hundred and eighty seven and of the independence of the United States the twelfth', but otherwise it can be read as keeping religion at arm's length. Article VI has: 'No religious test shall ever be required as a qualification to any office or public trust under the United States.' And the First Amendment says that: 'Congress shall make no law respecting an establishment of religion, or prohibiting the free exercise thereof.'

---

[4] *Ibid.*
[5] Jeffrey K. Hadden, 'Desacralizing secularization theory', in Jeffrey K. Hadden and Anson Shupe (eds.), *Secularization and fundamentalism reconsidered: religion and the political order* (New York: Paragon House, 1989), vol. III, p. 16.

Thomas Jefferson, in a famous letter in 1802 to the Danbury Baptist Association, glossed these constitutional elements in the following manner:

Believing with you that religion is a matter which lies solely between Man and his God, that he owes account to none other for his faith or his worship, that the legitimate powers of government reach actions only and not opinions, I contemplate with sovereign reverence that act of the whole American people which declared that their legislature should 'make no law respecting an establishment of religion, or prohibiting the free exercise thereof', thus building a wall of separation between Church and State. Adhering to this expression of the supreme will of the nation in behalf of the rights of conscience, I shall see with sincere satisfaction the progress of those sentiments which tend to restore to man all his natural rights, convinced he has no natural right in opposition to his social duties.[6]

This Jeffersonian opinion has been deeply influential, and has given rise to the widespread belief that the American Constitution, from the first and deliberately, mandated a 'separation of Church and State', that there is a high wall between these two realms, and that this has arisen because 'religion is a matter which lies solely between Man and his God'. More broadly, since Jefferson was arguably the founding father who was most sceptical of Christianity and, as the chief author of the Declaration of Independence, often used to personify the American founding, it also gave rise to the presumption that the United States was founded by those who wished to constrain religion, either because Christianity was untrue or because it occasioned civil strife.

This is wrong on almost all counts. The Constitution and its Bill of Rights nowhere mentions churches, separation or walls, and is silent on what may or may not lie between men and God.[7] Jefferson's opinion was but a retrospective and partisan interpretation, and very much a minority opinion, which was not accepted by the Supreme Court until the 1940s and, even then, with marked, not to say bizarre, selectivity.[8] The colder truth is that these passages in the Constitution said no more than what they said; that no federal official could be required to pass a religious test, that Congress could neither establish a religion nor

---

[6] Thomas Jefferson to Messrs Nehemiah Dodge, Ephraim Robbins and Stephen S. Nelson, a committee of the Danbury Baptist Association in the State of Connecticut, 1 January 1802, at www.loc.gov/loc/lcib/9806/danpre.html.

[7] Philip Hamburger, *Separation of Church and State* (Cambridge, MA: Harvard University Press, 2002) argues persuasively that Jefferson's doctrine does not become constitutional dogma until the mid twentieth century, though less persuasively that anti-Catholicism drove most nineteenth-century American attitudes towards religion and the state.

[8] Hamburger, *Separation*, pp. 422–92.

abridge religious freedom. The immediate referents, of course, were the English precedents of the Test Acts, the Church of England and the various laws forbidding blasphemy and the like. One might also think it was setting up the federal government's social ethics in opposition to the tests, establishments and statutes regulating religion that had been common in American colonial governments. In fact, this was little so. These clauses applied only to the federal government, not to the states. The Constitution presumed that, in the division of responsibilities within federalism, religion belonged to the states, not to the federal government. This expressed no innate hostility towards religion, merely an opinion about the appropriate level at which any legislation about the role of religion should be enacted.

At the end of 1791, when the First Amendment went into effect, five states (New Hampshire, Massachusetts, Connecticut, Maryland, South Carolina) had established churches and used tax revenues to pay ministers and twelve states out of the thirteen (New York was the exception) required religious tests for the holding of public office.[9] The Pennsylvania of 1776 required legislators, before taking their seats, to declare, 'I do believe in one God, the creator and governor of the universe, the rewarder of the good and the punisher of the wicked. And I do acknowledge the Scriptures of the Old and New Testament to be given by Divine inspiration', though it added, somewhat inconsistently, that 'no further or other religious test shall ever hereafter be required of any civil officer or magistrate in this State'.[10] The preamble to the 1780 Constitution of Massachusetts spoke of 'the goodness of the great legislator of the universe, in affording us, in the course of his providence, an opportunity, deliberately and peaceably, without fraud, violence or surprise, of entering into an original, explicit, and solemn compact with each other; and of forming a new constitution of civil government' and implored 'his direction in so interesting a design'.[11] John Adams, the chief author of that constitution, though he drifted into a vague Unitarianism, remained convinced that religion was essential. As president, in 1798 he proclaimed a fast day, in which he invited Americans to

acknowledge before God the manifold sins and transgressions with which we are justly chargeable as individuals and as a nation; beseeching him at the same time, of his infinite grace, through the redeemer of the world, freely to remit all our offenses, and to incline us, by his holy spirit, to that sincere repentance and

---

[9] Frederic Cople Jaher, *A scapegoat in the new wilderness: the origins and rise of anti-Semitism in America* (Cambridge, MA: Harvard University Press, 1994), p.121.

[10] See http://avalon.law.yale.edu/subject_menus/statech.asp.

[11] See www.nhinet.org/ccs/docs/ma-1780.htm.

reformation which may afford us reason to hope for his inestimable favor and heavenly benediction.[12]

Later, he observed to Jefferson,

Twenty times, in the course of my late reading, have I been upon the point of breaking out, 'This would be the best of all possible worlds, if there were no religion in it!!!' But in this exclamati[on] I should have been as fanatical as Bryant or Cleverly. Without religion this world would be something not fit to be mentioned in polite company, I mean hell.[13]

Gradually, to be sure, disestablishment was completed in the states.[14] The last two to go were the Congregationalist states of Connecticut in 1818 and Massachusetts in 1833, under pressure from coalitions of Methodists, Baptists and occasional ageing philosophical radicals. However, state constitutions continued routinely to speak of the connection between citizenship, religion and morality. The 1874 Constitution of Arkansas, which is still in effect, begins, 'We, the People of the State of Arkansas, grateful to almighty God for the privilege of choosing our own form of government; for our civil and religious liberty; and desiring to perpetuate its blessings, and secure the same to our selves and posterity; do ordain and establish this Constitution.'[15] The 1897 Constitution of Delaware (also still in effect) begins, 'Through divine goodness, all men have by nature the rights of worshiping and serving their creator according to the dictates of their consciences.'[16] Nor did religious tests for public office, militia and jury service necessarily disappear. As late as the 1830s, for example, four states (New Jersey, North Carolina, Rhode

---

[12] The text can be found in James D. Richardson, *A compilation of the messages and papers of the Presidents, 1789–1897* (Washington, DC: US Government Printing Office, 1896), 1:268–70; see also Charles Ellis Dickson, 'Jeremiads in the new American republic: the case of national fasts in the John Adams administration', *New England Quarterly* 60 (1987), 187–207.

[13] John Adams to Thomas Jefferson, 19 April 1817, in Lester J. Cappon (ed.), *The Adams–Jefferson letters: the complete correspondence between Thomas Jefferson and Abigail and John Adams* (Chapel Hill: University of North Carolina Press, 1959), p. 509. Lemuel Bryant ('a jolly jocular and liberal Schollar and Divine') had been the young Adams's parish priest, and Joseph Cleverly ('a biggoted episcopalian') his Latin master.

[14] It is worth noting that many Americans understood 'establishment' to mean the exclusive support of a single denomination, and hence a state that supported financially more than one sect could not be considered as having established a religion. As Jasper Adams put it, 'The meaning of the term "establishment" in [the First Amendment] unquestionably is, the preference and establishment given by law to one sect of Christians over every other:' Jasper Adams, *The relation of Christianity to civil government in the United States* (Charleston: A. E. Miller, 1833), reprinted in Daniel L. Dreisbach (ed.), *Religion and politics in the early republic: Jasper Adams and the church–state debate* (Lexington: University Press of Kentucky, 1996), p. 46.

[15] See www.stateconstitutions.umd.edu/Thorpe/display.aspx?ID=20. There is similar wording in the 1873 Pennsylvania Constitution and that of Virginia in 1903.

[16] See www.stateconstitutions.umd.edu/Thorpe/display.aspx?ID=122.

Island, New Hampshire) formally denied Jewish civil equality and it was only in 1876 that the last state – New Hampshire – removed such disabilities and permitted Jews to hold public office.[17] Since, during this period, US senators were elected by state legislatures, these disabilities structured one branch of the federal government.

It is worth noticing, too, that, characteristically, when toleration was extended, it was usual to deny it to atheists. So, when Maryland voted for Jewish emancipation in 1825 – Jews had been able to vote, but not hold office – it did so with the provision that an official 'must make and subscribe to a declaration of his belief in a future state of rewards and punishments'. The legislature had been offered a 'universal version' of this bill and this had, more plainly, said that 'no religious test shall ever be required as a qualification for any office or public trust under the state of Maryland'. But it had been objected that, with such generosity, 'Turks and atheists would rule the country', indeed that the campaign was using Jews as a front for 'pagan idolators and heathens'. So the enacted version excluded, as its historian notes, 'a non-conforming Jew or Christian, deists, and atheists'. Indeed, given that it is most common for Jews to be agnostic about the possibility of an afterlife, it is arguable that it excluded the conforming, rather than the non-conforming Jew. However that may have been, 'even the Maryland Constitution of 1867 ... required an office holder to believe in God'.[18]

In these matters, then, there were hierarchies of intolerance and mistrust. Dissenters, especially Baptists and Methodist, wished to take privileges from Episcopalians or Congregationalists and to establish a civic equality among Protestants. Protestants wished to deny equality to Roman Catholics, while Christians (Protestants and Catholics) wished to deny equality to non-Christians (Jews, Muslims, Confucians, Native Americans, atheists) or those thought to be only liminally Christians (deists, Unitarians). In so far as there was, at least until the Civil War, an American concept of toleration, it mostly hinged upon one Christian tolerating another, not upon the religious tolerating the irreligious. (The Virginia Statute of Religious Liberty of 1786, of which Jefferson was so proud, begins, 'Whereas almighty God hath created the mind free'.)[19] Hence there was little or no sense of the legitimacy of the secular. It was not that the public realm was secular, only that it was not sectarian. As is still the case, the US Congress had a chaplain and its proceedings, like

---

[17] Jaher, *Scapegoat*, pp. 121, 185.
[18] On this, see Edward Eitches, 'Maryland's Jew Bill', *American Jewish Historical Quarterly* 60 (1971), 258–79 (quotations on 279, 267, 272, 277).
[19] Henry Steele Commager (ed.), *Documents of American history*, 7th edition (New York: Appleton-Century-Crofts, 1963), p. 125.

those of the Supreme Court, were opened with religious invocations. Churches were granted tax-exempt status, first by the states who were following colonial precedents. In 1802, the glebe lands of the Episcopal Church in the district of Columbia were given exemption by Congress, and, later, the federal government granted an exemption to ministers when it started the income tax in 1913. Indeed, the federal government, before the Civil War, refunded tariff duties on imported plates for printing the Bible, as well as on vestments, church furnishings (including paintings) and bells.[20] It became immediately customary after 1789 for politicians to invoke the blessings of God on the enterprise of the United States, a precedent set by that deist George Washington and followed even by Jefferson, whose first inaugural ends with the admittedly perfunctory and vague words, 'May that infinite power which rules the destinies of the universe lead our councils to what is best, and give them a favorable issue for your peace and prosperity.' In his farewell address of 1796, Washington had observed that, 'Of all the habits which lead to political prosperity, religion and morality are indispensable supports.' He opposed those 'who should labor to subvert these great pillars of human happiness', and dismissed any suggestion that morality was sustainable without religion, at least for ordinary mortals. His phrasing was delicate, but unmistakable: 'Whatever may be conceded to the influence of refined education on minds of peculiar structure, reason and experience both forbid us to expect that national morality can prevail in exclusion of religious principle.' And morality, he argued, was 'a necessary spring of popular government'.[21] The American popular imagination and its iconography honoured this conjunction. Washington was Cincinnatus, but he was also portrayed in John James Barralet's *Apotheosis of Washington* (1800) as someone who had been carried up to heaven by angels.[22]

The mind of peculiar structure belonging to Thomas Jefferson did not significantly dissent from Washington's argument. Like Tom Paine and Ethan Allen, Jefferson did not like priests or churches, and he drew the line at declaring fast days, but he did believe in God and in the ethical

---

[20] See John T. Noonan, *The lustre of our country: the American experience of religious freedom* (Berkeley: University of California Press, 1998), p. 218. My attention was drawn to this book and these facts by the 'Testimony of Professor Patrick M. Garry before the subcommittee on the Constitution, US House of Representatives, Committee on the Judiciary, in support of H.R. 2679 (Public Expression of Religion Act of 2005)' online at http://judiciary.house.gov/media/pdfs/garry062206.pdf.

[21] Commager, *Documents of American history*, pp. 188–9, 173.

[22] Garry Wills, *Cincinnatus: George Washington and the Enlightenment* (Garden City, NY: Doubleday, 1984), p. 26.

importance (if not the divinity) of Christ.[23] Indeed, two days after writing his 1802 letter to the Danbury Baptists, he started attending church services at the US Capitol, though this seems to have arisen more from an anticipation of imagined political benefits than any new confessional interest (he had never been before).[24] It is very hard to find an atheist or even an agnostic in the United States before the middle of the nineteenth century. Most notable was the poet Joseph Barlow, who was briefly an atheist in the 1790s.[25] Hence the foundational debate about the link between the state, religion and society was effectively an intramural discussion among differing Christians, and was driven by what best served the interests of Christianity in a plural society. Another way of putting this is that the framework for American secularisation (to use the anachronistic term) was established very early, before the intellectual crisis of Darwinism and the professionalisation of intellectual disciplines, and achieved partly under the auspices of the conservative wing of the Enlightenment (Thomas Reid rather than Helvetius), partly under the auspices of evangelical Protestantism (Charles Grandison Finney rather than David Friedrich Strauss). A still stronger way of putting it is that it makes more sense to see this view of religion and secularism as the last act of the early modern world, rather than the first act of the modern, if there is such a thing.

So, as Philip Hamburger has reminded us, it was the standard presumption of the American nineteenth century that the Constitution did not mandate a separation of church and state, let alone of religion and the state. Hamburger has a fascinating narrative of attempts in the 1870s and 1880s by a small cadre of 'anti-Christian secularists', a new phenomenon, 'to obtain a constitutional amendment guaranteeing a separation of church and state', precisely because they believed the existing Constitution did no such thing. Mostly, these were believers in free religion and non-Christian theism, though they did include some atheists and agnostics. The proposed amendment took various forms, but the strongest version was drafted by the Liberal League in 1876. It required, among more familiar things, the federal government, the states and the territories to forbid: 'in any degree a union of church and State' or any grant of 'special privilege, immunity, or advantage to any sect or religious body'; any taxes of 'the people of any State, either directly or

---

[23] See, especially, Thomas Jefferson to Benjamin Rush, 21 April 1803, in Merrill D. Peterson (ed.), *Thomas Jefferson: writings* (New York: Library of America, 1984), pp. 1122–6.

[24] Hamburger, *Separation*, p.162.

[25] James Turner, *Without God, without creed: the origins of unbelief in America* (Baltimore, MD: Johns Hopkins University Press, 1985), p. 44.

indirectly, for the support of any sect or religious body'; and any deprivation of rights because of religious opinions. In addition to this, the Liberal League had a platform styled the 'Nine Demands of Liberalism': 1. the taxing of church property; 2. no government-paid chaplains; 3. no government funds for sectarian education; 4. no government-sponsored church services, including Bible reading in public schools; 5. no religious proclamations by federal or state officials; 6. abolition of judicial oaths and the substitution of affirmations; 7. the repeal of sabbatarian laws; 8. the repeal of laws 'looking to the enforcement of Christian morality'; 9. no privileges to Christianity or any religion, and founding the political system 'on a purely secular basis'.[26] Obviously, this got nowhere. What is interesting, however, is that, as Douglas Laycock has pointed out, almost none of these demands have been met to this day, the partial exceptions being items 3 and 4.[27]

The reasons for this failure are clear. Hardly anyone wished the United States to be secular, nor do they today. Even the freethinkers who semi-flourished between the 1865 and 1915 countenanced religion, if a religion that they curiously insisted needed to be 'rational'; hence, in the manner of Comte, they devised rituals, held camp meetings and wrote hymns that announced, 'Joy to the world, for reason reigns.'[28] In all this, the special configurations of American nationalism played a part. As Alexis de Tocqueville observed in the 1830s, a synergy had developed between the ideas of liberty, republicanism, democracy, the United States and religion. Each, by itself, was regarded as unstable and perilous. The republic could fail, democracy could be killed by mobs, liberty could become licence, the Union could unravel from sectional tensions and religion could be mutilated by sectarianism. Taken together, however, each might serve to ameliorate the centrifugal vices and amplify the tolerant virtues of the others. Just how these ideas converged has been much studied. Most historians give most credit to the evangelical churches, especially for effecting the far-from-easy and far-from-self-evident

---

[26] Hamburger, *Separation*, pp. 299–300, 294–5.

[27] Douglas Laycock, 'The many meanings of separation', *University of Chicago Law Review* 70 (2003), 1695–8.

[28] Evelyn Kirkley estimates that there were perhaps 'a few thousand' freethinkers in the antebellum United States, and that 'between 1865 and 1915 thirty to forty thousand people participated in the Freethought movement, with up to a hundred thousand fellow travelers'. A typical freethinker was 'an Anglo-American, middle-class married male professional who lived in a small town in the mid-west, with a Christian background and limited formal education'. See Evelyn A. Kirkley, *Rational mothers and infidel gentlemen: gender and American atheism, 1865–1915* (Syracuse, NY: Syracuse University Press, 2000), pp. 3–28 (quotations on pp. 5, 18–19, 27).

reconciliation between Christianity and democracy.[29] But equally significant were Whiggish elitists like Washington, Jefferson, John Quincy Adams and even Abraham Lincoln, who, for their varying reasons, had their sharp doubts about the viability of the American project and invoked God, sometimes more in hope than expectation. By themselves, it was argued, Americans would fail. Americans, plus God, would succeed. This became a central idea in the American resistance to systematic secularisation, at least as it touched the state, and this intermingling of the natural and supernatural speaks to an underlying pessimism in American ideology, too little emphasised. It is well to remember that the United States, in the half-century after 1776, was undertaking something thought to be exceptionally daring. Americans undertook to dismiss monarchy, aristocracy and many aspects of established religion, while asserting popular sovereignty, all at the same time. To be sure, many states kept slavery, which was understood as one way to salvage the comforts of hierarchy and to prevent federalists and even democrats from getting nose-bleeds. But the ancient lineage of Christianity was as important. Something old, it was presumed, was badly needed to balance something new. When it became wrong to kneel down before men, it seems to have been reassuring still to kneel down before God.

The half-century after 1865 is another matter, not for shifts in American public ideology, but for changes in American thought, society and education. Much that had previously been shaped by religion, increasingly was not. It is important to observe, however, that a few things (notably immigration) moved in the other direction. So this was a period when the boundary between religion and secularity moved, perhaps more so than at any other time in American history, but inconsistently, for there was not one boundary, but many, each specific to a place, an institution, a sect and a cultural logic.

Notably public education in schools, colleges and universities became semi-secular, not in the sense that religious studies were formally excluded, but that many forms of knowledge – natural science, social studies, and so forth – dispensed with the supernatural as a mode of explanation, at least explicitly. This was and is a very uneven business. Many rural schools, especially in the South, quietly ignored Darwinism. But, conversely, some colleges and universities officially sponsored by denominations were transformed; bishops and elders were expelled from boards of trustees, usually after a bitter struggle. Yet as colleges were lost to the faith, others were gained, for the sector of religious schools,

[29] See Nathan O. Hatch, *The democratization of American Christianity* (New Haven, CT: Yale University Press, 1989).

colleges and seminaries grew greatly and these lay (and lie) beyond the reach of a rigorous secularism. In 2003–4, there were 5.1 million children attending American private schools, these constituted about 10 per cent of all American schoolchildren, and 18 per cent of those private schools described themselves as non-sectarian, a category unlikely systematically to exclude religion.[30] As for colleges and universities, in the fall of 2003, there were 16.9 million students enrolled in them, and of these 1.6 million (about 9.5 per cent) were enrolled in 'religiously affiliated' institutions.[31]

However, even the early process of removing bishops was seldom if ever done in the name of secularisation, but as an application to higher education of the non-sectarian religiosity which had characterised the antebellum political order. Vanderbilt University in Nashville was a case in point. It had been founded in 1853 as a college of the Methodist Episcopal Church, South, but had drifted close to bankruptcy because of war and Reconstruction. In 1873 the railroad magnate Cornelius Vanderbilt furnished a generous endowment of a million dollars and it was renamed in his honour. He was not Methodist, indeed 'a very worldly and even profane man', but possessed of a young second wife, a Methodist from Alabama, whom he was eager to please. As a Methodist institution, the new university received from the church modest subsidies which were used to subvent a 'biblical department', which was a Methodist seminary. In addition, the church was officially represented on its board, and for some years, it was the custom to appoint Methodists to the faculty, unless a Methodist candidate was markedly inferior to a non-Methodist. But this preference was exercised with diminishing frequency. The Methodist Episcopal Church, South, became discontented and formally signalled this unhappiness in 1904, when the university's president James Hampton Kirkland, a classicist trained in Leipzig, wished to appoint a Presbyterian as a professor of history and a Baptist as a dean. The president was sternly warned by a bishop that, though the appointments might be made, Kirkland was being put on notice that the church was aware that eleven out of nineteen professors were now not Methodist, and six out of seven deans, and that such ways,

[30] S. P. Broughman and N. L. Swaim, *Characteristics of private schools in the United States: Results from the 2003–2004 Private School Universe Survey (NCES 2006-319)*, US Department of Education (Washington, DC: National Center for Education Statistics, 2006), pp. 2–3.
[31] 'Table 178: Fall enrollment and number of degree-granting institutions, by control and affiliation of institution: selected years, 1980 through 2003', online at http://nces.ed.gov/programs/digest/d05/tables/dt05_178.asp.

if continued, 'must necessarily tend to estrange the University from the Church and the Church from the University'. For ten years, there was a struggle, which the church lost. There was a formal divorce, the bishops left the board, and the biblical department was replaced by a non-sectarian 'School of Religion'. The nature of this struggle is instructive. The church did not contest the teaching of subject matters, did not demand that theology oust sociology, but instead cared for the denomin-ational identity of the professoriate and the behaviour of students, often no longer Methodist and, even when Methodist, often inadequately pious. There were condemnations of 'the frivolous worldliness of stu-dents, as reflected in intercollegiate athletics, fraternities, and officially sanctioned dances'. Conversely, Kirkland did not fight in the name of the secular, but for the university's 'friends in all denominations', against the 'bigoted and sectarian', and for a 'liberal Christian policy'.[32]

Nonetheless these were changes, gently inclining towards the secular, and this is not easy to explain, since atheists and agnostics were so thin on the ground and had negligible influence on education, and almost all the proponents of the new ways were religious, albeit people impressed by the internal logic of their professionalising disciplines, which were finding it difficult to develop when obedient to religious demands. The case of Vanderbilt University suggests one motive. Kirkland knew that there was not enough money or scope in a sectarian affiliation to sustain a modern university; foundation money and philanthropy demanded the non-sectarian. Not insignificant was the munificent endowment of the Carnegie Foundation, which was newly willing to underwrite professor-ial pensions, but only in public and non-sectarian private colleges.[33]

James Turner has shrewdly suggested another, less worldly concern. The new and peculiar authority of the liberal arts in collegiate and university curricula, established in the fifty years after the Civil War, arose precisely from the unease generated by this change. Gone, for example, was the old course on moral philosophy which had invariably culminated any antebellum education, in which one had read Joseph Butler's *Analogy of religion* and William Paley's *Evidences of Christianity*. Instead there came to be 'core' curricula, intended, however unsuccess-fully, to sustain the premise of coherence, mysteriously embedded in

[32] Paul K. Conkin, *Gone with the ivy: A biography of Vanderbilt University* (Knoxville: University of Tennessee Press, 1985), pp. 149–84 (quotation on p. 149); Edwin Mims, *Chancellor Kirkland of Vanderbilt* (Nashville, TN: Vanderbilt University Press, 1940), pp. 160–96 (quotations on pp. 162, 164); Michael McGerr, 'The Commodore's strange gift', *Vanderbilt Magazine* (Summer 2006), 47–53, 86.
[33] Conkin, *Gone with the ivy*, p.156.

'liberal culture'.[34] One might still read Paley, but no longer as a required author, instead as a text informally recommended by one's university president as a 'character forming book' to be read on Sundays, though less because Paley proved the existence of God and the cogency of Christianity, but because he had contributed to 'the religious thought of Anglo-Saxon people'.[35] Within the academy, God often became a historicised morality.

Partly such a limited secularisation, in the wider culture beyond the academy, is explicable by mass immigration and a shift in the character of religious diversity – the growing proportion and cultural influence of Roman Catholics, Greek and Russian Orthodox, and Jews expanded what was needed as neutral ground beyond what a Protestant ecumenalism had once required. This accelerated a partial exclusion of religion from the public sphere and its partial confinement to the private, though it is important to emphasise that the American stress on individualism and insistence that the public sphere is the creature of the private are but the expression of a myriad of private wills, which means that this distinction is less important to Americans than it might be to others. Nonetheless, mass immigration much complicated the matter of multiple boundaries between religion and secularity, in several senses.

First, these differing religions had differing notions of what might be conceded as legitimately secular, and frequently the secular became embroiled in internal disputes. This was especially so of Judaism, for secularity became a weapon in the warfares of Orthodox, Conservative, and Reform Jews. Second, the social experience of migration often deepened religious commitments, for Jews arriving in 1900 from Poland and entering the strange world of the Lower East Side, knew their selves partly through the synagogue, the rabbi, the cantor, the Torah, all of which served as anchors and helped in understanding the startling weirdness of Theodore Roosevelt, Tammany Hall and novels by Mark Twain. The same process worked for Roman Catholics, for Confucians, for Shintoists, in recent times for Muslims and Hindus, all of whom have had good reason to notice that, despite amiable disclaimers, the United States looks like a confessional state to most newcomers. Third, immigrants distributed themselves unevenly over the American landscape, so that what one American place might consider a defensible boundary

---

[34] James Turner, 'Secularization and sacralization: some religious origins of the secular humanities curriculum, 1950–1900', in *Language, religion, knowledge: past and present* (Notre Dame, IN: University of Notre Dame Press, 2003), pp. 50–68.

[35] D. G. Hart, 'Faith and learning in the age of the university: the academic ministry of Daniel Coit Gilman', in George M. Marsden and Bradley J. Longfield (eds.), *The secularization of the academy* (New York: Oxford University Press, 1992), pp. 120–1.

between religion and secularity might be unintelligible elsewhere. In 1928, Al Smith seemed to New Yorkers a plausible choice for president, because as a Roman Catholic he stood for Christianity against Judaism or atheist socialism, but for many Southerners he dangerously threatened the destruction of Virginia's Protestant order.[36] Fourth, the nativist reaction to mass immigration much deepened the sense of the United States as a culture peculiarly committed to Christianity, even to Protestantism, and the debates over immigration restriction were crowded with discussions of religious and social implications.

Nonetheless, there did painfully and unevenly emerge a tendency for American religion to sponsor tentative habits of religious toleration and zones of non-sectarianism. This came to mean that American religion was little able or even willing to resist an elision into a quasi-secularisation, and indeed came to be dependent upon that secularisation's existence. Hence secularisation has mostly existed in American culture under licence from the religious and, for the most part, has taken the form that suits the purposes of the religious. Ever since the Cane Ridge revival of 1801, if not before, an essential characteristic of mainstream American religion has been that it has been modern in organisation and anti-modern in rhetoric. Consistently, American churches, synagogues and temples have deployed all the techniques that modernity has successively invented – print culture, radio, television, the internet, marketing, advertising, corporate organisation – while decrying modernity (print culture, radio, television ...) and has offered itself as the solution to modernity, as a transcendence of the sinfulness spawned by the shock of the new.[37] In truth, nothing ought to appal a fundamentalist more than triumph. To achieve the repeal of the First Amendment, the restoration of prayer in schools, the control of all school boards, the teaching of intelligent design at Harvard, would be a grim scenario, far beyond the debacle of prohibition, for the religious would then be in charge of the public sphere, would be responsible for American culture, and so answerable for its failures and tensions. Becoming the problem, they could no longer offer themselves as the solution. For the most part, American religious leaders have understood this (less so, in recent

---

[36] By 1960 when John Kennedy ran for president, this logic had shifted, though the presidential election of 2008 indicates that it has little changed for Mormons.

[37] See, for example, Andrew Chamberlain Rieser, 'Secularization reconsidered: Chatauqua and the de-christianization of middle-class authority, 1880–1920', in Burton J. Bledstein and Robert D. Johnston (eds.), *The middling sorts: explorations in the history of the American middle class* (New York: Routledge, 2001), p. 150, which observes, 'religious organizations and motives were deeply ensconced in the organizational revolution'.

years, to be sure). Hence the American debate has hardly ever been about the religious sphere extinguishing the secular, or the secular sphere extinguishing the religious, only about, what might be termed, boundary disputes. Naturally, this dialogue has meant that American religion is less religious than it might be, the secular less secular than it might be. Theology, especially, has proved inconvenient when pleading the case for religion and has been in steady decline since the mid nineteenth century.[38]

This leads to a final observation, that the secularisation thesis is also mostly a function of the American religious imagination, and only episodically has it been a venture of the American sociological and historical imagination. That is, if you ask, who has most spoken of secularisation in American culture and most adduced evidence for it? the answer is not the secular people, but the religious. This goes back to the eighteenth century, when ministers pointed to the bloody carnage of the French Revolution as the fruit of atheism, and to the early nineteenth, when Jefferson was habitually abused as an infidel, whose influence needed resisting. In a sermon in 1833, Jasper Adams, then president of the College of Charleston, observed, with a footnote to Jefferson's works: 'It has been asserted by men distinguished for talents, learning and station, and it may well be presumed that the assertion is gradually gaining belief among us, that Christianity has no connexion with the law of the land, or with our civil and political institutions.'[39] This was a double bluff, for Adams's sermon gave ample evidence that the assertion had little cogency and was not gaining ground, but it was convenient to use Jefferson the bogeyman as an incitement to piety. To read American religious writings, of almost any period, is to be told that the American scene swarms with energetic sceptics and atheists, forever on the brink of a disastrous success. To look at American sceptics and atheists, however, upon their own terms is to observe a tiny and diffident band, well aware of their hopeless marginality.

Consistent with this, most of the secondary, scholarly literature on secularisation comes from authors who are religious. The best collection of essays on *The secularization of the American Academy*, for example, is co-edited by George Marsden, an American historian who is also an evangelical. The best book on the origins of American agnosticism – James Turner's *Without God, without creed* – is by a Roman Catholic. In contrast, with a few exceptions – Lester Frank Ward, Thorstein Veblen,

---

[38] As is forcefully argued by Mark A. Noll, *The scandal of the evangelical mind* (Grand Rapids: William B. Eerdmans, 1994).

[39] Dreisbach, *Religion and politics*, p. 42.

Theodore Dreiser, Clarence Darrow – American sceptics and secularisers have worked by stealth and kept their silence. Edward A. Ross, one of the founders of American sociology, observed in his autobiography: 'For years I felt bitter toward the clergy for "bulldozing" me. But after I found that I could ignore the preachers and still hold a university chair, I made a mute pact, "You leave me alone and I'll leave you alone."' This neglect affected the disciple of American sociology. James H. Leuba in 1916 estimated that only 29 per cent of American sociologists believed in God.[40] So William Graham Sumner was not alone for, as he put it, one day putting his religious beliefs in a drawer and, opening it some years later, to find it empty.[41]

It is tolerably clear, however, that the small amount of sociological research on religion done in the half-century after 1916 was disproportionately written by that 29 per cent. The rest averted their gaze and vaguely presumed that modernity would dispose of the problem without their conscious intervention. This was roughly the stance of Talcott Parsons, though he did late in life consent to being president of the Society for the Scientific Study of Religion, founded in 1949.[42] It was only later, notably with Gerhard Lenski's *The religious factor* (1961), that things began modestly to change. So, for most of American social science, secularisation has been an inactive presumption, but hardly ever a campaign, which is what it has often been in European cultures. If you look at Dorothy Ross's *The origins of American social science* (1991), a canonical work which covers the period from the late antebellum years to 1929, you will find in the index not a single reference to 'secularisation' or, indeed, to 'religion'. Indeed, the standard reference work on American intellectual history – Fox and Kloppenberg's *Companion to American thought* – contains no entry for 'secularisation'.[43] And scholarly work on the history of American atheism is very hard to find.

A passive circumspection did not arise without cause. After all, the profession of atheism or even agnosticism has habitually meant public death in American culture. Jefferson thought that even Christian scepticism needed to be expressed only in private. Today, though formal

---

[40] Hadden, 'Desacralizing secularization theory', pp. 8–10.
[41] Quoted in Turner, *Language, religion, knowledge: past and present*, p. 135.
[42] Hadden, 'Desacralizing secularization theory', 12–13, and www.sssrweb.org/past_presidents.cfm.
[43] Gerhard Emmanuel Lenski, *The religious factor: a sociological study of religion's impact on politics, economics, and family life* (Garden City, NY: Doubleday, 1961); Dorothy Ross, *The origins of American social science* (Cambridge: Cambridge University Press, 1991); Richard Wightman Fox and James T. Kloppenberg (eds.), *A companion to American thought* (Oxford: Blackwell, 1995).

disabilities have gone, no candid atheist or agnostic can be elected to high public office in the United States and, in practice, there are sharp limits on freedom of speech when speaking publicly of religion.[44] The woman whose lawsuit led to the 1963 Supreme Court decision on banning prayer in public schools was called 'America's most hated woman' by *Life* magazine and ended up buried on a Texas ranch, her body cut into small pieces by a saw. There are disputes over why Madalyn Murray O'Hair was murdered; mostly, it had to do with money.[45] But there is little disputing that most Americans felt she probably deserved being butchered, considering that she was a militant who had founded an organisation called American Atheists. On their present website, where her writings linger, you will find a section marked 'Coming Out', in which it is explained, 'Telling your religious friends and family that you are an atheist can be intimidating. The first article in this section is by Dave Silverman, and is appropriately titled *Atheism: the other closet.*'[46] But there is not going to be a Stonewall moment for American atheists any time soon.

---

[44] A notable and puzzling exception was Culbert Levy Olson, governor of California from 1939 to 1943; he was an ex-Mormon, a New Dealer, and an atheist who declined to say the words, 'So help me God', in the gubernatorial oath and instead affirmed his willingness to uphold the state's constitution. His administration met with little success.

[45] For an unclear account, see Ann Rowe Seaman, *America's most hated woman: the life and gruesome death of Madalyn Murray O'Hair* (New York: Continuum, 2005).

[46] See www.atheists.org/atheism/coming_out.

French Catholic political thought
from the deconfessionalisation of the state
to the recognition of religious freedom

Emile Perreau-Saussine

Liberty of conscience and liberty of the press were 'execrable' ideas, declared the encyclical *Mirari vos*, of 15 August 1832, dismissing brutally those who claimed that religion could gain anything from either idea. In the wake of *Mirari vos*, sovereign pontiffs thundered forth condemnations of the French Revolution and of the 'modern world'. Only truth (that is *Catholic* truth) had rights: there could not be a freedom not to be Catholic since recognition of such a freedom would entail a culpable indifference to revelation. In the course of the last centuries, the Catholic Church has been confronted with liberal democracy, a political regime whose triumph it had not foreseen, and with which, for this very reason, it was ill prepared to cope. With *Dignitatis humanae* (1965), the Catholic Church seemed to change its teaching in a fundamental way: the 'Vatican Council declares that the human person has a right to religious freedom'. Since then, there has been no serious attempt to return to the church's previous anti-liberalism. Catholics acknowledge the supremacy of the Catholic Church over the state, but regard themselves as powerless to implement Catholic rules and ideals at a national level except through the ballot box. This chapter sketches the reasons for this shift from a radical anti-liberalism to a certain type of liberalism. I focus in particular on the intellectual history of the Gallican Church since the internal debates of French Catholicism in this period have often turned out to be the debates about Catholicism as such. Even if their political teachings have not been officially recognised, and have at times been condemned by the papacy, Bossuet, de Maistre or Lamennais offer useful clues to the evolution of their church in its painful transition from an aristocratic age to a democratic one.

From Bossuet's Gallicanism to Joseph de Maistre's ultramontanism

In his *Letter concerning toleration*, Locke excluded Roman Catholics from the benefits of tolerance. He found the authority they recognised for the papacy incompatible with respect for the sovereignty of the state.

What can be the meaning of their asserting that kings excommunicated forfeit their crowns and kingdoms? It is evident that they thereby arrogate unto themselves the power of deposing kings, because they challenge the power of excommunication, as the peculiar right of *their* hierarchy ... These, therefore, and the like, who attribute unto the faithful, religious, and orthodox, that is, in plain terms, unto themselves, any peculiar privilege or power above other mortals, *in civil concernments*; or who upon pretence of religion do challenge any manner of authority over such as are not associated with them in their ecclesiastical communion, I say these have no right to be tolerated by the magistrate.[1]

Locke's point has become familiar again with the terrorism of radical jihadis. It is difficult to tolerate those who do not accept basic civil rules, who do not recognise, 'in civil concernments', the primacy of the crown over any international, 'foreign' authority ('*their* hierarchy'). Without such recognition, there cannot be any secure order or lasting tolerance.

Locke's point was well made, but it was not necessarily quite as anti-Catholic as it seems. In fact, many (if not most) Catholics agreed with him. Published in England in 1689, Locke's letter had already been fully answered in France by 1682. That year, Louis XIV had called a general assembly of the clergy to assert his own political rights against the papacy. The first article of the 1682 Declaration lays down that

the Pope has only received from God a spiritual power. Kings and princes are not subject in temporal matters to any ecclesiastical authority; therefore, they cannot be deposed in virtue of the authority of the Head of the Church, and their subjects cannot be released from the oath of loyalty.

Subject to the Pope as a Catholic Christian, the monarch contends that, as a sovereign, he is not a subject. Some of the other articles of the Declaration were contentious, but this one was not – at least, not in France. The clergy, including some Jesuits, were in broad agreement with it.[2] Bossuet, perhaps the greatest of Gallican theologians, took it for granted that the French did not need the help of Roman threats or censorship to behave in a Christian manner.

Locke nevertheless had a point. Traditional Catholic political teaching was not overwhelmingly respectful of national sovereignty. Temporal powers were limited by natural and divine law, and the church, as a transnational body, thought that it had a duty to assess whether princes respected that higher law – hence the right to excommunicate and depose kings. The papacy claimed, if not a 'direct' power, at least an 'indirect' one.

---

[1] The italics are mine, not Locke's.
[2] Victor Martin, *Le gallicanisme politique et le clergé de France* (Paris: Picard, 1929), pp. 314–22; Pierre Blet, 'Jésuites gallicans au XVIIe siècle?', *Archivum Historicum Societatis Jesu* 29 (1960), 55–84.

But Gallicans were not even prepared to accept this indirect power. To the extent to which traditional church teaching seemed to require a political power of some sort, either direct or indirect, Gallicans were prepared to get rid of that tradition. One way to part with tradition – Luther is a good example – is through a return to scripture itself. Bossuet's *Politics drawn from the very words of Holy Scripture*, which he started writing in the 1670s while educating the son of Louis XIV, pays little attention to philosophy or natural law: it seems to rely on 'Scripture alone'. Bossuet's book hardly mentioned the New Testament, drawing mainly on the Book of Kings, and seemed to prefer David to Christ the King. This prompts a simple question: why a *'Politics drawn . . . from Holy Scripture'*? And, more specifically, why from the Book of Kings? Bossuet's *Politics* justified the sovereignty of the French crown by giving a very specific status to the King. In the theocracies of David and Solomon, Bossuet finds the authoritative example he seeks: kings owe their legitimacy to God, without the direct or indirect mediation of the papacy. 'Princes act as God's ministers and as his lieutenants on earth.'[3] Directly appointed by God, kings did not owe their power to the Pope. The divine right of kings was supposed to buttress the position of kings against the papacy. Subjects were to obey monarchs without taking much notice of injunctions and excommunications from Rome.[4]

Bossuet finds in scripture the picture of a 'people whose legislator is God himself'.[5] In his book, through the constant reference to the Old Testament, he suggested that the French people were another chosen people.[6] 'The Gallican Church has carried the most knowledgeable, the most holy, the most famous bishops that there ever was.'[7] Bossuet's *Politics* can be seen as a manifesto of the French nation state, not only because its magnificent prose remains one of the most accomplished examples of classical French (the *national* language), but also because of the moral and theological importance he gives to 'love of one's country'.[8]

---

[3] Jacques-Bénigne Bossuet, *Politique tirée de l'Écriture sainte / . . . ouvrage posthume de messire Jacques-Benigne Bossuet* (Paris: Chez Pierre Cot, 1709), vol. III, 1, ii.

[4] John Neville Figgis, *The divine right of Kings* (Cambridge: Cambridge University Press, 1896).

[5] Bossuet, 'Dédicace', *L'Écriture sainte*.

[6] Joseph R. Strayer, 'France: the Holy Land, the chosen people and the most Christian King', in T. Rabb and J. Seigel (eds.), *Action and conviction in early modern Europe* (Princeton: Princeton University Press, 1969), pp. 3–16; Colette Beaune, *Naissance de la nation France* (Paris: Gallimard, 1985), pp. 75–229.

[7] Bossuet, *L'Écriture sainte*, vol. VII, vi, 14.

[8] *Ibid.*, vol. I, vi: 'De l'amour de la patrie' (cf. I, ii). Cf. Norman Ravitch, *The Catholic Church and the French nation (1589–1989)* (London: Routledge, 1990), pp. 1–41.

Bossuet is all the more prepared to assert the independence of the French crown as he is himself a 'Gallican', that is a patriot.

He defends political Gallicanism (the independence of the King in temporal matters) not because he is a Machiavellian who would like to free the crown from the constraints of natural and divine law, but because he is a religious Gallican. French kings were not absolute in the sense that they were free to do whatever they wanted ('*ab legibus soluta*'): they were still bound by higher laws. Bossuet distinguishes absolute from arbitrary power.[9] If one can safely take for granted that the King, his bishops and his magistrates were in some sense 'most Christian', then it is easy to see why the Pope has no good reason to intervene in temporal matters. The identification of France with the chosen nation justifies both the political and the ecclesiastical independence claimed by the French Church and body politic. Louis XIV does not need the Pope any more than Solomon did.

In the Old Regime, there was certainly no lack of tension between civil and ecclesiastical authorities. In a complex game, the political Gallicanism of the King or parliaments (keen to defend the primacy of lay authorities over ecclesiastical authorities), the religious Gallicanism of the bishops (keen to defend the primacy of councils against the primacy of the Pope) and ultramontanism could become opponents or allies in various combinations. The term 'ultramontain' ('beyond the mountains', that is 'beyond the Alps') was applied to those Catholics who maintained that the French Church was entirely subject to the authority of Rome. The blows were often brutal. But there were rules. Gallicanism rested on a subtle balance. Religious and civil authorities were too intertwined not to be aware of the need to limit the damage that could follow from their fights. The papacy was above all keen to prevent the Gallican Church from becoming autocephalous, and was attached to a policy which combined severe admonitions with flexibility and patience. As for the kings of France themselves, they had not much to gain from schism, because they had already obtained nearly everything they could aspire to with the Concordat of Bologna (1516), starting from the right to choose bishops. The Gallican Church was pushing independence in relation to Rome as far as it could. But, as it wished to remain both national and Catholic, it could not sacrifice its Catholic to its national component.

With Bossuet's theology of national sovereignty in mind, one can understand why the Catholic reaction to the French Revolution was at

---

[9] Bossuet, *l'Écriture sainte*, vol. IV, i and VIII, ii; Denis Richet, *La France moderne: l'esprit des institutions* (Paris: Flammarion, 1973), pp. 37–54.

best mixed. Religious liberty gained official recognition in France in 1789 with article 10 of the *Declaration of the rights of man and of the citizen*. The Old Regime, which had made full membership of the body politic depend upon Catholic faith (at least since the revocation of the Edict of Nantes in 1685), was thus radically overturned. The persecution of Protestants, of which Bossuet had approved to some extent, was prohibited. The crime of heresy was abolished. From now on, church and state would no longer have to be nearly coextensive. The French people need no longer be at one and the same time Christians and citizens, subjects of a monarch and children of the church. Even if the authors of article 10 had no formal intention of separating the state from the church, the recognition of religious liberty involved a measure of disestablishment of the church, which lost some of its privileges, and some of its centrality in the social and political life of the French. Matrimonial causes were to be heard by civil courts, and not in religious courts. Religious vows no longer had force in the eyes of the law. Canon law was no longer to be the concern of the state. Christian revelation was no longer a source of law.

When, later on, the Revolution turned against the church and the church against the Revolution, leading to persecution, massacres and even civil war, it became obvious to many Catholics that one could no longer trust the French nation and the French state in the way Bossuet had thought possible. In his *Considerations on France* (1796), de Maistre describes the French Revolution in the darkest possible tone, denouncing it as 'an anti-religious and anti-social insurrection', and, finally, a satanic movement. In *De l'église gallicane* (1821), he rejects violently the whole Gallican tradition, which he can no longer understand. In *Du Pape*, de Maistre writes that, in order to avoid tyranny, European peoples should turn to the papacy. 'There is a manifest contradiction between our contemporaries' constitutional enthusiasm and their animosity against the Popes.'[10] De Maistre does not ask explicitly for a papal power to dethrone monarchs, but he argues that the Pope should be made the final arbiter of political quarrels. We read, for example, from his pen: 'If the France of today, submissive under a divine authority, had received its excellent king from the hands of the Sovereign Pontiff, may we not believe that it would have been a little more content with itself and with others?'[11] De Maistre places his hopes in a kind of pontifical theocracy. Since the French state no longer considers itself limited by Catholic doctrine, the sovereignty that it claims becomes problematic for Catholics. In contrast, Rome should become a final guarantor which

---

[10] Joseph de Maistre, *Du pape* (Lyon: Rusand, 1813), II, 4.   [11] *Ibid.*, II, 10.

would return to post-revolutionary states a Christian sense of the limits of what is and is not permissible.

The authority of confessional states was constrained by their confessional nature. They had to respect their divine law. Temporal rulers were able to influence to their advantage the way that higher law was interpreted, but they still had to give the appearance of respecting it. In contrast, secular states were by their very nature no longer constrained by divine law. The deconfessionalisation of the state freed it from the constraints previously imposed by its religious identity. Celebrated by persecuted religious minorities and unbelievers, this deconfessionalisation raised fundamental difficulties from a political and from a theological point of view. Confessional states brought together religious and political considerations in such a way that they could claim authority over believers. But the deconfessionalisation of the state left the same believers uncertain as to whether they could respect the authority of a political body that is not itself committed to abide by divine law. In fact, more often than not, the deconfessionalisation of the state created a sentiment of panic among disoriented citizens who looked beyond the state for alternative sources of spiritual authority.[12]

One might have expected the pervasive victory of democracy in politics to lead the Catholic Church in a more Presbyterian direction, as the French revolutionaries who devised the Civil Constitution of the Clergy in 1790 were expecting. But this is not what happened. Historians of Roman Catholicism have often noticed that, in modern times, the papacy's spiritual authority has not diminished but grown. The more that secular states came under the influence of democracy, the more Catholics felt the need to turn to the papacy. The deconfessionalisation of the state led believers to look for a source of spiritual authority beyond their nation, which they found in Rome.

The deconfessionalisation of the state and the primacy of individual rights created among many believers a sentiment of anomie, as if there was no longer any agreement on who and what the moral authorities were. In a society in which each individual was supposed to decide for him or herself, it seemed difficult to maintain a spiritual unity. In particular, how was the tradition to be properly interpreted, if everyone could stick to his own subjective interpretation? It became necessary to agree on who the final authority was going to be.[13] The ultimate

---

[12] Paul Bénichou, *Le temps des prophètes: doctrines de l'âge romantique* (Paris: Gallimard, 1977).

[13] Yves Congar, 'L'ecclésiologie de la Révolution française au concile du Vatican sous le signe de l'affirmation de l'autorité', in Maurice Nédoncelle (ed.), *L'ecclésiologie au XIXe siècle* (Paris: Cerf, 1960), pp. 77–114.

authority could only be the papacy – an authority which de Maistre was very keen to describe as 'infallible'. The theme of papal infallibility was not new, but it had long coexisted with conciliarist themes putting forward the supremacy of universal councils, which de Maistre undermined with all the energy of his powerful rhetoric.

Setting out from France, the ultramontane movement spread to the whole of Europe. It recorded notable victories from the middle 1820s. Its triumph was complete in the 1840s. 'Notice what is happening in Catholic Europe' wrote Edgar Quinet in a book which was published in 1844.

You will very soon discover this noteworthy fact that everywhere the Church is aspiring no longer to support itself on anything but Rome. There is no need of startling insights in order to realise that in France, the Gallican Church no longer exists, except in name. In Spain too, where the clergy were until now so deeply embedded in the nation, all the voices that make themselves heard repeat one after the other the same cry: Rome! As I speak, all the Catholic clergy from the South to the North is vehemently stripping itself of the national characteristics which, in the past, have constituted its protection.[14]

In July 1870, the majority of bishops present at the first Vatican council voted in favour of the constitution *Pastor aeternus* which recognised the infallibility in matters of faith and morals of the bishop of Rome, when speaking 'ex cathedra'. *Pastor aeternus* appeared as a victory for the disciples of Joseph de Maistre and for the most extreme papalism. The opponents of the declaration of the dogma of pontifical infallibility, who joined the schismatic church of the 'Old Catholics', often lived in the most conservative parts of Europe, in which the church retained strong social roots, and where the effects of the French Revolution had not yet made themselves felt. This was notably the case in Austria, Bavaria and Switzerland, where the schism was more powerful than elsewhere. In contrast, ultramontanism was strong in France and Spain, where the impact of modern revolutions had been more decisive, and where the churches, in their own reactive manner, were more in tune with the way the world was going. In the wake of the French Revolution and of the transformation of the rest of Europe, Catholics turned to Rome because they felt uprooted in their own countries.[15] Gallican by its

[14] Edgar Quinet, 'L'ultramontanisme ou l'Église romaine et la société moderne', in *Œuvres complètes* (Paris: Pagnerre, 1857), vol. II, pp. 289–90. Cf. Hyppolite Taine, *Les origines de la France contemporaine: l'ancien régime* (Paris: Hachette, 1894), vol. III, p. 5; Austin Gough, *Paris and Rome: the Gallican Church and the ultramontane campaign (1848–1853)* (Oxford: Clarendon Press, 1986).
[15] Some anti-Catholics were eager to encourage this feeling, even as they were condemning ultramontanism. Jules Michelet, 'Notre nationalité non catholique', in *Cours au Collège de France, II (1845–1851)* (Paris: Gallimard, 1995), pp. 155–61.

property (which tied it to the national soil), royal by its privileges (which tied it to the monarchy), Catholic by its beliefs (which tied it to Rome), once it was deprived of property and privilege, and nothing tied it any longer to either soil or king, the church was tempted to remain nothing except Catholic, to detach itself from France and merge with Rome.

Not surprisingly, the opponents of ultramontanism were asking themselves whether 'a successor of Alexander VI would be going to redistribute the New World a second time'.[16] Ultramontanism was bringing back to life the legitimate concerns that Locke had expressed in his *Letter concerning toleration*. It seemed that the autonomy of the state was endangered. Gladstone feared that the papacy was renewing medieval claims to depose kings and to use force.[17] Had Catholics and the papacy lost all political sense?

Joseph de Maistre could be described as a staunch critic of Bossuet. However, their political thought belonged to the same authoritarian and absolutist family. They shared a similar dislike of individual freedom and democracy. The royal absolutism of Bossuet and the papal absolutism of de Maistre displayed a similar anxiety about the origins of authority and the crucial need for a top-down approach to politics and faith. Their visions of the world were equally hierarchical and anti-liberal. One of the first Catholic thinkers to break properly with this anti-liberalism was Lord Acton, who wrote famously that 'power tends to corrupt, and absolute power corrupts absolutely'.[18] Whereas Bossuet and de Maistre saw absolutism as a bulwark against corruption, Acton analysed absolutism as a source of corruption. Acton was himself at the centre of the fight against Vatican I, briefing Gladstone and others, while writing extensively against papal infallibility. In the wake of Acton, Catholics have asserted, discreetly to start with, but ever more strongly, the value of freedom. But, contrary to Acton's expectations, the assertion of the value of freedom has gone hand in hand with a reinforcement of the public role of the papacy.

Vatican I: a new role for the papacy

Absolutism presupposed the independence of the King from the Pope, and was thus an affirmation of sovereignty which assumed that the King was not necessarily a Catholic. At the same time, absolutism presupposed

---

[16] Lord Acton, 'The next general council', in H. A. MacDougall (ed.), *Lord Acton on papal power* (London: Sheed & Ward, 1973), p. 115.

[17] W. E. Gladstone, *The Vatican decrees and their bearing on civil allegiance* (London: John Murray, 1874).

[18] Lord Acton, 'Letter to Mandell Creighton, April 3, 1887', in L. Creighton (ed.), *The life and letters of Mandell Creighton* (London: Longmans, Green & Co, 1904), vol. I, p. 372.

that the King had control over the church. Political Gallicanism laid claim to the civil authority's independence from ecclesiastical authorities, and, in the same breath, to the dependence of the church on the state. On the one hand, the state sought to maintain or to re-establish the more or less unitary system of the Middle Ages, treating religion and politics as coextensive (*cujus regio*, ejus religio); on the other hand, it put an end to this unitary system by affirming the primacy of the state (cujus regio, *ejus religio*). However, under the Old Regime in France, this tension remained largely implicit, for the Most Christian Kings remained attached, if not to the substance, at least to the form of the Catholic faith.

With the Civil Constitution of the Clergy, the revolutionaries were proposing to undertake a wholesale reorganisation of the Church of France. Bishops and priests were to be elected locally by citizens, and the authority of the Pope over the appointment of the clergy was reduced to the right to be informed of the election results. After the declaration of religious liberty and the affirmation of popular sovereignty, which meant that the state had lost part of its Catholic identity, and after the refusal in February and April 1790 to declare that the Roman Catholic religion was the religion of the state, the revolutionaries proceeded to launch a more ambitious reform than had been envisaged by the Most Christian Kings of the Old Regime. Camus, one member of the Constitutional Assembly, went so far as to maintain that the nation should not only be able to reform the organisation of the clergy, but should also be able to change the established religion.[19] Without going to that extreme, the Civil Constitution still models the religious structure on the civil one, arranging for parish priests to be elected by citizens of *cantons*, and bishops by priests of *départements*.

From the secularisation of the state under the *Assemblée constituante*, three consequences were bound to follow. The clergy would cease to form an order in the state; the laws of the church would cease to be enforceable in the civil courts, and the state would cease to share in enacting them. Happy to acknowledge the first two consequences, the assembly denied the third. But the state could not at one and the same time forgo its essentially denominational character and maintain the practices and prerogatives of an essentially denominational state. How could a state maintain its authority over a church from which it had, to a large extent, separated itself? The revolutionary logic itself forbade the

[19] Armand-Gaston Camus, 'Discours du 31 mai 1790 sur la constitution civile du clergé', in M. J. Mavidal and M.E. Laurent (eds.), *Archives parlementaires de 1787 à 1860. Première série de 1787 à 1799* (Paris: Dupont, 1883), vol. XVI, pp. 6–7.

revolutionaries to undertake the reforms which they had every intention nonetheless of introducing. An assembly summoned in terms of orders would have been able to entrust the clergy with the task of undertaking the reforms of the church's laws. But the Constitutional Assembly was explicitly planned in opposition to the division into orders. This was indeed how the Revolution was started. This difficulty explains the condemnation of the Civil Constitution of the Clergy by a large part of the Catholic hierarchy. The bishops were not bound to object to the Civil Constitution of the Clergy, provided it was ratified by a national church council and/or by the Pope; that is to say, by authorities that were canonically competent.[20]

In 1815, the Restoration of the Bourbon monarchy could have been the occasion for renewing ties with a confessional state and with the Gallicanism that went with it. The accession of Louis XVIII, then of Charles X, brought back into power circles who sometimes boasted of having forgotten nothing and learned nothing since 1789, and who remained very attached to the religious policy of the old monarchy. Charles X intended to perpetuate the alliance between throne and altar. Legislation on sacrilege, enacted in 1825, created a new crime of profanation of consecrated hosts. The state thus adopted the Catholic dogma of the real presence. Charles X placed his reign in the lineage of the Most Christian monarchs of the Old Regime, and this alliance with the church was supposed to restore the continuity of centuries. It was a matter of preserving all of the Old Regime that could be preserved. However, Louis XVIII had sat on the throne not of Louis XIV, but of Napoleon. The government could not ignore the fact that the church's property had been sold, nor that religious liberty was now taken for granted.

The counter-revolution was condemned to inherit some of the features of the revolution it opposed. That is something seen very clearly by the opponents of the extremist tendency of the Restoration.[21] But it was also something that was understood by those who, like the impetuous Lamennais, maintained that neither Louis XVIII, nor even Charles X, were taking reaction far enough. An ultramontane and a reactionary like de Maistre, Lamennais published a book in 1825–1826, *On religion considered in its connection with the political and civil order*, in which chapter II is entitled: 'That religion in France is entirely separate from political

---

[20] Cardinal de Boisgelin, 'Discours du 29 mai 1790 sur la constitution civile du clergé', *Archives parlementaires*, vol. XV, pp. 724–31. Cf. Yann Fauchois, 'La difficulté d'être libre: les droits de l'homme, l'Église Catholique et l'assemblée constituante (1789–1791)', *Revue d'histoire contemporaine*, 48/1 (2001), 71–101.

[21] François Guizot, *Des moyens de gouvernement et d'opposition dans l'état actuel de la France* (Paris: Belin, 1988), pp. 135–48.

and civil society, and that the state in consequence is atheist'. Far from congratulating Charles X on the boldness of his reactionary policy, Lamennais found fault with him for his pusillanimity. He recalled – and lamented the fact – that the Most Christian monarchs of the Restoration owed their authority not to their coronation but to the Charter of 1815, which established their rights and duties on a contractual basis. *État civil*, births, marriage and deaths were withdrawn from the empire of the church. On 20 September 1792, *état civil* ceased to be in the hands of priests, passing from the sacristies to the town halls. Divorce, condemned by canon law, was recognised by civil law. On the whole, the church had lost the task of public instruction to the benefit of the state. It no longer enjoyed the official cure of souls to the exclusion of other denominations. In a word, for Lamennais, the Charter remained Republican.

The revolution has reached the stage of excluding God from the state and establishing atheism in the political order and in the civil order ... But from that point on, what is religion for the government? What must Christianity be in its eyes? Sad to say, it is an institution fundamentally opposed to its own, to its principles, to its maxims, it is *an enemy*; and that, whatever may be the personal sentiments of the men in power.[22]

Disappointed by the moderation of the government, which he considered insufficiently theocratic, Lamennais parted company with it. Since the regime remained under obligation to the Revolution, it was not open to it to legislate in religious matters, without its becoming tyrannical and in the last resort anti-Catholic.

By a curious paradox, it was *via* an out-and-out anti-liberalism that Lamennais was led to liberalism. The most reactionary government in the history of France not being sufficiently reactionary in his eyes, it lost the right to interfere in ecclesiastical matters. How could Catholics allow themselves to be guided by the state, knowing that 'one could search in vain in our legal codes for the name of God'?[23] Lamennais became a liberal to the extent that he came to realise that the church no longer had anything to hope for from the powers of this world.

None of the advantages which the state can offer has come anywhere near to compensate for the dangers of the way in which she must perpetually engage, in

[22] F. de Lamennais, *De la religion considérée dans ses rapports avec l'ordre politique et civil* (Paris: Mémorial Catholique, 1826), p. 97. Cf. J. Lecler, 'Les controverses sur l'église et l'état au temps de la Restauration (1815–1830)', in Nédoncelle, *L'ecclésiologie au XIXe siècle*, pp. 297–307.
[23] F. de Lamennais, *Des progrès de la révolution et de la guerre contre l'église* (Paris: Belin-Mandar, 1829), p. 50.

order to preserve her independence. She has consistently much more to fear than to hope for at the hand of princes.[24]

Starting from the quest for a spiritual authority worthy of this name, Lamennais came to realise that the alliance of throne and altar would no longer meet the case. It was expedient therefore that the church should abandon its dependence on the temporal power, and depend only on itself. Since the state was not being converted, it was imperative for the church to disengage itself from its embrace. The atheism of the law, which had led Lamennais into ultramontanism, likewise led him to liberalism. Lamennais was dissuading Catholics from putting their trust in a government which, under the pretext of protecting them, was intent on enslaving them. In 1830, he founded a journal, *L'Avenir*, whose motto was 'God and Liberty'. Around him gathered a group of young men attracted by his liberalism: Montalembert and Lacordaire among others. Their demand was for liberty and they rejected the divine right claimed by the Restoration.[25]

Initially very close politically to Joseph de Maistre, Lamennais soon discovered that their common plan to conflate the church and the state was actually pretty unsatisfactory from a Catholic point of view. In the 1820s, it did not make much sense to claim that the Pope could relate to kings in a top-down manner. In practice, the invitation to fuse religion and politics did not mean the subordination of the state to the church, but of the church (which was politically weak) to the state (which was politically strong). In other words, the ultramontanism defended by Maistre in *Du pape* was utopian. It had no chance of getting anywhere. Politically, the church was in no position to compete with the state for primacy. Lamennais' turn to liberalism was no accident: it was based on a realisation that the papacy could not claim to be the arbiter of European politics.

Even Vatican I, which saw the apparent triumph of de Maistre's disciples, could not do much to change these political realities. The constitution *Pastor aeternus*, the main document of the council, was the result of a compromise. Against the *zelanti*, the bishops had reached a *mezzo termino*. The ultramontanes had obtained most of what they could reasonably obtain, but nothing more, and in particular, not the political primacy of the papacy. Oddly enough, one could therefore argue that the anti-infallibilist minority had triumphed in its defeat.[26] In 1871, the

[24] *Ibid.*, pp. 99–100.
[25] Lacordaire, 'De la liberté de la presse', in *Articles de l'Avenir* (Louvain, 1831), vol. IV, pp. 505–6.
[26] Margaret O'Gara, *Triumph in defeat: infallibility, Vatican I and the French minority Bishops* (Washington, DC: Catholic University of America Press, 1988); Klaus Schatz, *Papal primacy: from its origins to the present* (Collegeville: Liturgical Press, 1996), pp. 179–82.

Holy See had to declare solemnly that 'it is a pernicious mistake to represent infallibility as entailing a right to depose sovereigns and to release peoples from their oath of allegiance'.[27] This was obviously in total contradiction with de Maistre's project. In fact, the declaration of papal infallibility did not change the relations of church and state: its effect was much less than reactionaries had hoped and liberals had feared.[28]

Paradoxically, the triumph of ultramontanism in the church paved the way for a liberalism like that of *L'Avenir*, which took the deconfessionalisation of the state for granted. In a speech to the Chamber of Deputies (Parliament) in July 1868 Emile Ollivier, who was to become a year later Napoleon III's chief minister, stated his views on the council that was yet to meet in the following terms:

Gentlemen, I know of no event since 1789 as important as this [declaration of papal infallibility]: it is the separation of the Church and state, and this effected by the Pope himself. The Church, for the first time in its history, through its chief pastor, says to the lay world, to lay society, to the lay powers: 'I wish to be, I wish to act, I wish to move, I wish to develop, I wish to assert myself, I wish to extend myself, apart from you, and without you. I have a life of my own, which I owe to no human power, which I hold from my divine origin, from my age-old traditions. This life is enough for me; I ask you for nothing, but the right to order myself as I think fit.' Gentlemen, I find this language striking in its boldness.[29]

A non-believer in the mould of the republican tradition, fervent admirer of the ideas of 1789, Ollivier could hardly be suspected of having any sympathy for any kind of papal despotism. 'The separation of Church and state effected by the Pope himself'! Ollivier's formula is particularly striking. It explains why European states, and France in particular, did not try seriously to prevent the declaration of the infallibility of the Pope. Emile Ollivier convinced the Emperor that there was nothing to be anxious about.[30] As a young man, Ollivier had visited the old Lamennais, and was indebted to his vision of a liberal ultramontanism.[31]

In his effort to reassure the British against claims such as Gladstone's, Cardinal Manning could argue similarly that ultramontanism was a not a form of authoritarianism, but the very opposite. 'The natural antagonist

---

[27] 20 July 1871, quoted by Emile Ollivier, *L'église et l'état au concile du Vatican* (Paris: Garnier Frères, 1879), vol. II, p. 374.

[28] Jean-Rémy Palanque, *Catholiques libéraux et Gallicans face au concile du Vatican (1867–1870)* (Gap: Ophrys, 1962), pp. 177–91.

[29] Ollivier, *L'église et l'état*, vol. I, pp. 399–400.

[30] Roger Aubert, *Vatican I* (Paris: l'Orante, 1964), pp. 172–8.

[31] Jacques Gadille, 'Emile Ollivier et l'église Catholique' in Anne Troisier de Diaz (ed.), *Regards sur Emile Ollivier* (Paris: Publications de la Sorbonne, 1985), p. 288.

of Caesarism is the Christian Church with all its liberties of doctrine and discipline, of faith and jurisdiction; and the vindication of those liberties of the church in their highest and most sacred form is Ultramontanism.' Ultramontanism was associated with political liberalism. 'Ultramontanism consists in the separation of the two powers and the vesting them in different persons.'[32]

There was religious intolerance when believers only recognised their own religious community, and ignored the body politic. Conversely, there was a patriotic sectarianism when citizens acknowledged only one community, the civil one. On the subject of the Civil Constitution of the Clergy, Madame de Staël remarked: 'It put political intolerance in the place of religious intolerance.'[33] By withstanding the pretensions of the 'enlightened' state which was persecuting them, Catholics paved the way for a limitation of the state. An observer who can hardly be suspected of being biased in favour of the Catholic Church, Ernest Renan, expresses himself in the following terms:

There is no longer any place for the state in the absolute sense in which French politicians understood it, and in which Prussian politicians [Bismarck] still understand it, and I am delighted by this, and I am grateful to Catholicism for having done in this case what it has already done more than once, that is preventing states from getting too strong. The *doctrinaire* state is always tyrannical.[34]

The victory of ultramontanism marked the full realisation, on the part of Catholics, of the end of the confessional state, a victory which has left a decisive mark on the modern church. On the one hand, popular devotion towards the papacy has kept in the twentieth and twenty-first centuries all the vitality that it acquired under Pius IX.[35] Catholics tend to go to Rome not to pray on the tombs of martyrs, as in the past, but 'to see the Pope'. On the other hand, it is now taken for granted that 'the supreme Pontiff freely appoints bishops'.[36] The only great exception remains China, but it is an exception that confirms the rule. More generally, the primacy of jurisdiction of the papacy, long contested but

[32] H. E. Manning, *Caesarism and ultramontanism* (London: Burns & Oates, 1874), pp. 58–9, 40. Léon Duguit, *Le régime du culte catholique antérieur à la séparation et les causes juridiques de la séparation* (Paris: Sirey, 1907), pp. 33–7.
[33] Mme de Staël, *Considérations sur les principaux événements de la révolution française* (Paris: Delaunay, 1818),vol. II, p. 13.
[34] Ernest Renan, 'La crise religieuse en Europe', in *Mélanges religieux et historiques* (Paris: Calmann-Lévy, 1904), p. 63.
[35] Bruno Horaist, *La dévotion au pape et les catholiques français sous le pontificat de Pie IX (1846–1878)* (Rome: École Française de Rome, 1995).
[36] *Code of canon law* (London: Collins, 1983), canon 377, §1.

solemnly affirmed at Vatican I, is now at the heart of canon law. By virtue of his office, the Pope 'possesses supreme, full, immediate, and universal ordinary power in the Church, which he is always able to exercise freely'.[37] Lastly, whereas the doctrinal teaching of the popes had only a minor place under the Old Regime, their 'ordinary magisterium' has become increasingly important in the life of the church.

However, the political position of the church at Vatican I was not very coherent. The council had condemned the separation of church and state, as well as the intrusions of civil powers in religious matters. These two condemnations could not sit easily side by side. The council was too dependent on those reactionary ultramontanes who had tried to separate the church from the state, but not the state from the church. At the council, the church was asking freedom for itself, but certainly not freedom for all. It demanded respect for its corporate autonomy while hoping to maintain some kind of rule over the state and its citizens. The political teaching of the Catholic Church regained its coherence with Vatican II's affirmation of the primacy of religious freedom. Vatican II brings to Vatican I a political unity that it did not have.

Put together, the two councils may be seen as part of the same 'Vatican Reform', which echoes the Gregorian Reform of the eleventh century, when the church, in order to recover its freedom, felt the need to reassert the centrality of the papacy. John Courtney Murray, a theologian of particular influence on the drafting of the Declaration on religious freedom, has himself related that declaration to the Gregorian Reform.[38] Bossuet had been very harsh in his assessment of Gregory VII, while Lamennais had seen in him the 'great patriarch of European liberalism'.[39] Modern ultramontanism proceeds from the same political logic as Gregory's assertion of the authority of the papacy. In both cases, what is at stake is the constitution of an independent spiritual authority.[40] Papal primacy is indeed a threat to the sovereignty of states, but no more than the declarations of human rights that put religious freedom to the fore. Properly understood, liberal democracy is not compatible with the cult of the state or with a blind patriotism – 'my country, right or

[37] *Ibid.*, canon 331. Cf. *Vatican I: Pastor aeternus*, chap. 3; Schatz, *Papal primacy*, pp. ix–x.
[38] John Courtney Murray, 'The issue of church and state at Vatican II', in *Religious liberty: Catholic struggles with pluralism* (Louisville: John Knox Press, 1993), pp. 207–8.
[39] Jacques-Bénigne Bossuet, *Défense de la déclaration de l'assemblée du clergé de France de 1682* (Amsterdam: Aux Dépens de la Compagnie, 1745) I, i, pp. 7–13; Lamennais, 'De la position de l'église de France', *Articles de l'Avenir*, vol. II, p. 149.
[40] Russell Hittinger, 'Introduction to modern Catholicism', in John Witte and Frank Alexander (eds.), *Teachings of modern Christianity, on law, politics and human nature* (New York: Columbia University Press, 2006), vol. I, pp. 3–38.

wrong'. Liberal democracy presupposes a disposition to defend individual freedom against the natural authoritarianism of states.

The spiritual authority of the papacy is all the more striking as the deconfessionalisation of the state has gone together with the depoliticisation of the clergy and the acknowledgment of the political centrality of the laity. In a democratic regime, the clergy as clergy does not have any specifically recognised political authority. The church can only hope to implement Catholic rules and ideals at a national level through the ballot box and thanks to the civic commitments of citizens whose votes and actions are informed by their faith.

Vatican II: a new role for the laity

Lamennais' own liberal moment had only been a moment, a passing phase in his life because of the condemnation of *L'Avenir* by the Pope himself, in the encyclical *Mirari vos*, but also because of the tensions at the heart of *L'Avenir*'s doctrines. Ultramontane liberalism cannot account easily for the autonomy that it grants to the state. Lamennais and his followers were liberal because they thought that the church had to be protected from the state, but their liberalism remained one-sided. They had to take the independence of the state from the church as given, not as something that could be explained, let alone fully justified. Ultramontane liberalism remained intellectually fragile. It emphasised the need to limit the temporal power, but it had no account of what the temporal power was, and above all no real idea of how to make sure that, as far as possible, it would act in a Christian manner.

Lamennais found an answer to this problem after the condemnation of *L'Avenir*. He became a radical democrat, assuming that genuine Christianity was to be found among those who were genuinely humble: the people. He discovered that, thanks to its Christian people, French society could remain Christian even without the direct intervention of the clergy. Strangely enough, this discovery brought him closer to the Gallican tradition that he had initially rejected. It brought him closer to the idea that the temporal power could be autonomous because of the Christian character of the nation itself.

In fact, the French Revolution killed off a certain type of absolutist Gallicanism without killing off Gallicanism as such. Those Catholics who felt that there was something satanic about the Revolution were bound to feel disenfranchised and to turn to an ultramontane point of view. In contrast, those Catholics who were at least somewhat sympathetic to the message of 1789 felt that they could remain politically attached to their nation, and that their duty was precisely to keep their nation broadly speaking Catholic. For them, in contrast with the young Lamennais, the state had not become 'atheist'.[41] The bulk of the French had remained at least nominally Catholic, and state policies remained indebted to a Christian culture.

Recalling the first article of the 1682 Declaration, Henry Maret, the dean of the Sorbonne in the second half of the nineteenth century, an early Christian democrat, as well as a liberal Gallican, notes:

> To the extent to which this article confines itself to asserting the independence of peoples and their magistrates in the civil and political sphere, and enclosing the ecclesiastical authority within its just limits, then this doctrine seems one of the most glorious achievements of the French clergy and of Bossuet.[42]

In retrospect, some have seen Gallicanism as an origin of liberalism.[43] In contrast with Bossuet's Gallicanism, liberal Gallicanism does not put the divine right of kings at its very centre. It relies not on the Christian character of the crown, but on the political commitment of ordinary Catholics. When Maret writes that the first article of the 1682 Declaration asserts 'the independence of peoples and their magistrates in the civil and political sphere', he is replacing the 'Kings and princes' by the 'peoples and their magistrates'. Now that the sovereign is no longer the King, but the people, Gallicanism is no longer to be associated with monarchism, but with democracy. Maret was not only a Gallican, he was also an admirer of 1789, a liberal and a Christian democrat keen to put the laity to the fore.[44]

A Catholic Gallican was also a citizen, and he did not understand his duties as a citizen to be unrelated to his duties as a believer. He did not want to isolate the church for the sake of a more or less illusory purity, but to keep Christianity at the centre of the political and intellectual life of the nation. As a form of patriotism, Gallicanism implied the active

[41] Royer-Collard, 'Discours du 12 avril 1825, contre la loi dite du sacrilège', in Léon Vingtain, *Vie publique de Royer-Collard* (Paris: Michel Lévy, 1858), pp. 272–3; Henry Maret, *L'église et l'état, cours de Sorbonne inédit (1850–1851)* (Paris: Beauchesne, 1979), pp. 171–2.
[42] Maret, *L'église et l'état*, p. 113.
[43] Lamennais, *Des progrès de la révolution*, pp. 47, 49–50, 56–7. In his Republican *Histoire de l'idée laïque en France au XIXe siècle* (Paris: Felix Alcan, 1929), Georges Weill considers Gallicanism to be one of the four sources of the *idée laïque* (the three others being evangelicalism, deism and free thinking). Pierre Manent's *Intellectual history of liberalism* (Princeton: Princeton University Press, 1994) starts significantly with a long-time hero of Gallicans, Marsilius of Padua, and shows how intimate the relation is between liberalism and the political form of the nation state.
[44] Claude Bressollette, *L'abbé Maret: le combat d'un théologien pour la démocratie chrétienne, (1830–1851)* (Paris: Beauchesne, 1977); Hans Maier, *Revolution and church: the early history of Christian democracy (1789–1901)* (Notre Dame: University of Notre Dame Press, 1969).

civic participation of believers to contribute in the formation of the Christian character of the nation. A form of patriotism had been essential to the age of absolutism; it became even more fundamental to a democratic age tied up with the ideal of popular self-determination. In many cases, Catholics have become more nationalist than before.[45]

Whereas Bossuet wrote his *Politics drawn from the very words of Holy Scripture* for the education of the future King, one of the great debates of the nineteenth century would concern the education of the people. In order to bring truth and charity to the world, the Catholic Church could not rely exclusively on its monks, priests or bishops. Lay people had a specific vocation and they could not be the foot soldiers of the papacy: they were meant to take their own decisions enlightened by their own informed conscience. Hence the church's desire to be free to educate and inform.[46]

In order to enlighten the world, the church did not need a direct power. An indirect power sufficed. That was the discovery of Alexis de Tocqueville in the United States.

If the spirit of the Americans were free of all impediment, one would soon find among them the boldest innovators and the most implacable logicians in the world. But American revolutionaries are obliged ostensibly to profess a certain respect for Christian morality and equity, and that does not allow them easily to break the laws when those are opposed to the execution of their designs; nor would they find it easy to surmount the scruples of their partisans even if they were able to get over their own. Up to now, no one in the United States has dared to profess the maxim that everything is allowed in the interests of society.[47]

De Tocqueville's religious faith was uncertain, but he identified himself with liberal Gallicans against ultramontanes, whom he found politically imprudent and unwise. It was foolish and utopian to pretend that the papacy could govern Europe; it was sensible to expect that ordinary Catholics would defend society against a crude utilitarianism.

As it has become more liberal, the teaching of the Catholic Church has ended up including some of the dimensions of Gallicanism that it initially rejected, starting with the political role of the laity. Ultramontanism initially went together with a clericalism ill adapted to the

---

[45] Raoul Girardet, *Le nationalisme français (1871–1914)* (Paris: Armand Colin, 1966). Compare with Dorothy Dohen, *Nationalism and American Catholicism* (New York: Sheed & Ward, 1967).

[46] *Syllabus of Errors* (London: George Cheek, 1864), pp. 45–8.

[47] A. de Tocqueville, 'Indirect influence of religious opinions upon political society in the United States', in *Democracy in America* (London: Saunders & Otley, 1835), vol. I, 2, p. ix. Cf. Pierre Manent, *Tocqueville and the nature of democracy* (London: Rowman & Littlefield), pp. 88–127.

democratic age. The long battle from Philip the Fair to the Declaration of 1682 and the Civil Constitution was not a battle between the 'church' and the 'state' but between the clergy and the laity, members of the same church.[48] Once a very controversial point between Gallicans and the papacy, the central role of the laity, is now taken for granted by Rome itself. Here is what Vatican II has to say on the matter:

> To be secular is the special characteristic of the laity. Although those in holy orders may sometime be engaged in secular activities, or even practice a secular profession, yet by reason of their particular vocation they are principally and expressly ordained to the sacred ministry ... It is the special vocation of the laity to seek the kingdom of God by engaging in temporal affairs and directing them according to God's will.[49]

The church no longer exerted political influence on the world mainly or directly through the clergy, but through those who were meant to be in power in a democratic regime: citizens who happened to be Catholic.

The central insight behind liberal Gallicanism is that non-Christians can make a valuable contribution to the political life of their nation. The emphasis on the dignity of the political life opens the eyes of believers to the good that those who do not formally belong to the Church can do. Those who are not co-religionists can be excellent fellow citizens. The awareness of the moral and political virtues of non-Catholics or non-Christians brings home a basic but forgotten point: the city of God is not coextensive with the institutional and empirical reality of the church here and now. Christians are also sinners, and conversely some true citizens of the city of God do not belong formally to the institutional church.[50]

A Catholic and a nationalist, Charles Péguy did his best to put Joan of Arc, both a very political and a very religious figure, at the centre of national self-consciousness. But Péguy was neither another Bossuet, nor a bigoted believer harking back to the Middle Ages and incapable of understanding the Revolution. A republican convert to Catholicism, he was keen to emphasise the continuity between the Old Regime and the

---

[48] George de Lagarde, *La naissance de l'esprit laïque au déclin du Moyen Age* (Paris: Presses Universitaires de France, 1934–46); Jean Mesnard, 'La monarchie de droit divin, concept anti-clérical', in Gérard Ferreyrolles (ed.), *Justice et force:politiques au temps de Pascal* (Paris: Klincksieck, 1996), pp. 111–38. The lay dimension of the *Constitution civile du clergé* is what some of its advocates have put forward – see Bordas-Demoulin, *Œuvres posthumes* (Paris: Ladrange, 1861).

[49] Vatican II, *Lumen Gentium*, §31. Cf. Yves Congar, *Jalons pour une théologie du laïcat* (Paris: Cerf, 1953) and *Code of canon law*, §285.3 and 287.2.

[50] Augustine, *City of God*, XVIII, 47.

Revolution, keen to show that even if superficially, 'politically', Catholics and Republicans were at odds, their 'mystiques' could be reconciled. The temporal is the natural dwelling place for the spiritual – a theme to which Péguy devoted many pages.[51] If Catholics abandoned the attitudes that had led to their opposition to individual rights, if Republicans abandoned their crude anti-clericalism, a real understanding was possible. If Catholics were faithful to the best of their religious vocation and to their sense of community, if Republicans were faithful to their political ideals of heroism and justice, reconciliation was unavoidable.

This sense of the generosity and moral excellence that was displayed outside the church, as well as his sense of the unity of the destiny of humanity, led Péguy to contend that everyone would be saved. The Catholic Church has not followed Péguy that far. But, in contrast to the time when its condemnation of religious freedom was closely associated with the belief that most people outside the formal boundaries of the visible church were bound to eternal damnation, the Catholic Church now acknowledges explicitly that even those who are not baptised can be saved.[52] And, whereas the church used to condemn religious freedom in the name of truth, it has now embraced religious freedom because it considers that in modern circumstances, truth is better served by freedom than by intolerance.

The neo-Gallicanism which has developed in the democratic age is indebted to the Gallicanism of the pre-democratic age. But, beyond the acceptance of democracy itself, the Gallican tradition has changed in at least one other fundamental way: in its recognition of religious freedom. Locke had two concerns when it came to the Catholic Church: its inability to recognise national sovereignty, and its condemnation of religious tolerance. Bossuet's political thought was an answer to the first concern, but not to the second: he was comfortable with national sovereignty because he thought of the French nation as a Catholic nation, as a nation which could not easily welcome non-Catholics. Liberal Gallicanism has turned this way of thinking upside down.

To conclude: the tension that was at the heart of the French Catholic Church has become the tension at the heart of the Universal Catholic Church, not least because the French Catholic Church has turned out to be, between 1650 and 1950, its main political laboratory. The Catholic Church's adaptation to the deconfessionalisation of the state has

---

[51] Charles Péguy, *Temporal and eternal* (Indianapolis: Liberty Fund, 2001).

[52] Vatican II, *Gaudium et spes*, §22 and *Ad gentes*, §7. On Péguy's views, see Hans Urs von Balthasar, *The Glory and the Lord* (Edinburgh: T. & T. Clark, 1986), vol. III, pp. 435–65.

entailed, as well as a major reinforcement of the public role of the papacy, a reinforcement of the political responsibilities of the laity. These two trends do not sit easily together, but it is not clear whether the Catholic Church can avoid committing itself to both of them, if it is to remain Catholic, that is both rooted in the life of the nations and universal in a concrete, tangible way, in contrast with the Protestant idea of an 'invisible' universal church.

(Sadly Emile Perreau-Saussine died in 2010.)

8   Religion and the origins of socialism

Gareth Stedman Jones

Socialism has rarely if ever been treated as part of the religious history of Europe and the wider world. Through most of the twentieth century, political and intellectual historians, particularly those writing about the modern period, tended to leave the study of religion to sociologists and psychologists. In the face of philosophical criticism, scientific advance and large-scale social change, religious mentalities and beliefs, it was assumed, were receding. Socialism, it was thought, belonged to that cluster of modern ideas which took the place of religious conceptions of the world. It was considered a 'social' movement and essentially secular, the expression of an urban and industrial working class and the growth of class-consciousness.

But in 1979, the world changed. With the unanticipated triumph of the Iranian Revolution, and the resurgence of religious fundamentalism in different parts of the world, conflicts between temporal and spiritual authority once again came to fore. These developments in turn have provided a different and arguably more appropriate framework, within which to examine the history of socialism. For socialism was above all a product of the fundamental crisis of spiritual authority created by the French Revolution. It was the outcome of a critique, not so much of the state, but of the church, and of the unsuccessful revolutionary attempts to find a replacement for it.

This framework also suggests different questions to be asked about the religious history of Europe. Putting socialism back into western Europe's religious history highlights what was distinctive about that history from the mid sixteenth to the mid twentieth century. It suggests that what was decisive in the first instance was not so much the advance of scientific ideas, be it those of Galileo or of Darwin, nor the particular character of European social-economic change, be it industrialisation, the growth of large cities, the rise of mass literacy or the exodus from the countryside. Least of all was it a steadily developing, if largely invisible, 'disenchantment' of the world. To appeal to these factors as the underlying causes of change is to miss the most salient and obvious fact: that

Europe's religious physiognomy has been shaped and driven by the character of its political development. The different relationships between church and state in Europe since the Reformation have been productive, not so much of secularisation as of distinctive and lasting forms of political antagonism and cultural polarisation. The continuing political insistence by states upon the control of national churches and their creeds, however divisive, inspired the development of heterodox movements and sects; and these in turn articulated that antagonism in increasingly cosmic forms.

This chapter relates the inception of socialism from around 1800 to different manifestations of a Europe-wide religious crisis. 'Socialism' in its different varieties presented itself as the universal replacement for the old religions of the world built upon a new 'science'-based cosmology and a new ethical code. There is unfortunately no space here to trace in detail the subsequent relationship of socialism to the various Christianised forms of radicalism and republicanism that flourished in the 1815–48 period. Nor can there be any analysis of the different kinds of relationship which developed between socialism and religion in France, Britain and Germany after 1848.[1] But it is clear that the degree to which socialism became associated with the construction of alternative cosmologies depended upon differences of political situation. Such a development was minimal in post-1848 Britain, where there was no revolution, but an increasing incorporation of the working class within the polity and a shift in the church's attitude towards 'the social question'. Nor did a distinctively socialist cosmology become prominent in post-1848 France. Hostility to the Catholic Church, strong in Paris, Lyon and parts of the south, was largely articulated either within a Christianised form of democratic republicanism or within a positivist framework shared with Liberal and Radical supporters of the post-1870 Republic. By contrast, there was the striking development of an alternative socialist creed and cosmology in post-1870 imperial Germany, where socialists like Catholics were treated by Bismark as *Reichsfeinde* (enemies of the state). There, the Social Democrats, while ostensibly maintaining that religion was a private matter, did proclaim an alternative evolutionary cosmology, outlined in August Bebel's best-selling *Woman and socialism* of 1879. Finally, the fullest development of an alternative cosmology and theory of man occurred in the Soviet Union after 1917. Rigorously policed by Communist parties throughout the world between the 1920s and 1950s, 'dialectical materialism' like the

---

[1] This chapter is a shorter version of a forthcoming study, 'The place of socialism in the religious history of western Europe'.

'Cult of the Supreme Being' of 1794 served to provide a distinct identity to a new theocratic regime obsessed by internal enemies and surrounded by hostile powers until its final collapse at the end of the 1980s.

The sources of the antagonism, which produced socialist religions or cosmologies, were political rather than intellectual or social. Discourses of secularism and low levels of male working-class church attendance, which characterised post-1870 Europe, were symptoms rather than causes of this antagonism. Conversely, it was the gradual receding of the sources of this antagonism and the corresponding blurring of confessional boundaries which, in addition to more visible and direct causes, brought about the decline and virtual disappearance of socialism as a religious phenomenon during the second half of the twentieth century.

'Socialism', which entered common parlance in the 1830s, was universally recognised to derive from the work of three founding prophets: Henri de Saint-Simon and Charles Fourier in France; Robert Owen in Britain.[2] In standard accounts of its history, it is usually assumed that the birth of socialism was connected with the awakening consciousness of a new working class created by the 'industrial revolution'.[3] Such an approach began with Engels, for whom the history of socialism was a transition from 'utopia' to 'science'. 'Utopianism' was the unavoidable cost paid by ideas which appeared ahead of their time – ahead, that is, of the historical appearance of the new proletariat. Accordingly, the writings of Saint-Simon and Fourier were boiled down into a small selection of suggestive insights and prophetic thoughts. Everything else was dismissed as unavoidable fantasy, which 'belonged entirely to the past'.[4] As late as the 1960s, the histories of G. D. H. Cole, Jacques Droz and George Lichtheim were still largely conceived within such a framework.[5]

This highly filtered reading rendered the whole phenomenon of early socialism historically unintelligible, or even absurd. Its real genesis

---

[2] For France, see the articles of Louis Reybaud on the 'socialistes modernes', a survey of the thought of Saint-Simon, Fourier and Owen, which first appeared in *La revue des deux mondes* in 1836 and 1838.

[3] This argument was first clearly put forward in the writings of Friedrich Engels between 1842 and 1845. See F. Engels, 'The condition of England. I. The eighteenth century. II. The English constitution' (May–June 1844), in *Karl Marx Friedrich Engels collected works* (hereafter *MECW*), (London: Lawrence & Wishart, 1975–2005), vol. III, pp. 469–514.

[4] Engels, 'Socialism: utopian and scientific', *MECW*, vol. XXIV, pp. 281–326.

[5] G. D. H. Cole, *A history of socialist thought*, 5 vols. (London: Macmillan, 1953), vol. I, 'The forerunners 1789–1850'; G. Lichtheim, *The origins of socialism* (London: Weidenfeld & Nicholson, 1969); J. Droz (ed.), *Histoire générale du socialisme*, 3 vols. (Paris: Presses Universitaires de France, 1972), vol. I. See, for example, Lichtheim's *Origins*, in which part 1 is devoted to 'heirs of the French Revolution', part 2 to 'critics of the Industrial Revolution', and the conclusion to 'the Marxian synthesis'.

belonged to the deeply perturbed aftermath of Jacobinism and the Terror in France and, more widely, to the religious and philosophical controversies of Europe from around the end of the eighteenth century. What came to be called 'socialism' originated neither as a new theory about the economy nor as a concern about the plight of the working class. In France, socialism began as one particular answer to a question debated with increasing urgency after the fall of Robespierre in 1794: how to bring the French Revolution to an end?

Later assumptions about the nature of socialist politics have also obscured what was most distinctive about the 'socialist' answer to that question. The concern was not about too little equality, but too much; not about the pursuit of virtue, but about the attainment of harmony; not about popular sovereignty, but the reign of truth; not about the extension of politics, but its subordination; not about the extension of the revolution or the consolidation of the republic, but about the foundation of a new global order. That order would be based upon a new creed or 'spiritual power' (*pouvoir spirituel*), no longer based upon unfounded and out-moded Catholic belief, but upon newly discovered scientific truths about nature, human and cosmological. Both in England and in France, socialism was conceived as a replacement of the Christian Church and all other religions.[6] Therefore, the original and most enduring ambition of 'socialism' was not to displace the state, but the church.

In this chapter, I shall outline the founding proposals of each of the major 'utopians' in order to substantiate these claims. But I shall also extend the analysis to Germany in order to argue that the affinity between socialism and religion was as much a characteristic of so-called 'scientific' socialism as of its 'utopian' counterpart. Let us therefore begin with a very brief *résumé* of the original claims made by each of the founders of so-called 'utopian socialism'.

Saint-Simon, who first set forth his agenda in his *Letters from an inhabitant of Geneva* (1802), began with an apparently bizarre propos-ition. Open a subscription at Newton's tomb; each subscriber to nomin-ate three scientists or artists to sit on the *Council of Newton* and oversee the progress of the world. Arguments for the subscription were addressed to 'scientists', property owners and 'the third which rallies under the word equality, and encompasses the rest of humanity'.[7]

---

[6] On the relationship between socialism or communism and religious reform, see G. Stedman Jones, 'Introduction' to K. Marx and F. Engels, *The communist manifesto* (London: Penguin, 2002), pp. 8–10, 74–84, 140–5.

[7] C. H. de Saint-Simon, 'Lettres d'un habitant de Genève à ses contemporains', *Œuvres de Claude-Henri de Saint-Simon* (Paris: Anthropos, 1966), vol. I, p. 26

If these rival classes agreed to raise above themselves that interest which they all possessed in common – the progress of science – and if, therefore, all obeyed the spiritual rule of scientists, social conflict would cease. Then followed a dream, in which Rome had abandoned its religious pretensions and instead, a peaceful and orderly humanity worshipped Newton under the aegis of the committee of twenty-one persons of 'genius', which presided over his tomb. Previous religions, Saint-Simon claimed, had missed the essential point, which was the 'founding of an establishment which would lead human intelligence along the shortest path towards some approximation of my divine foresight'. They had not followed the scientific path, and had not seen that instead of chastity, continence and all other meaningless religious injunctions, mankind need only obey a single commandment: 'all men shall work'. After 1815 in the revamped version of his proposal, now prudently renamed *The new Christianity*, Saint-Simon proclaimed that religion could be distilled into two messages: 'men must treat each other as brothers'; 'religion must direct society towards the great aim of the most rapid possible amelioration of the poorest class'. 'I am convinced', he concluded, 'that I myself am accomplishing a divine mission in summoning peoples and kings to the true spirit of Christianity.'[8]

Fourier's crucial discovery, 'the science of passionate attraction', also dated from the late 1790s. He claimed that the course of the French Revolution proved the incompetence of Jacobins, republicans, political economists and all other theorists.[9] He had reached his 'Columbus'-like discovery by applying the principle of 'absolute doubt' to such alleged knowledge. His basic point was that the passions so despised by the 'philosophers', with their hateful cult of virtue and equality, were God-given. It was the repression of passions that explained the 'incoherence' of civilisation. Like Saint-Simon, Fourier considered the Catholic Church 'decrepit' and, like him, he imagined the need 'to found a new religion', 'a religion of voluptuousness' which would 'activate desires and passions for which mythology created the taste in pictures'. Fourier's theory was cosmic. Attraction moved both the passions and the planets. He had concluded that 'the attractions and properties of animals, vegetables and minerals were perhaps co-ordinated according to the same

[8] C. H. de Saint-Simon, *Œuvres de Saint Simon* (Paris: Dentu 1868–1875), vol. XXIII, p. 104.
[9] 'What else can one expect from the writings of these *savants*, who, having assembled all enlightenment, ancient and modern, engendered in their debut, as many calamities as they had promised benefits and moved civilised society towards a barbarous state?' See G. Stedman Jones and Ian Patterson (eds.), *Fourier: the theory of the four movements* (Cambridge: Cambridge University Press, 1996), p. 6.

plan as those of men and the stars'. Hence the title of the book: *The theory of the four movements*. Fourier also ascribed to himself a special status. As he later wrote, 'John the Baptist was the prophet, precursor of Christ. I am the prophet, post-cursor, announced by him and completing his work of the rehabilitation of men.'[10]

Finally, Owen, who in the decade from 1812 to 1822 applied his own newfound principle with increasing boldness to the solution of the problems of industrial Britain during the French wars and after. From 1812 to 1817, the immediate object of his preoccupations passed from crime, through the misery of factory children to the increase of pauperism and the problem of post-war unemployment. His increasingly radical solutions started from a new national system of education, proceeded through fiscal reforms and factory legislation, and culminated in a national, and indeed global, network of 'villages of co-operation' in 1817. All these proposals were, supposedly, applications of his new principle of the formation of character, first set down in 1812 and 1813 and fully published in 1816 in *A new view of society*.

Owen claimed, 'all men are ... erroneously trained at present, and hence the inconsistencies and miseries of the world'.[11] In particular, individuals were subjected to the fundamental error, 'that they form their own individual characters, and possess merit or demerit for the peculiar notions or opinions impressed on the mind during its early growth'.[12] Man's ignorance of his own nature, the belief that he himself rather than outside circumstances was responsible for his character, had in turn led him to devise false laws and 'social arrangements'. This was the reason why Man's pursuit of happiness only took selfish and destructive forms. But history would now take a new direction, for knowledge of the science of 'the influence of circumstances' was itself a new circumstance.[13]

Owen's claims for 'the science of the influence of circumstances over the whole conduct, character and proceedings of the human race' were even loftier than those of the French. When Owen laid the foundation of his community at Queenwood in 1839, the stone was inscribed 'C.M'.

[10] Cited in H. Desroches, 'Messianismes et utopies. Note sur les origines du socialisme occidental', *Archives des sciences sociales des religions* 8 (1959), 38.
[11] R. Owen, 'A new view of society, or essays on the principle of the formation of the human character, and the application of the principle to practice', in G. Claeys (ed.), *Selected works of Robert Owen*, 4 vols. (London: Pickering & Chatto, 1993), vol. I, p. 70.
[12] *Ibid.*, p. 71.
[13] 'When these truths are made evident, every individual will necessarily endeavour to promote the happiness of every other individual within his sphere of action; because he must clearly and without doubt, comprehend such conduct to be the essence of self-interest, or the true cause of self-happiness.' *Ibid.*

(Commencement of the Millennium); and this was not a metaphor. Its meaning was spelled out in a 'Recapitulation' at the end of Owen's most systematic treatise, his *Book of the new moral world*. The knowledge imparted to mankind by Owen was 'the second coming of truth'.[14]

In order to understand the centrality of this focus upon religion and science, it is necessary to return to the course of religious reform at the end of the eighteenth century, and in particular to the French Revolution and what became its bitterest source of conflict. Part of the reason for the persistence of the Engels interpretation of utopian socialism through to the 1960s was its underpinning up until that time by a Marxian-inspired 'social' interpretation of the Revolution, found in the works of Albert Mathiez, Georges Lefebvre and Albert Soboul. If ideology were the product of social situation, and if 1789 were a 'bourgeois revolution' directed against a feudal monarchy and aristocracy, then questions about politics, religion and science were secondary, and the writings of 'the utopians' indeed anomalous and eccentric.

Clearly the dismantling of the 'social interpretation' was a necessary condition of any attempt to restore historical intelligibility to these first 'socialist' writings. But it was not a sufficient one. For competing forms of revisionism have been no more successful than the preceding 'social interpretation' in reconstructing an intelligible context for the first writings of Fourier and Saint-Simon. This is true, whether we start from Cobban's picture of unchanging agrarian predominance, Tocqueville's emphasis upon the continuity of the centralised state, Habermas's foregrounding of new forms of sociability or Furet's positing of the autonomisation of politics.[15]

---

[14] 'The First Truth, given through the spirit of the most advanced mind in former periods of the history of humanity, declared that to make the population of the world wise, good and happy, there must be universal charity and universal kindness – men must be trained to love one another as they love themselves, and then there will be peace on earth and good will towards men', and not before. This is the announcement of the First Great Truth to Mankind. But the causes which continually prevented the creation of universal charity, – which kept men, ignorant, wicked and miserable, – which made men hate and dislike each other, and maintained war and ill-will among the human race, were hidden until now in impenetrable darkness; and, much more, the *causes* which can alone create universal charity and universal love, make men wise, good and happy, and ensure forever, peace and good-will amongst mankind. The Second Coming of Truth is to announce this all-important knowledge to the human race.' R. Owen. *Book of the new moral world* (London: Home Colonisation Society, 1842–4), book VII, p. 65.

[15] A. Cobban, *The social interpretation of the French Revolution* (Cambridge: Cambridge University Press, 1964); A. de Tocqueville, *L'ancien régime et la révolution*, 4th edition (Paris: M. Lévy, 1856); J. Habermas, *The structural transformation of the public sphere: an enquiry into a category of bourgeois society* (Cambridge, MA: MIT Press, 1989); F. Furet, *Interpreting the French Revolution* (Cambridge: Cambridge University Press, 1981).

None of these prevalent forms of historical revisionism fully addresses the significance of the battle over the church, arguably the central polarising issue of the Revolution and a fundamental reason for the instability of its outcome through to the Third Republic. The birth of French socialism in the 1790s was one result of this battle. For the extraordinary proposals found in the first writings of Saint-Simon and Fourier were attempts to address these concerns in the immediate aftermath of Robespierre and the Terror, the years of *Thermidor* (1794–1802).

The equation of the Revolution with modernity makes it easy to forget that the years between 1789 and 1802 could be viewed as the last in a series of reformations and religious wars, which had rent Europe apart since the beginning of the sixteenth century. Looked at that way – and many contemporaries, both inside and outside France, did look at it that way – the Revolution could equally be viewed as a failed Reformation. The history of church and state in France before 1789 reinforces that interpretation. For the criminalisation of the Huguenots, the repression of the Jansenists and the successive purges of the *ancien régime* church necessary to enforce the *religion royale* suggested that in crucial respects, the wars of religion never came to an end.[16]

Such an impression was greatly strengthened by the course of the Revolution itself. If the problem of ecclesiastical reform in 1789 seemed minor and soluble, that appearance was deceptive. For, by 1791, it was the religious issue which polarised opinion more than any other, and by 1793–4, what had begun as an optimistic and consensually intended reform of the church had ended in the violent ambition first to overthrow Catholicism, and then, Christianity itself.[17]

The seignorial rights of the church were abolished on 4 August 1789. Its land and property were put at the disposal of the nation and were to be employed in paying off the nation's debts. Since the church was now declared to be at one with the nation, the church also lost its right to meet as a separate order and its clergy were transformed into salaried employees of the state. The new priority accorded to work was made clear in 1790 in the suppression of religious orders 'composed of *fainéants* who passed their time in prayer'. According to the Civil Constitution of Clergy passed by the National Assembly between 29 May and

---

[16] Dale K. van Kley, *The religious origins of the French Revolution from Calvin to the civil constitution, 1560–1791* (London: Yale University Press, 1996).

[17] The only French historian in the nineteenth century who adequately grasped the importance of this issue was Edgar Quinet in *Le Christianisme et La Révolution Française* (Paris 1845). There is a useful discussion of Quinet's importance in F. Furet, *La gauche et la Révolution française au milieu de XIXe siècle: Edgar Quinet et la question de Jacobinisme 1865–1870* (Paris: Hachette, 1986), pp. 1–117.

12 July 1790, the number of sees was reduced to eighty-three, one for each *département*. Priests and bishops were to be elected by lay assemblies, the Pope simply to be informed of the elections when they had taken place. The incomes of higher clergy were slashed. Monks and nuns were made redundant.

These measures encountered resistance. The National Assembly therefore made the clergy swear a loyalty oath to the new constitution. Widespread refusals to take the oath together with deep-seated royal hostility towards the new Constitutional Church were among the most important causes of the civil war, which broke out in 1793. In the ensuing polarisation, the Constitutional Church was itself marginalised. Paris fell under the sway of the 'Cult of Reason' propagated by its Commune; campaigns of de-Christianisation were carried into the countryside by the revolutionary armies. In the summer of 1794, the Commune's 'Cult of Reason' was displaced by Robespierre's 'Cult of the Supreme Being'. Only with the fall of Robespierre and the end of the Terror was an unstable truce achieved on the basis of the separation of church and state and the establishment of freedom of religious worship. Finally, in 1801, for purely pragmatic reasons – not least the pacification of the Vendée – Napoleon made a Concordat with the Pope. His justification was that 'the people must have a religion. This religion must be in the control of the government.'[18]

If in one sense the attempt to replace the church looked like a continuation of the wars of religion of early modern Europe, in other respects, it inaugurated something wholly new: one of the most radical, if least remarked, breaks with the past. The initial concerns in France in 1789 were practical and pragmatic: could the Catholic Church be refashioned to meet national needs? It soon emerged however that immediate issues of reform raised more basic questions, which were inescapably political and theological, and had been present since the original adoption of Christianity as a state religion by the Emperor Constantine. Who had the right to exercise spiritual authority, and on what basis? These very old question were now re-raised in a drastically novel form.

The novelty arose in the aftermath of the American Revolution and the transformation of the Estates General into the National Assembly. Spiritual authority, which in the sixteenth century had been transferred

---

[18] See J. McManners, *The French Revolution and the Church* (London: SPCK, 1969), p. 140. Napoleon's accommodation with Catholicism was an acknowledgement that the Catholic religion could not be eradicated. Napoleon stated, 'my policy is to govern men as the majority wish to be governed. That is the way, I believe, in which one recognises the sovereignty of the people ... If I ruled a people of Jews, I'd rebuild the Temple of Solomon.' *Ibid.*, p. 142.

from the papacy to the Catholic monarch, now was to be transferred to the 'nation' or 'the people'. In practical terms, this meant that the laity (many of whom were not members of the church) would be entrusted with the power to elect the clergy. Not surprisingly, substantial numbers of the clergy resisted, and that set the Catholic Church and the new French Republic upon a disastrous collision course.

It was the frightening failure of the Revolution's original programme of religious reform which led to Jacobin attempts to devise an alternative 'Cult of Reason' or, in 1794, Robespierre's 'Cult of the Supreme Being'. This brief reversion to a theocratic solution to the problem of the relationship between church and state drew heavily upon Rousseau's discussion of 'civil religion' in the *Social Contract*, a proposal which had been greeted with horror by Voltaire.[19] It lasted only a few weeks, but cast a long shadow over nineteenth- and twentieth-century Europe.

If the states of Protestant Europe had reached a situation in which religious questions became second-order issues (ceasing to pose a direct threat to the character of the state), it was because to a greater or lesser extent their policies were based either upon the basic Protestant principle that there was no intermediary between man and God and therefore that individual reason must be free in religious matters (providing it posed no political danger), or upon the idea spelled out by Hobbes and others, that politics concerned actions, not sentiments and therefore that the state should not make windows into men's souls. The Jacobins of 1793–4 adopted neither of these positions. Instead, like Rousseau they subscribed to a contradictory blend of *philosophe* and ancient republican ideals. Rousseau's 'civil religion', while according religious freedom on questions with no bearing on 'morality', contained a capacious set of dogmas pertaining to the 'religion of the citizen'. These included not only the existence of a beneficent deity and personal immortality, but also 'the sanctity of the social contract and the laws', and they were buttressed by punishments for non-compliance ranging from exile to death. For those keen to establish forms of civic religion appropriate to twentieth-century Communist or fascist regimes, Robespierre's cult, brief though it was, offered an ominous precedent.

But whatever the long-term legacy of the Revolution, what struck contemporaries in its immediate aftermath – even those who supported

---

[19] See 'Of civil religion' in 'Of the social contract, book IV', in V. Gourevitch (ed.) *Rousseau: the social contract and other later political writings* (Cambridge: Cambridge University Press, 1997), pp. 142–51. On Voltaire's reaction, see P. Gay, *The Enlightenment: an interpretation*, vol. II: *The science of freedom* (London: Wildwood House, 1973), p. 528.

the Revolution – was its failure. The attempt in 1789 to found a new order based upon the 'Declaration of the Rights of Man and the Citizen' had ended in the Terror and the Jacobin dictatorship. During the years immediately after Robespierre's fall, between 1794 and 1802, all who had supported the Revolution, whether moderates or radicals, had to face the shocking fact that the majority of the population remained attached to Catholicism and probably monarchy as well. The Republic had not taken root in the hearts and minds of the people. What had gone wrong? It was from these questions that it is possible to trace the origins of socialist thought, and its development, both immediate and long-term.

During *Thermidor*, the once unbounded faith in political institutions was replaced by the realisation that the Revolution had been unable to establish reason without bloodshed. The Revolution had failed to capture the hearts and minds of a large part of the French people. If the Republic were to survive, there would have to be a change in the manners and beliefs of the people. Some, notably the *Idéologues*, believed that this could be achieved by a secular reform of education, which would transform the process of reasoning. Others, especially in the years of the July Monarchy between 1830 and 1848, pushed further the democratic logic contained in the original Civil Constitution of Clergy of 1790. Not only was Christ a man of the People, preaching equality and fraternity, Christ was the People. Christ was the divinely appointed embodiment of the democratic people. Some variant of this belief was held by most of the leaders of *Démocratie Sociale*, the main grouping of republicans and democrats during the revolution of 1848.[20]

Others – and here lies the origin of socialism in France – believed that the power of the Catholic Church over people's minds would have to be replaced by a new *pouvoir spirituel*, a new 'spiritual power', and that this new spiritual power was embodied in the discovery of a new 'social science'. Saint-Simon and Fourier focused upon a new science, which would at the same time serve as a new religion, as the only means of producing effective political and cultural change, given the failure of revolutionary Jacobinism to discover a form of *pouvoir spirituel* equivalent to the Catholic Church. This is why in France, the birth of socialism was at the same time the birth of positivism and Comte's later 'Religion of Humanity'.

But how then is the parallel growth of socialism in Britain to be explained? One link was the generally shared expectation, particularly marked from the 1770s and still present in the 1830s, of apocalyptic

---

[20] E. Berenson, *Populist religion and left-wing politics in France, 1830–1852* (Princeton: Princeton University Press, 1984).

change, of a providentially guided progress, of 'the last days' or of the imminent fall of Anti-Christ. Such expectations were especially prominent in Protestant countries. Both in Britain and Germany, religious radicals hailed the world crisis created by the events in France. In Germany, they presaged the completion of the sixteenth-century doctrinal Reformation by a Second Reformation, a 'reformation of life'. In Britain, the late eighteenth-century revolutions fuelled many forms of millennial expectation. Owen's 'second coming of the truth' was one eccentric example. Such expectations were by no means confined to the poor, the uneducated or the philosophically naive; they also informed the calculations of prominent government ministers, the bulk of the established clergy, and the evangelically enthused middle class.

To make this claim in Owen's case might seem strange, in the light of his repeated denunciations of 'all the religions of the world'. But Owen's diagnosis of the obstacles to human emancipation, his providential sense of the laws of nature and of the significance of his 'science', his idea of 'truth' and his millennial conception of the future of mankind were all recognisable modifications of a discourse which eighteenth-century historians have defined as 'rational dissent'.[21]

Unlike France where secular history had rarely been imbued with providential meaning, millennial thought in Protestant countries had been defined by the sixteenth-century Reformation. This had introduced a connection with secular time. For orthodox divines the millennium had been inaugurated with the establishment of the Church of England at the beginning of Elizabeth's reign in 1558. But since for many, the millennium could only begin with the destruction of Anti-Christ, and since Anti-Christ still ruled in Rome, the millennium belonged to the future. Clues about that future might be assembled from a study of the prophetical books of the Bible.

For example, during the Cromwellian Protectorate of the 1650s, when the millennium was thought to be imminent, great importance was attached to the prophecy in Daniel 12.4 that during the time of approaching apocalypse, 'knowledge shall be increased'. This inaugurated an association between science and millennial thinking, which was to last for two centuries. Another example was Cromwell's readmission of the Jews, a decision based at least in part upon the prophecy that Jews would be present at the Second Coming. Similarly, from the time of the Spanish Armada and Foxe's *Book of martyrs* in the 1580s, the end of Anti-Christ was coupled with England's mission as the chosen

---

[21] K. Haakonssen (ed.), *Enlightenment and religion: rational dissent in eighteenth-century Britain* (Cambridge: Cambridge University Press, 1996).

Protestant nation to bring about the downfall of the main supports of Anti-Christ, first Spain, and then especially from the time of Louis XIV and the Revocation of the Edict of Nantes, France.

This helps to explain why the French Revolution provoked such excitement in Britain. For, as Locke had argued, Revelation did not end in biblical times, it was an unfolding process. Each new event might possess hidden theological significance. Major Protestant or Dissenting thinkers in the eighteenth century, including Newton, Hartley and Priestley, anxiously scanned events for 'signs of the times'.

Much also depended upon whether England had undergone a true reformation. A refusal to accept the Anglican liturgy and prayer book in 1662 had been the original reason for the formation of organised dissent. But disagreement over practice soon came to encompass disagreement over doctrine. Many like Newton and Hartley – outwardly Anglicans – maintained the corruption of the Christian message by all ecclesiastical establishments. What came to be called 'rational dissent' emerged after 1700 when the threat to Christianity derived as much from Deism as from Catholicism. It dissociated itself from a stark fundamentalist Calvinism based upon God's incomprehensible power, emphasising instead the rationality of God's creation and the duty to employ reason and natural philosophy in the study of the Bible. It was on these grounds that Newton's friend Samuel Clarke rejected the Trinity in 1712, thus preparing the way for the main grouping of rational dissenters, the Unitarians.

What, then, are the grounds for connecting an avowed Deist and anti-Christian, like Owen, with the millennial vision of Christianity found in rational dissent? First, the similarity of Owen's approach to that of the millennial optimism and scientific rationalism of Joseph Priestley, the Unitarian preacher, famous chemist and champion of the associational psychology of David Hartley. Hartley's theory of the association of ideas, which was directed against the Calvinist picture of original sin, formed the basis of Owen's famous law of the formation of character. Owen also followed Priestley in believing human progress was not solely a human project. Humanity's duty was to co-operate with the divine plan for the arrival of the millennium by removing all obstacles to 'the truth'. According to Priestley, church and state should be separated; religious establishments were objectionable because they used their association with civil power to enhance their authority. They thus inhibited 'candour', the means by which honest citizens reached agreement and therefore the truth. The best way to hasten the millennium was by removing all obstacles in the way of the truth. Governments, republican or otherwise, were to be judged according to whether they assisted progress towards 'the end of all things'.

In Owen's writings, many of Priestley's assumptions reappear, but now shorn of their explicitly Christian reference. Just as the Dissenters had broadened the Anglican definition of Anti-Christ from the Pope to all ecclesiastical establishments, so Owen extended it to all religions. Similarly, he enlarged the dissenting conception of the original purity of Christianity into that of the original purity of human nature. Finally, while it is generally accepted that Owen owed his absolute and singular notion of truth to William Godwin, Godwin himself was an ex-Dissenting minister and his own conception of Truth, as Mark Philp has shown, was also a thinly disguised inheritance from rational dissent.[22] What it implicitly referred to was God's purposes, both in nature and ethics. It was in this way that liberty of private judgement led to the triumph of one indivisible truth.

In Germany, the connection between religion and socialism was more oblique, if not later deliberately concealed. For Marx made every effort to cover his tracks, and Marx's followers, like the followers of Owen, loudly proclaimed their distance from any religious source. But despite these protestations, it is equally clear that German socialism like 'utopian socialism' in Britain and France emerged from a movement of religious reform.

A major reformulation of religious thought in Germany was already under way in the decade before the outbreak of the French Revolution. Lessing's *Education of the human race* (1780) was important because it restated in the language of the *Aufklärung* the expectation of a *Lebensreformation* – a Reformation of life, originally voiced by religious radicals at the time of the Lutheran Reformation and reiterated in the aspirations of seventeenth-century Pietists. The 'Age of the Son' characterised by the New Testament promise of heaven as a reward for virtue was now superseded by the 'Age of the Spirit', in which virtue would be pursued for its own sake. In Kant's writings, there was a comprehensive destruction of the prudential basis of Christian ethics. Traditional proofs of God and immortality were removed; and in their place was constructed a rational ethics based upon moral autonomy and expressed in the categorical imperative. The replacement of the otherworldliness of conventional Christianity by a vision of an ethical commonwealth, which could be the result of 'the victory of the good principle in the founding of a kingdom of God on earth', was set down in *Religion within the boundaries of mere reason*.[23] The attempts to combine these new notions with

---

[22] M. Philp, *Godwin's political justice* (London: Duckworth, 1986), pp. 35–6.
[23] Immanuel Kant, *Religion within the boundaries of mere reason and other writings*, ed. Allen Wood and George di Giovanni (Cambridge: Cambridge University Press, 1998), pp. 105–12.

the ideals of the French Revolution pursued by Hegel and his fellow theological students at Tübingen was set back by the Terror, but the enlarged hopes of spiritual transformation remained. For, as Hegel later stated, the mistake of the French Revolution was to assume that political reform was possible without the reform of religion, 'to make a revolution without having made a reformation'.[24] 'Spirit', as he told his friend, Niethammer, would now migrate from the land of revolution to the land of self-consciousness, and this would be its more appropriate home.[25]

In the 1810s, Hegel thought that his philosophy had laid the basis for *Lebensreformation*. He had shown how once the Reformation occurred, 'divine spirit introduces itself into actuality' and 'the divine spirit must interpenetrate the entire secular life'.[26] But as reaction triumphed in Germany after 1819, and a reactionary religious fundamentalism gained ground at the Prussian court, Hegel's vision of a transfigured and rationally grounded Protestantism lost ground. For radicals after 1830, Christianity even in its speculative shape was no longer identified with emancipation, freedom or the age of 'spirit', but instead, with the bleak individualism and moral authoritarianism of *Vormärz* Prussia. A drastic reformulation of the rational kernel of the Christian promise was necessary, and this was provided by a former student of Hegel, David Strauss, whose *Life of Jesus* appeared in 1835.

Strauss introduced 'the human species' or 'Man' in place of the Christ of the New Testament in his attempt to construct an enlightened and rationalised successor to Christianity. Christ's reconciliation between the human and the divine, Strauss maintained, could only be accomplished by the whole human race in the whole course of its history. In this way, the sacredness of Christ was transferred to the history of 'Man' and human history acquired a providential meaning.

The Young Hegelians, a group of Hegel's followers who started from Strauss's idea, believed they were now living in an age of 'crisis' engendered by the imminent fall of Christianity, and its replacement by this new humanist faith. They added the thought that in worshipping the Christian God, man had worshipped himself in alien form, and, in so doing, had abased himself by ascribing his own capacities to a supernatural being. Marx fully shared this conviction and believed that this recovery of the true conception of 'Man' created a moral obligation

---

[24] G. W. F. Hegel, *Philosophy of mind*, trans. W. Wallace (London: Oxford University Press, 1971), para. 552, p. 287.

[25] 'Hegel to Niethammer, April 29, 1814', in C. Butler and C. Seiler (eds.), *Hegel: the letters* (Bloomington: Indiana University Press, 1984), p. 307.

[26] Hegel, *Philosophy of mind*, para. 552, p. 286.

(a 'categorical imperative') to combat every sphere – whether in religion, politics or material life – in which 'Man' had been 'degraded'. In this way, the criticism and replacement of Christianity became linked with a form of socialism imported from France.

But this vital link connecting Marx's communism with the Young Hegelian movement for religious reform became invisible as a result of what happened next. One of the Young Hegelians, Max Stirner, attacked this humanism as yet another variant of Christianity. The mere individual was now being enjoined to act in the name of 'Man', just as he or she had once acted in the name of Christ. Stirner protested that if one removed this notion of duty inherited from religion, then no such obligation remained. The individual ego need only have concern for him- or herself.

This drastic challenge posed Marx with a dilemma. If he accepted Stirner's point that humanist or communist theorising rested upon religious presuppositions, how could he avoid the conclusion that these were merely matters of individual belief or aspiration and not the product of some higher necessity? Marx's solution was to deny that any idea played an innovatory or independent role in history. 'Morality, religion, metaphysics and all the rest of ideology' . . . merely expressed 'in general terms, actual relations springing from an existing class struggle'. In this way, communist goals could be retained, but any connection between communism and ethics peremptorily denied. Once ideas became merely expressions of the 'real' movement of history and class struggle, it was not too difficult to detach ideas from their actual creators and reassign them to appropriate classes appointed to bear them. In this way, communism was ascribed to the vocation of the proletariat, and the crisis originally imagined by the Young Hegelians as the approaching end of Christianity was reshaped to describe the final crisis of capitalism.

Marx's manoeuvre was very successful. Marxists came to refer to this volte face as 'a great theoretical revolution', while non-Marxist commentators found a way of translating Marx's claim into the language of common sense. As A. J. P. Taylor put it, 'nearly everyone now accepts the principle that ideas and beliefs grow out of and reflect existing society rather than lead an independent life'. The evidence of what had really happened was very deeply buried in the obscurely written polemics of the mid 1840s, especially, *The German ideology*. In that text, Marx denounced Stirner over 200 pages, while never referring to the real point at issue.

The history of Marxian socialism in the nineteenth and twentieth centuries is not merely suggestive of a religious movement. Once the texts which describe its founding moment are properly scrutinised, it is clear that Marx's socialism was an offshoot of a humanist creed, designed both to complete and replace Christianity. What Marx called 'the criticism of religion' had not resulted in agnosticism, but in vision of human history resting upon the theological underpinning of a teleology, reminiscent of Protestant Christianity, in which the exploited were given a sacred vocation and certainty about the future. Hence the paradox of a movement as fervent as any creed, equipped with its church fathers, its priests, its dogma and its holy books, yet proclaiming itself militantly secular, uncompromisingly materialist and vehemently 'scientific'.

In what ways did the religious origins of socialism continue to affect its subsequent character? I would like to suggest that socialism's religious genesis was not merely a contingent feature of its prehistory, but continued to shape the subsequent nineteenth- and twentieth-century development of socialism in all its forms.

Perhaps most important was the place assigned by socialism to politics. For socialism was not simply a form of politics as many commentators have assumed. One feature common to all the founding works of 'socialism' was the relegation of politics to a subordinate or derivative status. Socialism was never primarily interested in the state. What mattered was the social terrain, whether defined in terms of mentality (religion, 'spirit', superstition) or everyday practice (economy, household, family). Put differently, its ambition was either to establish a new religion ('the rational religion' of the Owenites, Saint-Simon's 'religion of Newton' or 'New Christianity', the Saint-Simonian 'religion of Saint-Simon', Fourier's 'religion of voluptuousness', etc.) or else in Marx's case to take the place of religion by standing in its place.[27]

Different constitutions or forms of government were therefore of interest to socialists only in as far as they offered the means to forward this end. The relationship of socialism with politics was strictly instrumental. Once understood in this way, it becomes easier to understand the inadequacy of attempts to present socialist thought in conventional political or economic terms. 'Socialism' is better understood as a self-proclaimed, science-based post-Christian religion or as a novel cosmology to which diverse forms of politics were at different times attached. An awareness of the cosmological dimension of socialism helps to make more sense of the zigzag trajectory between purist abstention and opportunist endorsement so often followed by socialist movements and parties

[27] As Karl Marx put in 1844, 'the criticism of religion ends with the teaching that *man is the highest being for man*, hence with the *categorical imperative to overthrow all relations* in which man is a debased, enslaved, forsaken, despicable being'. K. Marx, 'Contribution to the Critique of Hegel's Philosophy of Law: Introduction', *MECW*, vol. III, p. 182.

during the nineteenth and twentieth centuries. Anecdotes about Saint-Simon's appeal to the Pope and the massed ranks of scientists in 1813, Fourier's appeals to Louis Philippe, the Rothschilds and other philanthropic millionaires, Owen's appeals to Metternich and the Congress of Vienna, or in 1848 to 'Queen Victoria and the red republicans', or Lassalle's proposals to Bismark are perhaps familiar. The reckless encouragement of European war by Marx and Engels before 1870, the extraordinary faith in dictatorship as a prelude to the disappearance of the state found in Lenin's *State and revolution*, the guileless endorsement of Stalinism or fascism by prominent Fabians, the unblinking defence of the Hitler–Stalin pact by tens of thousands of Communists or the brief love affair between *gauchiste* French intellectuals and the Chinese Cultural Revolution, only make sense because politics was subordinated to larger historical and cosmological scenarios.

If the metaphysical core of socialist ambition is accepted, it becomes easier to understand why early socialists characteristically constructed not merely a theory of society, but also a whole theory of the cosmos to underpin it. This aspect of the socialist past, while not unknown, has generally been treated as part of a comic prehistory – Fourier's talk of a 'lemonade sea' or the Saint-Simonian orientalist quest for a female messiah, for example. Supposedly, a fantastic prologue before the real history of socialism began. But in fact a cosmological framework remained central to the definition of socialism, whether of its internationalism, its scientific ambition or of its determination to capture the religious terrain. Its cosmopolitanism also strongly contrasted with the many varieties of republicanism, whose common emphasis was upon the primacy of the *res publica* and the cultivation of patriotic virtue.

The ambition to provide a cosmological foundation for socialism was by no means confined to its 'utopian' founders. A similar quest impelled by the desire to distinguish the 'materialist conception of history' from other conceptions of popular materialism underlay both Engels's *Anti-Dühring* and his unfinished *Dialectics of nature*. The subsequent fate of these writings – the enthronement of Engels even above Marx as the philosopher of the Second International, and the enshrinement of the doctrine of 'dialectical materialism' as the official cosmology of the Soviet Union and the Third International – only underlines the continuing significance of socialism's starting point as a science-based cosmology underpinning a post-Christian religion.

If this was the appeal of socialism, it is easier to understand its post-1960s demise. Its declining appeal was most obviously the result of a sequence of catastrophic political events, which highlighted the repressive social order that 'actually existing socialism' had brought into being – from the repression of the Hungarian Uprising by the Soviets in 1956 to the Tiananmen Square massacre, the fall of the Berlin Wall and the collapse of the Soviet Union in 1989–91. Less dramatic, but no less disenchanting, were the failures of democratic socialism in western Europe, in particular, that of the British Labour government's 'social contract' in the 1970s, and of socialist economic policy of the 1981–6 Mitterrand government in France.

But there were other equally potent, if less visible, reasons for decline. The appeal of socialism had rested upon its claim to scientific truth. Science was to lead the way to a new world order. But from the 1960s onwards it was not simply the perversions of 'Soviet' science which invited ridicule. After Auschwitz and Hiroshima, science itself had lost its emancipatory lustre, and this loss in turn stripped socialist leaders and thinkers of their aura of scientific authority. Other cultural changes strongly reinforced this decline in stature. Of great importance was the growing moral and cultural individualism of the young, made possible by rising standards of living, better education, less cramped housing, new forms of popular culture and a growing migration from country to town.[28] Connected with these changes were fundamental shifts in confessional and socialist politics: the post-war growth of Christian Democracy as Catholic or interconfessional parties in France, Italy and West Germany; the revision of attitude of the German Protestant Churches towards Social Democracy, confirmed by the Social Democrats' Bad Godesburg programme of 1959; and most spectacularly Vatican II (1962–5). With the decline of political and cultural confrontation, the polarised and seemingly immobile political and cultural communities of the 1890–1950 era, Catholic as much as socialist, became permeable and began to break up. In the fifteen years following World War II, these shifts had largely occurred beneath the surface. But from the mid 1960s to the mid 1970s they acquired a radical and articulate existence in a proliferation of anti-authoritarian movements globally dramatised by the theatrical events of 1968.

It was barely a decade before the visionary hopes of the 1960s gave way to a harsher economic climate and the resurgence of conservatism. The anti-authoritarian trend continued, but now was increasingly inspired by a neo-liberal agenda. Visions of a socialist utopia did not return. Even the worldwide capitalist crisis of 2008 failed to revive them. But that was because socialism had never been simply an economic doctrine, nor had the movement which it had inspired.

---

[28] Hugh McLeod, *The religious crisis of the 1960s* (Oxford: Oxford University Press, 2007).

9   From 1848 to Christian Democracy

Christopher Clark

This chapter focuses on the relationship between the processes of secularisation and Catholic religious revival that have shaped Europe's transition to modernity. The chapter falls into two parts. The first explores the deepening tension between an anti-clerical European liberalism at the height of its powers and confidence and a revitalised Catholic Church determined to mobilise the masses of the faithful in support of its objectives. The second part of the chapter explores the dialectical relationship between secular (liberal, republican) and clerical forms of mobilisation. Secularising movements and initiatives, it argues, triggered waves of confessional mobilisation and vice versa. In this process of challenge and response the two processes evolved in tandem. The chapter closes with a reflection on the significance of this paradoxical intertwining of opposed phenomena for the shaping of modern Europe.

Even the most cursory overview of the history of Catholicism in nineteenth-century continental Europe reveals an apparently contradictory state of affairs. On the one hand, church properties were seized and sold off; ecclesiastical privileges (fiscal, political, juridical) were removed or curtailed; clerical authorities came under pressure to retreat from their commanding positions in education and charitable provision; liberal, national, radical and socialist political discourses were marked by an uncompromisingly anti-clerical rhetoric and Masonic and free-thinking associational networks sprang up to combat the influence of church institutions and doctrine over human affairs. On the other hand, this was an era that witnessed a remarkable burgeoning of religious energies: the proliferation of popular devotions, church buildings, religious foundations and associations, a correspondingly dramatic rise in the number of religious vocations (especially among women) and the establishment of confessionally motivated newspapers and journals.

Although signs of incipient polarisation can be discerned across western Europe before 1848,[1] the revolutions of that year marked a new departure. In the 1840s and even during the revolution itself, as one study of provincial south-western France has shown, there was still little sign in France of principled anti-clericalism in the political rhetoric of most republicans; on the contrary, most were still 'full of solicitude and even of a certain hope' vis-à-vis the clergy and Catholicism in general during the events of 1848. But from the elections of May 1849 onwards, a 'resolute anti-clericalism' came to be one of the signature tunes of the republican left.[2] In Italy, the emergence of radical secular republican movements in the summer and autumn of 1848 and the conservative turn in papal policy demolished the illusion that the church could be part of a liberal, nationalist solution to the Italian question. In the German states, too, 1848 produced a hardening of anti-clerical attitudes within the revolutionary left, as reflected, for example,

---

[1] On religious revivals during the late enlightenment, see Louis Chatellier (ed.), *Religions en transition dans la seconde moitié du XVIIIe siècle* (Oxford: Voltaire Foundation, 2000), p. 74; for the revolutionary and post-Napoleonic periods, see Jacques Godechot, *La Contre-Révolution: doctrine et action (1989–1804)* (Paris: Presses Universitaires de France, 1961); T. C. W. Blanning 'The role of religion in European counter-revolution, 1789–1815', in D. E. D. Beales and G. Best (eds.), *History, society and the churches: essays in honour of Owen Chadwick* (Cambridge: Cambridge University Press, 1985), pp. 195–214; D. Beales, 'Joseph II and the monasteries of Austria and Hungary', in Nigel Aston (ed.), *Religious change in Europe, 1650–1914* (Oxford: Clarendon Press, 1997), pp. 161–84; J. McManners, *The French Revolution and the church* (London: SPCK, 1969); J. McManners, *Church and society in eighteenth-century France*, vol. I: *The clerical establishment and its social ramifications* (Oxford: Clarendon Press, 1998), pp. 216–17, 308, 332–46; C. Naselli, *La soppressione napoleonica delle corporazioni religiose: contributo alla storia religiosa del primo ottocento italiano 1808–1814* (Rome: Gregoriana, 1986), pp. 203–5; on pre-1848 polarisation in Switzerland, see Josef Lang, '"Die Firma der zeitverständigen Geistlichen stirbt aus": die Ultramontanisierung des Schweizer Klerus im langen Kulturkampf von 1830–1880', *Traverse. Zeitschrift für Geschichte* 3 (2000), 78–89; on Spain, see J. Callahan, *Church, politics and society in Spain, 1750–1874* (Cambridge, MA: Harvard University Press, 1984), pp. 169–72; Frances Lannon, *Privilege, persecution and prophecy: the Catholic Church in Spain, 1875–1975* (Oxford: Clarendon Press, 1987), p. 2; Stanley G. Payne, *Spanish Catholicism: an historical overview* (Madison: University of Wisconsin Press, 1984), p. 98; on Belgium, Els Witte (ed.), *Documents relatifs à la franc-maçonnerie belge du XIXe siècle 1830–1855* (Leuven: Nauwelaerts, 1973), p. 11; John Bartier, 'La franc-maçonnerie et les associations laïcques en Belgique', in Hervé Hasquin (ed.), *Histoire de la laïcité, principalement en Belgique et en France* (Brussels: Renaissance du Livre, 1979), pp. 177–99, 179–82; on Germany, Friedrich W. Graf, *Die Politisierung des religiösen Bewusstseins: die bürgerliche Religionsparteien im deutschen Vormärz: das Beispiel des Deutschkatholizismus* (Stuttgart: Fromann-Holzboog, 1978); Andreas Holzem, *Kirchenreform und Sektenstiftung: Deutschkatholiken, Reformkatholiken und Ultramontane am Oberrhein (1844–1866)* (Paderborn: Schöningh, 1994).
[2] Jean Faury, *Cléricalisme et anticléricalisme dans le Tarn (1848–1900)* (Toulouse: Université de Toulouse, 1980), pp. 37–8.

in attacks on the homes of prominent Berlin clergymen, or in the demand that religious instruction be removed from school curricula. In Prussia especially, the churches paid a price for the political alliance between political conservatism and Protestant orthodoxy that had been an abiding feature of the 1830s and 1840s.[3]

It was not just that the revolutions radicalised liberal and anti-clerical politics; they also removed many of the formal constraints on religious revival. In Germany, for example, the upheavals of 1848 led to a relaxation of the legal constraints on association and a phase of accelerated Catholic self-mobilisation, as witnessed in the rapid proliferation of the *Piusvereine*.[4] In the France of the Second Empire, the administration maintained a policy of conciliation that encouraged the expansion of the church's institutional basis and the consolidation of its place in education and social provision, despite the persistence of strong anti-clericalism in broad sections of the population. Here, as in many other parts of Europe, the church was the indirect beneficiary of the revolution, in the sense that it commended itself to the post-revolutionary administration as an organ of social control and a bulwark against further upheaval.[5]

In the Netherlands, too, the revolution strengthened the standing of the church, though through a different mechanism. The separation of church and state accomplished by liberal constitutional reformers in 1848 meant that the Catholic Church could now organise itself as it wished. In 1853, Pope Pius IX capitalised on the new situation by announcing unilaterally the reintroduction to Dutch territory of the Catholic hierarchy. In a country whose myths of origin were rooted in the bitter early modern struggle against Catholic Spain, this re-Catholicisation of Dutch territory was seen as an intolerable

---

[3] Hugh McLeod, *Secularisation in western Europe, 1848–1914* (Basingstoke: Macmillan, 2000), pp. 31–51.

[4] On the *Piusvereine*, see Ernst Heinen, *Katholizismus und Gesellschaft: das katholische Vereinswesen zwischen Revolution und Reaktion (1848/49–1853/54)* (Idstein: Schulz-Kirchner, 1993); Jonathan Sperber, *Popular Catholicism in nineteenth-century Germany* (Princeton: Princeton University Press, 1984).

[5] On the place of the church in education, see R. D. Anderson, 'The conflict in education. Catholic secondary schools (1850–1870): a reappraisal', in Theodor Zeldin (ed.), *Conflicts in French society: anti-clericalism, education and moralism in the nineteenth century* (London: Allen & Unwin, 1970), pp. 51–93; and R. D. Anderson, *Education in France, 1848–1870* (Oxford: Clarendon Press, 1975); R. Gildea, *Education in provincial France, 1800–1914: a study of three departments* (Oxford: Clarendon Press, 1983); James McMillan, '"Priest hits girl": on the front line in the "war of the two Frances"', in Christopher Clark and Wolfram Kaiser (eds.), *Culture wars: secular–Catholic conflict in nineteenth-century Europe* (Cambridge: Cambridge University Press, 2003), pp. 77–101; John K. Huckaby, 'Roman Catholic reaction to the Falloux Law', *French Historical Studies* 4 (1965), 203–13.

provocation. The consequence was the 'April movement', a dramatic mobilisation of anti-Catholic sentiment centred in the city of Utrecht, seat of the new Catholic archbishop. In an effort to contain and neutralise the resulting tensions, the government enacted a law imposing stricter regulations on (by implication Catholic) religious processions, a law that reflected Protestant, rather than authentically secular, priorities.[6] In many areas of mixed Catholic and Protestant confession, the revolutions intensified the linkage between nationalism and Protestantism: for Prussia, 1848–9 brought into view the as yet unrealisable prospect of a Protestant-dominated and (relatively) ethnically homogenous 'lesser Germany' that would exclude Catholic multi-ethnic Austria. In Switzerland, as Heidi Bossard-Borner has observed, the federal state that emerged in 1848 after a phase of civil war and revolutionary upheaval 'owed its origin not least to anti-Catholic emotions'.[7]

As these constellations suggest, the religious conflicts of mid and late nineteenth-century Europe cannot be explained solely in terms of the tension between secular and clerical interests. Any account that adopts the concept of secularisation as a causal driver will find it difficult to discriminate between conditions in Catholic states like Spain, where the key cleavage was between seculars and clericals, and the more complex triangulated relationships that obtained in multi-confessional states like the German territories, Switzerland or Holland. Here, the conflict was characterised by an unstable fusion between genuinely secularising liberal forces and interconfessional antagonisms that dated back to the Reformation. How the two factors are weighed up against each other varies from historian to historian.[8] Victorian England was a special case. The absence of an 1848 on mainland Britain may help to explain why

---

[6] Peter Jan Margry and Henk te Velde, 'Contested rituals and the battle for public space: the Netherlands', in Clark and Kaiser (eds.), *Culture wars*, pp. 132–3; A. J. Bronkhorst, *Rondom 1853. De Invoering der Rooms-Katholieke hiërarchie: de April-Beweging* (The Hague: Boekencentrum, 1953), pp. 67–8; J. P. de Valk, *Roomser dan de paus? Studies over de betrekkingen tussen de Heilige Stoel en het Nederlands katholicisme, 1815–1940* (Nijmegen: Valkhof, 1998), pp. 172, 347–8; Rob van der Larse, 'De deugd en het kwaad: liberalisme, conservatisme en de erfenis van de Verlichting', in J. H. C. Blom and J. Talsma (eds.), *De Verzuiling voorbij: godsdienst, stand en natie in de lange negentiende eeuw* (Amsterdam: Het Spinhuis, 2000), pp. 24–9.

[7] Heide Bossard-Borner, 'Village quarrels and national controversies: Switzerland', in Clark and Kaiser (eds.), *Culture wars*, p. 262; on Swiss confessional conflict more generally, see Peter Stadler, *Der Kulturkampf in der Schweiz: Eidgenossenschaft und katholische Kirche im europäischen Umfeld 1848–1888* (Zurich: Chronos, 1996); Victor Conzemius, 'Der Kulturkampf in der Schweiz – Sonderfall oder Paradigma?', *Rottenburger Jahrbuch für Kirchengeschichte* 15 (1996), 27–42.

[8] In the case of the German *Kulturkampf*, for example, some historians have focused on secular, others on (Protestant) religious patterns of motivation. David Blackbourn's *Marpingen: apparitions of the Virgin Mary in Bismarckian Germany* (Oxford: Clarendon

the polarisation of secular and confessional politics that was such a striking feature of life in some continental states was so much less marked in Britain, where religion and politics remained entangled in complex ways that may constitute a British *Sonderweg*. In Victorian England, the agitation for ostensibly secularising initiatives, such as the removal of religious instruction from school curricula, was more likely to be driven by nonconformist desire to stem the influence of the Anglican clergy.

'Secularisation' was in this sense a process licensed by believers as a means of protecting their confessional subcultures against infiltration by agents of the established church. Even here, however, concern over the growing confidence and strength of Roman Catholicism in Europe (and Ireland) goes a long way towards explaining the sharpness of the conflicts between Anglicans and nonconformists over issues such as schooling and the relationship between church and state; these were in many respects variants of the clashes occurring elsewhere in Europe.[9]

Although there had been occasional bursts of polemic from parts of the ultramontane press in the 1830s and 1840s, most Catholic journals had striven to avoid political controversy and focused on religious questions in the narrower sense. The revolutions of 1848 produced a less restrained climate. The lifting of press restrictions in many countries encouraged the launching of new journals and removed some of the constraints on tone and content. More importantly, the secularising and sometimes anti-clerical thrust of liberal demands across Europe opened a gap between liberals and ultramontanes that had previously been cloaked by a shared rhetoric of 'liberty' in the face of repressive state measures. One of the most important ultramontane voices of the post-revolutionary era was that of the French publicist Louis Veuillot, editor of the profoundly influential journal *L'Univers*. In his journal and through his prolific occasional writings, Veuillot applied a style honed in his youthful days as a theatre critic (before his adult 'conversion' to ultramontane Catholicism) to the purposes of religious polemic. The rhetoric and arguments of liberalism were subjected to forensic analysis,

---

Press, 1993) stressed the anti-clerical, post-Enlightenment impulse underlying liberal anti-Catholic sentiment in later nineteenth-century Germany; by contrast, Helmut Walser Smith, *German nationalism and religious conflict: culture, politics and ideology, 1870–1914* (Princeton: Princeton University Press, 1995) focused on the role played by confessional antagonisms.

[9] On these conflicts, see J. P. Parry, 'Nonconformity, clericalism and "Englishness": the United Kingdom', in Clark and Kaiser (eds.), *Culture wars*, pp. 152–80; for a more general treatment: E. R. Norman, *Anti-Catholicism in Victorian England* (London: Allen & Unwin, 1968); D. G. Paz, *Popular anti-Catholicism in mid-Victorian England* (Stanford: Stanford University Press, 1992).

their inconsistencies and lacunae sarcastically exposed. What emerged were the outlines of a coherent 'clericalism' that did not simply rearticulate Catholic theological and moral positions but defended the church – under papal authority – as a social institution.[10] In Italy, too, the ultramontane press now issued blanket condemnations of republicanism and nationalism and their fellow travellers in clerical garb, expressed in a new mordant style exemplified by the writing of Giacomo Margotti, editor of the Turin paper *L'Armonia*.[11] The note of intransigence and polemical sharpness sounded during the months of revolution was to remain a defining feature of much ultramontane publicistic activity.

The papal curia, too, emerged from the revolutions more attuned to public opinion, more demotic, more plebiscitary in its approach to public relations. It was only after 1848, under the pressure of the dramatic expansion in political print that accompanied the revolutions, that the papacy actually developed a broad-circulation press organ of its own.[12] *Civiltà Cattolica*, launched in April 1850, was a nominally independent, self-funding enterprise, yet it was produced under the close supervision of the curia and, in particular, of Pius IX himself, who frequently examined the proofs of the journal before publication. As a consequence, *Civiltà Cattolica* came to occupy a unique place in the panorama of the international press as the 'semi-official voice of the Pope'.[13]

In short, the new post-revolutionary Catholic Church equipped itself for the battle against European liberalism by acquiring many of the attributes of a modern multi-national corporation: a press and information policy; focus-grouped initiatives designed to secure mass appeal; and a more tightly organised executive structure capable of policing the mass membership, securing compliance and purging or marginalising unreliable elements. The loss of temporal sovereignty after the truncation and annexation of the Papal States by the new kingdom of Italy in

---

[10] On Veuillot, see James F. McMillan, 'Remaking Catholic Europe: Louis Veuillot and the ultramontane project', *Kirchliche Zeitgeschichte* 14 (2001), 112–22; Marvin L. Brown, *Louis Veuillot: French ultramontane journalist and layman, 1813–1883* (Durham: Moore, 1977); Benoît Leroux, *Louis Veuillot: un homme, un combat* (Paris: Téqui, 1984); Pierre Pierrard, *Louis Veuillot* (Paris: Beauchesne, 1998).

[11] Full title 'L'Armonia della Religione colla Civiltà'; Angelo Majo, *La stampa cattolica in Italia: storia e documentazione* (Milan: Piemme, 1992), pp. 31–5.

[12] Majo, *Stampa cattolica*, p. 49; R. Aubert, *Le Pontificat de Pie IX (1846–1878)* (Paris: Bloud & Gay, 1963), p. 39; F. Dante, *Storia della 'Civiltà Cattolica' (1850–1891): il laboratorio del Papa* (Rome: Studium, 1990), pp. 57–63, 141–52.

[13] Dante, *Storia*, pp. 66, 67, 71.

1859/70 merely facilitated and accelerated this reconfiguration of the church as an authentically transnational entity.[14]

These developments set the stage for the church–state conflicts that were such a conspicuous feature of European politics in the second half of the nineteenth century. Across the continent, the rise of liberal nation states placed Catholic institutions and Catholic loyalties under increasing pressure. In Prussia, following the foundation of the German Empire in 1870/1, Otto von Bismarck's government launched a salvo of laws intended to neutralise Catholicism as a political force, triggering a 'struggle of cultures' (*Kulturkampf*) that shaped the contours of German politics and public life for more than a generation.[15] In Italy, the annexation of the Papal States and the city of Rome in 1870, and the 'imprisonment' of the Pope within the walls of the Vatican produced a stand-off between the church and the secular kingdom of Italy, with far-reaching consequences for Italian political culture. In France, the elite of the Third Republic and the forces of clericalism waged bitter rhetorical battles, to the point where it seemed that secular and Catholic France had become two separate social realities. In Belgium, a long period of growing friction between liberals and Catholic political interests culminated in the 'school war' of 1879–84, during which liberal and Catholic crowds clashed in the streets of Brussels, again with lasting repercussions for Belgian society and political culture. In the Netherlands, heated conflict over Catholic processions, which were legally forbidden, together with the pressurising impact of the *Kulturkampf* underway in neighbouring Germany, accelerated the articulation of Dutch society into discrete sociocultural milieus. In Switzerland, confessional and secular–Catholic tensions at local and cantonal level became intertwined with the most important issues in national politics. In Austria and Hungary, Catholics and Liberals clashed over civil marriage, schooling and Protestant burials in the aftermath of the new political settlement established by the Compromise of 1867.

---

[14] Francisco Colom González, 'El hispanismo reaccionario. Catolicismo y nacionalismo en la tradición antiliberal española', in Francisco Colom González and Ángel Rivera (eds.), *El altar y el trono: ensayos sobre el Catolicismo político iberoamericano* (Barcelona: Anthropos, 2006), p. 47.

[15] Useful studies include: Eleonore Föhles, *Kulturkampf und katholisches Milieu in den niederrheinischen Kreisen Kempen und Geldern und der Stadt Viersen* (Viersen: Kreisversen, 1995); Christoph Weber *'Eine starke, enggeschlossene Phalanx': der politische Katholizismus und die erste deutsche Reichtagswahl 1871* (Essen: Klartext, 1992); see also the relevant chapters in Margaret Lavinia Anderson's important study *Practicing democracy: elections and political culture in Imperial Germany* (Princeton: Princeton University Press, 2000).

There had of course always been intermittent institutional friction between church and state in central and western Europe, but the conflicts that came to a head in the 1860s and 1870s were of a different kind. They involved processes of mass mobilisation and societal polarisation. They embraced virtually every sphere of social life: schools, universities, the press, marriage and gender relations, burial rites, associational culture, the control of public space, folk memory and the symbols of nationhood. They acquired this ubiquity and depth because the mobilisation of clerical (and liberal anti-clerical) allegiances became interwoven with broader processes of social and political change, most importantly, the expansion of political participation that occurred within the European states in the middle and later decades of the century. It is noteworthy that in many countries the most intense phase of secular–clerical conflict followed a moment of historically significant constitutional innovation – the Compromise of 1867 in Austria–Hungary, franchise reform in Belgium and Britain, the formation of new partly democratic national polities in Italy and Germany, or the establishment of the Third Republic in France. In an environment where franchises were opening up and parliaments were acquiring more power, institutions that had been locked into relatively stable systems of representation – marriage and burial, schooling, dress, the use of public space, even the sacral quality of royalty or the state – were now up for grabs. In such a setting, it was possible for conflicts between Catholic and anti-clerical (or Protestant) pressure groups to escalate into 'culture wars', in which the values and collective practices of modern life appeared to be at stake.

One consequence of this epochal struggle was a discursive escalation in both camps. The papal declarations of Pius IX were marked by a stridency of tone that set them apart from their eighteenth-century predecessors (with the possible exception of *Unigenitus*).[16] The Catholic polemic of the culture wars era projected a Manichaean vision of a world in which the forces of Christ were arrayed against those of Satan. 'This is no time for half measures', one anonymous author declared in *De Katholiek*, an ultramontane journal published in s'Hertogenbosch. 'Everyone is forced openly to take up a position with or against

---

[16] Owen Chadwick, *A history of the popes* (Oxford: Oxford University Press, 2003), p. 235; Frank J. Coppa, *Pope Pius IX: crusader in a secular age* (Boston: Twayne, 1979), pp. 140–53; Roger Aubert, Johannes Beckmann, Patrick J. Corish and Rudolf Lill, *The church in the age of liberalism*, trans. Peter Becker (London: Burns & Oates, 1981), pp. 293–9; Klaus Schatz, *Vaticanum I, 1869–1870*, 2 vols. (Paderborn: Schöningh, 1992), vol. I, p. 32.

Christ – there is no middle way.'[17] In this Manichaean worldview, the forces of 'obedience' – one of the cardinal virtues celebrated by the papalist camp – were ranged against the forces of 'Satanic rebellion' unleashed by the revolutions of 1789 and 1848, and the Italian unification of 1859.[18]

The first casualties of such a worldview were naturally the conciliatory Catholics, the *transigenti* who sought to defend a range of positions between the ultramontane and the anti-clerical camps. The denigration of Catholic liberalism had long been a central theme of the ultramontane press, but it became more strident after the revolutions of 1848 and more strident again after the formation of the kingdom of Italy in 1859, the defeat of the Papal States in 1866 and the annexation of Rome in 1870. A recurring strategy was to define liberal Catholic positions in a way that made them appear self-contradictory. In an essay of 1866, Louis Veuillot declared that liberal Catholicism was 'nothing but an illusion, nothing but a piece of stubbornness – a pose'. It was an ideological disease that had infected weak minds seduced by the 'false spirit of conciliation'.[19] The very concept of the 'liberal Catholic', *Civiltà Cattolica* declared in 1869, was 'not only a bizarre and monstrous, but also an entirely repugnant combination', since liberalism implied the exclusion of any religious influence from social relationships. Not only, the article argued, was an accord between liberalism and Catholicism impossible, war between the two was inevitable.[20] In an echo of earlier Spanish Catholic preoccupations with 'purity of blood', Cándido Nocedal, editor of the integralist journal *Siglo futuro*, denounced liberal Catholics as *mestizos* (half-breeds). The same line was taken up by many Spanish provincial papers.[21] Sardà i Salvany's *Liberalism is sin*, expounded the thesis that liberalism was a worse evil than blasphemy,

[17] 'Rd.', 'Een enkel woord over Döllinger', *De Katholiek* 60 (November 1871), 278; 'R.', 'Der vijand van de heilige Kerk', *De Katholiek* 66 (August 1871), 49–61. On this theme more generally, see Giacomo Martina, *Pio IX (1851–1866)* (Rome: Gregoriana, 1986), pp. 433–9.

[18] See 'Waartoe zijn de Katholieken in den tegenwoordigen Strijd verpligt?', *De Katholiek* 56 (July 1869), 1–21; also 'La Civiltà Cattolica nel 1860', *Civiltà Cattolica* 10 (1859), 641–56.

[19] Louis Veuillot, *The Liberal illusion*, trans. G. B. O'Toole (Washington, DC: National Catholic Welfare Conference, 1939), pp. 62–4, 76–7.

[20] 'Ripugnanza del Concetto di Cattolico liberale', *Civiltà Cattolica* 8 (1869), 5; see also Alvaro Dioscoridi, 'La rivoluzione italiana e "La civiltà cattolica"', in *Comunicazioni del XXXI Congresso di storia del Risorgimento*, published as a thematic issue of *Rassegna storica del Risorgimento* 42 (1955), 258–66; C. L. van Rijp, 'De Toestand der katholieke liberalen in 1872', *De Katholiek* 62 (July–December 1872), 222, 223.

[21] M. Cruz Seoane, *Historia del periodismo en España*, 3 vols. (Madrid: Alianza, 1983), vol. II: *El siglo XIX*, p. 175.

adultery or homicide and was dedicated entirely to proving the impossibility of any accommodation between Catholics and liberals.[22] Special vituperation was reserved for those 'Old Catholics' who publicly doubted the wisdom of declaring infallibility in 1870 or rejected the doctrine in principle; they were 'chorus-leaders in the camp that Satan commands against the eternal, infallible church'.[23] Since the world was perceived as divided into two opposing camps, the dissenters within Catholicism (liberal Catholics, Jansenists, Febronians, anti-infallibilists, etc.) were no less dangerous than its enemies without. 'The Holy Father said', one eye-witness reported in the early days of the Vatican Council of 1870, 'that the most pernicious enemies of the church are the liberal Catholics, because [these are] internal.'[24]

Pressured to choose sides, many middle-class Catholics (including many who had counted themselves 'liberals') renounced their opposition to papal centralisation. A case in point are those educated Catholics in the Rhineland who initially opposed the doctrine of papal infallibility announced in Vatican I (1870), but later swallowed their doubts because they saw in Rome the best safeguard against the apparently limitless hegemonial ambition of the new Bismarckian nation state. In opposing the pretensions of the liberal nation states, themselves in many respects the creations of 1848, political Catholicism in western and northern Europe became the credo not of the nation, but of the region, and specifically of those regional redoubts (Alsace, the Rhineland, Limburg, the Tyrol and many others) in which Catholic observance and Catholic loyalties remained intact. In refusing to renounce their commitment to the Universalist, transnational identity of their faith they placed themselves above the nation-building process, while at the same time aligning themselves with its victims.

Among the church's liberal and republican antagonists, too, there was a prolonged phase of rhetorical radicalisation. Anti-Catholicism became one of the defining strands of later nineteenth-century liberalism. Liberals (and their French Republican counterparts) held up Catholicism as the diametrical negation of their own worldview. A bestiary of anti-clerical stereotypes emerged: the satires in liberal journals thronged with wily, thin Jesuits and lecherous, fat priests – amenable subjects because the cartoonist's pen could make such artful play with the solid black of their garb. By vilifying the parish priest in his confessorial role or

---

[22] Sardà i Salvany, *El liberalismo es pecado: cuestiones candentes* (Barcelona: Coimbra, 1884).
[23] 'Rd.', 'Een enkel woord', 278.
[24] G. G. Franco, *Appunti storici sopra il Concilio Vaticano*, ed. G. Martina (Rome: Gregoriana, 1972) pp. 75–6.

impugning the sexual propriety of nuns, such caricatures articulated through a double negative the liberal faith in the sanctity of the patriarchal nuclear family. In contradistinction to the image of the depraved nun or the 'rotund, simpering, effeminate monk', liberals constructed a pantheon of ideal types: 'the industrialist, the entrepreneur, the banker, the scientist, and the civil servant'. Through their nervousness about the prominent place of women within many of the new Catholic orders and their prurient fascination with the celibacy (or not) of the priest, liberals revealed a deep-seated preoccupation with 'manliness' that was crucial (though not always explicitly) to the self-understanding of the movement.[25]

Of all the goods for which Catholics and anti-clericals contended during the culture wars era, the most encompassing was the nation itself and the collective identity that attached to it. Anti-clericals across Europe aligned themselves with the cause of the nation, which was imagined as an autonomous collectivity of unbound (male) consciences. The ideas of nation, science, rationality coalesced to form the 'common sense' of a self-confident European bourgeoisie that regarded itself as the antipode of Catholic obscurantism and the embodiment of modernity.[26] Liberals were entirely unable (or unwilling) to perceive the modernity of Catholic revival, which they insisted on viewing as a bizarre and distasteful survival from the medieval world.[27] Indeed, the equation of secularism with modernity, which passed via the brilliant Protestant National Liberal political theorist Max Weber into the fabric of the 'modernisation theory', has underwritten so much of the most authoritative writing on European history since the 1960s. In this way, as Manuel Borutta has observed, sociology 'objectivised the confessionalist paradigm, transforming it into a scientific premiss'. The 'epistemological anti-Catholicism' of the liberal concept of modernity was concealed beneath a 'veneer of objectivity'. The result was, until well into the 1980s, the virtual disappearance of Catholicism from 'history'. Within

[25] On liberal anti-Catholicism in Germany, see Michael Gross, *The war against Catholicism: liberalism and the anti-Catholic imagination in nineteenth-century Germany* (Ann Arbor: University of Michigan, 2004), p. 296; for similar observations regarding French republican anti-clericalism, see Ralph Gibson, 'Why Republicans and Catholics couldn't stand each other in the nineteenth century', in Frank Tallett and Nicholas Atkin (eds.), *Religion, society and politics in France since 1789* (London: Hambledon, 1991), pp. 107–20.
[26] Manuel Borutta, 'Das Andere der Moderne: Geschlecht, Sexualität und Krankheit in antikatholischen Diskursen Deutschlands und Italiens (1850–1900)', in Werner Rammert (ed.), *Kollektive Identitäten und kulturelle Innovationen: ethnologische, soziologische und historische Studien* (Leipzig: Leipziger Universitätsverlag, 2001), pp. 59–75.
[27] Gross, *War against Catholicism*, p. 296.

mainstream historical practice (the picture was different, of course, among the church historians and the theologians), Catholicism was for a long time discernible only as an obstacle on the road to modernity, and the culture wars only as efforts to circumvent it.[28] The result was (until the 1980s) a persistent historiographical neglect of Catholic political and spiritual movements.[29]

In reality, of course, European political Catholicism had more future locked up inside it than the terminal diagnosis of secularisation theory suggested. The thesis that the nineteenth-century culture wars are best understood as the clash between liberal or republican 'modernity' and a reactionary, regressive or obscurantist Catholicism has long ceased to persuade. The means adopted by the nineteenth-century Catholics – mass-circulation media, voluntary associations, demonstrative forms of mass action, the expansion of schooling among deprived social groups[30] and the increasingly prominent involvement of women in positions of responsibility[31] – were quintessentially modern. Moreover, it is far from clear that Catholic mobilisation hindered or delayed processes of political modernisation in the European states. In a number of European countries, confessional conflict contributed to the broadening of political participation by providing Catholics (especially rural ones) with the language and argument of collective interest and thus with a reason for entering the political arena as activists, deputies or voters.[32]

---

[28] Michael Borutta, 'Enemies at the gate: the moabit klostersturm and the Kulturkampf: Germany', in Clark and Kaiser, *Culture wars*, p. 253.

[29] Martin Conway, 'Introduction', in Tom Buchanan and Martin Conway (eds.), *Political Catholicism in Europe, 1918–1965* (Oxford: Clarendon Press, 1996), p. 4.

[30] On Catholicism and schooling in Spain, see Payne, *Spanish Catholicism*, p. 100.

[31] On the role of women in Catholic associational culture, see Gibson, 'Why Republicans and Catholics', J. F. McMillan, 'Religion and gender in modern France: some reflections' and Hazel Mills, 'Negotiating the divide: women, philanthropy and the "public sphere" in nineteenth-century France', all in Tallett and Atkin (eds.), *Religion, society and politics*, pp. 107–20, 29–54, 55–66; Caroline Ford, 'Religion and popular culture in modern Europe', *Journal of Modern History* 65 (1993), 152–75; Caitriona Clear, *Nuns in nineteenth-century Ireland* (Dublin: Gill & Macmillan, 1987); Claude Langlois, *Le catholicisme au féminin: les congrégations françaises à supérieure générale au XIX siècle* (Paris: Cerf, 1984). For an account that denies the 'emancipatory' potential in Catholic female voluntarism arguing that it merely consolidated patriarchal power relations, see Irmtraud Götz von Olenhusen, *Klerus und abweichendes Verhalten: zur Sozialgeschichte katholischer Priester im 19. Jahrhundert: die Erzdiözese Freiburg* (Vandenhoeck und Ruprecht: Göttingen, 1994), pp. 19–20, 397–8.

[32] These themes are explored in Anderson, *Practicing democracy*, pp. 69–151, and broadly supported by the statistical analyses presented in Jonathan Sperber, *The Kaiser's voters: electors and elections in Imperial Germany* (Cambridge: Cambridge University Press, 1997). See also M. L. Anderson, 'Clerical election influence and communal solidarity: Catholic political culture in the German Empire, 1871–1914', in Eduardo Posada-Carbó (ed.), *Elections before democracy: the history of elections in Europe and Latin*

Particularly striking, as Margaret Lavinia Anderson has shown, was the integration of Catholic women in the process of confessional and political mobilisation.[33] For all the anti-modernism of its rhetoric, the Catholic Church, its lay auxiliaries and its political allies were deeply implicated in processes of rapid social and political transformation.

We need therefore to move beyond a binary conception of the culture wars as a confrontation between 'modern' and 'anti-modern' forces. As Alfonso Botti has suggested, the traditionalist ideology espoused by the new Catholicism of nineteenth-century Europe was 'neither archaising nor anti-modern, but was instead concerned, through a process of continuous scrutiny, to filter out incompatible elements of modernity'.[34] And once we move beyond this notion of the secular–clerical culture wars of the nineteenth century as a binary stand-off between modernising and retrograde forces, it becomes easier to see how the intermittently fractious conversation between Catholic and secularising forces might have become a constitutive feature of modernity in western Europe. In an influential essay published in 1903, the sociologist Georg Simmel speculated that 'conflict itself' could function as a 'form of sociation' capable over the longer term of heightening the cohesion of the society within which it takes place. Social cohesion, Simmel observed, does not come into existence through the triumph of 'positive' social forces and the neutralisation of 'negative' ones, but rather through the playing out of antagonistic relations between opposed groups. It was a feature of such social conflicts, Simmel suggested, that they accelerate the process by which the initially diffuse commitments of each camp are raised to the level of ideological coherence.[35] Although in the short term this process of ideological clarification might produce an intensification of hostility between opposed interest groups, the resulting conflict, provided it takes place within a universe of shared norms, can also stimulate the establishment of 'new rules, norms, and institutions, thus serving as an agent of socialisation for both contending parties'. At the same time, conflict had the potential to 'reaffirm dormant norms and

America (New York: Macmillan, 1996), pp. 139–62; M. L. Anderson, 'Voter, junker, landrat, priest: the old authorities and the new franchise in Imperial Germany', *American Historical Review* 98 (1993), 1448–74; for a similar argument applied more broadly and less tentatively to the European states, see Raymond Grew, 'Liberty and the Catholic Church in nineteenth-century Europe', in Richard Helmstadter (ed.), *Freedom and religion in the nineteenth century* (Stanford: Stanford University Press, 1997), pp. 229–30.

[33] Anderson, *Practicing democracy*, pp. 126–31.

[34] Alfonso Botti, *Nazionalcattolicesimo e Spagna nuova (1881–1975)* (Milan: Franco Angeli, 1992), p. 18.

[35] Georg Simmel, 'The sociology of conflict, I', *American Journal of Sociology* 9 (1903), 490–525.

thus intensify participation in social life', while giving rise to broader associations and coalitions and thereby 'binding the various elements of society together'.[36]

That this is true for the Catholic–secular conflicts of nineteenth- and early twentieth-century Europe is borne out not only by the extraordinary associational and partisan networks that were forged on both sides during the culture wars, but also by the reality of compromise that underlay the polemical rhetoric of the partisan media. The struggle waged by the papacy against the Italian state was fought over real issues and genuine abuses, but the tacit acceptance on both sides of the 'Laws of guarantee' as the 'constitutional' basis of the Vatican's status within the new Italian nation state was an important act of compromise. In the 1880s, one historian has argued, a 'tacit alliance' developed between the church authorities and the French state, based on habits of inconspicuous collaboration.[37] Catholics and secular nationalists worked in tandem to sustain the *Italianità* of the Italian diaspora, even while the culture war was at its height, and a recent study has highlighted the extent to which the Italian Catholic church accepted and supported the legitimacy of the nation state, even as it opposed the activities of the liberal elites who dominated the public life of the kingdom.[38] In Germany, too, Catholic reading clubs nurtured a progressive and even increasingly nationalist ethos among German Catholics without arousing the ire of the hierarchy.[39] As these transitions suggest, a foundation of shared assumptions underlay the façade of bitter polemic between Catholics and their anti-clerical opponents.[40]

There were, of course, limits to the applicability of Simmel's paradigm of a beneficent conflict generating new and salutary forms of social synthesis. Spain is one important boundary case. Here, the stand-off between liberal/radical and Catholic constellations produced (or intensified) deep and abiding divisions that were ultimately profoundly

---

[36] Commentary on Simmel in Lewis A. Coser, *The functions of social conflict*, (London: Routledge & Kegan Paul, 1956), pp. 128, 141.

[37] Livio Rota, *Nomine vescovili e cardinalizie in Francia alla fine del secolo XIX* (Rome: Gregoriana, 1996), p. 357.

[38] R. J. B. Bosworth, *Italy and the wider world, 1860–1960* (London: Routledge, 1996), p. 121; for a powerful reassessment of Catholic attitudes to the nation, see Francesco Traniello, *Religione cattolica e stato nazionale* (Bologna: Il Mulino, 2007).

[39] Jeffrey T. Zalar, '"Knowledge is power": the *Borromaeusverein* and Catholic reading habits in imperial Germany', *Catholic Historical Review* 86 (2000), 20–46; see also Barbara Stambolis, 'Nationalisierung trotz Ultramontanisierung oder: "Alles für Deutschland, Deutschland aber für Christus". Mentalitätsleitende Wertorientierungen deutscher Katholiken im 19. und 20. Jahrhundert', *Historische Zeitschrift* 269 (1999), 57–97.

[40] Thus Theodor Zeldin on the polemic between the 'two Frances' in *France, 1848–1945*, 2 vols. (Oxford: Clarendon Press, 1973–7), vol. II, p. 994.

destructive of social cohesion. A proper analysis of the reason for this must lie beyond the compass of this chapter, but it is worth drawing attention to several points of contrast that touch on our story. First, there is the fact that the formal secularisation of Spain, in the sense of the expropriation of church properties and their transfer to non-ecclesiastical ownership, was a later and more protracted process in Spain than in most other European states. Between 1836 and the end of the nineteenth century over 600,000 properties were sold under secularising legislation, amounting in total to a value of more than eleven billion reales.[41] It was a process that imposed a persistent burden on the relationship between liberal administrations and the Spanish church. Second, Spanish Catholicism was marked by a stronger and more radical reactionary political orientation than the national churches in France, Germany and Belgium. It is striking that when Leo XIII attempted, after the death of Pius IX in 1878, to cool the culture wars raging across Europe by reigning in the Catholic press, he found this especially difficult to accomplish in Spain, where extremist Catholic journals like the *Siglo futuro* continued to mount furious attacks on the more moderate Spanish bishops. By contrast with Germany, Catholic activists in Spain faced no Protestant rival forcing them to bid competitively for the support of voters in a dynamic and expanding political marketplace by staying focused on issues of practical import.[42] By contrast with French ultramontanism, which drew its strength and confidence from its identity as a social movement, conservative Catholic political thought in Spain had always tended to focus on the state; only an authoritarian Catholic regime, the celebrated conservative writer and diplomat Juan Donoso Cortes observed in 1849, could arrest the process of de-Catholicisation which had deprived Spanish society of its values and organic structures.[43] Appalled by the French upheavals of 1848–9, Donoso Cortes argued that free parliamentary discussion was incompatible with the quest for truth and sure to lead to social ruin. The very idea of a public sphere was charged with menace in the eyes of the Spanish traditionalists, since the existence of newspapers and the publication of parliamentary debates appeared merely to accelerate the circulation of erroneous and damaging ideas. The extremism of these nineteenth-century antecedents laid the foundations for the integralist

---

[41] Francisco Simón Segura, *La desamortización Española en el siglo XIX* (Madrid: Instituto de Estudios Fiscales, 1973), p. 273.

[42] Margaret L. Anderson, 'The limits of secularisation: on the problem of the Catholic revival in nineteenth-century Germany', *Historical Journal* 38 (1995), 657.

[43] Juan Donoso Cortes, *Discurso sobre la dictadura* (1849), discussed in 'Introducción', in González and Rivera (eds.), *Altar y trono*, pp. 10–11.

'national-Catholicism' of twentieth-century Spain – there was little room here for the kind of bargaining and compromise on the basis of shared norms and procedures that helped other European societies to absorb and transcend the antagonisms of secular–clerical conflict.[44]

Also anomalous, though for different reasons, are Ireland and Poland. Neither was a sovereign state in the nineteenth century. The struggle between legislatures, executives and constituencies that was a defining feature of the culture wars thus took place within the framework of other states – Prussia–Germany and Austria in Poland's case (conditions in Russia being such as to prevent the triangulation of the conflict in this sense) and Britain in the case of Ireland. Most important, however, was the fact that the conditions of 'foreign' dominion obtaining in these two nations on the opposite peripheries of Catholic Europe militated against the unfolding of a secular–clerical struggle. Neither in Poland nor in Ireland was the Catholic identity of the nation plausibly contested by a powerful secular or heterodox competitor (despite the presence of Protestant Irish patriots in the early Irish national movement). In both cases, the divisive questions posed by such conflicts in other states were overshadowed by the quest for national autonomy. In both countries, the national identity was so pervaded with confessional substance that the emergence of a separate Catholic social formation to pursue specific religious objectives was unnecessary.

But where the polarisation of Catholic and liberal-secular/Protestant camps did take place, and where the conditions existed for repeated negotiations at many levels of the terms of conflict, processes of confessional revival and secularisation could and did interweave and shape each other. The two had always been locked into a dialectical relationship. The trauma of revolution and de-Christianisation in France shaped the contours of the subsequent revival, dividing communities around the choice between collaboration and resistance and generating more 'baroque' and communally based forms of piety than had been the norm at the end of the *Ancien Régime*.[45] By seeking to confine the activity of the clergy to its core religious functions and redistributing church

---

[44] Ángel Rivero, 'La reacción católica: el peccado liberal y la constitución tradicionalista en la España del siglo XIX', in González and Rivera (eds.), *Altar y trono*, p. 26; see also Antonio Rivera Garcia, 'Los orígenes contrarrevolucionarios de la nación católica', in Francisco Colom González (ed.), *Relatos de nación: la construcción de las identidades nacionales en el mundo hispánico*, 2 vols. (Madrid: Iberoamericana, 2005), vol. II, pp. 1023–44; Antonio Rivera Garcia, *Reacción y revolución en la España liberal* (Madrid: Biblioteca Nueva, 2006).

[45] M. Vovelle, *The revolution against the church: from reason to the Supreme Being* (Cambridge: Polity Press, 1991); S. Desan, *Reclaiming the sacred: lay religion and popular politics in revolutionary France* (Ithaca: Cornell University Press, 1990); O. Hufton, 'The reconstruction of a church 1796–1801', in C. Lucas and G. Lewis

incomes towards parochial provision, secularising regimes encouraged the development of more close-knit relationships between the clergy and the faithful.[46]

Developments in western Germany in the late 1830s illustrate the interlocked character of secularising and revivalist initiatives. Efforts by the Protestant authorities to regulate clerical management of Catholic–Protestant 'mixed marriages' in the late 1830s generated a wave of Catholic confessional mobilisation that continued well into the 1840s that culminated in the remarkable Trier Pilgrimage of 1844, in which some 500,000 Catholics participated. This spectacle of a resurgent mass Catholicism in turn triggered the emergence of the first anti-ultramontane mass movement, in the form of the 'German Catholics' (*Deutschkatholiken*). And this latter movement, in its turn, provided the mid-century German revolutions with some of their most important radical leaders.

The papal cults that were such a striking feature of nineteenth-century Catholicism were also in large part a response to the challenges posed by secularising regimes. Their apogee came during the pontificate of Pius IX, when the annexation of the northern Papal States by the kingdom of Piedmont/Italy and the reduction of the Pope's temporal domains to a rump territory around Rome triggered outrage among Catholics. A wave of addresses to the Pope followed, gathering 5,524,373 signatures. Among the most dramatic expressions of Catholic solidarity with the pontiff was the revival – on a voluntary basis – of the levy known in the Middle Ages as the 'Peter's Pence' (*Deniers de Saint-Pierre, Peterspfennig, Obolo di San Pietro*).[47] Although the Peter's Pence movement was encouraged by elements of the ultramontane clergy and

---

(eds.), *Beyond the Terror: essays in French regional and social history 1794–1815* (Cambridge: Cambridge University Press, 1983).

[46] R. Gibson, *A social history of French Catholicism 1789–1914* (London: Routledge, 1989), pp. 78–80; D. Beales, 'Joseph II and the monasteries of Austria and Hungary', in N. Aston (ed.), *Religious change in Europe, 1650–1914* (Oxford: Clarendon Press, 1997), p. 162; on the wealth gap, J. McManners, *The French Revolution and the church* (London: SPCK, 1969), pp. 18, 39; and *Church and society in eighteenth-century France*, vol. I: *The clerical establishment and its social ramifications* (Oxford: Clarendon Press, 1998), pp. 216–7, 308, 332–46. On the popular impact of secularising measures: C. M. Naselli, *La soppressione napoleonica delle corporazioni religiose: contributo alla storia religiosa del primo ottocento Italiano 1808–1814* (Rome: Gregoriana, 1986), pp. 203–5.

[47] On the wave of addresses in 1859, see Vincent Viaene, 'The Roman question: Catholic mobilisation and papal diplomacy during the Pontificate of Pius IX (1846–1878)', in E. Lamberts (ed.), *The black international. L'internationale noire, 1870–1878* (Kadoc Studies 29) (Leuven: Leuven University Press, 2002), p. 143; Martina, *Pio IX*, p. 22; Hartmut Benz, 'Der Peterspfennig im Pontifikat Pius IX: Initiativen zur Unterstützung des Papsttums (1859–1878)', *Römische Quartalschrift* 90 (1995), 90–109; on the personal charisma of this pope, see Schatz, *Vaticanum*, vol. II, p. 22.

by ultramontane press organs, it was driven above all by a spontaneous wave of lay activism in which women played a prominent role. Papalist voluntarism took other forms as well – Catholic volunteers flocked to join the Zouave army of the Pope during the 1860s, there were successive waves of mass petitions supporting the Pope in his struggle with the kingdom of Italy and there was a surge in pilgrimages to the Holy See, especially after the seizure of Lazio and Rome in 1870.[48] Among Protestants and secular liberals and republicans, this mass response inspired a deepening hostility and paranoia whose imprint can be seen in the culture wars of the 1860–70s, the century's most violent spasm of secularisation.

In other words, the impact of government campaigns against the church and its personnel was equivocal. Secularising campaigns in Piedmont, Prussia, Belgium and elsewhere projected the confidence of a liberal elite at the height of its powers. At the same time, however, they reinforced the social and moral authority of the church amongst its mass membership and galvanised Catholic political solidarity. A good example is the German Centre Party (*Deutsche Zentrumspartei*), the party of Catholics. Although Bismarck did succeed in isolating the Centre Party politically – at least for a time – he could do nothing to prevent it from increasing its share of the popular vote in national elections.[49] The existence of a successful German Catholic mass party was not a cause, but a consequence, of the initiatives launched by Bismarck and his Liberal allies.[50]

Secularisation and confessional revival thus fed each other, not only because liberals/republicans and Catholics remained locked for some decades in a kind of rhetorical arms race, but also because while assaults on religious privilege stimulated confessional solidarities within and between the nation states, the process of religious political mobilisation itself had – over the longer term – a secularising impact. The mass-membership Catholic parties that emerged in Belgium, the Netherlands, Austria, Germany and Italy to defend the interests of European

---

[48] Pieter de Coninck, 'En les uit Pruisen. Nederland en de kulturkampf 1870–1880', PhD dissertation, Rijksuniversiteit Leiden (1998), pp. 48–9, 51–3; Aubert, *Pie IX*, pp. 88–90; Bruno Horaist, *La dévotion au pape et les catholiques français sous le pontificat de Pie IX (1846–1878) d'après les archives de la bibliothèque apostolique vaticane* (Rome: École Française de Rome, 1995), pp. 22–5, 34–6, 43; Urs Altermatt, *Katholizismus und Antisemitismus: Mentalitäten, Kontinuitäten, Ambivalenzen: zur Kulturgeschichte der Schweiz, 1918–1945* (Frauenfeld: Huber, 1999) pp. 257–60.

[49] This argument is detailed in Sperber, *Kaiser's voters*.

[50] One of the central arguments of Anderson, *Practicing democracy*; see also R. Morsey, 'Der Kulturkampf', in A. Rauscher (ed.), *Der soziale und politische Katholizismus*, 2 vols. (Munich: Olzog, 1981), vol. I, p. 126.

Catholics against liberal, Protestant or anti-clerical elites soon emancipated themselves from clerical control. They gradually distanced themselves from the church, defining their identity and that of their
constituencies in terms that de-emphasised religion. The struggle to
safeguard Catholic interests in an environment of expanding political
participation produced lay Catholic mass movements that were capable
in the longer term first of balancing and later of challenging the authority
of the hierarchy. Paradoxically, as one historian of the Catholic parties
has observed, the organisations formed to bring religion into politics
actually ended by taking it out. In these ways, liberal democracy in
Europe was 'expanded and consolidated by its enemies'.[51]

We can follow this argument through into the later twentieth century.
The interwar years saw a formidable upsurge of Catholic political organisation across western Europe. To the long-established German Centre
Party, the Austrian Christian Social Party and the Belgian Catholic Party
were added a range of more recent foundations: the *Partito Popolare* in
Italy, the Roomsch-Katholieke Staatspartij (RKSP) in the Netherlands,
the *Partido Social Popular* in Spain and the *Parti Démocrate Populaire* and
the *Fédération Nationale Catholique* in France. Alongside these formations, there also flourished a diffuse array of Catholic social movements,
ranging from the militant Catholic Action groups that attracted younger
members of the Catholic bourgeoisie to Catholic trade unions and
affiliated workers' organisations. Catholic organisations were thus a
more prominent feature of European politics after 1918 than they had
ever been before.[52]

Whether these parties constituted a single political movement
during the interwar era can be doubted. They were certainly, as Wolfram
Kaiser has shown, becoming more densely networked in a European,
transnational sense.[53] But they were also profoundly fractured. Some
Catholic groups were drawn to the new fascist parties of the extreme
right, others embraced an authoritarian politics focused on the creation
of Catholic political regimes, and yet others remained committed to a
variety of corporatist, socialist or conservative positions. The rise of
Nazism and the advent of World War II had a traumatic but clarifying
effect. In Germany and in Austria, the rise of the Nazis placed Catholic
organisations and the Catholic Church under unprecedented pressure.

---

[51] S. N. Kalyvas, *The rise of Christian Democracy in Europe* (Ithaca: Cornell University
Press, 1996), p. 262.
[52] Conway, 'Introduction', pp. 21–5.
[53] Wolfram Kaiser, *Christian Democracy and the origins of European Union* (Cambridge:
Cambridge University Press, 2007).

In Italy too, Catholic groups faced state harassment in the 1930s, despite the protections granted under the Lateran Treaties of 1929. As Martin Conway has observed, the advent of war forced politically minded European Catholics to choose between the liberal and putatively secular regimes of Britain and France and the fascist or racist experiments unfolding in Germany and Italy. Across Europe (with the unlovely exceptions of Croatia and Slovakia) Catholic political activists were gradually alienated from the politics of the 'New Order' and Catholic groups were conspicuous for their role in active resistance. The consequence was a profound disillusionment with the kind of authoritarian politics that had still been attractive to many Catholics in the interwar years, and a reawakening of interest in democratic and participatory politics. In Belgium, France, Germany, Italy and Austria Catholics once again aligned themselves (I am speaking here of mentality, not of concrete resistance activity) with the victims of the prevailing form of state power.

The European carnage of 1939–45 represented – or at least could be construed as – the absolute bankruptcy of the liberal-nationalist project. And this nadir in turn created an unprecedented opportunity for the Catholic political movements and networks. Although the post-1945 Christian Democratic parties succeeded in acquiring a more secular and interconfessional image than their interwar predecessors, they remained absolutely dependent on the support of Catholic voters. In the French elections of 1946, 75 per cent of practising Catholics voted for the *Mouvement Republicain Populaire* (MRP); in the early 1950s the figure was still 54 per cent, despite the fact that the Gaullists were now competing energetically for Catholic votes. According to a survey of 1952, 66 per cent of practising Catholic women claimed to vote MRP.[54] In Italy, Catholic Action, with some help from the Pope and the hierarchy, played a crucial role in mobilising support for the *Democrazia Cristiana*.[55] In West Germany, 60 per cent of all Catholics voted for the *Christlich Demokratische Union* (CDU)/*Christlich Soziale Union* (CSU) until the 1960s. No wonder Martin Niemöller condemned the West German republic as 'a Catholic state . . . begotten in the Vatican and born in Washington'.

To be sure, these parties were in many respects new formations dominated by a younger generation whose attitudes had been shaped

[54] James F. McMillan, 'France', in Buchanan and Conway (eds.), *Political Catholicism*, p. 61; for electoral statistics, see also R. E. M. Irving, *Christian Democracy in France* (London: Allen & Irwin, 1973), pp. 91–6.
[55] John Pollard, 'Italy', in Buchanan and Conway (eds.), *Political Catholicism*, p. 87.

by the experiences of the war years. They eschewed the paranoid fortress mentality of the interwar parties and abandoned the authoritarian corporatist visions of their predecessors to embrace democracy and market economics. Nevertheless, the new Christian Democratic parties dug deep into the repertoire of Catholic political tradition to assemble a policy amalgam that stood a reasonable chance of seeing off the competition. One important resource was the corpus of social thought that the church had developed in order to fight off the challenge posed by the rise of the socialist parties and reinforce its influence among Catholic workers. Among the most important texts that the future German Chancellor Konrad Adenauer read during his period of 'inner exile' at the monastery of Maria Laach in 1933–4 were the two papal encyclicals *Rerum novarum* (1891) and *Quadragesimo anno* (1931). The first was Leo XIII's profoundly influential declaration of solidarity with the plight of the poorest in society 'who are tossed about helplessly and disastrously in conditions of pitiable and undeserved misery'; the second, published during the pontificate of Pius XI and subtitled 'On reconstruction of the social order', developed the rather diffuse arguments of the earlier encyclical in the direction of a kind of welfare statism.[56] The CDU's Ahlener Programm of 1947 took up this impulse, articulating a detailed critique of the 'unlimited domination of private capitalism' and advocating a third way combining state buy-outs with a regime of extended intervention in the economy. In the Austrian elections of 1945, the *Österreichische Volkspartei* campaigned under the slogan 'Austria's Labour Party' in order to wean voters away from the Marxist *Sozialdemokratische Partei Österreichs* (SPÖ).

In addition to these echoes of Catholic anti-mammonism, we should note the emphatically European frame of Christian Democrat politics. Here again, we discern clear traces of the Catholic political tradition, whose orientation had always been European rather than global, unlike that of its competitor, internationalist socialism.[57] In West Germany, it is worth noting, the dominant faction of the socialist leadership remained committed to the consolidation of a reunified German nation state. The Catholics, by contrast, had no love for the all-devouring nation state, which they saw as a liberal invention whose credit was all but exhausted after six catastrophic years of war. In its place they could

---

[56] *Rerum Novarum*, trans. J. Kirwan (London: Catholic Truth Society, 1983); 'Quadragesimo Anno', in Francis J. Haas and Martin R. P. McGuire, *On reconstruction of the social order* (National Catholic Welfare Conference, 1942).

[57] Wolfram Kaiser, *Christian Democracy and the origins of European Union* (Cambridge: Cambridge University Press, 2007), p. 189.

mobilise the pre- and transnational idea of a Catholic (or, to broaden the appeal, 'Christian') 'civilisation' – *civiltà cristiana* that was so prominent in the rhetoric of the Italian Christian Democrat De Gasperi (itself an ecumenical redaction of the earlier ultramontane concept *civiltà cattolica*) was easily refashioned into a *civiltà europea*, for the awakening of Europe 'unitary energy' could only be accomplished, De Gasperi argued, by harnessing the resources of 'our shared civilisation [*nostra civiltà commune*]'.[58] What horrified liberal Protestant nationalists like Martin Niemöller, or unificationist socialists like Kurt Schumacher in West Germany was precisely Adenauer's ability to turn his back on the nation state in the quest for a broader alignment with Catholic western Europe – and with France, Belgium and Luxemburg in particular. The Catholic distrust of the over-mighty nation state was not the expression of an unchanging Catholic 'tradition', but a consequence of the nineteenth-century culture wars and the experience of liberal-dominated national integration, whose most recent perversion was the pagan, racial state of the National Socialists.[59]

Finally, it is worth drawing attention to the strong regional anchoring of the European political Catholicisms. To some extent, these regionalisms reflected the patterns of Catholic observance, which had always been geographically uneven, but they also were an ideological response to the centralising nationalism of the liberal elites. In Germany, regionalist politics and a determination to discipline the unruly demands of the centralising nation state had been a defining feature of Catholic politics since the foundation of the empire in 1871. A strong regional colouring had always been a feature of the French Catholic press, too – the most important organ of Catholic Christian-Democrat opinion before 1914 was *L'Ouest-Éclair*, founded by Désgrées du Loû, the descendent of an old Breton family, to galvanise support among Catholics in the west of France.[60] In the *Parti Démocrate Populaire* (founded 1924), a party with strong social Catholic and Christian democratic commitments, regional caucuses – especially Breton and Alsatian – played an important role, and the electoral basis of the post-war MRP was concentrated in the

[58] De Gasperi, *Scritti e discorsi di politica internazionale*, p. 386, cited in Traniello, *Religione Cattolica e stato nazionale*, p. 306.
[59] Kaiser, *Christian democracy*, p. 189.
[60] McMillan, 'France', p. 39; P. Delourme, *Trente-cinq années de politique religieuse ou l'histoire de 'l'Ouest-Eclair'* (Paris: Fustier, 1936); on the religious geography of France more generally, see Gérard Cholvy and Yves-Marie Hilaire (eds.), *Histoire religieuse de la France contemporaine*, 3 vols. (Toulouse: Privat, 1989), vol. II, pp. 171–218; Ralph Gibson, *A social history of French Catholicism* (London: Routledge, 1989), pp. 170–7.

west, Champagne, Alsace-Lorraine and the south-east.[61] The Italian Catholic movement was likewise marked by its concentration in specific regions – Venetia, north-eastern Lombardy and southern Piedmont, plus the Marches on the Adriatic coast, the province of Lucca in Tuscany, the eastern seaboard of Calabria, parts of the Sicilian interior and the province of Lecce in Apulia.[62] And regional power bases were important for many of the other parties: the south-western provinces of Limburg and North Brabant in the case of the *Katholische Volkspartij*, for example, or Flanders in the case of the *Christelijke Volkspartij* and the Rhineland and Bavaria in the case of the German Christian Democrat and Christian Social parties. These were not just external geographical facts; they played a constitutive role in shaping the politics and outlook of the Catholic parties. In Belgium, the demand for Flemish regional autonomy and a more federal organisation of the Belgian state was a central theme in post-war Catholic politics; in France the 'departmental Federation' was intended to serve as the basic unit of the MRP, ensuring that policy-making processes flowed from the base to the summit, as well as in the other direction; in Germany, the CDU and its Bavarian sister the CSU were committed to a federal system, in which the *Länder* enjoyed extensive autonomy.[63]

In the labile, open-ended political condition of an early post-war Europe still reeling from six years of war, the Catholic political movements benefited from the fact that Catholicism was, in John Boyer's words, 'both a local and a universal phenomenon'. On the one hand, there was the relative solidity and cohesion of the Catholic regions, with their webs of parochial personnel and institutions. On the other, there was the identification with a transcendent civilisation that 'helped to compromise all other universalisms'.[64] The transnational European organisation of the Christian Democratic parties was facilitated by the survival of networks that had linked the Catholic *petites patries* since at

---

[61] M. Fogarty, *Christian democracy in Western Europe, 1820–1953* (London: Routledge & Kegan Paul, 1957), pp. 331–2; on Alsace as a regional centre of French Catholicism, see D. P. Silverman, 'Political Catholicism and social democracy in Alsace-Lorraine, 1871–1914', *Catholic Historical Review* 52 (1966), 39–65; C. Baechler, *Le parti Catholique alsacien 1890–1939: du Reichsland à la République jacobine* (Paris: Ophrys, 1982); McMillan, 'France', p. 61.

[62] Pollard, 'Italy', p. 71.

[63] Martin Conway, 'Belgium', in Buchanan and Conway (eds.), *Political Catholicism*, pp. 187–218; Irving, *Christian democracy*, pp. 63, 95–6.

[64] John Boyer, 'Catholics, Christians and the challenges of democracy: the heritage of the nineteenth century', in Wolfram Kaiser and Helmut Wohnout (eds.), *Political Catholicism in Europe, 1918–45*, 2 vols. (London; Routledge, 2004), vol. I, pp. 7–45.

least the 1870s.[65] These lesser Catholic fatherlands, with their trans
national affiliations, were an important frame of reference for men like
Bidault, de Gasperi, Schuman, architects of the new Europe. This
pattern of affiliations goes some way towards explaining how political
Catholics – unlike socialists – could come to see the supranational,
continental organisation of western Europe as a way of safeguarding
regional identities.[66]

It would be grossly misleading to extrapolate from these elective
affinities a cheerful, whiggish narrative in which the persecuted
Catholics of the nineteenth century come to the rescue of democracy
in the twentieth. To do so would be both to ignore the spectrum of anti-
democratic thought that underlay so much European Catholic activism
before 1939 and to conceal the contribution of other traditions – notably
the Social Democratic – to the reconstruction of Europe after 1945.
Nor am I entering here a plea on behalf of a Catholic 'contribution' to
modern Europe, in the sense of the survival of an abiding theological,
philosophical or ecclesiastical tradition. My claim here is rather that the
long struggle between Catholics and secularisers of various stripes
altered the structure and substance of Catholicism as a social and
political phenomenon in ways that allowed it to become a transformative
agent in European affairs. Europe's modernity was not the consequence
of the victory of secular over Catholic forces, but a product of the long,
fractious and intermittently violent conversation between them.

---

[65] Robert Schuman used the term 'petite patrie' for his home country of Lorraine and his
experience of political division in this bicultural region endeared him to the 'overarching
value of the unification of Europe'; see Rudolf Mittendorfer, *Robert Schuman – Architekt
des neuen Europa* (Hildesheim: Olms, 1983), pp. 16–18.

[66] Kaiser, *Christian democracy*, p. 190.

10   The disciplining of the religious conscience in nineteenth-century British politics

Jonathan Parry

The most important variable in the relationship between religion and politics in modern British history has not been the strength of religion but the strength of politics. The key question is not the extent of 'secularisation' at any one time – which is fortunate, given how tricky and unstable a concept it is. Religion has not played as destabilising a role in British mainland politics over the last two centuries as it has in some other countries. But it does not follow that religion has been a marginal influence in a 'secular' political culture. This chapter argues that, on the contrary, religion has often been a major theme in politics, certainly in the nineteenth century. However, religious disagreements were confined and muted by political processes. In Britain, the religious conscience was disciplined to accept the legitimacy and primacy of political institutions, even while it remained vibrant within the broader public culture.

Most prominent in asserting a religious conscience were evangelical Protestant Dissenters, for whom opposition to state support for religion was a basic principle. As soon as the political reforms of 1828–32 gave them a national political presence, they started agitating against the requirement to pay rates for the upkeep of the local Anglican Church, their exclusion from Oxford and Cambridge universities, and the existence of the Anglican Church establishment itself in England, Wales and Ireland. They also quickly joined vehement protest movements against the continuation of the slave system, against the Corn Laws, against state support for religious education, and in favour of international peace. Between 1850 and 1875 they increased their efforts for church rate abolition and for disestablishment in England and Ireland, and were also involved in other vocal pressure group action, for example demanding the right of voters to veto the sale of alcohol locally. Each of these campaigns was conducted with the zeal that one would expect from a body that combined an intense purifying fervour, a rigorous anti-statist feeling, a sense of social inferiority vis-à-vis the 'upper ten

214

thousand', and a righteousness based on strong middle-class backing. Each crusade was intended to be a potent, insistent challenge to the political and social establishment.

There often appeared to be a fundamental incompatibility between this focus on particular ends derived from religious principle, and the compromises inherent in a mature party political system. The temperance activist William Hoyle spoke for many in describing his cause in 1873 as a question of 'right and wrong, and therefore political-expediency doctrines, ... cannot, except in a secondary way, be taken into the account'.[1] Yet this chapter argues that the long-term political disruption from these campaigns was surprisingly small. Nonconformists never achieved the outcomes for which they fought most strongly, such as disestablishment in England, and the end of state funding of religious teaching. This was not because the 'Nonconformist conscience' was weak, vacillating or hypocritical.

Nonconformity retained a seminal role in British public life; 185 Nonconformist MPs were returned at the 1906 election. What it suggests instead is the strength of the British political system: its ability to integrate strongly opposing religious sentiments, whether held by Nonconformists or by the Anglicans who resisted them. In particular, it indicates the importance of two unglamorous but crucial political phenomena: Whiggish ideas of politico-religious relations, and political party.

I

In 1848 the *Nonconformist* newspaper declared war on the irreligious 'English oligarchy' and its hold over national politics. Twenty-four years later, its long-standing editor, Edward Miall, announced that 'if Christianity is not to be killed by the Establishment, Christianity must kill the Establishment'.[2] Miall, the leading radical Nonconformist agitator of his generation, was not a man for half-measures. Nor were other leading political Dissenters like Joseph Sturge or Edward Baines. They entered politics in order to root out the corrupting impurities of conventional elite rule, and to create a more virtuous Christian nation, founded on Dissenting principles of mutual self-reliance and respect for God's law, unfettered by state power.

[1] D. A. Hamer, *The politics of electoral pressure: a study in the history of Victorian reform agitations* (Hassocks: Harvester Press, 1977), p. 16.
[2] Jonathan Parry, *The politics of patriotism: English Liberalism, national identity and Europe, 1830–1886* (Cambridge: Cambridge University Press, 2006), pp. 173, 307.

Dissenting fervour for political engagement built up in ever-stronger waves during the course of the three most severe economic depressions of the nineteenth century. These depressions – of 1829–30, 1839–42 and 1847–8 – punctuated the later stages of the 'age of atonement', forcing many evangelically minded Britons to ask where the nation had gone wrong and what action was necessary in order to restore God's favour. Each crisis, as a result, saw the emergence of important political movements that were characterised by a zealous advocacy of urgent purifying reforms, and by an insistence that concerns about party convenience or worldly advantage must not stand in their way. Evangelical Nonconformists – for our purposes, mostly Congregationalists and Baptists – were particularly susceptible to such notions because they were heirs to the 'protesting mentality' which had historically attached importance to truth-seeking and principle at all costs, rather than cosy compromise.

This emphasis on the need for the individual to take responsibility for, or to crusade against, political and moral practices of the day was the distinguishing feature of the new phase of the anti-slavery movement, which began in 1829–30 and which made abolition such a high-profile movement over the following three years. In autumn 1830, 2,600 petitions against slavery were presented to Parliament, of which 2,200 were sponsored by Nonconformists. Voting was seen as a matter of personal responsibility not to tolerate an amoral MP. From 1830 anti-slavery campaigners placed great emphasis on forcing prospective members to pledge to support abolition, and after the election of 1832, 104 MPs were committed to the total and immediate abolition of slavery. The first major act of the new parliament was to abolish slavery in the British colonies in 1833. This seemed a victory for an aroused 'religious world'.[3]

Then the very deep depression of 1839–42 gave birth to a number of movements that sought to rally popular sentiment for a purifying cause combining religious and class fervour. The most famous was the Anti-Corn Law League, which sought to elevate its campaign with a religious claim: that only free trade could rescue the economy from the bungling of vested interests that sought to obstruct the free flow of resources by which God had intended mankind to prosper. In 1840 its leader Cobden argued that 'the religious and moral feelings must be appealed to, and the energies of the Christian world must be drawn forth by the

---

[3] D. B. Davis, 'The emergence of immediatism in British and American anti-slavery thought', *Mississippi Valley Historical Review* 49 (1962), 229; Howard Temperley, 'Anti-slavery', in Patricia Hollis (ed.), *Pressure from without in early Victorian England* (London: Edward Arnold, 1974), pp. 30–9; Izhak Gross, 'The abolition of Negro slavery and British parliamentary politics, 1832–1833', *Historical Journal* 23 (1980), 65.

remembrance of the anti-slavery and other struggles, and by being reminded that the cause of truth and justice must prosper in the end'.[4] Meanwhile the alarming state of the nation, and the example of the Anti-Slavery movement (which had just succeeded in getting apprenticeship in the West Indies abolished in 1838) paved the way for other, more directly religious-minded pressure groups. Sturge set up the British and Foreign Anti-Slavery Society in 1838 in order to foster anti-slavery activity internationally, while Buxton's African Civilisation Society aimed to implant free commerce in West Africa. The Peace Society, driven by anger at the wars and tensions of 1839–41 over France, Spain, Afghanistan and China, began a new, more political strategy of petitioning the Commons. A number of Dissenters took their struggle against church rates to a new level, refusing to pay, and earning martyrdom status when imprisoned. Moreover, two committees were formed to lobby for Church disestablishment: the Evangelical Voluntary Church Association in December 1839 and the Religious Freedom Society in May 1840.[5]

However, Anglicans and Roman Catholics also reacted to the severe social and economic tension of this decade by making clashing demands for a moralised politics, thus heightening political tension. Church of England electoral and educational activity led to a Conservative Party victory at the 1841 election and a reactionary educational policy from Peel's government of 1841–6. Its plan of 1843 to give the Church of England an institutional advantage in schools in heavily Dissenting manufacturing districts prompted massive and successful Nonconformist counter-petitioning. High Church Anglicans and Catholics also resisted attempts by both Whig and Tory governments to increase state influence over educational institutions in ways that threatened their freedom; hence the growing vehemence of the Oxford Movement and the growing unwillingness of the Irish Catholic hierarchy to co-operate with the British government. Nonconformists, in turn, were alarmed *both* by state interference in religion and by the high political profile of High Churchmen and Roman Catholics. The result was a major crisis when, in 1845, Peel's government increased and made permanent the official grant to the Irish Catholic priestly training college at Maynooth, in an attempt to keep the Irish priesthood loyal to the state.

---

[4] Hollis, *Pressure*, p. 10.
[5] Stephen Conway, 'The politicisation of the nineteenth-century Peace Society', *Historical Research* 66 (1993), 274–6; Richard Brent, 'The Whigs and Protestant Dissent in the decade of reform: the case of church rates, 1833–1841', *English Historical Review* 102 (1987), 906–7; Timothy Larsen, *Friends of religious equality: Nonconformist politics in mid-Victorian England* (Woodbridge: Boydell Press, 1999), p. 80.

Nonconformists argued that Whig and Tory measures supporting religion were aiding error in order to shore up the authority of wrong-headed government. To make matters worse, in 1846–7 the incoming Whig government significantly increased state funding for English religious groups involved in education.[6]

Together these policies unleashed a passionate Nonconformist crusade against the principle of state financial support for religion. This had two elements: Miall's Anti-State Church Association (founded in 1844) and Baines's plan for Nonconformists to reject all state funding for schools and to rely instead on denominational effort: on 'voluntaryism'. At the 1847 election these two campaigns throve off each other, and off the success of the Anti-Corn Law League in getting publicity for its cause by attempting to secure pledges from by-election candidates to vote for Corn Law repeal. In April 1847 a Dissenters' Parliamentary Committee was formed to organise a campaign to withhold Dissenting votes from candidates who would not resist new state religious funding.[7]

These movements were a declaration of hostility to establishment politics in two ways. First, they were imbued with a strong suspicion of state authority and patronage. They used the Radical language of 'old corruption' to insist that those in charge of government were elitist and sectional representatives of vested interests, at odds with the needs and spirit of the best part of the nation. They meshed with the secular Radical critique of the early nineteenth-century state in so far as they focused on issues of taxation, patronage and spending: they claimed that church rates were not a legitimate charge on non-Anglicans, and that the state used the wealth of the Church establishment as a political tool to reward toady families rather than to promote true religion. State funding for education was also seen as a political strategy, bribing schoolmasters to impose a religion which they did not need to believe in their hearts, and muzzling Irish Catholics from expressing their real social grievances. In Britain and Ireland, the endowment of religion would make it 'an instrument for political and aristocratical, and often unjust purposes', in Miall's words. The only proper conception of the church was as a community of the faithful, zealously defending and spreading religious truth. National establishments were the opposite, an unchristian political coalition for purposes of social control and ideological persuasion.[8]

[6] For Nonconformist political activity in the 1840s, see Parry, *Patriotism*, pp. 161–9.
[7] Derek Fraser, 'Voluntaryism and West Riding politics in the mid-nineteenth century', *Northern History* 13 (1977), 207.
[8] Parry, *Patriotism*, pp. 114, 163–4, 168–9; Larsen, *Friends*, pp. 86–8.

Secondly, in consequence, the campaigns of 1847 were opposed to party interests. Vehemence against the Whigs, the nominal allies of Dissenters, was particularly strong. The voluntaryists succeeded in getting the prize scalp of Macaulay, defeated at Edinburgh. Though they claimed to have secured the return of twenty-six MPs pledged to disestablishment and sixty more who would oppose further state endowments, their main impact was negative, in splitting the Liberal vote and handing seats to Conservatives. Damage was most spectacular in Baines's heartland in the West Riding of Yorkshire: safe Liberal seats were lost that way in Halifax, Leeds and Wakefield. Not only the principal Whigs, but also the Radical Cobden, MP for the Riding, were furious at the damage done to Liberal interests by voluntaryism. But Miall saw it as an example of a new, higher spirit in politics.[9]

II

On the face of it, this use of the electoral system to promote righteous crusading for truth and faith, despite the damage to party interest, continued for several decades. In 1853 the United Kingdom Alliance was formed, inspired by the Maine Law passed in that state in 1851, prohibiting the sale of alcohol. The Alliance worked for legislation allowing local populations to vote for prohibition, and this interest in using the electoral process to pursue righteousness influenced its own early campaigning tactics, which relied on small blocs of temperance activists threatening to withhold their votes in election contests and thus holding the balance of power between candidates. To this end it established a network of local electoral agents.[10]

However, it was the campaign against the church–state connection that captured most Dissenting enthusiasm. The Anti-State Church Association changed its name to the Liberation Society in 1853, and a permanent Electoral Committee of the Society was set up in 1855. Despite its efforts, and the emergence of a united Liberal government under Palmerston in 1859, Parliament could not be persuaded to pass a Church Rate Abolition Bill. The lack of a vigorous Liberal Party leadership on this and other issues forced many Nonconformists, along with other dissatisfied Radicals, to channel their energies into grassroots campaigns to change opinion. Even Robert Vaughan, the leading

[9] G. I. T. Machin, *Politics and the churches in Great Britain, 1832 to 1868* (Oxford: Clarendon Press, 1977), p. 192; Fraser, 'Voluntaryism', 215–16, 226; A. Miall, *Life of Edward Miall* (London: Macmillan, 1884), pp. 125–6.
[10] Hamer, *Politics*, ch. 9.

Nonconformist moderate and editor of the traditionalist *British Quarterly Review*, decided to throw his influence behind the agitators for disestablishment in 1862: 'the present state of things throws upon US a totally new responsibility'.[11]

In October 1863, therefore, Miall began a campaign for a more aggressive Liberation Society election strategy, calling on supporters of religious equality to put the cause first and to give 'only subordinate importance to the ascendancy of the Liberals'. Rather than placing themselves at the service of aristocratic MPs, they should use the 'power placed in our hands by the wisdom of God to bring advantage to his church'. Nonconformist voters should withhold their electoral influence if election candidates did not accept the religious equality programme. His strategy was endorsed at meetings in several large towns, though some leading Nonconformists, such as James Guinness Rogers and R. W. Dale, expressed anxiety that, like the 1847 initiative, it might backfire and help the Conservatives.[12] As it happened, the Society built up its electoral influence – it had 6 electoral agents in 1866 and 13 by 1871 – cautiously and constructively, by concentrating its efforts on persuading candidates to favour their programme rather than putting independents up against them, so that Conservatives opposed to church rate abolition did not benefit. The pattern was different, and more significant, in Wales, where Society influence contributed to a decisive improvement in the fortunes of Nonconformist representatives at the general election of 1868, challenging the Anglo-Welsh Whig and Tory gentry with the aid of the expanded franchise of 1867, and ensuring that Welsh Nonconformist interests were strongly expressed in the Parliament of 1868–74.[13]

The Liberation Society believed that its electoral apparatus had a major impact at the election of 1868, when it worked with the Liberal Party to campaign successfully for the newly adopted policy of its new leader Gladstone, for the disestablishment of the Church of Ireland – a cause that Liberationists had espoused since the mid 1850s. The electorate's enthusiasm for this policy, coming after the large franchise extension of 1867, convinced many Nonconformists – and many fearful Anglicans – that post-Reform Act politics would give a great fillip to their programme of religious equality. Church rates had already been abolished in the 1868 session; the Irish Church was disestablished with little effective political resistance in 1869. Radicals generally believed that

---

[11] *Ibid.*, p. 98; Larsen, *Friends*, p. 72.   [12] Hamer, *Politics*, pp. 102–7.

[13] I. G. Jones, 'The Liberation Society and Welsh politics, 1844–68', *Welsh History Review* 1 (1961), 193–224.

the politics of 'old corruption' was gone for ever, and many assumed that the logical next page in the Liberal programme was an assault on all remaining forms of state patronage, with disestablishment in England to the fore. Nonconformist excitement at the prospect was all the stronger because the new generation of leading Dissenting ministers, men like Dale, Rogers and Joseph Parker, had been enthused, as students in the mid-to-late 1840s, by Miall's firebrand campaigning, and converted to political activism by him.[14]

This exuberance explains the extraordinary events of the next few years, the so-called 'Nonconformist revolt' against Gladstone's Liberal government. The immediate context was the 1870 Education Act, which many of them felt gave unfair advantages to Church of England schools. This seemed a sudden reversal of the positive trend about which they had felt so confident. What began as a campaign against specific sections of the Act turned into something much broader, a campaign to restrict state funding for elementary education to purely secular objects, leaving all religious teaching to be provided by the various denominations' voluntary efforts. Nonconformists seemed convinced that their moral energy in this direction could convert the country. The 'secular solution' was adopted at a conference of 1,885 Nonconformists at Manchester in January 1872, which pledged Nonconformists to withhold their votes from candidates who did not support that policy. Dale urged 'the necessity of having regenerate persons to teach Divine truth'.[15] In parallel, Miall, now an MP, brought three motions in Parliament for church disestablishment between 1871 and 1873. Meanwhile the National Education League, founded in 1869, developed under the aegis of the young Joseph Chamberlain into an aggressive electoral agency pressing for very similar changes to the Education Act. The League supported a strategy of putting up its own candidates at by-elections in order to publicise the issue, damage the government, and persuade Liberal MPs to accept their policy demands.

This revolt of the conscience-ridden proved catching. In the same years, two other movements, both largely staffed by Nonconformists, also used by-elections as a means of attempting to protest at the failures of Gladstone's government and to impose their views on the political classes. One fought for the repeal of the Contagious Diseases Acts, which allowed authorities to incarcerate prostitutes in eighteen protected

[14] Larsen, *Friends*, p. 71.
[15] J. P. Parry, 'Nonconformity, clericalism and "Englishness": the United Kingdom', in C. M. Clark and W. Kaiser (eds.), *Culture wars: secular–Catholic conflict in nineteenth-century Europe* (Cambridge: Cambridge University Press, 2003), pp. 165–7.

districts of Britain around army garrison stations, if they were suspected of carrying venereal disease. Supporters argued that the legislation not only discriminated against women but condoned prostitution and deprived individual citizens of their Christian duty to patrol moral standards themselves, thus weakening the sense of individual responsibility without which a virtuous polity could not exist. The other was the United Kingdom Alliance, which moved into a more aggressive electoral strategy in protest at the inadequacy of the 1872 Licensing Act, and in an attempt to defeat the brewing interest which seemed to be mobilising on the other side of the temperance debate.[16] What is striking about all three movements is their deliberate rejection of compromise legislation proposed by the Liberal government. For activists in all three organisations, it seemed that nothing should be allowed to interfere with the free expression of the aroused conscience.

So there would appear to be continuity between the extremism of 1847 and 1870–3. In both cases religious-minded campaigners for reforms, convinced about the right course of action, refused to tolerate anything short of their ideal, and refused to accept the legitimacy of a party system that would have subordinated it to the interests of a broader Liberal coalition. In both cases they were prepared to do great damage to a Liberal government which was already in trouble – the Gladstone government lost twenty-four of the fifty-one English Liberal seats contested at by-elections between 1870 and 1873. Here, one might think, is evidence of the immaturity of the British political system in the face of aroused religious principle and earnestness.

However, this is a very partial truth. Loyalty to party and to the political process was much stronger than this rather heroic reading of Nonconformist activism suggests. Two other themes need to be grasped in order to explain why this was.

III

First, we need to situate Nonconformist political responses in the context of broader Radical responses to the question of government authority and state legitimacy. Perhaps the most important development in nineteenth-century politics was the waning of the old Radical critique of the state. This critique held that the state was a collection of vested interests, towards which the patriotic voter should behave very warily. He should assume that government would naturally tend to favour

---

[16] Parry, *Patriotism*, p. 113; Hamer, *Politics*, pp. 185–6.

particular classes and groups rather than the national interest, and should exert himself to oppose measures that favoured such groups at the expense of the taxpayer, or liberty, or the general health of the economy. This Radical hostility to 'old corruption' was reinforced, in the case of many religious-minded people, by an evangelical anxiety to purge public life of sinful practices, which is why many Nonconformists, particularly of the Miall–Baines generation, identified strongly with the Radical agenda.

Between 1820 and 1870 the force of that agenda was greatly weakened. Major reductions in the national debt and in state patronage, the virtual abolition of the protectionist system in the fifteen years after 1840, and the increase in government accountability over finance, destroyed the major part of the economic case. The reform of the representation in 1832 and especially in 1867, and major changes in the tone of politics associated particularly with Peel, Palmerston, Cobden and Gladstone, undermined the political case. Radicalism was further enfeebled in the 1850s by general confidence that the British polity was better run than the over-governed continental states. From around 1850, and certainly from 1867, it was very difficult for Radicals to find a major example of state illiberalism or vested interest to campaign against.

In the 1860s Radicals generally assumed that further parliamentary reform would come soon and would lead to a final assault on the old vested interest state, because that was the traditional direction of their thinking. They duly geared up for this fight. Many Radicals entered with zeal into arguments that the Church establishment, the army, the colonial system and the monarchy should be scrutinised and fundamentally reformed – particularly after 1870, when the Gladstone government's programme ran out of steam. What they noticed only slowly was that the country was not with them. Perhaps it never had been with them, but the major extension of the franchise in 1867 cooled reforming ardour and made many feel that the forces of the establishment had already been sufficiently liberalised, and should be supported as a bulwark of legitimate authority. Therefore there was a major reaction in defence of the church, the monarchy, the army and the empire, which helped return the first majority Conservative government for thirty-three years in 1874.[17]

---

[17] On this process, see Philip Harling, *The waning of 'old corruption': the politics of economical reform in Britain, 1779–1846* (Oxford: Clarendon Press, 1996); Miles Taylor, *The decline of British radicalism, 1847–1860* (Oxford: Oxford University Press, 1995); Jonathan Parry, 'Whig monarchy, Whig nation: crown, politics and representativeness 1800–2000', in A. Olechnowicz (ed.), *The monarchy and the British nation, 1780 to the present* (Cambridge: Cambridge University Press, 2007), pp. 47–75.

Indeed after 1867, Radicals themselves gradually became much less rigorously critical of the state, now that it seemed more accountable to a mass electorate. This trend was noticeable among Nonconformists, for all their instinctive, centuries-old suspicion of government authority. In October 1867 Miall and Baines dramatically abandoned the policy of voluntaryism, explicitly because control of the state was passing from one class to another, so that there were no longer grounds for working-class suspicion of it.[18] This reflected a confidence in the good sense of a parliament that could be swayed by Nonconformist pressure: the number of Dissenting MPs doubled between 1865 and 1868, to seventy. It also reflected growing Nonconformist power in urban local government, which had great influence on educational matters after 1870. But on the other hand there was also a fear of atheism and of a secularised democracy, shared by many middle-class and propertied people after the unexpectedly large franchise extension of 1867. Dale and Baldwin Brown talked of religion, together with intelligence, as crucial 'counter-balancing centrifugal forces' to the 'menacing ... centripetal force in Democracy' which posed a 'terrible danger to the higher freedom and life of mankind'. They wanted Nonconformist political and religious activity to turn democracy into Christian paths, thus allowing it to fulfil its 'sacred mission'.[19] Few Nonconformist leaders were enthusiastic democrats: they had a tendency towards a residual Calvinism, with the emphasis on the leadership qualities of a responsible elect. The Reformed state could be a useful ally against potential disorder.

On the whole, the political changes of the 1860s seemed very positive to Nonconformists, because they pushed national affairs away from aristocratic coteries and in the direction of manly earnestness and moral pressure. They gave more influence to provincial common sense, to men like the Quaker John Bright. In other words, they increased the weight of the England that had existed for centuries and to which they felt most attached: the England of Cromwell and conscience. In new northern town halls – such as Rochdale and Leeds – Cromwell was portrayed in a line of English rulers, as a symbol of the nation's civic republicanism. By the 1870s and 1880s, most Nonconformists saw themselves as a crucial force in national history, 'English of the English'.[20] They had little reason still to regard themselves as outsiders. The passage of the

---

[18] Miall, *Miall*, p. 273; Edward Baines, *National education: address* (London: Jackson, Walford, & Hodder, 1867), p. 8.

[19] Parry, *Patriotism*, p. 118.

[20] Raphael Samuel, 'The discovery of Puritanism, 1820–1914: a preliminary sketch', in Jane Garnett and Colin Matthew (eds.), *Revival and religion since 1700: essays for John Walsh* (London: Hambledon, 1993), pp. 214, 220; Parry, *Patriotism*, p. 116.

Burials Act in 1880 removed the last of the second-order civil grievances for which they had lobbied in the 1830s. Political pluralism was a fact of life, and so was social recognition. By the late nineteenth century, the traditional after-dinner toast of 'church and state' had in many contexts given way to the more inclusive 'ministers of all denominations'.[21]

Nonconformist approval of the improved tone of national politics was apparent in their admiration for the ethical earnestness of Gladstone, even though they had no sympathy with his High Church Anglican theology. John Clifford said of a Gladstone speech of 1876: 'The hearer felt he was witnessing a fight for righteousness, for humanity, for God.' Gladstone in turn told Nonconformists that he appreciated them for consistently applying 'the principles of the Kingdom of God to the business of public life'.[22] Gladstone sympathised with Nonconformists in significant ways, particularly in seeing Erastianism as a deadening influence on religious life. But they also admired the honesty with which he disagreed with them. Gladstone represented a politics in which conscience seemed to count for more than it had in the days of elitist aristocratic rule. One supporter remarked in 1883 that it was chiefly owing to him that 'there never was a time when drawing-rooms, and snobberies of all kinds, had less practical influence than now'. In fact this trend to cross-class honest manliness in political discourse predated Gladstone and can be detected from the early 1850s. But he certainly did a great deal to promote it.[23]

This cult of earnest manliness not only encouraged general Nonconformist loyalty to the state; it also had a specific effect in weakening their hustings campaigns to require candidates to pledge support for specific measures. Such campaigns implied that MPs could be persuaded to vote against their own preferences by the threat to withdraw electoral support. Increasingly, however, this did not seem such an appropriate relationship between an MP and his constituents. The rising young Nonconformist MP Henry Winterbotham argued against pressure for pledges in 1871, saying that it was important to trust him, as an honest MP,

[21] James Munson, *The Nonconformists: in search of a lost culture* (London: SPCK, 1991), p. 127.

[22] David Bebbington, 'Gladstone and the Baptists', *Baptist Quarterly* 26 (1976), 233; Stephen E. Koss, *Nonconformity in modern British Politics* (London: Batsford, 1975), p. 17; Munson, *Nonconformists*, p. 221.

[23] E. H. Coleridge, *Life and correspondence of John Duke Lord Coleridge*, 2 vols. (London: Heinemann, 1904), vol. II, p. 322; Parry, *Patriotism*, pp. 69–71; John Tosh, 'Gentlemanly politeness and manly simplicity in Victorian England', *Transactions of the Royal Historical Society* 12 (2002), 455–72.

to 'follow the dictates of my conscience freely'. The emphasis of Nonconformist pressure groups increasingly came to be the less confrontational tactic of 'educating up' politicians by seeking to persuade them of the superior rationality and morality of their arguments. After 1874 the pressure groups made very few attempts to run independent candidates against official Liberals. 'Educating up' was necessarily a slower and more consensual process – and one that also reflected the general acceptance of the idea that legislative process in Britain now required the prior maturation of public opinion; there was no point in an advanced polity seeking to change morals simply by fiat, as continental autocracies might do.[24]

Greater confidence in the tone of politics meant that Nonconformists' assertiveness on disestablishment declined. This was not to say that they ceased to believe in its inherent attractiveness; there was no recession from the belief that free churches were purer and more Christian agencies than state ones. But the question was always whether to mount a political campaign of attack on the established status of the Church of England, and from the mid 1870s this ceased to be a priority, both because the purification of church and state did not seem so urgent, politically or socially, and because it was unpopular electorally and hence politically counter-productive. It was the Conservatives who stoked, and benefited from, the cry of the 'church in danger' in 1885.

If we see Nonconformity as engaged fundamentally not in a permanent hostility to the state, but in the defence and promotion of the idea of a spiritual and moral community against threats to it, then we can appreciate better the turn in Nonconformists' politics in the 1880s. They moved towards tackling the more urgent threat to that community – from social and moral decay, particularly in the inner cities. This meant some attention to the social problem, since lack of education, poor housing and hygiene obviously contributed to the 'bitter cry of outcast London' identified by Andrew Mearns of the London Congregational Union in his famous 1883 pamphlet. It meant concern with social purity, as indicated by the increased profile of the temperance campaign in the 1880s and the crusades of Stead and others against child prostitution, brothels and the general incursion of 'French morals'. And it meant stern action to protect the morality of politics itself. Nonconformists were to the fore in ending the high-flying careers of Sir Charles Dilke and Charles Stewart Parnell when both were embroiled in embarrassing divorce cases in 1886 and 1890.

---

[24] Hamer, *Politics*, pp. 32–5, 51.

It was the Parnell affair that led to the coining of the term 'Nonconformist conscience'.[25]

Everything said so far makes the point that, at any rate once the excited millenarian overtones of the 1840s had faded, there was no significant Nonconformist disillusionment with the basic structure of politics. One aspect of their strong national loyalty was their intense dislike of Catholicism (and Anglo-Catholicism), which in fact was arguably the major cause of their brief mid-century militancy. It drove the strategy of electoral assertiveness in 1847 and 1870–3. These were times when the theological and international climate seemed threatening to the maintenance of sound Protestant values: atheism and Catholicism both appeared to be gaining ground, spiritually and politically, at home and abroad. Educational voluntaryism in 1846–7, and the secular solution in 1872, were adopted specifically in order to find a coherent nationwide policy that would justify the withholding of state funding from Irish Catholic educational institutions. In the light of Maynooth and the apparent willingness of the Whig and Tory political elite to offer concurrent endowment of all religions both in Britain and Ireland, the withdrawal of that endowment seemed necessary. Similarly it was the power of Cardinal Cullen and the Irish hierarchy, in the context of the Vatican Council of 1870 and the Gladstone government's apparent favouritism to the Irish and willingness to fund Catholic schools and universities that led Dale and his allies to press for secularism in 1871–2. Subsequently, once the Catholic threat had receded, the urgency of withdrawing state funding from religious education receded with it. The crises of 1847 and 1870–3 were exceptional, not typical. Only a few years after Maynooth and the 1847 election, most Nonconformists supported, however reluctantly, the idea of legislation vetoing the Pope's power to appoint bishops in the United Kingdom without seeking prior approval from the state. This was a telling outcome for a body that venerated denominational freedom from state control – but venerated national identity more.[26]

After the mid 1870s, as the pressure for educational secularism and disestablishment slackened, it could be seen more clearly that Nonconformists had implicitly accepted the Church establishment and state funding for the teaching of religion. In essence the policy of the other major wing of the Victorian Liberal Party, often described in shorthand as the Whigs, had triumphed, though it was wise of them not to brag

---

[25] Parry, *Patriotism*, pp. 120–2; Koss, *Nonconformity*, p. 27; Munson, *Nonconformists*, p. 213.
[26] Larsen, *Friends*, pp. 230–41.

about it. In the Whig tradition, the state played a crucial role in disciplining the potential extremism and zeal of religious sects. Most Whigs believed that the Church establishment was invaluable because it supplied moral teaching on a nationwide basis. In Whig eyes, its bishops and clergy were the spiritual equivalent of the propertied classes in politics: an intermediate layer between divine authority and popular passion, which had a duty to teach and to behave responsibly and accountably. They should be subject to the guidance of Parliament – of the representatives of the people – because this would provide a safeguard against clergymen's potentially intolerant or reactionary views, and clerical abuses such as plurality and non-residence. A national establishment on a broad, inclusive basis guaranteed rights of private judgement and helped the church to remain more or less in harmony with the evolution of intellectual opinion, rather than clinging to meaningless formularies reflecting the superstitions of less progressive times. However broad the church, it would nevertheless not be broad enough to represent a pluralistic nation, which was Parliament's duty; so there should be no civil disabilities on members of any sect. Allegiance to the nation state was to be on the basis of its representative constitution, not to any doctrinal or ethnic idea. Catholics, Jews and atheists should sit at Westminster so that their legitimate grievances could be represented. If Irish Catholics could express themselves there, and if their MPs swore allegiance to the crown, then there was no danger in practice from the Pope's aspirations for ultramontane political influence.

In other words, a liberal parliamentary state could project support for religion and morality on a pluralistic basis, against anarchy, and yet at the same time could follow an anti-clerical policy of criticising every expression of anti-social religious assertiveness or extremism. Religious groups, unable to overthrow the liberal state, would accept its benefits. For many Whigs, these benefits should ideally extend to concurrent endowment of all sects in order to bind them more effectively to the state. That was the policy they tried and failed to implement in Ireland, having to accept disestablishment there instead, because of the weight of Catholic opinion. In heavily Nonconformist Wales, too, pressure for disestablishment and for secular education remained too strong to be suppressed. But in England and Scotland, more of the Whig model has survived than has disappeared.[27] To this day the state maintains religion in a number of ways: through its alliance with the Church of England; through obligatory religious worship in schools, reinforced by the overtly

[27] Parry, *Patriotism*, ch. 2.

Christian Butler Education Act of 1944 (and its hardly less Christian successor of 1988); through a monarch who remains Defender of the Faith and whose coronation was an explicit dedication of her life to God on behalf of the nation; and through a national anthem which in effect requires English football fans to plead with God to support her in that task, something they seem very willing to do.

IV

Not the least of the successes of this Whiggish approach was to maintain a rough-and-ready political alliance, in a Liberal Party, with Nonconformists who in theory differed from them on so much. A political party structure – the Liberal Party in this case – was able to subordinate and yet in important ways to satisfy the religious conscience.

All the militant Nonconformist initiatives discussed above were dogged by internal disputes about how far it was wise for them to damage the Liberal Party. At the 1841 election, despite dissatisfaction at the slow legislative progress of church rate abolition, Nonconformist voters were generally loyal to Whig candidates. By the next contest, in 1847, relations had clearly broken down badly in places, owing to the influence of men like Miall and Baines, but even in the heartland of the revolt, the West Riding, the party held together in important towns where an influential local figure, such as William Byles in Bradford, exerted pressure for that outcome.[28] Both in 1863–4, in the discussion over Miall's new strategy, and in 1872, during the secularist revolt, moderates succeeded in watering down the strategy declaration so as to give leeway to Nonconformists to decide to support the party leadership in cases where national factors required it. The reason why pressure groups focused so much on by-elections was because they recognised that these, rather than general elections, were the contests at which there was the best chance of persuading supporters to vote on a single issue rather than on straightforward party lines. Even so, they often failed to make much headway, as is shown by the various contests of 1863–4 and 1871–3. The League had to call off its strategy in autumn 1873, using the excuse of John Bright's return to the Cabinet. The introduction of the secret ballot in 1872 was a significant blow to the temperance strategy of trying to organise electors into a bloc which could visibly withhold its votes until the candidate gave a pledge to support their

---

[28] Machin, *Politics and the Churches*, pp. 73–4; A. Jowitt, 'Dissenters, Voluntaryism and Liberal unity: the 1847 election', in J. A. Jowitt and R. K. S. Taylor (eds.), *Nineteenth-century Bradford elections* (Bradford: Bradford Centre, 1979), pp. 7–23.

campaign. Moreover, Nonconformists tended to be unhappy about pursuing a merely negative strategy of abstention, since most Liberals and Radicals prized possession of the vote and political participation.[29]

The obvious reason for this general loyalty to the Liberal Party was the identification of the Conservative Party with the maintenance of the privileges of the Church of England, and with other interests of which Nonconformists usually disapproved (such as landowners and publicans). In most towns and counties with a substantial electorate some version of the two-party system had developed at a local level at an early stage, based very largely on religious affiliation. Even before 1830, Nonconformists had formed a significant element in the local coalitions that challenged the dominance of Tory–Anglican borough corporations. Locally and nationally, there was a natural trend towards an alliance of religious and political 'outsiders', under Whig leadership. The one issue on which the alliance could always unite was in opposing the narrow ecclesiastical basis of the Tory state, by proposing to repeal the Test and Corporation Acts and other civil disabilities, and introducing Catholic Emancipation. This alliance survived after 1832 owing to the threat from its Tory–Anglican opponents. Nonconformist indiscipline was greatest at times when the electoral threat from Toryism had waned but the social influence of Anglicanism had not. On the whole, Nonconformist electoral strategy was at its most assertive between 1863 and 1873, a time of maximum confidence about Liberal electoral invulnerability and about the onward march of political progress. The extent of the Conservative reaction in 1874 was a great shock, and thereafter none of the Nonconformist pressure groups behaved so cavalierly. The expression of an independent Nonconformist conscience, which began as an evangelical move for urgent social purification in the 1840s, became by the 1860s a luxury born out of a confidence in Liberal dominance. In 1880 the Liberal Party was united and on its best behaviour during the drive to defeat Disraelian Conservatism after its alarming six years of majority government. Throughout the 1880s both the Liberation Society and the United Kingdom Alliance were generally keen not to play into the hands of their newly powerful political opponents.[30]

In fact Nonconformists' assertive electoral strategy can be seen as a political tactic within Liberalism: a contribution to a broad Liberal debate about policy and organisation, given the looseness of the party's

[29] Hamer, *Politics*, pp. 22, 29, 111–12, 122–38.
[30] Frank O'Gorman, *The emergence of the British two-party system 1760–1832* (London: Edward Arnold, 1982); John Vincent, *The formation of the British Liberal party, 1857–68* (Harmondsworth: Penguin, 1972), pp. 101–3; Hamer, *Politics*, pp. 154–5, 227–38.

structure. It was motivated by frustration at their failure to wrest command of the party away from its aristocratic leaders, and by a desire to impose an alternative vision of party based on mobilisation of the protesting mentality. Though there was a good deal of conscience in the Nonconformist vision of electoral activity, there was also a good deal of the caucus. The two most significant figures in Nonconformist electoral strategy were Miall and Joseph Chamberlain. Both were intensely anti-aristocratic, had clear political ambitions, and were visionaries for the use of large-scale electoral mobilisation to change the balance of power in the party and the nation. Chamberlain succeeded: he turned the National Education League into a precursor of the National Liberal Federation, the body through which he sought to impose a radical programmatic policy on the Liberal leadership, and which he used to leapfrog so dramatically into the Cabinet in 1880. Similarly, the struggle over voluntaryism in the West Riding in the 1840s should be seen in large part as a struggle for control of local Liberal politics by urban radicals challenging the traditional dominance of the Fitzwilliams and other county families. I have argued elsewhere that the so-called 'Nonconformist revolt' of 1870–3 did very little damage to Liberal Party performance at the 1874 election and indeed strengthened the Nonconformist activists' grip on local Liberal Party organisations in a lot of towns. This was because they used the furore over section 25 of the 1870 Act, and secularism, to assert their organisational influence over other elements in local Liberalism.[31]

In the 1870s and 1880s party organisation developed rapidly, driven by the need to mobilise a much larger electorate. For religious groups with experience of electoral politics, this was both an opportunity and a check. The emergence of formal Liberal Party associations in constituencies, and of more centralised bodies such as the National Liberal Federation, involved the disciplining of sectional groups within the party, to force them to accept the value of unity. Yet at the same time the growth of formal organisation increased the weight of constituency activists, many of whom pressed for the adoption of several of these sectional demands. The result was that more and more Liberal candidates felt it prudent to express support for the issues about which their organisers felt most strongly – a task made easier because a consensus emerged that for the sake of party unity those demands should be expressed less contentiously than in the past. For example, from the

---

[31] P. Auspos, 'Radicalism, pressure groups, and party politics: from the National Education League to the National Liberal Federation', *Journal of British Studies* 20 (1980), 184–204; Parry, 'Nonconformity'.

1880s, instead of requiring candidates to support legislation for a local veto on the sale of alcohol, the United Kingdom Alliance was willing for them just to support the idea of a resolution on the subject, leaving it to the party leadership to determine the timing of actual legislation. As long as leaders were given this power, more and more Liberal MPs were willing to express support for the abstract principles demanded by faddist groups, for example the idea of disestablishment in Scotland and Wales. Something approximating an informal legislative programme emerged – briefly made formal in the Newcastle Programme of 1891. This process allowed Nonconformists and other faddist groups to feel that their wishes were fully integrated within Liberal Party decision-making structures – even though the prospect of disestablishment had hardly increased.

Nonconformists could therefore vote Liberal with some hope that their legislative desires might eventually be met. But that was not, in fact, the main point of voting. Supporting the Liberals could be seen as a righteous act – especially when leaders like Gladstone and Lloyd George expressed themselves in quasi-evangelical language.[32] Above all it was a satisfying declaration of war against the enemy, the Anglican Tory establishment – for, after all, in a two-party system the strongest emotion of voters is usually their determination to vote against something unpleasant rather than to vote for an ideal. Two-party politics meant identity politics, tribal politics. The greater evil in 1880 and 1906 was Tory misrule, not the state of religion and morals. The party system was so effective between 1874 and 1914 because it produced high participation levels – turnout averaged 84 per cent in the three general elections of 1906–10 – while usually defusing rather than heightening tension between opposing social groups. This was because, in general, neither party pursued an extremist religious policy during these years. Governments of both camps recognised that religious issues were so divisive that to pander to the wishes of their extreme supporters would risk a damaging counter-agitation from opponents. Liberal ministries did not push for disestablishment, while Conservatives on the whole accepted the constraints on Anglicanism imposed by the 1870 Education Act, for fear of giving the anti-clerical Liberal alliance an effective rallying-cry. The necessity of overhauling the 1870 Act in 1902 was the exception that proved the rule: it prompted a massive and emotive Nonconformist reaction to the idea of putting 'Rome on the rates', giving Liberal

[32] Boyd Hilton, 'Gladstone's theological politics', in M. Bentley and J. Stevenson (eds.), *High and low politics in modern Britain: ten studies* (Oxford: Clarendon Press, 1983), pp. 52–7.

religious zealots all the excuse they needed to dust off venerable anti-Tory criticisms. Yet even this crusade would have been much weaker had it not also involved secular criticisms of a stale, blundering and ineffective Conservative regime. And the true political importance of the education issue was revealed by Nonconformists' inability to persuade the 1906 Liberal government, despite its massive majority, to commit enough resources to amending the 1902 Act.[33]

V

This chapter has argued that the Victorian polity came to channel the energies of Nonconformists effectively. This was firstly because of increasingly general confidence in the basic fairness and historical legitimacy of the political system, which Nonconformists shared not least because of their sense of history. Nonconformity was inherently a political movement; it defined itself by its view of the relationship between religion and the state. The key judgement required of it was always a political one: how zealous did the religious conscience need to be in protesting about the behaviour of those in power? Secondly, and building from that, Nonconformists recognised that the existing party system could express their identity and grievances. It allowed them to define themselves directly against their political opponents, giving them a sense of engagement in a virtuous battle which produced frequent uplifting victories. It also produced occasional defeats, but the tendencies towards consensus within a mature party system meant that these defeats never threatened their basic liberties or undermined their social status. At the beginning of the Victorian period, the act of voting could be seen as a pious declaration of the regenerate voter's responsibility to purge the nation of its sins. But forty years later, the sense of evangelical urgency had been subsumed in an avowedly political struggle, even though that struggle was still genuinely seen as one between right and wrong, particularly at set-piece elections like the fight against un-Christian Disraeli in 1880. The political process had found a way of transplanting religious concerns onto a stage where they could be acted out with fewer apocalyptic consequences for social stability.

A liberal political order is perfectly compatible with a strong religious culture as long as that culture accepts the primary legitimacy of that order. Political parties which appeal strongly to religious groups have often played a valuable role in defusing the potential tensions between

---

[33] D. W. Bebbington, *The Nonconformist conscience: chapel and politics, 1870–1914* (London: Allen & Unwin, 1982), pp. 141–60.

religion and politics, by involving those groups in the excitements of contested politics but confining the effects of their enthusiasm within safe limits. The compromises inherent in representative politics operate both within large organisations like mass parties and between the parties in a contest for power – since there is a natural tendency for political leaders to aim to maximise electoral appeal by trying to occupy the middle ground of public opinion and accusing their opponents of being unattractive extremists. Thus the continental parties which sought to represent Roman Catholic interests, such as the Centre Party in Germany, played a key part in defeating any ultramontane sympathies which German Catholics may have had and persuading them of the legitimacy of German political institutions. A more contemporary example would be the religious right in America, whose high profile has excited much alarmist commentary from opponents. Despite that, it seems unlikely that the Republican Party will win enough power to be able to implement a shift in social values, unless it shows itself consistently willing to make compromises with other elements of an extremely diverse nation.

Even in the nineteenth century, of course, religion was far from being the only determinant of voting. Parties were vehicles for other social groups to declare their identities. They also allowed expressions of support for or opposition to various economic and social ideals: low taxes, independence from overbearing authority, redistribution of wealth, protection for various interests and trades. In the twentieth century, as state spending has increased, the importance of economic and social identity has undoubtedly come to outstrip the importance of religious identity in explaining party fortunes – though until 1945, and in some parts of Britain later than that, the electoral significance of religion should not be underestimated.[34] The genius of the British party system, historically, has been to offer voters choices which, most of the time, have seemed meaningful to them in both economic and religious terms. Conversely, parties weaken their appeal when they cease to be able to provide an attractive moral narrative of any sort. In such a climate, there will be alienation from the political system, whether from those who feel marginalised socially or those who feel that their spiritual or intellectual worldview is not embraced by it. In considering the apparent recent increase in religious controversy and political instability in the West, the crucial question may be less how to deal with the alleged 'extremism' of religious opinion than how to ensure a more effective and integrative politics.

---

[34] D. W. Bebbington, 'Nonconformity and electoral sociology, 1867–1918', *Historical Journal* 27 (1984), 633–56; David Butler and Donald Stokes, *Political change in Britain: forces shaping electoral choice* (Harmondsworth: Penguin, 1971), pp. 159–71.

11 Colonial secularism and Islamism in North India: a relationship of creativity

Humeira Iqtidar

This chapter is concerned with excavating the historical context that gave rise to Islamism,[1] particularly in North India,[2] and the paradoxes that surround its self-defined antagonistic relationship to secularism. I focus here on the Jamaat-e-Islami (JI), an Islamist party founded in 1941 that has been particularly influential in not just the South Asian context but in inspiring similar groups around the world. My point of departure is Asad's[3] insight that secularism is not a one-time separation of church and state, but a constant remodelling and refashioning of religious practice by the state, giving rise to new versions and forms of religion. I propose here that Islamism is closely related to the secularism that helped define its limits, its contentions and its focus; the relationship between Islamism and secularism is not one of straightforward antagonism but a dialectical and creative one. Critically, I propose that the type of secularism that the British sought to impose in colonial India created the possibility of this novelty in Muslim thought and practice that is called Islamism.

Versions of this chapter were presented at the South Asia History Seminar, Oxford, the Secularism and Religion Network Seminar, King's College, Cambridge and the Annual Social Science Conference at LUMS, Lahore. I am grateful to the audience for their comments and questions, but particularly to Asef Bayat and David Gilmartin for their incisive feedback as commentators in the Cambridge and LUMS sessions respectively. Ira Katznelson, Gareth Stedman Jones and Joya Chatterji provided encouragement and feedback at just the right junctures. Justin Jones and Veronique Altglass have both provided close readings and many helpful comments.
[1] Islamists are distinguished from the other Muslim revivalists by their insistence on engagement with the political structures and state apparatus as a means of establishing a Muslim society. See Olivier Roy, *The failure of political Islam* (London: Tauris, 1994); Graham Fuller, *The future of political Islam* (New York: Palgrave, 2003).
[2] That colonial India, bigger in physical size and population, vastly more varied in terms of ethnic, linguistic and religious diversity than all of Europe combined, was termed a subcontinent, while Europe was conceived of as a continent, is part of imperial hubris. I focus here on North India (generally conceived of as the part of India stretching from Bengal to Punjab).
[3] Talal Asad, *Formation of the secular: Christianity, Islam and modernity* (Stanford: Stanford University Press, 2003). See also his *Genealogies of religion: discipline and reasons of power in Christianity and Islam* (London: Johns Hopkins University Press, 1993).

Tradition, modernity and secularism
in Muslim societies

Before we proceed, it would be useful to complicate our understanding of tradition and modernity, particularly with reference to Islamism. Islamism is often conceived of as a 'traditional' reaction against 'modernity' and secularism is seen to be an integral part of this modernity. It is useful to remind ourselves here that in the case of Muslim societies the *need* for the kind of secularism that took shape, at least in its reified version, in western Europe, with the insistence on a sharply delineated public and private sphere, and a clear separation between church and state, did not exist.[4] There was no single centralised authority such as the Pope and historically the *ulama* have operated as a diverse, decentralised group of scholars and practitioners.[5] At the same time pre-colonial, primarily Muslim states had evolved other mechanisms for managing the diversity of religious and ethnic communities, and supporting mostly peaceful coexistence (see Barkey in this volume). For these primarily Muslim societies, the rupture in tradition as a result of the colonial encounter was very intense, but, I contend, has been creatively approached by different individuals and groups within these societies in rethinking religious belief and practice – their agency exhibited in the range of responses to the structures of colonialism.

Marshall Hodgson[6] pointed out at the end of his history of Islamic civilisation that western societies have managed to retain a deeper and more continuous link with their traditions than the Muslim societies. Charles Taylor's magisterial *Sources of the self: making of modern identity*[7] alludes to this particular religious – Christian – and philosophical continuity in Europe. In the sense of a relatively continuous philosophical dialogue, dependence upon largely the same authors, books and philosophers, western societies are more traditional than non-western, including predominantly Muslim ones. At the same time, emerging scholarship on tradition, particularly influenced by Hobsbawm and Ranger's widely quoted edited volume,[8] has alerted us to the possibility

---

[4] Carl L. Brown, *Religion and state: the Muslim approach to politics* (New York: Columbia University Press, 2000).

[5] Mohammed Qasim Zaman, *The ulama in contemporary Islam: custodians of change* (Princeton: Princeton University Press, 2002).

[6] Marshal Hodgson, *The venture of Islam: conscience and history in a world civilization* (Chicago: University of Chicago Press, 1974).

[7] Charles Taylor, *Sources of the self: the making of modern identity* (Cambridge: Cambridge University Press, 1989).

[8] Eric Hobsbawm and Terence Ranger (eds.), *The invention of tradition* (Cambridge: Cambridge University Press, 1983).

that many traditions, while retaining some link with past practices and modalities, are very recent creations.

In this context, it is important to realise, first, that the 'tradition' put to the service of legitimising competing claims of authenticity, whether by Islamists or others, may be of very recent origins. Second, and more importantly, contrary to a particular stream of scholarship on Islamic tradition, and indeed the claims of many Islamists, 'traditional' Muslim society was not rigid and static.[9] Hallaq, Cook, Zaman and Brown,[10] among others, show that adaptive creativity, dissent and rethinking have been an integral part of traditional Islamic legal and theological thought. The imposition of colonialism and the introduction of a particular model of the state that we call 'modern' led to much rethinking and re-evaluation within the non-western, and not just Muslim, societies. While the impact of colonisation in terms of its disruptions was tremendous, we can see individuals and groups selectively appropriating and braiding together elements of existing ideas and practices with newer impositions leading often to unforeseen and unexpected combinations. Thus, contrary to established understanding we should see this engagement as one of great creativity, where new schools of thought (such as the Deoband in South Asia) and new forms of organisation (such as the Jamaat-e-Islami and the Tablighi Jamaat, also in South Asia) emerged. I want to suggest then that the relationship between 'modernity' and 'tradition' is not one of linear antagonism but of accommodation, suggestion and creation.

Differentiated and intrusive state structures, institutions of mass education, and critically, changes in the relationship of religious identity to political structures are a hall-mark of the modern period. I follow Asad[11] in his suggestion that the very unevenness and variation in the manifestations of modernity require that we recognise it as a project with strong aspirational aspects to it as well as a historical period. This is not to suggest

[9] Movements of renewal have been a continuous feature of Islamic 'tradition'. In the centuries preceding European colonialism, several revivalism movements (Wahabi, Mahdi, Fulani, Padri and others) were initiated in Muslim societies as diverse as those in Africa and South-East Asia. See John Esposito, 'Contemporary Islam: reformation or revolution?', in John Esposito (ed.), *The Oxford history of Islam* (Oxford: Oxford University Press, 1999), p. 645. My argument here is that Islamism draws upon this 'tradition' of revivalism, but is of course, shaped by the context in which it arose.

[10] Wael Hallaq, *Authority, continuity and change in Islamic Law* (Cambridge: Cambridge University Press, 2001); Michael Cook, *Commanding right and forbidding wrong in Islamic thought* (Cambridge: Cambridge University Press, 2000); Zaman, *Ulama in contemporary Islam*; Brown, *Religion and state*.

[11] Talal Asad, 'From the history of colonial anthropology to the anthropology of western hegemony', in G. Stocking (ed.), *Colonial situations* (Madison: University of Wisconsin Press, 1991).

a complete abandonment of the term modernity, but to propose the abandonment of associating normative values with the 'modern' and to focus on substantive changes in Muslim practices as a result of the colonial encounter in North India. As I discuss in the next section, the profound impact of this encounter was based not just on outright rejection or opposition, but on negotiation, absorption and subtle reframing of earlier discourses. In the process, I lend further support to the contention that political fundamentalism in general,[12] and Islamism in particular, is a modern phenomenon rather than a traditional response to modernity.

What does it mean to suggest that Islamism is a particularly modern phenomenon? Are the Islamists not, by their own definition, hoping to go back to the glorious first days of Islam under the prophet Mohammed? It is the path and not just the destination that makes the Islamists modern – the ways in which they aim to get back to a 'purified' Islam and their reasons for wanting to do so that give us an insight into why Islamism would not have been possible in any other historical period. Eisenstadt[13] suggests that religious fundamentalisms constitute a distinctive form of modern political movements. To him fundamentalism is a variant of the Jacobin tendencies that are an intrinsic part of modern political movements, and that arise, in part, because of an inherent contradiction within modern polities between totalising and more pluralistic conceptions, between reflexivity and active construction of nature and society, between autonomy and control. In similar vein, Bruce Lawrence[14] has argued that Islamism would have been inconceivable in any age but the modern one: not only do the Islamists use modern ways of organising and communicating, but the very categories, notions and laws that they hope to defy or modify are modern constructs. In this chapter I single out the emergence of the intrusive modern state and its attempts at managing religion within a colonial context in North India as a key development that made Islamism conceivable.

The intrusive modern state

The colonial imposition, albeit one that proceeded unevenly in different parts of India, of a modern state, with its constant interference in everyday

---

[12] S. N. Eisenstadt, *Fundamentalism, sectarianism and revolution: the Jacobin dimension of modernity* (Cambridge: Cambridge University Press, 1999); Bruce Lawrence, *Defenders of God: the fundamentalist revolt against the modern age* (London: Tauris, 1990).
[13] Eisenstadt, *Fundamentalism*, p. 62.
[14] Bruce Lawrence, *Defenders* and *shattering the myth: Islam beyond violence* (Princeton, Princeton University Press, 1998).

life, was a major break from the past. Sudipta Kaviraj has argued that, as in the case of pre-modern Europe, the pre-colonial Indian state was of limited significance in quotidian life. 'The state had', he suggests,[15] 'the discretion to tax severely or leniently. It could cause or end wars, but its power to reorder the structure of productive roles which determined everyday destinies of individual men and social groups was severely restricted.'[16] No doubt the colonial state built upon previous structures of power, domination and information collection that existed in pre-colonial India, especially in the earlier years.[17] Yet something new was also being created – this state was different both in the quality and the quantity of its intrusion into individual lives. The colonial state's interference in daily life operated on two parallel and intertwined levels. One encompassed the politically motivated, sometimes cynical but mostly self-righteous attempts at social and political 'reform'. This included the attempts at banning practices like *sati*, the introduction of electorates along religious lines, etc. The other and perhaps more critical was the less self-conscious, although admittedly no less self-righteous, ontological remapping of the individual, community, society and polity.[18] Included in this is, for instance, census activity that divided individuals into neat and hermetically sealed categories.

It is in this specialisation as well as increased reach that the colonial state betrays its 'modernness'. This interest in categorising and shaping individuals and communities is a defining characteristic of not just the colonial state but of the modern state generally. In a perceptive analysis of this inherent compulsion within the modern state, James Scott has observed:

The aspiration to such uniformity and order alerts us to the fact that modern statecraft is largely a project of internal colonization, often glossed, as it is in the imperial rhetoric, as a 'civilizing mission'. The builders of the modern

---

[15] Sudipta Kaviraj, 'The modern state in India', in Martin Doornbos and Sudipta Kaviraj (eds.), *Dynamics of state formation: India and Europe compared* (Delhi and London: Sage, 1997), p. 229.

[16] Sumit Guha in 'The politics of identity and enumeration in India c.1600–1990', *Comparative Study of History and Society* 45/1 (2003), 148–67, among others, has objected that Kaviraj's view under-represents the complexity of the Mughal state and does not take into account the extensive enumeration strategies that the Mughal Empire undertook to extract revenues. However, this does not significantly alter the crux of Kaviraj's argument. His main concern is to show that the intensity of state intrusion and its impact on cognitive structures was much more pronounced within the modern colonial state.

[17] Chris Bayly, *Empire and information: intelligence gathering and social communication in India 1780–1870* (Cambridge: Cambridge University Press, 1996).

[18] Bernard Cohn, *Colonialism and its forms of knowledge: the British in India* (Princeton: Princeton University Press, 1996); Kaviraj, 'Modern state', 1997, p. 231.

nation state do not merely describe, observe and map; they strive to shape a people and landscape that will fit their techniques of observation.[19]

The intrusion of this state, modern and colonial, was not targeted specifically at Muslims. Rather it touched all religious practices. Indeed, one of the central planks of colonial sociology was the codification of diverse practices across the geographical and social landscape of India as a single coherent whole, creating 'religion' as an analytical category. For instance, it is often pointed out that Hinduism was not conceived of as a unified 'religion' until colonial times.[20] Yet, until recently, a similar analysis has not been extended to Islam, and its dramatic reconstruction during colonial times not adequately recognised. This may in part have to do with the wider geographical spread of Muslims, some structural similarity to Christianity, and the vague notions of a Muslim *'ummah'* that percolated at various levels in pre- and early colonial periods. However, recent research is beginning to question this assumption of a coherently Islamic imaginary, as well as the specific implications of this imagination in the early colonial period.[21] For the major religious groups, the diverse, regionally specific activities that were classified, under colonial rule, as one religion were often mutually contradictory, with irreconcilable social and economic differences.

The idea of a unified religion was closely linked to legal codification. The contradictions and 'looseness' of Indian textual and customary judicial practices remained a source of anxiety for early colonial administrators, such that authoritative compilations that would not just represent, but rationalise and reconstruct Indian jurisprudence, were commissioned.[22] The early colonial jurist William MacNaghten appears representative of the administrators' interest when he states that his *Principles and precedents of Moohummudan law* was intended to 'fix' the many areas 'where a contrariety of opinion has hitherto prevailed' to allow a clear determination of the case at hand.[23]

[19] James C. Scott, *Seeing like a state: how certain schemes to improve the human condition have failed* (New Haven: Yale University Press, 1998), p. 82.
[20] Thomas Blom Hansen, *The saffron wave: democracy and Hindu nationalism in Modern India* (Princeton: Princeton University Press, 1999); Peter Van der Veer, *Imperial encounters: religion and modernity in India and Britain* (Princeton: Princeton University Press, 2001); see also Kaviraj in this volume.
[21] Ayesha Jalal, *Self and sovereignty: individual and community in South Asian Islam since c.1850s* (New York: Routledge, 2001); Faisal Devji, 'Apologetic modernity', *Modern Intellectual History* 4/1 (2007), 61–76.
[22] Jon Wilson, 'Anxieties of distance: codification in early colonial Bengal', *Modern Intellectual History* 4/1 (2007), 7–23.
[23] *Ibid.*, 18.

Not surprisingly, legal codification and homogenisation, important for the modern state's effective administration, was introduced in India by the British administration in a manner that was shot through with their own assumptions and perceptions. An interesting example in this context is the case of Muslim personal law. Sharia had been practised in India based on a diversified, subjective and localised interpretation.[24] Due to their anxieties as rulers and the precariousness of their rule, the East India Company and colonial administrators started a process of codification as early as the late eighteenth century. However, the very process of such codification meant that certain views were excluded and others highlighted, distortions magnified by the interests of the administration and lack of knowledge among the administrators.

Paradoxes of colonial secularism

In terms of an explicit policy regarding religious belief and practice, the colonial administration was concerned, particularly in the later half of the nineteenth century, with maintaining an official distance from religious identities that were seen as particularistic in the Indian context. Of course, the policy went through several reversals and modifications, as well as regional variations in how it was implemented.[25] However, even as secularism was broadly conceived of as a position of equal distance from the different religions, the very constitution of 'religion' was different from the administrator's own experience. The boundary-less and pervasive nature of practices and norms, alien and strange to the British sensibilities, demanded, nevertheless, some recognition. The resulting codification of religious laws, political constituencies and census activity meant first that religion emerged as a unified cohesive category of identification, and second that it attained a political prominence it had previously lacked. Much of this line of reasoning is familiar to scholars, particularly historians of South Asia, in the context of a rich collection of research on communalism and religious nationalism, particularly Hindutva. In the context of Islam, this literature is largely

---

[24] Mohammed Khalid Masud, Brinkley Messick and David Powers, *Islamic legal interpretation: muftis and their fatwas* (Cambridge, MA: Harvard University Press, 1996); Zaman, *Ulama in contemporary Islam*; Scott Alan Kugle, 'Framed, blamed and renamed: the recasting of Islamic jurisprudence in colonial South Asia', *Modern Asian Studies* 35/2 (2001), 257–313.

[25] While her research is focused primarily on education policies during colonial rule, Nandini Chatterjee, 'State, Christianity and the public sphere in India, 1830–1950', unpublished PhD thesis, University of Cambridge (2007), pp. 6–10, identifies four stages of what she calls the 'British religious policy'. See also Van der Veer, *Imperial encounters*, pp. 21–5, for some discussion of regional and temporal variations.

concerned with the demand for a separate Muslim homeland, Pakistan.[26] However, Islamism has not been analysed by embedding it in this context, nor have the insights generated in the study of communalism been carried over to think through Islamism.[27] My argument about the creation of Islamism in relationship to colonial secularism goes beyond the claim that the British introduced politicised religious identities in India to entrench their own rule; not because the British did no such thing – 'divide and rule' was a policy prescriptive,[28] and not just in India – but because colonialism was a variegated multidimensional relationship which resulted in many unplanned and unforeseen developments. I want to suggest that as a result of a multilayered, long-term and multidimensional interaction certain processes were set in motion that have resulted in Muslims, among others, having to define, rationalise and engage with aspects of their belief and practice in ways they did not need to before. Of the various responses generated, Islamism mirrors the key concerns of colonial secularism closely but by shifting the focus on Islam rather than Christianity.

Recent historical research[29] has shown that religious identity was one of the many identities in a hugely diverse India. Indeed, the idea of an integrated 'India' should be treated with some caution and it is useful to remind ourselves here that under the Mughals its population was only nominally unified under an empire, with different languages, ethnicities, princely states, castes, class positions and religious practices exerting competing pressures. For instance, Vasudha Narayanan[30] has

---

[26] Incidentally, Maududi had rejected the demand for Pakistan as a means of dividing Muslims. It was only after Pakistan became a reality that Maududi decided to acknowledge it. He moved to Pakistan after partition because he calculated that the chances of setting up an Islamic state would be higher there.

[27] In part this is a result of trajectories of western scholarship. 'Islam' has been studied primarily in the context of the Middle East while India/South Asia was conceived of as home primarily to the Hindus. The very presence of Islamism, and indeed Islam beyond India has led many to study it without embedding it in the South Asian context. Tribal boundaries around disciplinary specialisations may also have some role to play in this context.

[28] Francis Robinson, 'The British Empire and Muslim identity in South Asia', *Transactions of the Royal Historical Society* 6/8 (1998), 277.

[29] Barbara Metcalf, *Islamic contestations: essays on Muslims in India and Pakistan* (Delhi: Oxford University Press, 2004); Francis Robinson, 'Review: *Islamic revival in British India: Deoband, 1860–1900* by Barbara Daly Metcalf', *Modern Asian Studies* 18/2 (1984), 337–45; David Gilmartin and Bruce Lawrence (eds.), *Beyond Turk and Hindu: rethinking religious identities in Islamicate South Asia* (Gainesville: University Press of Florida, 2000); Bayly, *Empire and information*; Catherine Asher and Cynthia Talbot, *India before Europe* (Cambridge: Cambridge University Press, 2006).

[30] Vasudha Narayanan, 'Religious vocabulary and regional identity: a study of the Tamil *Cirappuranam*', in Gilmartin and Lawrence (eds.), *Beyond Turk and Hindu*.

shown in the context of South India that Muslim invaders from the North were distinguished, not through their religious beliefs, but on the basis of their ethnic origins – as Turks rather than Muslims. C. A. Bayly[31] is representative of the emerging consensus that 'pre-colonial social enquiry and representation were never communal in the sense that they saw India as a field of conflict of two irreconcilable faiths'.[32] This is not to imply that Indo-Muslim political practices or 'governing principles' were secular in that there was a conscious separation of religion and the state, but rather that they were 'a matter of indifference'.

Under colonial rule such identities were no longer matters of indifference. The colonial administration's stated policy of neutrality towards religious 'belief' was negated by an active practice of highlighting and utilising religious difference where it seemed beneficial to the interests of the East India Company and later the British Empire. This difference between the stated policy and actual practice created a tension that, at the very least, did not exist previously. Ayesha Jalal presents a rather understated case:

The colonial state's avowed policy of neutrality based on political indifference toward religion was easier to proclaim than translate into practice. As a moral stance, it clashed with the imperatives of ruling a culturally alien society. The British needed to appropriate existing symbols of cultural legitimacy, so for them religion could never be a matter of political indifference. Intrinsic to the search for collaborators and the organization of social control, religion was in the service of the colonial state's political purposes and thus had qualitatively different consequences from the political treatment of religion in the preceding centuries.[33]

Quite apart from a distinct equation of Christianity with modernity that I discuss later, the colonial administration made sometimes contradictory, often temporary, but nevertheless discernable shifts in its dealings

---

[31] Bayly, *Empire and information*.

[32] The term 'communal' has a particular history in South Asia. Its use by colonial administration and later application to present day tensions between Hindu and Muslim groups in India has led to a largely negative association with it. For an overview and critique of the term see Dilip Menon, 'An inner violence: why communalism in India is about caste', in T. N. Srinivas, *The future of secularism* (New Delhi: Oxford University Press, 2007). Ayesha Jalal, 'Negotiating colonial modernity and cultural difference: Indian Muslim conceptions of community and nation, 1878–1914', in Leila Tarazai Fawaz and C. A. Bayly (eds.), *Modernity and culture, from the Mediterranean to the Indian Ocean* (New York: Columbia University Press, 2002), p. 236, points out that the use of negatively associated communalism was important as a foil for the 'lauded sentiment' of nationalism.

[33] Jalal, 'Negotiating colonial modernity', p. 235.

with particular religious communities. After the rebellion ('mutiny' in British records) of 1857 against the increasing British imperial presence and under the nominal patronage of the last Mughal king, Bahadur Shah Zafar, Muslims were treated by the colonial administration as a potential threat. Such a view tended to gloss over the very real and deep divisions that existed between Muslims of different regions, classes and ethnicities, to highlight the threat posed by their putative allegiance to the same faith. Governor-General Mayo deputed W. W. Hunter to investigate the possibility of a religious duty binding Muslims to disloyalty to the British rule. Hunter's report *The Indian Musalmans*, published in 1871, denied such a link, but highlighted that there were 'fanatical' elements which, unless checked, would lead to greater uprising among the ignorant Muslims.[34] This report and the policies that flowed from it had an impact in shaping Muslim perceptions of their victimhood, as well as a separate community.[35]

A related and critical development was the shift from qualitative notions of dominance to quantitative ideas (see Kaviraj in this volume). Democracy and secularism are often intertwined in liberal theory. Yet the contradictory pressures that the notion of democracy exerts on identities and communities remain important – on the one hand, there are pressures to distinguish groups and, on the other, to expand membership within that group to be able to claim a majority. Moreover, the type of democracy that the colonial administration finally conceded to in the Indian context requires further analysis. David Washbrook[36] distinguishes between the 'representative' forms of government that the colonial state established to strengthen its own power and the 'democratic' forms that would have entailed transferring significant power to the elected representatives. These representative forms were designed to co-opt elites through engaging them in an advisory and administrative role rather than a policy-making and directional role.

---

[34] *Ibid.*, p. 237 (quotation). The similarities and continuities of this position with the current US regime are made all the more striking for the century and half that separates them. See Mahmood Mamdani, *Good Muslim bad Muslim: America, the Cold War, and the roots of terror* (New York: Pantheon/Random House, 2004) for an analysis that speaks of similar arguments in the current context. In particular, it is interesting to note the gullibility associated with the 'ignorant' average Muslim at the hands of the 'fanatics'.

[35] Amir Mufti, 'Secularism and minority: elements of a critique', *Social Text* 45 (1995), 75–96; Farzana Shaikh, *Community and consensus in Islam: Muslim representation in colonial India, 1860–1947* (Cambridge: Cambridge University Press, 1989).

[36] David Washbrook, 'The rhetoric of democracy and development in late colonial India', in S. Bose and A. Jalal (eds.), *Nationalism, democracy and development: state and politics in India* (Delhi: Oxford University Press, 1998).

David Gilmartin[37] has argued persuasively that we need to analyse the very structure and concept of elections, understood to be the vehicles of democracy, as introduced under colonial rule, to understand the formation of Muslim identity and nationhood in modern South Asia. Rather than a non-problematic structure for the expression of popular views, elections called forth 'a distinctive pattern of community rhetoric – a pattern whose analysis . . . gives new insight into the relationship between religion and nationalism'.[38] The introduction of the Minto-Morley reforms in 1909 that instituted the principle of separate electorates to Muslims at all levels of representation can be seen not as the culmination of a process that started in 1880 with the introduction of religion-based electorates in municipal elections, but one more step in a rather long process of defining political communities along religious lines. Once started, the process created an impetus for individuals and groups to sharply define their allegiances, practices and beliefs, at the same time as claiming members from different parts of India. Existing in a twilight zone between the two starkly defined identities of Muslim and Hindu was no longer possible for those who had previously done so.[39] Their identity had to be defined, enumerated and rationalised.

Critically, the norms associated with their lives in Britain became the standards through which religious belief and practice, and their relationship to modernity were measured by the colonial administrators. There was a distinctly religious aspect to modernity as it was presented to Indians during the colonial rule and through establishment-supported missionary activity; the Christian way of being was presented as the modern way of being.[40] Moreover, the colonial administration's policy proclamations regarding secularism aside, the rhetoric of civilising missions was not inaccessible to the literate Indian population; they could

---

[37] David Gilmartin, 'A magnificent gift: Muslim nationalism and the election process in colonial Punjab', *Comparative Studies in Society and History* 40/3 (1998), 415–36.

[38] *Ibid.*, 416–17.

[39] For instance, Mohammed Khalid Masud (ed.), *Travellers in faith: studies of the Tablighi Jama'at as a transnational Islamic movement for faith renewal* (Leiden: Brill, 2000), p. xxxiv, documents the combination of Hindu and Muslim practices, ideas and celebrations among the Meos of Delhi right up to the twentieth century. On p. xxxv he contends that use of both Hindu and Muslim names for individuals was quite common amongst North Indian communities in Awadh, Balgaram, Kashmir, Sind and Bengal.

[40] Peter Van der Veer, 'The moral state: religion, nation and empire in Victorian Britain and British India', in P. Van der Veer and H. Lehmann (eds.), *Nation and religion: perspectives on Europe and Asia* (Princeton: Princeton University Press, 1999), p. 39; 'Secrecy and publicity in the South Asian public arena', in Armando Salvatore and Dale Eickelman (eds.), *Public Islam and the common good* (Leiden: Brill, 2004); and *Imperial encounters*.

not fail to grasp at least intuitively the contradictions inherent in this policy, nor the thinly veiled contempt towards their own practices and beliefs. The colonial administration's support for missionary activity in India has received some scholarly attention recently.[41] Many of the groups collectively associated with religious fundamentalism in South Asia today, such as the Arya Samaj (Hindu), and Jamaat-e-Islami and Tablighi Jamaat (Muslim), not only started in direct response to the activities of the Christian missionary groups but also adapted many of their techniques and operational strategies.[42] The key difference was that these newly founded Hindu and Muslim groups focused primarily on their co-religionists with the idea of reintroducing a true religion to them, and bringing them back to a purified mode of practice and belief.[43] Certainly, Jamaat-e-Islami, founded in the last years of colonial rule in India, was originally conceived of as a *dawa* or proselytising organisation by Maududi, but organised on the lines of a Leninist party.[44]

A central tension within the colonial administration's policy of secularism was that even as local religions were proclaimed parochial and particularistic, the traditions of Christianity informing its reading of secularism were raised to the pedestal of universal values. That British and European secularism was the result of a particular historical trajectory, in which a structured, hierarchical church conceded its control over property and society only after a protracted, often violent struggle with the emerging modern state,[45] did not seem to distract the colonial

---

[41] Masud (ed.), *Travellers in faith*; Lata Mani, *Contentious traditions: the debate on sati in colonial India* (Berkeley: University of California Press, 1998).

[42] *Ibid.*, pp. xlvi–lvi; Barbara Metcalf, *Islamic revival in British India: Deoband 1860–1900* (Princeton: Princeton University Press, 1982); Van der Veer, *Imperial encounters*.

[43] The contemporaneous impact of non-European influences such as Wahabism on the revitalising and rethinking of many Islamic practices was also significant and led to considerable rethinking among the Muslims of North India. The Wahabi movement was a movement of puritanical revivalism that originated in present-day Saudi Arabia. In India, a significant response was mounted by the Barelvi *ulama* to the Wahabi challenge. Barelvis are associated with more popular practices of saint worship, religious festivals and rituals. As a result of their resistance, the term Wahabi continues to carry substantial negative connotations, and in contemporary Pakistan, Wahabis tend to refer to themselves as Ahl-e-Hadith. See Metcalf, *Islamic revival*, for a detailed analysis of the Ahl-e-Hadith reformism in North India.

[44] S. V. R Nasr, *The vanguard of the Islamic revolution: the Jama'at-I-Islami of Pakistan* (Berkeley: University of California Press, 1994) and also his *Mawdudi and the making of Islamic revivalism* (New York: Oxford University Press, 1996); Masud, *Travellers*; Humeira Iqtidar, 'Jama'at-e-Islami Pakistan: learning from the left', in Naveeda Khan (ed.), *Crisis and beyond: Pakistan in the 20th century* (Delhi: Routledge, 2010).

[45] Armando Salvatore, 'The Euro-Islamic roots of secularity: a difficult equation', *Asian Journal of Social Science* 33/3 (2005), 412–37.

administration from imposing its notions of 'religion' and 'secularism' in a very different context. It is this rendering of all other religions as particularistic that made it difficult for them to aspire to the secular-universal. David Gilmartin[46] has quite correctly pointed out that 'the meaning of "public" has to be understood in the Indian colonial politics not primarily in contrast to the "private" but to the "particular"'.

This tension is particularly apparent in the legal and juridical norms that the British established in colonial India. At the initial stages of colonial rule they assumed that all Indians acted out of 'inherent religiosity and orthodoxy, so the codes of religious law were sufficient to adjudicate in all their crises'.[47] At the same time they attributed to their own legal traditions the 'principles of universal jurisprudence'.[48] This provided the backdrop to the persistent attempts at the codification of Islamic laws, binding their practice through the use of precedents and increasingly limiting their application to the point that in the early twentieth century Islamic law could rightly be termed static and out of date. Thus, in the process of codification, what was a dynamic and variegated practice was stunted so that it was of little use in contemporary life.[49] Meanwhile, public matters, and those of universal application, were to be adjudicated by laws of an English provenance.[50] It is this very

[46] David Gilmartin, 'Democracy, nationalism and the public: a speculation on colonial Muslim politics', *South Asia* 14/1 (1991), 125.

[47] Kugle, 'Framed, blamed', 270.   [48] *Ibid.*, 281.

[49] Kugle, 'Framed, blamed', 258 fn. 3, is worth quoting here in detail: 'The shariah is a notoriously difficult concept to define. In broadest terms, the shariah is the accepted custom of the Muslim community in doctrinal belief, ritual action, commercial transaction and criminal punishment. More technically, the shariah consists of a network of decisions by jurists on whether a specific action is obligatory, recommended, permissible, discouraged or forbidden when compared against the known sources of revelation. As such, the shariah is a wide umbrella of moral sanctions, covering other theoretical possibilities as well as practical exigencies. The shariah embraces contradictory juridical decisions and a multiplicity of juridical methods, insisting only that they be based on certain authentic sources and reasoned deduction. This crucial element of flexibility and multiplicity is often lost when the term shariah is translated as "the law of Islam" or even "Islamic law". Rather, shariah is a broad set of customs authenticated and sanctified by legal decisions. The principles and institutions of legal specialists, who make such decisions generally know as *fiqh*, should be understood as "Islamic law."'

[50] See also David Skuy, 'Macaulay and the English penal code of 1862: the myth of inherent superiority and modernity of the English legal system compared to India's legal system in the nineteenth century', *Modern Asian Studies* 32/3 (1998), 513–57. Skuy argues that while most historians have assumed that Indian law was primitive compared to British law, this simply is not the case. English legal system was no more 'modern' than the Indian one. In fact, struggles to modernise the legal system in England were more easily realised in India, illustrating that 'imperial powers were often able to do in their colonies what they were unable to do at home' (514). I am grateful to Justin Jones and Eleanor Newbigin for suggesting these works by Kugle and Skuy.

claim to universalism made by colonial secularism, embedded in legal practices, cultural norms and political structures, that Maududi and the Islamists destabilised by their insistence on the universalism of Islamic laws. In a mirrored reversal they claimed the compatibility of Islamic cultural norms, legal practices and political concepts with the modern state and its effective running.

Muslim responses to colonial secularism

Our understanding of the origins of Islamism in North India would be incomplete without understanding the range and diversity of options being discussed by North Indian Muslims. The multifaceted interaction with a new way of conceptualising religion and its relationship with the political and public spheres led to a plethora of responses from the Muslims of India. I hesitate to use the term Muslim community, lest I give the impression of a coherent, internally unified group. Indeed, the huge variety of responses from Muslims is not surprising if we keep this diversity in their social positions, educational backgrounds, regional affiliations and cultural trajectories in mind. From Syed Ahmed's emphasis on modern education to the Nadwa *ulama*'s insistence on a stronger base in Islamic education before allowing modern education to 'corrupt' young minds, from the Indian nationalism and 'secularism' of the traditionally trained *alim* Maulana Azad to the religious nationalism of the uncommonly westernised Mohammed Ali Jinnah, from the political opportunism of Punjabi feudal lords to the pan-Islamism of Mohammed Iqbal (Pakistan's national poet), the variety of ways in which Muslims responded to the changes brought upon by new legal, political, social and economic changes under colonial rule makes sense only if we recognise this internal diversity within the Muslim 'community'.

While Muslims formed a diverse and internally fractured group[51] at the start of colonial rule, the very homogenising impulse of the modern state structure operative during British rule facilitated an emergent imagery of Muslim community and nationhood that gained momentum during the early years of the twentieth century. In particular, the shift from a qualitative notion of dominance to a quantitative notion of minority and majority (Kaviraj in this volume) was critical in underpinning a new political imaginary. Academic writings of the late 1980s and

[51] Jalal, *Self and sovereignty*, highlights the controversies surrounding Ahmedi Muslims to bring out precisely this lack of internal cohesion that is often glossed over in discussions about Muslims.

1990s[52] that focused on Muslim nationalism leading to the formation of Pakistan convey the reluctance with which the Muslims of North India rose to appropriate a collective identity; there is a sense of having exhausted other options, of being pushed into a corner. In his article, Amir Mufti brings to the fore a particularly difficult dilemma faced by the Muslims of North India by juxtaposing their situation with the 'Jewish Question' in Germany. He suggests that, '"German Jew" and "Indian Muslim" are names not merely of social groups but of entire cultural and political problematics and trajectories; names, furthermore, of the respective torments of European and Indian modernity.'[53] Mufti traces the formation of the Muslim subject in colonial sociology as primitive/religious/anti-modern, and connects it to the crisis of representation within Indian nationalism, where the nationalist claim for the existence of a singular Indian nation seeks to accord the 'Muslim' the role of the national minority. Thus, Mufti claims,[54] it asks the Muslim to explain himself, and the question is experienced as a trap: 'If "Muslim outright" then how can he be an Indian in the modern sense? And if "no Muslim" at all, then why not a "bare and blank" citizen?' Thus, if nothing else, this body of writings from the late 1980s onwards that I mentioned above sensitises us to the dilemma faced by Muslims in first recognising themselves as a group and then defining a relationship between their beliefs, practices and the state.

Islamists as modernists

Islamism is a particularly modernist way of defining this relationship between belief and the state. Islamism's focus on the state is generally understood to be the result of an internal compulsion within Islam. This has been a result of taking at face value the Islamist's claim that in Islam there is no distinction between religion and state. The vast majority of Muslim opponents of the Jamaat-e-Islami have tended to prove the contrary through recourse to Quranic texts and Hadith (sayings of the prophet). Irfan Ahmed[55] rightly points out that both the western academics (Ernest Gellner, Bernard Lewis, Myron Weiner, etc.) and Muslim critics of Maududi's focus on the state rely on theological arguments to explain or criticise Islamism. Quite clearly though,

---

[52] Ayesha Jalal, *The sole spokesman: Jinnah, the Muslim League, and the demand for Pakistan* (Cambridge: Cambridge University Press, 1985); David Gilmartin, *Empire and Islam: Punjab and the making of Pakistan* (London: Tauris, 1988); Mufti, 'Secularism'; Shaikh, *Community*.
[53] Mufti, 'Secularism and minority', 85.   [54] *Ibid.*
[55] Irfan Ahmed, 'The state In Islamist thought', *ISIM Review* 18 (2006), 12–13.

the centrality of the state in Islamist thought is a result not of a theological compulsion within Islam, but due to the historical context in
which Islamism was founded.

Formation of Islamist groups like Jamaat-e-Islami is part of the multifaceted response generated as a consequence of the 'colonial encounter'.
The response, alluded to above, was not limited to Islamism, but
included a variety of positions taken up by different, and sometimes
even the same, Muslims, including those of Indian nationalism, communal nationalism, pietism and socialism. That these various responses
should operate in an intersubjective, dialectical manner, refining and
redefining their positions based on the interaction with others, should
therefore come as no surprise. Maududi himself went from espousing
secular nationalism to religious nationalism, and then radical organisation.[56] He operated in a period that was particularly thick with debate
and discussion. His interaction with socialists (particularly the Khairi
brothers in Delhi), mostly nationalist traditionalists such as Jamiat-
ulema-e-Hind, and communal political forces in Hyderabad constituted
a context in which he was able to articulate a particular vision of political
engagement. It was in part a result of these influences and the context
of his involvement that the structure of Maududi's ideology is radically
different from the traditionalist *ulama*, and the organisation of his party
is based on the modernist notions of the Leninist party. His conception
of history is very much a modernist one and the JI was formulated as
a 'vanguard' party primarily to engage in the project of modernity.
My argument here, however, goes beyond Maududi to highlight the fact
that Maududi's ideas gained popularity precisely because of the context
in which they found resonance within a certain segment of Muslims of
North India: those who were determined to be part of the project
of becoming 'modern', of running a modern state, but without letting
go of their 'Muslimness' in the public arena.

The traditionalists claim[57] that in his attempt to provide logical
reasons for following Islam, and in his engagement with the modern
state, Maududi and the Islamists despiritualised Islam. They claim that
rather than Islamising politics, he politicised Islam. At the heart of
Maududi's endeavour was an effort to present Islam as a rational religion
that was not outdated as the 'naturalists' (or *nechari* in Urdu) claimed it

[56] Nasr, *Mawdudi*.
[57] Cook, *Commanding right;* Seyyid Hossen Nasr, *Islam and the plight of the modern man* (London: Longman, 1975); Taqi Usmani, *Hakeem ul Ummat kay Siyasi Afkar* [Political Thoughts of Maulana Ashraf Ali Thanvi – text in Urdu] (Maktaba al-Ashrafiya, n.d.); For a quick overview, see also Timothy Winter, 'Understanding the Four Madhabs', n.d. web article available at www.masud.co.uk/Islam/ahm/madhab.html

to be.[58] In attempting to rebut the secularist *necharis*, Maududi never-theless had to take on the structure of their arguments and their think-ing, and to thus reproduce it to some extent. He made an explicit effort to decrease the role of spirituality and miracle in South Asian Islam and was vehemently opposed to various customary and ritualistic practices. These included saint worship, visits to cemeteries to pray for the deceased, and extended social ceremonies surrounding life-cycle events such as marriage, death and birth. A key element of Maududi's innov-ations was his opposition to the role of the *ulama*.

In this sense Islamism was an innovation, a break from the past. At the same time, the innovation took place by creatively reworking ideas and practices within an existing repertoire. The oppositional stances of Islamists and traditionalists should not blind us to the fact that Maududi built on a reformist tradition in South Asian Islam that spanned a range of movements, from Syed Ahmed Barelvi's to changes within sufi *tariqat* among the *pirs* in Sind, the Chishtiya in Punjab and the Naqshbandiya in Delhi, as well as Wahabism.[59] Reform movements in the late pre-colonial and early colonial period were concerned not so much with the European presence but with the decay in social and political life within Mughal India. These attempts at reform included movements of polit-ical change and social renewal as well as the establishment of institutions like the Farangi Mahal School. The Farangi Mahal aimed to systematise scholarship in Islamic texts, through the Dars-e-Nizami, but also to provide registrars, judges and revenue agents for the Mughal and other courts. In the nineteenth century, the madrasa at Deoband, with which Maududi and Jamaat-e-Islami are sometimes mistakenly linked, drew upon the achievements of the Farangi Mahal and further standardised the study of Islamic texts.

Maududi's approach to religion and its practice then translated into innovations at various levels, while building upon earlier vocabularies and 'traditions'. The key innovation, though, was at the level of political engagement. Maududi's vision of worship inverted the emphasis on personal piety and made political engagement central to religious prac-tice. In this he not only responded to the intrusive nature of the modern state, but also drew upon the leftist notion of a 'vanguard' party

---

[58] Syed Abul A'ala Maududi, *Jihad kiya hai?* [What is jihad?] (n.d,n.p); *Musalman aur maujooda siyasi kashmakash* [Muslims and the current political struggle] (Pathankot: Maktaba Jama'at-e-Islami, 1937, 1942); *Islam ka nazariya siyasi* [The political view of Islam] (Lahore: Manshoorat, 2000). Texts all in Urdu.

[59] Metcalf, 'Islamic contestations'; Robinson, 'Islamic revival'.

transforming the state. Moreover, he inverted the British/Christian claim to universalism by claiming the same privilege for Indian/Muslim. Thus his notion of an Islamic state duplicated, assimilated and modified western political concepts, structures and operations, producing a theory of statecraft that, according to one influential commentator, 'save for its name and its use of Islamic terms and symbols, showed little indigenous influence'.[60] Paradoxically, this is a source of comfort for some like Roxanne Euben,[61] who argue that precisely because Islamist political thought 'betrays a Western influence inconsistent with the stated attempt to cleanse an Islamic concept of foreign corruption' it renders arguments of incommensurability implausible.

Conclusion

My intention here has been to destabilise the automatic assumption of incompatibility and negation between secularism and Islamism by showing that Islamism is creatively linked to the secularism that formed the context and impetus for its origins. The emergence of Islam as a unified category of analysis and belonging, an engagement with modernity as a project, the impetus created by an intrusive and seemingly all-encompassing modern state, a notion of secularism that attributed universality to its own unself-conscious traditions and particularity to others, created a context which generated the innovation in Muslim thought and practice that is Islamism. Of the various responses possible and produced, Islamism replicates these concerns most closely by inverting them in an Islamic idiom through its focus on the state, its conception of Islam as a cohesive system that is central to political life and its aspirations to universal application.

Islamism has, since these early years, gone through several important changes driven both by local trajectories and global imperatives. Elsewhere, I have looked at the impact of leftist mobilisations on the organisation and strategies of Islamists in Pakistan during the 1960s–70s, as well as the long-term impact of Islamist mobilisations in contemporary Pakistan.[62] My intention here has been to recognise the close relationship between secularism and Islamism. This in turn allows us to be wary of ideologising secularism by reminding ourselves,

[60] Nasr, *Mawdudi*, p. 90.
[61] Roxanne Euben, 'Premodern, antimodern or postmodern? Islamic and western critiques of modernity', *The Review of Politics* 59/3 (1997), 429–59, here, 165.
[62] Humeira Iqtidar, *Secularising Islamists? Jamaat-e-Islami and Jamaat-ud-Dawa in Pakistan* (Chicago: University of Chicago Press, 2011).

as Masud does, that these processes work in a dialectical manner, '[T]hese discourses on secularism also suggest that the more secularism and Islam are ideologized, the more difficult it is to speak of change and reform.'[63]

The western European experience, albeit one with much variation internally (see various contributions to this volume, in particular Klausen), has been idealised to produce an image of secularisation and secularism working in tandem. Elsewhere I have looked at the theoretical problems with this assumed relationship between secularism and secularisation.[64] In the case of colonial India, the universal pretensions of official secularism were instrumental in codifying and highlighting as particularistic local religious affiliations, and paradoxically also giving them salience through the attribution of authenticity to religion in the political sphere. Ultimately, this defeated any potential for secularisation, particularly in terms of relegating religion to the private sphere. I have focused here on two key components of colonial secularism that I believe were critical in supporting the rise of Islamism. The first is the structural vehicle of this secularism: the modern state that was engaged in an ontological remapping of the population as part of the practice of modern statecraft. The second is the substantive aspects of this policy that I suggest allowed only particularistic attachment to Muslim practices, attaching universalism to those modes of belief and behaviour that seemed secular to the colonial administrators but particularly Christian to others. The specific modalities of colonial secularism created real difficulties for the large majority of Muslims to own the notion precisely because of the codification of a Muslim particularistic identity that could not aspire to identification with the universalist secularism without letting go of its 'Muslimness' completely. The real relationship of incompatibility, then, was between colonial secularism and secularisation among Indian Muslims.

---

[63] Mohammed Khalid Masud, 'The construction and deconstruction of secularism as an ideology in contemporary Muslim thought', *Asian Journal of Social Science* 33/3 (2005), 363–83.
[64] Iqtidar, *Secularising Islamists?*

12   The 1960s

Hugh McLeod

Historians of the future may come to rank the 1960s alongside the 1520s and the 1790s among the great revolutionary decades of Europe's religious history. Indeed, the religious significance of the 1960s is even wider, since equally radical changes were taking place in North America and Australasia. And the atmosphere of the 1960s also had much in common with that of those other revolutionary decades. History moved faster during these years, and a dynamic of change built up which old institutions and traditions were powerless to withstand. For some people, a new era of apparently limitless possibilities was opening up. As in many other periods, the rebels and nonconformists had an influence out of proportion to their numbers. However, this was also a period of profound yet unspectacular social changes. In focussing on flamboyant manifestations of the counter-culture or the most trenchant forms of political radicalism, there is a danger of overlooking more mundane developments which were changing the lives even of the conventional majority.[1]

I

The importance of the 1960s in the religious evolution of the western world is widely recognised and there is a growing body of historical and sociological literature describing and explaining the changes in that period.[2] There is also considerable agreement as to the main directions of change at that time, in spite of significant differences of emphasis. But there is no consensus at all as to the causes of change. For instance, those historians who focus principally on events within the church, such

---

[1] For development of these arguments, see Hugh McLeod, *The religious crisis of the 1960s* (Oxford: Oxford University Press, 2007), and 'Why were the 1960s so religiously explosive?' *Nederlands Theologisch Tijdschrift* 60 (2006), 109–30.

[2] See McLeod, *Crisis*, and Patrick Pasture, 'Christendom and the legacy of the sixties: between the secular city and the age of Aquarius', *Revue d'histoire ecclésiastique* 99 (2004), 82–117.

as the Second Vatican Council (Vatican II) or the impact of such books as John Robinson's *Honest to God* are divided between those who think reform in the 1960s went too far and too fast and those who think it did not go far enough.[3] Historians who focus mainly on the impact of social and political change on religion are divided between, for instance, those like Callum Brown who see the key changes as taking place in the areas of gender and sexuality, those, like the French sociologist Henri Mendras, who dwell mainly on changes in the economy and social structure, and those, like Denis Pelletier, who emphasise the political context and especially the impact of 1968.[4] One thing that many writers in this field share, in spite of their differences, is the search for a master-factor to explain changes that are both momentous and mysterious. This search is mistaken. The 1960s were religiously explosive not because of one key ingredient, but because so many currents of change, initially separate, interacted with one another. Most important was the impact of affluence, because the changing economic climate affected so many other areas of people's lives and opened up new possibilities. However, this affluence is not a sufficient explanation of what happened in the decade. At least five other factors made an essential contribution to the story. There was the decline from the later 1950s of the ideologically based subcultures which had been central to life in many parts of Europe since the later nineteenth century; there was the theological radicalisation beginning in the early 1960s; there was the 'sexual revolution' gathering pace from the mid 1960s; there was the political radicalisation of the mid and later 1960s, stimulated above all by opposition to the Vietnam War; there was women's search for greater freedom, self-fulfilment and independence.

Historians of this period also differ in their chronologies. One fundamental division is between those, such as Alan Gilbert, who see the 1960s as the culmination of long processes of change over several decades or even centuries, and those, like Callum Brown and Peter van Rooden, who emphasise the suddenness of change in the early 1960s and the degree to which that decade was a reaction against, rather

---

[3] Compare Gérard Cholvy and Yves-Marie Hilaire, *Histoire religieuse de la France contemporaine, 1930–1988* (Toulouse: Privat, 1988), with Andrew Greeley, *The Catholic revolution: new wine, old wineskins and the Second Vatican Council* (Berkeley: University of California Press, 2004).

[4] Callum Brown, *The death of Christian Britain* (London: Routledge, 2001), and *Religion and society in twentieth-century Britain* (Harlow: Pearson, 2006); Henri Mendras, *La seconde révolution française* (Paris: Gallimard, 1990); Denis Pelletier, *La crise catholique: religion, société et politique en France, 1965–1978* (Paris: Payot, 2002).

than a continuation of, trends in the decades preceding.[5] Neither the 'evolutionary' nor the 'revolutionary' approach to religious change in the 1960s is entirely satisfactory. The 1960s were indeed a time when history moved faster and the former approach, as well as being excessively teleological, tends to gloss over the specificity of particular periods. On the other hand, the latter approach underestimates the extent to which the ground for spectacular changes in the 1960s was prepared by changes, often less highly visible, in earlier decades. In understanding both the nature and the pace of change in the 1960s, we need a chronology that operates at three different levels. First, there are long-term preconditions, including, for instance, the legacy of the Enlightenment, of the French Revolution and of changes in thinking about sexuality that were developing in western societies since the later nineteenth century. Second, there are short-term triggers, including most notably the impact of increasing affluence from the mid 1950s. Third, there is the impact of specific events and movements, including most notably the American civil rights movement, the Vietnam War and Vatican II.

The religious situation in western Europe in the later 1950s was highly variegated. Except in the Netherlands, the overwhelming majority of the population belonged at least nominally to one of the Christian churches, and most children were receiving some kind of religious upbringing, whether directly through parental teaching, by being sent to Sunday school or catechism classes, or through day school. Christian Democratic or other confessional parties habitually received 40–50 per cent of the votes in large parts of continental Europe, and even in countries where politics was apparently more secular, politicians commonly referred to the fact that they were living in a 'Christian country' and that the laws should reflect that fact. In fact in the years after World War II the churches were enjoying enhanced prestige and a modest increase in churchgoing, partly in reaction to Nazi 'paganism' and Soviet atheism, and partly because of a desire to return to 'normal' after the horrors of World War II. Christianity had also been enjoying an intellectual revival,[6] and in some countries, such as Britain, students were the most religiously active sections of the population.[7] However, levels of active religious involvement varied hugely, both between countries and

[5] Alan D. Gilbert, *The making of post-Christian Britain: a history of the secularisation of modern society* (London: Longman, 1980); Brown, *Death*; Peter van Rooden, 'Oral history and the strange demise of Dutch Christianity', www.xs4all.nl/~pvrooden/Peter/publicaties/oral%20history.htm
[6] Adrian Hastings, *A history of English Christianity, 1920–2000* (London: SCM, 2001), pp. 288–301, 491–504; Cholvy and Hilaire, *France*, pp. 24–9.
[7] McLeod, *Crisis*, pp. 37–8.

between regions of the same country. The widest differences were seen in France, where regular attendance at mass ranged from over 90 per cent in parts of Brittany to less than 5 per cent in the Limousin. While a lot of the older literature made exaggerated claims for the extent of secularisation, 'revisionists', such as Callum Brown and Olaf Blaschke,[8] have gone too far in the opposite direction. It is the uneasy balance between the strength of religion and the secularising forces that needs to be stressed. Three long-standing 'problem areas' for the churches may be mentioned. First, there was the intertwining of religion and politics: the identification of most of the churches with political conservatism clearly strengthened their links with certain sections of the population, but it alienated others. Second, there was the question of class: partly for these political reasons and partly for other reasons, the working class in many parts of Europe was largely detached from the church. Third, there was sex. This was the area of Christian ethics where practice differed most widely from theory.

In retrospect, the 1950s have been seen by some as a period of prosperity and relative calm for the churches, and by others as a period of stifling complacency and conformism. Yet it was also a time of new problems which would be fully confronted in the 1960s, and of new beginnings which would take full shape in the years following. For many Catholic bishops the biggest problem was the decline in vocations.[9] For many Catholic intellectuals and students the biggest problem was their bishops. In the Netherlands, Catholic intellectuals were increasingly critical of the system of 'pillarisation' in their country and of the authoritarian style of episcopal leadership, including instructions on how to vote. In France the Algerian war led to a major confrontation in 1957 between the strongly pro-nationalist Catholic students' movement and the bishops, who were tending to sit on the fence.[10] In Britain two pointers to the 1960s were the Wolfenden Report of 1957, which recommended the legalisation of homosexual acts 'between consenting adults in private', and the formation in the same year of a theological discussion group in Cambridge[11] out of which much of the more radical Anglican theology of the 1960s would grow.

[8] Olaf Blaschke (ed.), *Konfessionen im Konflikt: Deutschland zwischen 1800 und 1970: ein zweites konfessionelles Zeitalter* (Göttingen: Vandenhoeck und Ruprecht, 2001).
[9] Wilhelm Damberg, *Abschied vom Milieu? Katholizismus im Bistum Münster und in den Niederlanden 1945–1980* (Paderborn: Schöningh, 1997), pp. 184–91.
[10] Cholvy and Hilaire, *France*, pp. 254–5; John A. Coleman, *The evolution of Dutch Catholicism* (Berkeley: University of California Press, 1978), pp. 48–57.
[11] Keith W. Clements, *Lovers of discord: twentieth-century theological controversies in England* (London: SPCK, 1988), pp. 143–77.

The late 1950s and early 1960s were a time of questioning, in which some of the ideas and movements and trends that would be characteristic of the years following began to be seen and heard. The 'Christendom' of the post-war years was still intact, but it was being undermined by satirists who laughed at all established institutions; by church reformers critical of the power of the clergy and the ecclesiastical hierarchy; and by taboo-breakers determined to speak the unspeakable. Perhaps the most notable example of the latter was Rolf Hochhuth's play *Der Stellvertreter* (The representative), first performed in West Berlin in February 1963. At a time when the prestige of the Catholic Church was high, and Catholics were still congratulating themselves on their creditable role during the Nazi period, Hochhuth was the first influential writer to accuse Pope Pius XII of 'silence' in the face of Nazi crimes. The play acted as a catalyst for criticism of the record of the churches more generally during the Third Reich, which in turn fed into criticism of their continuing authority in contemporary Germany.[12] In Britain the new mood was represented by the satire movement, at its peak between 1960 and 1963, and embodied most influentially in the magazine *Private Eye* and the TV programme *That was the week that was*. The monarchy, the military, the empire, politicians and national icons such as Winston Churchill were all among the targets – as were the Church of England and the Roman Catholic Church.[13]

The pace of change increased in the course of the decade. To appreciate the atmosphere of the time we need to note not only the broad social trends, but also the changing mood of these years and the impact of specific events. The cautious openness to change, which characterised the 'early' sixties between about 1958 and 1962, evolved into the optimistic reformism of the 'mid' sixties between about 1963 and 1966, and finally the apocalyptic and polarised atmosphere of the 'late' sixties between about 1967 and 1974. There was a palpable change in the religious atmosphere in the course of the 'long sixties', to borrow a phrase from Arthur Marwick,[14] who defines it as the period between about 1958 and 1974. Broadly speaking, one can distinguish between the religious 'ferment' of the early and mid sixties and the religious 'crisis' of the late sixties. In the first half of the decade church attendance was falling, at least in England, France, West Germany and

---

[12] Dennis L. Bark and David R. Gress, *Democracy and its discontents*, 2 vols. (Oxford: Blackwell, 1989), vol. II, pp. 73–4.

[13] See Humphrey Carpenter, *That was satire that was* (London: Gollancz 2000).

[14] Arthur Marwick, *The sixties: cultural revolution in Britain, France, Italy and the United States, c.1958–1974* (Oxford: Oxford University Press, 1998).

the United States,[15] but there was widespread hope that the churches were responding effectively to these challenges through church reforms, new theologies and pastoral innovations. The biggest factors were Vatican II and the immense popularity of Pope John XXIII. Also important were new developments in Protestant theology, popularised by such best-selling writers as John Robinson and Harvey Cox, and the successes of the American civil rights movement, where the influence and prestige of Martin Luther King reached a peak in 1964–5. Nor should one ignore the impact of ambitious building projects, such as the completion of magnificent new cathedrals, Anglican and Catholic respectively, in Coventry and Liverpool. And in spite of some disturbing statistics, there were others which gave grounds for optimism. For instance, the Church of England enjoyed a boom in ordinations, peaking in 1963, when the number was higher than at any time since before World War I. By 1967 and 1968, however, the scale of the crisis faced by the Christian churches was clear. By now the decline in religious practice was more rapid, it was affecting Catholics as much as Protestants, and nearly every western country was affected. Indeed, the biggest drops in churchgoing were taking place in areas previously noted for their staunch Catholicism, such as the southern Netherlands, Flanders or Quebec. Most churches were suffering a decline in the numbers of ordinands and, in the case of the Roman Catholic Church, the problem was exacerbated by mass movements of resignations by priests and nuns. Meanwhile, a wide range of alternative faiths were becoming more readily accessible, ranging from the newly fashionable 'eastern' religions to the political faiths of Marxism, anarchism and feminism.

In these years, distancing from the church was a mass phenomenon across the western world. Yet it was not an organised movement, comparable to the movements of mass exit from the churches orchestrated first by the Social Democrats and later by the Communists and Nazis in Germany, and it happened in different ways and for many, often quite different, reasons. For instance, there was a 'coming out' by those who had never had any Christian commitment but in the atmosphere of the 1960s felt free to declare their atheism or agnosticism. This was probably a significant factor in the decline in infant baptisms, which in England was already underway in the 1950s: especially in the larger cities and in

[15] Brown, *Death*, p. 188; Yves-Marie Hilaire, 'La sociologie religieuse du catholicisme français au vingtième siècle', in Kay Chadwick (ed.), *Catholicism, politics and society in twentieth-century France* (Liverpool: Liverpool University Press, 2000), pp. 255–6; Damberg, *Milieu*, pp. 417–21; Dean Hoge, *Commitment on campus* (Philadelphia: Westminster, 1974), pp. 165–6. See also Dean Hoge and David Roozen, *Understanding church growth and decline 1950–78* (New York: Pilgrim Press, 1979).

other areas with a mobile population,[16] there was less social pressure on agnostics or those uninterested in religion to conform. There was also a 'dropping out' by those who made no conscious decision to leave the church, but who found that changing patterns of family life or new leisure opportunities were leaving less time for religious activities. Then one can speak of a distancing from the institution of those who remained Christians but chose to practise their Christianity in other ways – often through political activism. There was also disillusion or loss of faith by those, including many political activists, who rejected Christianity, pinning their hopes on more secular routes to salvation. And there were those who never made the transition from attendance at Sunday school in childhood and membership of church youth organisations in early adolescence to adult churchgoing. The relative importance of these different patterns of disengagement from the church probably varied from country to country. In England this last group of those who did not so much 'leave' the church as never join it may have been particularly numerous. For instance, between 1956 and 1973, though Anglican communicants as a percentage of adult population declined by a third, confirmations in relation to the teenage population declined by more than half. Particularly revealing are the statistics of Methodist membership, which break down the factors contributing to growth and decline in each year. Between 1960 and 1970 there was a 14 per cent decline in British Methodism, which was overwhelmingly due to a crisis of recruitment. The number of Methodists who resigned during the 1960s was only slightly higher than the number doing so in the 1950s; but the number of new members had dropped by 30 per cent.[17] In England churchgoing was already relatively low, but in countries or regions where churchgoing had been high, the drop in this period was steeper. In the Netherlands 64 per cent of Catholics attended mass on an average Sunday in 1965, but by 1975 this had fallen to 31 per cent.[18] The rate of decline was probably highest among those in their teens and twenties, but in view of the scale of this decline there must also have been many adults who had been regular churchgoers for most of their lives but who gave it up largely or entirely in the 1960s and early 1970s.

In the next section I show how social changes contributed to the crisis of the church; then I will look at the role of political and religious

---

[16] See McLeod, *Crisis*, pp. 62–4.

[17] Clive D. Field, 'Joining and leaving British Methodism since the 1960s', in Leslie J. Francis and Yaacov J. Katz (eds.), *Joining and leaving religion: research perspectives* (Leominster: Gracewing, 2000), pp. 57–85.

[18] Jan Kerkhofs (ed.), *Europe without priests?* (London: SCM Press, 1995), p. 11.

movements; and finally I will consider some of the alternative ways of conceptualising religious change in the 'long sixties'.

II

Among the social changes, the most important was the onset of 'affluence'. The 'long sixties' saw dramatic improvements in the standard of living throughout the western world. This affluence affected all sections of the population, though in different ways. The rising earnings of working-class and lower-middle-class youth from the later 1950s funded the youth culture, focused on rock 'n' roll, new fashions in clothes, and often on motorbikes and scooters. Full employment emboldened students, who had often been rather conformist in the 1950s and early 1960s, but who became the pace-makers of political radicalism and cultural experimentation in the middle and later 1960s. Family lifestyles changed with the acquisition of cars, television sets and washing machines, with the availability of foreign holidays, and most important of all, with higher-quality housing (and often home ownership). And the biggest changes of all were seen in the many rural regions which saw both the mechanisation of agriculture, the increasing incursion of urban cultural influences, and large-scale migration to seek better-paid work in the cities.

All of these changes potentially had implications for religion and the churches. To begin with the most obvious case, there is no doubt as to the scale of change in this period in many rural regions. According to Henri Mendras, 'The decline of the Catholic Church can in large part be explained by the disappearance of the peasantry, just as the decline of the Communist Party can be explained by the disappearance of the proletariat.'[19] He goes on to admit that this is an over-simplification. But there is an important element of truth in what he is saying. Rural depopulation had a devastating effect on many communities, but there were also radical changes in the lives of those who remained in the countryside, as is shown in Yves Lambert's brilliant account of religious change in the Breton village of Limerzel.[20]

The developing youth culture posed both a direct and a more indirect threat to the churches. The indirect threat lay in the fact that their youth work, still very extensive in the 1950s, faced increasingly strong competition as young people could afford an increasingly wide range of alternatives. Oral history interviews with the generation born in the 1940s

[19] Mendras, *Révolution*, p. 79.
[20] Yves Lambert, *Dieu change en Bretagne* (Paris: Cerf, 1985), pp. 237–69.

show a common pattern whereby young people who had gone to church and belonged to a church youth group in their early and mid teens, drifted away in their later teens, not through any conscious decision, but because more and more of their time was being taken up by concerts, coffee bars and pubs, or going out with friends on their motorbikes. The youth culture could pose a more direct threat in so far as it nurtured values or forms of behaviour which were at odds with those prescribed by the churches.

Affluence also had more subtle and intangible effects on the life of families. The main overall effect was to weaken ties to local communities, as, on the one hand, life became more focused on the home and the nuclear family, and, on the other, families became more open to wider influences. Here Elizabeth Roberts's oral history-based research on working-class families in the north-west of England between 1890 and 1970 provides good examples of the trends[21] A central theme of her work is the enormous importance of the neighbourhood, and of the conformist pressures exercised by the combined influence of 'neighbours, teachers, clergymen and policemen'.[22] Neighbours could be very supportive in situations of need and could also play a key role in, for instance, finding work. At the same time, neighbourhood gossip placed strict limits on the individual's freedom of action. The norms of behaviour were well established, and could not be lightly disregarded: interviewees often explained their actions by simply saying 'It was the thing to do.'[23] Included in these norms of respectable behaviour were, for instance, the churching of mothers after childbirth, the baptism of the baby, their subsequent religious education in Sunday school, and eventually a church wedding.

By the later 1950s a multitude of small changes were underway, the cumulative effect of which could be very considerable.[24] Neighbourhood and family networks were becoming less necessary in the search for work, since full employment meant that it was easy to throw up a job and find a new one. Rising earnings for young workers made it easier for teenagers to defy parental authority. 'Experts' were increasingly influencing such things as the upbringing of children, and overriding the influence of neighbours and grandparents. Corner shops, centres of neighbourhood gossip, were being replaced by supermarkets.

[21] Elizabeth Roberts, *A woman's place: an oral history of working-class women, 1890–1940* (Oxford: Blackwell, 1984), and *Women and families: an oral history, 1940–1970* (Oxford: Blackwell, 1995).
[22] Roberts, *Women and families*, p. 162.
[23] *Ibid.*, p. 160.   [24] *Ibid.*, pp. 13–17, 45–51, 56, 92–3, 141–57.

Above all, 'making a beautiful home' was becoming a principal objective for many people.

A second kind of social change which was happening at this time was the weakening of the collective identities rooted in confessional and ideological subcultures, which had dominated many western societies in the period from about the 1880s to the 1950s.[25] The full consequences of this became apparent in the 1970s and 1980s, but signs of change were already appearing in the 1950s and especially the 1960s. There was a blurring of ideological boundaries because of the realisation by political parties and churches that they had alienated specific social or confessional groups, and that any advance in membership or influence would depend on a broadening of their appeal. Meanwhile, at the local level, changes in social structure were also having an impact. In the Flemish strongholds of political Catholicism, Conway notes 'the emergence of a more educated and self-confident laity reluctant to accept uncritically the guidance of the ecclesiastical hierarchy' and the development of 'a more integrated and fluid society in which the isolation of the Catholic community no longer seemed to many Catholics to be either feasible or desirable'.[26] And Communist and Socialist, as much as Catholic parties, were being weakened by increasing individualism and diminishing ideological militancy.[27]

A third major area of social change concerned family and sexual relationships generally and the position of women in particular. These included a continuing rise in the proportion of married women doing paid work, the availability from 1961 of the contraceptive pill, the 'sexual revolution' and the increasing influence of the ideal of the 'companionate marriage'. The changes which had the biggest effects on religious behaviour were those concerning the relationship between husband and wife, especially in working-class families. In Britain the years 1945–70 have been seen as the golden age of companionate marriage.[28] If at the time of World War II this was a mainly middle-class ideal, by the 1960s it had also been adopted by wide sections of the working class. While newspapers, magazines and the publications of such bodies as the

---

[25] See Hugh McLeod, *Religion and the people of western Europe, 1789–1989* (Oxford: Oxford University Press, 1997).

[26] Martin Conway, 'Belgium', in Tom Buchanan and Martin Conway (eds.), *Political Catholicism in Europe, 1918–1965* (Oxford: Clarendon Press, 1996), p. 214.

[27] See Edgar Morin, *Plodemet: a report from a French village* (London: Allen Lane, 1971).

[28] Marcus Collins, *Modern love: an intimate history of men and women in twentieth-century Britain* (London: Atlantic, 2003). See also the more sceptical assessment by Jenny Finch and Penny Summerfield, 'Social reconstruction and the emergence of companionate marriage', in David Clark (ed.), *Marriage, domestic life and social change* (London: Routledge, 1991), pp. 7–32.

National Marriage Guidance Council played a part in the diffusion of this ideal, rising living standards made its realisation much more possible. In particular, the home was becoming the focus of life, with the television set at its centre, and couples or even whole families habitually devoting large parts of their free time to watching it together.[29] At the same time, there was a growing tendency for leisure habits once deemed suitable only for courting couples to continue into married life. That is, instead of leisure being gender specific, with married men meeting other married men in a pub or at a football match, and women meeting other married women at, for instance, a cinema or a church, married couples were doing things together. Oral history interviews with women born in the 1940s show many examples of those who had gone to church regularly in their teens, but whose attendance dwindled when they started courting, or after they married, a non-churchgoing man. Increasingly the tendency was for couples to go to church together, or to stay away together. Ian Jones, in his oral history of Birmingham churches since 1945, found that out of 47 married interviewees, 39 had a churchgoing spouse.[30]

Although the precise nature of the 'sexual revolution', and still more its causes, continue to be debated, the period between about 1955 and 1970 clearly saw significant changes both in sexual behaviour and in the extent and nature of public discussion of sex.[31] These included an increase in the numbers of those having sex before marriage, a reduction in the age at which people first had sex, and a modest increase in the proportion of children born outside wedlock. While the extent of the changes in behaviour during the 1960s may have been exaggerated, it is incontestable that there were huge changes in the legal status of sexual activities and in the treatment of sex by the media. Much less evident is the impact of these changes on other areas of people's lives, including their religion. It is clear that the counter-culture rejection of Christianity and Judaism (though sometimes a positive view of 'eastern' religion) went hand in hand with rejection of all conventional sexual morality, and a major emphasis on the beneficial results of 'sexual liberation'.[32] In the population at large sexual nonconformity took much milder forms. There is a correlation between attitudes to religion and to sex in this

---

[29] Roberts, *Women and families*, pp. 103–4.
[30] Ian Jones, The 'mainstream' churches in Birmingham, c.1945–1998: The local church and generational change, PhD thesis, University of Birmingham (2000), pp. 139–41.
[31] Marwick, *Sixties*, p. 18 and passim, provides an international overview.
[32] See Jonathon Green, *Days in the life: voices from the underground 1961–1971* (London: Heineman, 1988), pp. 296–7 and passim. This is based on interviews with veterans of the British counter-culture.

period, but the precise nature of the relationship is unclear because of the paucity of evidence on such intimate areas of people's lives. Michael Schofield in a survey of older teenagers, mainly in London, in 1964, found that boys and girls who never went to church were much more likely to have had sexual intercourse than those who were regular churchgoers. He speculated that sexually experienced teenagers had been alienated from the churches by finding what they were doing condemned by church teachings. However, it is equally possible that those already alienated from, or simply uninvolved in, the church simply had fewer inhibitions. Indeed, Schofield's later survey of young adults, based on research in 1972, suggested that churchgoers, though less sexually precocious than their non-churchgoing peers, were able to reconcile their religious practice with sexual practice that their church might consider deviant. Among those who were regular churchgoers 59 per cent said they had had pre-marital intercourse, as against 75 per cent of non-churchgoers.[33] There was still a difference, but not a big one. A survey of former students at Girton, a Cambridge women's college, provides some chronology. Among students who came to Girton between 1950 and 1954, 33 per cent said they had had pre-marital sex; among those starting in 1971 and 1972 it was 63 per cent. The increase seems to have come in two phases. In the later 1950s and early 1960s it was mainly among the less religious students, who were both increasing in numbers and becoming more sexually active; the later increase was mainly explained by increasing levels of sexual activity among the more religious students.[34] Except in the specific case of Catholics and contraception, there is little evidence that rejection of church teachings on sex was itself a cause of alienation from the churches. However, as the sexual climate changed during the 1960s, and even more in the 1970s, those already detached felt increasingly free to ignore church teachings, while those who remained in the church claimed a greater freedom to make their own judgements on questions of ethics.

Callum Brown has argued that the 'de-feminisation of piety' and the 'de-pietisation of femininity' were the key to the religious crisis of the 1960s.[35] Brown overstates the suddenness of religious change in that decade and underestimates the importance of other elements in the

---

[33] Michael Schofield, *The sexual behaviour of young people* (London: Longmans, 1965), pp. 148–9, 216, 254; and *The sexual behaviour of young adults* (London: Allen Lane, 1973), p. 169.

[34] *University and life experience* (Girton College Archives, Cambridge). I am grateful to the Mistress and Fellows, Girton College, Cambridge, for permission to refer to this material.

[35] Brown, *Death*, p. 192.

crisis, enumerated in this chapter. He also overstates the extent to which piety was 'defeminised': the 1960s saw declining church involvement by both women and men, but women continued to be more religiously active than men. For instance, the English church census of 1979 showed that 58 per cent of churchgoers aged fifteen and over were female and that women were overrepresented in all age-bands.[36] Such evidence as we have for individual motivation suggests that the reasons for women leaving the church in the 1960s were broadly similar to the reasons for men doing so, and, in one of the few cases where clear evidence of this exists, Lambert's study of a Breton village, quoted above, showed that it was men who initiated the movement away from the church. However, Brown is right to stress the strategic role which women have played in the religious life of western Christian countries, and the consequent significance of changes in women's religious outlook.[37] Women had been the mainstay of most congregations: nuns or women volunteers had been key players in the parish; at home, it was usually mothers who taught their children prayers and sent them to church, and who stuck up pictures of Mary or biblical texts on the walls. As fewer mothers have found the time or had the inclination to do these things, the religious socialisation in childhood, which remained normal up to the 1950s, has become less common. The detachment of many women from the church in the 1960s has thus had an important influence on changes *since* that time, but it does not provide an explanation for the crisis *during* the 1960s.

III

The undermining of traditional authorities in the early 1960s prepared the ground for the political and religious radicalisation which was well underway in the mid 1960s, and reached its climax in the last years of the decade. By 1968, expectations of imminent and drastic change in church and society had reached a very high level. There were also growing numbers of conservatives who believed that change had already gone much too far. Revolutions are nearly always a bad time for churches, as the revolution tends itself to become sacralised and all other loyalties

---

[36] Peter Brierley (ed.), *Prospects for the eighties* (London: Bible Society, 1980), p. 23.

[37] Apart from Brown's own work, see Hugh McLeod, *Piety and poverty: working-class religion in Berlin, London and New York, 1870–1914* (New York: Holmes & Meier, 1996), chapter 7; Ruth Harris, *Lourdes: body and spirit in the secular age* (London: Allen Lane, 1999).

become relativised and often discredited as a result. Moreover, larger churches are almost inevitably divided in such situations.

A combination of factors placed strain on those whose radicalism had Christian roots, especially from 1968 onwards. One was the magnetic attraction of Marxism and the belief that it offered the only truly scientific understanding of the world. Its withering critique of capitalism had a strong moral appeal, and by legitimating political violence and fostering a language of attack and struggle it was readily compatible with older styles of masculinity. For some, Marxism simply replaced Christianity, and for others it showed how Christian ideals could become a reality. Those who remained Christian believers often became disillusioned with the church, which seemed too slow to change and which, with its varied social and political constituency, was difficult to mobilise for revolution.[38] The critique of Christianity and Judaism as legitimators of patriarchy was an important theme – though one that has so far been relatively little explored by historians. Certainly there were some feminists for whom this critique was central, such as the American theologian Mary Daly.[39] Feminist discourse had a much wider impact, influencing the thinking of women who never joined any women's group, including those who stayed in their churches. It is, however, striking when reading transcripts of interviews of oral history projects relating to religious change in the 1960s and 1970s that very few of those interviewed gave the influence of feminist ideas or sexism in the church as a reason for leaving their church or rejecting their religion. There is a contrast here with interviews with those brought up in the early twentieth century, who quite often give class discrimination in the church or the influence of radical politics as a reason for leaving. Among those mainly working-class and lower-middle-class Lancashire women interviewed by the Centre for North-West Regional Studies, who had attended a church as teenagers but had later left, there is only one whose departure had a feminist or partly feminist motive. And she, on leaving her Anglican church, had not rejected Christianity, but had become a Quaker.[40] In the Millennium Project, a vast oral history project conducted by local radio stations, there were, in a sample of 167 interviewees born between 1935 and 1954, 38 people, of whom 19 were women, who gave reasons

---

[38] Danièle Hervieu-Léger, *De la mission à la protestation: l'évolution des étudiants chrétiens* (Paris: Cerf, 1973).

[39] Sara Maitland, *A map of the new country: women and Christianity* (London, Routledge & Kegan Paul, 1983), pp. 141–2.

[40] 'Social and family life, 1940–1970', transcripts of interviews by Lucinda Beier and Elizabeth Roberts at the Centre for North-West Regional Studies, University of Lancaster, interview with Mrs R4B, p. 52.

for having temporarily or permanently rejected religion or the churches. Men and women gave broadly similar reasons, and only one woman explicitly connected her rejection of Christianity with feminist arguments.[41] The link between sex, gender and rejection of the church was much clearer in predominantly Catholic countries, both because of *Humanae vitae*, the papal encyclical of 1968 condemning the use of contraceptives, and because of the confrontations between the Catholic Church and the women's movement over abortion.

The 1960s were a time of ferment for both Catholics and Protestants. It was a time of hope and, especially in the latter part of the decade, a time of intense conflict within the churches. The hopes, the disappointments and the conflicts all played a part in the crisis faced by the churches in the later 1960s and early 1970s. In particular, Vatican II raised intense expectations among Catholics, including many younger priests and nuns. But the radicals faced powerful opposition from conservatives or moderates; many of them well entrenched in positions of authority. Already in 1967, Paul VI's encyclical reaffirming the rule of clerical celibacy offered a major blow to the reformers. But worse was to come, most notoriously *Humanae vitae* – not the least of the shocks which hit the world during the fateful year of 1968. The reasons for the sharp drop in Catholic religious practice between about 1967 and 1974 continue to be hotly debated. Traditionalists blame the church's problems on the Council, while progressives blame them on *Humanae vitae*. Even if the Council had never taken place, the church would have had to face many of the same issues, certainly including contraception, and probably a decline in the number of priests. However, the fact that the Council did happen shaped the specific form that the crisis took. It raised hopes very high – often for them to be dashed when it became clear that actual results would fall far short of what seemed to have been promised. At the same time, reforms alienated some working-class and peasant Catholics – not so much the vernacular liturgy as the removal of statues from churches, the discouragement of various forms of folk Catholicism, and the dropping of such badges of identity as the eating of fish on Fridays. In the years following the Council congregations not only became smaller – but following Protestant trends they also became more middle class.[42]

[41] McLeod, *Crisis*, p. 181.
[42] Michael Hornsby-Smith, *Roman Catholics in England* (Cambridge: Cambridge University Press, 1987), pp. 61, 66; Cholvy and Hilaire, *France*, pp. 320–4.

IV

In this chapter I have been focusing mainly on one particular aspect of religious change, namely the reasons for the distancing of many individuals from the church. I have shown that this could happen in many very different ways, ranging from changing lifestyles as a result of social change, to the rival attractions of radical political movements or new kinds of religion and 'spirituality', to the effects of conflicts within the church. I have highlighted the parallels between the problems faced at this time by the churches and those faced by political parties. Both depended for their mass membership partly on family and community loyalties at a time when individual freedom and individual rights were coming to be valued above collective identities. I have not attempted to assess how far individual religious belief changed during this period. That is an aspect of religion which is particularly difficult to assess – certainly the questionnaires used in some of the literature on contemporary religious change seem too blunt an instrument. Nor have I broached the important topics of the relationship between church and state and the role of religion in public institutions. In fact, there was much less change in these areas than in the relationship of individuals to the church. Perhaps the biggest changes in this period were in the cultural role of Christianity. In spite of the decline of churchgoing in many western countries in the later nineteenth and early twentieth centuries, Christianity continued to provide a 'common language', which was to some degree shared by all but the most convinced and committed unbelievers.[43] Even the latter tended to regard themselves as 'Catholic', 'Protestant' or 'Jewish' atheists, and most people, whatever their personal beliefs, continued to participate in the rites of passage, which provided generally accepted ceremonies for marking the great turning points of life. In the 1960s this common language was breaking down. Confessional identities weakened, as did the sense of Sundays, saints' days or even the major Christian festivals as special. Those without personal belief saw non-participation as more 'authentic'. Religious language played less part in political rhetoric, as politicians tried to appeal to an audience that was assumed to include both believers of many different kinds and unbelievers.

The most influential way of summing up these changes continues to be 'secularisation' – though there remains a fundamental disagreement between those who see this secularisation as just a part of a much longer history and those who see the 1960s as 'the secularisation decade'.

---

[43] Hugh McLeod, *Secularisation in western Europe, 1848–1914* (Basingstoke: Macmillan, 2000), pp. 12–14.

However, this approach is open to various objections. Some historians reject the idea that there has been a general shift towards secularity. They argue that the period since the 1960s has seen a lack of consensus and the coexistence of many contrasting belief systems: they therefore suggest that increasing pluralism is the central theme of this period. Some writers discard 'secularisation' in favour of 'de-Christianisation',[44] arguing that Christianity has declined, but that society has not thereby become secular. On the other hand, a recent collection of essays on British Christianity since 1945 was given the title *Redefining Christian Britain* (in explicit contrast to the 'death' posited by Callum Brown), in order to emphasise what the authors see as the resilience of the churches and the pervasive cultural influence of Christianity even in a period of institutional decline.[45] Others suggest that while older forms of belief have declined, new beliefs, more in tune with the zeitgeist, have taken their place. Thus they speak of a 'spiritual awakening'[46] or 'the spiritual revolution'.[47] In two recent books I have taken 'the decline of Christendom' as a central theme, and I have defined the 1960s as 'the end of Christendom'.[48]

Each of these descriptions has its value, though none tells more than part of the story. 'Secularisation', as I have argued elsewhere, is a useful description of some of the most important trends in European history over the last three centuries.[49] However, it has often been used in misleading ways, which partly explains why so many scholars have preferred to use other terms. One problem is that secularisation as a descriptive term is often confused with the 'secularisation thesis', according to which there is a general relationship between the 'modernisation' of societies and the declining significance of religion. The most familiar criticism of this thesis is that it attempts to generalise about the world on the basis of the European case; my own main objection is that it does not provide an accurate explanation of how secularisation has happened in Europe. Focus on secularisation has

---

[44] For 'pluralism', see Gerald Parsons and John Wolffe (eds.), *The growth of religious diversity in Britain from 1945*, 3 vols. (London: Routledge, 1993); for 'de-Christianisation', see Jean-Louis Ormières in *L'Europe désenchantée*. (Paris: Fayard, 2005).

[45] Jane Garnett *et al.* (eds.), *Redefining Christian Britain: post 1945 perspectives* (London: SCM Press, 2007).

[46] Robert Ellwood, *The sixties spiritual awakening: American religion moving from modern to post-modern* (New Brunswick: Rutgers University Press, 1994).

[47] Paul Heelas and Linda Woodhead, *The spiritual revolution* (Oxford: Blackwell, 2005).

[48] Hugh McLeod and Werner Ustorf (eds.), *The decline of Christendom in western Europe, 1750–2000* (Cambridge: Cambridge University Press, 2003); McLeod, *Crisis*, chapter 11.

[49] For fuller discussion, see McLeod, *Secularisation*, pp. 1–15.

sometimes led to a narrow kind of religious history, in which other aspects of religious change are ignored. Indeed, what is best described as religious change is often seen as another manifestation of secularisation, as if religions were definitively constituted at one point in their history and any subsequent development should be regarded as decline. Here a polemical agenda often comes into play, whether consciously or, more often, unconsciously – sometimes bringing together unlikely bedfellows. Conservative Christians, suspicious of any kind of 'modernism', have been ready to brand any theological innovation as an example of secularisation. Meanwhile, those who regard any progressive reform as a result of beneficial secularist influence are inclined either to ignore religiously motivated contributions to such reforms or to see them as a manifestation of 'internal secularisation'.

A case in point is the revolution in the relationship between law and morality which took place in many western countries in the 1960s and 1970s. The drive for greater individual freedom in the 1960s was not only the work of rebellious youth – some of the most important changes were brought about by middle-aged and elderly legislators. Two of the widest-ranging programmes of liberalisation were in England and Wales between 1959 and 1969 and in Canada between 1967 and 1969. In England and Wales these years saw the liberalisation of the laws relating to the censorship of books (1959), betting and suicide (1961), abortion, contraception and homosexuality (1967), theatre censorship (1968) and divorce (1969), as well as suspension (1965) and abolition (1969) of the death penalty. In Canada a similar package of reforms was included in one large omnibus bill, introduced in 1967 and passed into law in 1969. Historians coming from opposite directions have agreed in seeing these reforms as symptoms of 'de-Christianisation' (the term used by Callum Brown) or 'secularisation' (the word used by the French Catholic historian René Rémond).[50] Yet it is worth noting that both in Canada and in England and Wales many of these reforms had official church support and that individual Christians were sometimes among their most significant advocates. For instance, Trudeau's political philosophy was rooted in a liberal Catholicism which gave primacy to the individual conscience, and he justified the proposed reforms by reference to the pluralistic nature of Canadian society and the inappropriateness of giving civil law a theological basis.[51] Already in 1954, when the

---

[50] Brown, *Religion and society*, p. 267; René Rémond, *Religion and society in modern Europe* (Oxford: Blackwell, 1999), p. 199.
[51] George Egerton, 'Trudeau, God and the Canadian constitution: religion, human rights and the making of the 1982 constitution', in David Lyon and Marguerite van Die (eds.),

whole subject was still taboo, the Church of England's Moral Welfare Council was advocating reform of the laws on male homosexuality, and when in 1966–7 the issue was debated in Parliament and a reform finally enacted, Archbishop Michael Ramsey spoke strongly in favour. The Church of England played a major part too in the process leading to reform of the divorce laws in 1969 – though Ramsey himself was dissatisfied with the law that eventually resulted. Most of the Protestant churches agreed on the need for reform of the laws on abortion – though there was disagreement as to how far the reform should go.[52] The overwhelming church support for abolition of the death penalty might also be mentioned, since this is sometimes presented as part of a liberalising 'package', though in fact it was a very different issue.[53]

At least five kinds of consideration played a part in Christian support for these reforms. One was the argument that a Christian's first duty is compassion, rather than the laying down of moral absolutes. So, for instance, the bishop of Carlisle, in advocating the decriminalisation of attempted suicide, declared that the suicidal needed compassion and not punishment.[54] This kind of argument often proved to be the clincher in the debates of the 1960s, but it might not have been decisive, but for several other developments. Second, there was an increasing readiness by the Anglican leadership to draw on the advice of 'experts', such as doctors, psychiatrists and sociologists, who tended to highlight the practical consequences of particular laws, rather than the ethical principle that they were intended to uphold. Third, there was what was sometimes called the 'new morality' based on situation ethics, of which John Robinson, bishop of Woolwich, was the most influential advocate.[55] Robinson's ethical creed was based on what he called 'Christian freedom', by which he meant acting responsibly and in a spirit of love, but without a legalistic code of morality. In the light of this, liberal

Rethinking church, state and modernity: Canada between Europe and America (Toronto: University of Toronto, 2000), p. 96; Pierre Elliott Trudeau, *Memoirs* (Toronto: McClelland & Stewart, 1993).

[52] Peter G. Richards, *Parliament and conscience* (London: Allen & Unwin, 1970), pp. 63–84; Jane Lewis and Patrick Wallis, 'Fault, breakdown and the Church of England's involvement in the 1969 divorce reform', *Twentieth-century British History* 11 (2000), 308–32; G. I. T. Machin, *Churches and social issues in twentieth-century Britain* (Oxford: Clarendon Press, 2000), p. 200.

[53] Hugh McLeod, 'God and the gallows: Christianity and capital punishment in the nineteenth and twentieth centuries', in Kate Cooper and Jeremy Gregory (eds.), *Retribution, repentance and reconciliation* (Woodbridge: Boydell & Brewer, 2004), pp. 346–7.

[54] Mark Jarvis, *Conservative Governments, morality and social change in affluent Britain* (Manchester: Manchester University Press, 2005), p. 95.

[55] Eric James, *A Life of Bishop John A. T. Robinson* (London: Fount, 1989).

Christians like Robinson argued that some of the existing laws were based on concepts of morality that were outdated and not truly Christian. Fourth, there were those whose own moral principles were more conservative than Robinson's, but who recognised that in a society without any consensus on some key ethical issues compromises might be necessary. Indeed, as long ago as 1937 this point had been conceded by Archbishop Cosmo Gordon Lang, the archbishop of Canterbury, in reluctantly accepting a modest liberalisation of the divorce laws.[56] There may be a connection with the fact that Lang was also preaching a 'recall to religion' during which he deplored 'a slackening, sometimes even a scorning, of the old standards of Christian morality', especially in the field of sex and marriage. In 1909–12 as a member of the Royal Commission on the Divorce Laws he had opposed any extension of the grounds for divorce. While the published sources offer no clear explanation for the changes in Lang's thinking, it seems most likely that the clearer indications of secularisation in English society in the 1920s and 1930s were influencing his thinking. And fifth, bishops, like, for instance, judges and academics, were influenced by the principle laid down in the Wolfenden Report that the sphere of morality, which encompasses the whole of life, is different from the sphere of law, which covers only those areas where it is necessary for the state to intervene. Thus Sir John Wolfenden disapproved of homosexuality as much as did the archbishop of Canterbury, Geoffrey Fisher. But both agreed that so long as it involved only 'consenting adults in private' it should not be a concern of the law. (It should be noted, incidentally, that the Wolfenden Report was in no sense a product of or a response to the 'swinging sixties' and the committee was meeting at a time when the Church of England appeared to be enjoying a revival.) In summary, we have several different kinds of change here: changes in Christian thinking both about ethical principles and about ethical priorities; changes in Christian thinking about the relationship between law and morality; and a recognition that on some key moral issues there was no longer any consensus and that the law should reflect this increasing pluralism. While the third of these might be seen simply as a response to secularisation, this is not an adequate explanation of the first two developments. 'The end of Christendom' offers a more precise description of the context in which these changes were happening.

To speak of 'the end of Christendom' leaves open the question of what will replace it. But it establishes several important points. Christendom

[56] J. G. Lockhart, *Cosmo Gordon Lang* (London: Hodder & Stoughton, 1949), pp. 233–4, 235, 267.

marked a phase in the history of Christianity and a phase in the relationship between state, society and religion. But Christianity is not dependent on the existence of a Christendom, and it will find ways of adapting
to the changed environment. At the same time, the growth of atheism,
agnosticism or religious indifference since the 1960s is only one dimension of the changing religious situation. Also significant has been the
growth of conservative forms of Christianity, most notably Pentecostal-
ism, and of non-Christian faiths, whether through immigration or
through conversion, and the proliferation of 'alternative spiritualities'.
Each of these (and indeed more liberal and moderate forms of
Christianity) have major centres of influence. For instance, the Catholic
and Protestant churches continue to have an enormous role in the
education and welfare systems of most European countries and in a
range of voluntary agencies; conservative forms of Christianity are
strong at either end of the social spectrum, among working-class immigrants and members of ethnic minorities, and also in the medical
and legal professions; secularism is especially influential in the world
of the media; and 'alternative spiritualities' have a big influence on
popular culture. Meanwhile, Islam and other non-Christian faiths,
though still small in numbers in the western world, benefit from the
high level of commitment of many of their adherents, and also from their
value as allies: in earlier times secularists saw them as allies in their
campaigns to cut back Christian influence; now they are more likely to
be seen by Christians as allies in the battle against secularism. Here we
have an ongoing contest, and it is not yet clear who the winners and
the losers will be.

13 Gendering secularisation: locating women in the transformation of British Christianity in the 1960s

Callum G. Brown

The marginalisation of gender

Of all the ways in which secularisation has been imagined and studied by scholars, the least explored has been gender. As a category of analysis, it is now pretty standard across the historical and sociological professions, and has transformed areas of study, established entirely new ones, and generally invigorated intellectual thought about past and present societies. But few studies of religious change and secularisation in the twentieth century have considered gender seriously.[1] Some of those, notably by Hugh McLeod, have concluded that class remained more important than gender in differentiating people's religious behaviour.[2] Peter van Rooden has conducted a small-scale oral-history project in the Netherlands to test the involvement of women in the 1960s in the 'strange demise of Dutch Christianity'.[3] This chapter explores further gendered aspects of the British experience of secularisation since the 1960s. It does this through a reading of both women's and men's autobiographies as a source revealing the transformation of the place of religion in British culture. Like any approach, this has its difficulties. The voices heard recalling mid-twentieth-century Britain tend to lean strongly towards a group of people involved in the political and cultural changes represented by the term 'the sixties' and its counter-culture. Many of the people who talk of the cultural transformation were participants in it, and seemed to be inhabiting a world predominantly of London and the south-east of England; the term of choice was,

---

[1] But see C. G. Brown, *The death of Christian Britain: understanding secularisation 1800–2000*, 2nd edition (London: Routledge, 2009) and P. Heelas and L. Woodhead, *The spiritual revolution* (Oxford: Blackwell, 2005).

[2] H. McLeod, *Religion and society in England 1850–1914* (Basingstoke: Macmillan, 1995); S. C. Williams, *Religious belief and popular culture in Southwark c. 1880–1939* (Oxford: Oxford University Press, 1999). See also Sean Gill, *Women and the Church of England: from the eighteenth century to the present* (London: SPCK, 1994).

[3] Peter van Rooden, 'The strange demise of Dutch Christianity', in C. G. Brown and M. Snape (eds.), *Secularisation in the Christian world* (Farnham: Ashgate, 2010).

after all, 'swinging London'. Moreover, a criticism often levelled at voices to be heard expounding on these matters is that they are wholly or mainly middle class. But most began in humble working-class homes, many outside London, and for others membership of the middle classes is not an argument of exceptionality but, indeed, of commonality in mid and late twentieth-century Britain. We hear the voices of people from the English midlands and north, including Lorna Sage, Sheila Rowbotham, Joan Bakewell and Paul McCartney, some from Scotland, such as Lulu and Donovan Leitch. Many of these are middle class, from provincial towns and schools in which the place of religion was deeply embedded in most people's lives and from which, to a very great extent, the sixties represented an escape. There are those from London and the south-east, like Carolyn Steedman, who were from working-class families as alienated from the bohemian classes of London as it was possible to be. The distance being travelled from 'religion' was for many of these people also a distance from provincial cultures towards another 'thing' that included affluence, London-centred lives, as well as sexual liberation and women's liberation. Cultural battles were underway in all sorts of provincial contexts. Sexual promiscuity was hardly off the lips of commentators in Scotland in the mid to late 1960s, and Edinburgh University became a byword for student sex (Malcolm Muggeridge resigning as University Rector in 1968 over the installation of a condom machine in the Men's Union, and the Student Health centre opened in 1969 being immediately dubbed 'the Pill Centre').

Sexual change was nationwide; statistics on illegitimacy show that England, Wales and Scotland experienced a parallel revolution in premarital sex, with Northern Ireland trailing perhaps six years behind.[4] Indices of religious change are equally indicative of the extent of change in the 1960s. After being relatively stable during 1920–60, Protestant Church adherence across mainland Britain plummeted in the 1960s. Similarly, religious marriage had been fairly stable in the 1950s but fell between 1962 and 1975 from 80 to 64 per cent of all marriages in Scotland, and from 70 to 52 per cent in England and Wales.[5] Though Northern Ireland's experience is a little different (with change starting from a higher level of religiosity and coming six or seven years behind mainland Britain), the evidence suggests that the 1960s cultural change was one that was being felt across much of mainland Britain. This did not mean that liberal cultural and sexual freedom, and anti-authoritarian

[4] See the graph in C. G. Brown, *Religion and society in twentieth-century Britain* (London: Pearson Longman, 2006), p. 32.
[5] Data from graph, *ibid.*, pp. 25, 34.

revolt erupted everywhere equally; but it did mean the forces fostering swinging London were strongly influenced by an inflow of émigré young people from the provinces channelling their desire for change. And a central element in this was a flight from traditional organised religion, led more especially by young women.

Autobiographical and oral testimony is exceptionally important to the study of gender in religious change because of the paltry volume of statistical information on gender collected by historians and sociologists of religion. For instance, the massive Economic and Social Research Council (ESRC) project which collected historical data on British church statistics, published in 1977, contained none on gender, and this has been largely replicated in church-based and other studies since.[6] For historians, social class remained the number one category of analysis in the British historical study of secularisation. The imagining of secularisation has tended to conceive of it in patriarchal terms within patriarchal frameworks – the loss of church authority, the sale of church land, the decline of religious taxes and the dissolution of state or estab-lished churches. Secularisation has often been imagined as a story of power change in a world dominated by men. It is imagined as a struggle between civil and religious institutions, as a struggle between institutions of state, of power politics played out virtually entirely between men over institutions they have controlled. In this way, secular-isation has in some studies been imagined as a rearranging of the ecclesi-astical deckchairs on the good ship patriarchy.

One of the reasons for this has been the dominance of a strongly *secular* feminism within the history community. The secular feminism that drove feminist historians of the 1960s to explore the role of religion in the subordination of women in discourse and experience in the nineteenth century and before seems to have been the very same femi-nism that caused them, as individuals, to lose interest in the course of religion after the 1950s. In a sense, feminism was itself part of a struggle with religion in the 1950s and 1960s. Once that 'battle' was perceived to have been won, interest was lost.

These may not be the only factors in gender blindness on secularisa-tion. Yet, these, on their own, seem to have been powerful enough to have diverted interest from gender. For many in religious studies, church history and sociology, the evidence that women had been and remained in the late twentieth century much greater churchgoers, more interested in religious voluntary organisations, in prayer, and belief in

---

[6] R. Currie, A. Gilbert and L. Horsley, *Churches and churchgoers: patterns of church growth in the British Isles since 1700* (Oxford: Clarendon Press, 1977).

God and the afterlife, underpinned what has seemingly been widely accepted as an inherent 'gender law' of religion – that women are naturally more religious, and the least likely to secularise. Thus, reflecting focus back onto men, the issue became trapped in a traditional structuralism. Secularisation studies have remained one of the firmest redoubts of a traditional scholarship, resistant to postmodern perspectives and even a pretty basic linguistic turn.[7] Listening through a gender framework to the voices of secularising change in the mid twentieth century is one way that opens a different understanding.

Remembering before the 1960s

One of the stunning changes in the British autobiography from the 1960s was the way in which the representation of religion was transformed. The transformation was a highly gendered one, and placed religion at the heart of remembrance of pre-1960s lives and society.

Until the 1950s, the British autobiography was dominated by a central role for religion. This did not apply to every autobiography, but it was an extremely common phenomenon that defined the nature of the conventional remembered life. In this it reflected the place of religion in British popular culture. But in the mid twentieth century, the way in which the autobiography introduced religiosity underwent dramatic change, reflecting changes in discourse (and remembrance of it); in how the 'self' was composed from discourse, and in the structuring of the life narrative and religiosity's place within it.

It is hard to find a single autobiographer from any social class born between 1800 and 1930 who did not discuss religion and the moral construction of the individual – whether it was themselves, their parents or others in their community. Many male socialist autodidacts recorded their repulsion with religion and their journeys into atheism.[8] But more commonly, the Victorian and Edwardian 'life' was habitually a journey away from, or in fear of, moral and economic destruction. The male artisan commonly portrayed himself as respectable, pious and home-loving, avoiding drink and gambling to find redemption in a wife-centred religious life at home. For women, the religious was an even stronger element in the autobiography of this period. Women's accounts of their

---

[7] C. G. Brown, 'The secularisation decade: what the 1960s have done to the study of religious history', in H. McLeod and W. Ustorf (eds.), *The decline of Christendom in western Europe 1750–2000* (Cambridge: Cambridge University Press, 2003), pp. 29–46.

[8] J. Rose, *The intellectual life of the British working classes* (New Haven and London: Yale University Press, 2002), pp. 58–92.

lives were used in various formats as evangelising literature to both women and to men. Indeed, it was more to men that the image of the woman struggling with a drunken husband, poverty and ill-fortune was held up in literature as a guiding example to follow. Femininity in both fictional and autobiographical literature of the nineteenth and first half of the twentieth century was bound up with a pious respectability; female literature, and literature for women, tended to centre on a conjunction of piety and femininity that had to be negotiated and only rejected with the direst of social consequences for a women's reputation.[9] It was a minority of female autobiographers who experienced religious crises, for few lost Christian faith completely, rebelling more against the churches than against belief and the narrative of the moral life.[10] The autobiography was a location for the evangelical narrative of descent and redemption. For women, the descent was usually because of male fecklessness or misfortune; for men, it was because of temptation to drink, gambling or sex.

The first changes to the female autobiography came in the mid twentieth century. If the pre-1940 autobiography focused on the subject (the writer) as on a life-journey of personal salvation, autobiographies of the second half of the twentieth century form a revealing contrast in structure and treatment. This may be detected in the late 1940s in Flora Thomson's famous autobiography set in Oxfordshire, but it became a standard feature in the mushrooming female autobiographies of the 1950s, 1960s, 1970s – such as in autobiographies by Margaret Penn (Manchester), Molly Weir (Glasgow), Lillian Beckwith (Scottish Highlands) Dolly Scannell (London), Victoria Massey (London), Kathleen Woodward (London), Betsy White (Scottish travellers), Margaret Powell (London), Winfred Foley (New Forest), Celia Davies (Essex) and Rose Gamble (London). These books treated lives begun in the main between 1880 and 1930, placing great emphasis on religion through discussion of Sunday school and church, temperance activities, and the impact of religion on leisure and recreation. Some of these books were not sympathetic to religion, yet few failed to recall the impact of religion in their communities and families. What was going on was the commodification of religion as part of 'the world we have lost' – a literature of remembrance that appealed to readers hankering after an old-time religiosity that was beginning to fade. In a sense, the appearance of the literary genre was itself a marker of secularisation, and the

[9] Brown, *Death*, chapter 3.
[10] D. Vincent, *Bread, knowledge and freedom: a study of nineteenth-century working-class autobiography* (London: Methuen, 1981), pp. 179–81, 188.

fact that the output peaked in the early and mid 1970s was indicative of the realisation of what was sliding rapidly from British culture. But though the genre has not totally lost its appeal, it has been in noticeable decline since the 1980s. The level of interest in religion-fuelled nostalgia is losing its market as the British buyer has become increasingly someone born since the 1950s, without knowledge of religion, and for whom the world being recalled in such works has little resonance.

So, the British female autobiography changed again, mostly in the 1980s, 1990s and 2000s, with a new generation which came of age in the late 1950s or 1960s, and who became part of a new world for women. These are the women who became embroiled in the swinging sixties, in some way or other, to some extent or other, or in the feminist movement that sprang up in the early 1970s. For them the autobiography became something which reconfigured remembrance of religion.

Unlike their predecessors, autobiographies recalling the 1950s and 1960s in Britain are not stories of 'lost' community. The decline of 'golden ageism' in the autobiography as it transits the middle of the century is quite pronounced. These autobiographies are not about the demise of rustic villages torn asunder first by out-migration and then by suburbanisation, nor about urban communities torn down by slum clearance and the formation of cold, isolated peripheral estates and new towns. Nor are they about the mythical 'golden age' of marriage.[11] This genre for the most part does not exist in relation to the 1960s – which, it must be argued, is indicative of the absence of a cultural place for it in British memory and nostalgia. Indeed, the autobiographies remembering the 1950s and 1960s are of a hue by and large unseen before outside the narrow confines of the labour-movement memoir. They are autobiographies of revolution – in this case, of women's gender change.

The genre developed under the Virago imprint in the 1980s, notably in two volumes of extracts – *Truth, dare and promise* about the 1950s, and *Very heaven* about the 1960s.[12] These two books established that there was a pattern to remembering these two decades. The 1950s were recalled as a decade of female repression, and the 1960s as a decade of liberation. Angela Carter set the tone when she wrote: 'I grew up in the fifties – that is, I was twenty in 1960, and, by God, I *deserved* what

---

[11] C. Langhamer, 'Sexual politics in mid twentieth-century Britain: adultery in post-war England', *History Workshop Journal* 62 (2006), 87–109.

[12] L. Heron (ed.), *Truth, dare or promise: girls growing up in the fifties* (London: Virago, 1985); S. Maitland (ed.), *Very heaven: looking back at the 1960s* (London: Virago, 1988).

happened later on. It was tough, in the fifties, girls wore white gloves.'[13]
Liz Heron summarised the view of the fifties:

It is seen as the time when women, yielding their jobs to the returning male
population as soon as the war was over, lost the paid employment that had given
them independence; as the time when the family was re-cemented, when women
were re-domesticated, their role redefined as that of home-maker; when progress
itself had a domestic incarnation, with the kitchen as the centre of the new
developments in consumer technology. It is seen as the time when all the
outward signs of sexual difference were re-emphasised through style and
fashion, and women's femininity pronounced in the clothes of the New Look.[14]

Helpful to understanding the change to the remembrance of life is the
work of Penny Summerfield on discourse change. Summerfield's study of
oral-history narratives showed how two dominant discourses of women's
experience existed of the wartime years and their aftermath: the modernising woman and the traditional woman. The first of these was a discourse
that empathised with the impact of war in opening opportunity for
women, and instigating the prospect of liberalisation of women's lives.
The second interpreted women's experience as an interlude to be endured
before women returned to traditional roles in house, home and mother-
hood. But Summerfield concluded that 'the discourse of modernisation
was in fact riddled with traditionalism'. Few of those who pushed, or
identified with, the discourse of modernisation 'departed from the dominant, traditional view that women's main purpose at the end of the war
was to "return home" and recreate a domestic haven'. 'The contradiction', Summerfield continued, 'between this representation and the idea
that the war had liberated women was resolved by the suggestion that,
later in the post-war years, women would turn their backs on the domestic
"cage" and demand the freedoms made available by the war'.[15] From
this work arises the argument that there was a deferment to women's
liberation from the late 1940s and 1950s to the next generation – to
the 'daughters' of World War II – whilst women's 'return to the doll's
house' was heavily propagandised in the late 1940s and 1950s.[16]

The idea of deferment is critical to understanding the reaction of
younger women, growing up in the 1950s and reaching their late teens
and twenties in the 1960s, to the experience of their mothers. Whether
directly or indirectly, there is a sense in which mothers thwarted one

---

[13] Maitland (ed.), *Very heaven*, p. 210.   [14] Heron (ed.), *Truth, dare*, p. 4.
[15] P. Summerfield, *Reconstructing women's wartime lives* (Manchester: Manchester
University Press, 1998), p. 259.
[16] A good summary of this is to be found in E. Wilson, *Only halfway to paradise: women in
postwar Britain, 1945–1968* (London: Taylor & Francis, 1980).

way or another in ambition in the 1940s and 1950s passed to their daughters a sense of the liberation they should now grab for themselves. Carolyn Steedman's part-autobiography, part-historical research book *Landscape for a good woman* (from which an extract appeared in *Truth, dare and promise*) pursued this story in a self-analysis of accepted discourse on a woman's role in society. She showed how girls and women in the mid twentieth century displayed an economic understanding of their identity – similar to that found in Henry Mayhew's famous 1849 encounter with an eight-year-old watercress-seller in East London, who defined herself in the economic terms of shrewdness and 'street-wise' economic sense with which to sustain her very poor family. Steedman says that 'her labour was not an attribute, nor a possession, but herself'.[17] Steedman then shows that by the 1950s, this vision of a girl's capacity for economic independence had been swept out of society for good social-welfare reasons and for the protection of children, but it left older women like Steedman's own mother misunderstood, leading to her searing, guilt-ridden account of autobiographic remembrance of her mother's very difficult economic circumstances. 'Women are the final outsiders', she wrote.[18]

What Steedman started opened up with other autobiographies of the generation of women who 'found themselves' in the later 1960s and early 1970s. A wider sense that the 1950s was a supreme moment of girls' subordination becomes evident, and at its heart lay the cultural power of a religious-based guilt that transcended the experiences of the working and middle classes. In Carter's case, the Sunday-best dress of frilly frock and white-lace gloves is recalled with a horror that the previous generation of women, for the most part, did not share; indeed, Sunday-best dress was recalled in oral-history testimony and autobiography with fervent enthusiasm by elderly women in the 1970s and 1980s.[19] Sheila Rowbotham was sent by her Methodist-hating father to a Methodist boarding school in North Yorkshire. 'We were meant to be pure as well as tough', she recalled of the school's cold dormitories. 'At school assembly tapers would be lit and passed round like a lamp of purity.' Even as a rebellious sixth-former there, she was intensely acculturated to guilt: 'Beneath my overt rejection of conventional morality, I continued to be haunted by the fear of condemnation, a fifties hangover which remained powerful in 1960.'[20] The power of guilt, indeed,

[17] Carolyn Steedman, *Landscape for a good woman* (London: Virago, 1986), pp. 129, 136.
[18] *Ibid.*, p. 144.   [19] Brown, *Death*, pp. 128–32.
[20] Sheila Rowbotham, *Promise of a dream: remembering the sixties* (London: Verso, 2001), pp. 2, 4, 6.

was central to recollections of later feminist autobiography. Its basis was laid in the fifties' culture. Valerie Walkerdine recalled: 'The ordinariness of manners, or please-and-thank-you'd politeness, of being a nice girl, who went to the Brownies and Guides, and for whom the competitions in the annual Produce Association show provided one of the most exciting occasions of the year.'[21] The 1950s was a decade when sub-urbanism reached its highest expression, enjoyed by the generation who had fought two world wars and survived depression, but who now imposed their 'victory' on their own children through 'Sunday-school respectability, the Cubs' "Bob-a-job-week" and the Brownie's "Purpose Day"'.[22] This was intensely oppressive for young girls. These values were propagandised amongst the young with a vengeance in this decade, underpinned by a manic religious state of anxiety about worthiness: 'I see now', wrote Carolyn Steedman three decades later, 'the relentless laying down of guilt'.[23]

The guilt was greatest over pregnancy outside wedlock. There were few, perhaps no, liberal institutions in 1950s Britain that would coun-tenance this. Universities were hostile; a pregnant student was sent down or left in the face of the shame. At Glasgow's Royal College (shortly to be Strathclyde University) in the late 1950s, sexual relations were very few, but one 'more fashionable' student who 'had boyfriends', and 'went places at night' got pregnant, had to marry and 'caused a real stooshie'. Her fellow women students spoke of her with hushed tones: 'we all spoke about it with a low voice'; 'you only whispered it to your pal'; 'you wouldn't have spoken about it to anyone else'.[24] Women lost education, careers, prospects and respectability through pregnancy. Many lost their families – both the child and their parents. One woman who experienced the ferocity of unmarried pregnancy was Lorna Sage, a feminist academic, who recalled the 1950s as the period of 'post-war moral rearmament, with everyone conscripted to normality and standing to attention'.[25] Sage was destined by family culture to early marriage, but she resisted in her mid teens, planning with her best friend to stay unmarried. Her scheme failed when she became pregnant at the age of seventeen, and faced the prospect of being sent by her parents to a Church of England Home for Unmarried Mothers, 'where you repented

[21] V. Walkerdine, 'Dreams from an ordinary childhood', in Heron (ed.), *Truth, dare*, p. 65.
[22] *Ibid.*, p. 72.
[23] Carolyn Steedman, 'Landscape for a good woman', in Heron (ed.), *Truth, dare*, p. 117.
[24] Testimony of Pat Fraser and Elizabeth McCudden, quoted in C. G. Brown, A. McIvor and N. Rafeek, *The university experience 1945–1975: an oral history of the University of Strathclyde* (Edinburgh: Edinburgh University Press, 2004), p. 100.
[25] Lorna Sage, *Bad blood* (London: Fourth Estate, 2001), p. 89.

on your knees (scrubbed floors, said prayers), had your baby (which was promptly adopted by proper married people) and returned home humble and hollow-eyed'.[26] Like Rowbotham at exactly the same time, Sage educated herself in a different vision of women through reading Simone de Beauvoir. In 1959, she and her boyfriend pre-empted parental action by getting married to end her mother and father's guardianship; it was, she said, 'an insult to matrimony', and for her parents made the family seem shamed and 'look lumpen, real white trash, common as muck'.[27] In London in 1965, Janet Street-Porter took a different route to solving the same problem; unable to face telling her parents she was pregnant, and also fearing loss of her place as an architectural student, she paid £25 to have an illegal abortion.[28]

In Stockport in Cheshire, Joan Bakewell also grew up in the 1940s and early 1950s in a world of sexual guilt. From an early age she felt a personal relationship to Jesus. 'It was quite a personal matter, directly between myself and Him. I knew what He looked like from the picture on the wall at Sunday school, which we attended every week as routinely as we went daily to school.'[29] She said prayers nightly kneeling either in the bedroom or living-room, and her mother listened to these and was the focus for the cultivation of her sense of guilt. 'I knew that home, the Church and school all talked the same language of morality with absolute certainty, and much of it was directed at me.'[30] Though her parents hardly ever went to church, she did throughout her teenage years as an act of personal seriousness. Together with home and school, 'the three presented a formidable array of pressure, overlapping and reinforcing the only values I knew'. And what she calls the 'combined fire-power' of the three institutions was directed 'with particular keenness and unanimity at one ambiguous target: sex'.[31] And from that point on, her mother impressed a tremendous guilt over even the mildest and non-physical of relationships with boys, her mother shaming her for a holiday romance:

I didn't know what to do with the shame. I went upstairs, sat on the bed and stared out of the window for a long time. There were no tears, just shock ... Suddenly I was savagely and tremblingly angry. All the judgements being passed, the controls inflicted, must be defied and defeated. I could assess as well as she what was good or bad, right or wrong. In all my childhood, that was the moment when I had a sense of growing, of my essence under pressure to change, and

---

[26] *Ibid.*, p. 237.   [27] *Ibid.*, p. 244.
[28] Janet Street-Porter, *Baggage: my childhood* (London: Headline, 2004), pp. 209, 221.
[29] Joan Bakewell, *The centre of the bed* (London: Sceptre, 2003), p. 72.
[30] *Ibid.*, pp. 73–4.   [31] *Ibid.*, p. 75.

deciding to be myself. That was the end of innocence, not the loss of virginity or any fumbling that fell short of it. It was when I crossed into adulthood, knew my own mind and was sure of who I was.[32]

Despite this decisiveness, the guilt kept returning, induced by her mother with a frosty silence at various turns in her teenage and student years.

This was the oppressive mental world that enveloped much – arguably most – of 1950s and early 1960s Britain. It was one that we can trace most readily in the written memoirs of those who were, or became, either famous or middle class. But those from poorer backgrounds, like Steedman and a number of pop stars, can be found also amongst working-class testimony. Young girls from all social classes were especially loaded with guilt and apprehension about sexual matters – even when they might know absolutely nothing about it. Indeed, this was the greatest, ironic way in which the guilt worked. What it was that the young woman was to have feelings of guilt about was unknown. She was expected to be ignorant about sex, to be literally unknowing of the facts of life; to admit knowledge of them was in itself a sign of unrespectability. Also, what was extremely common was ignorance about sex – on the marriage night – and ignorance about childbirth itself. In her oral history of birth control, Kate Fisher says quite a lot about sexual ignorance. One of her respondents described this as 'a curiously sexless world', where sexual material went unrecognised even when it appeared in popular culture and in conversation between the knowing; warnings over VD, for instance, were often completely ineffective because both men and especially women just did not understand the euphemistic terms used. This instilled a women's world of anxiety and incomprehension in the mid twentieth century, leading to men being more knowledgeable than women, and to chastity being much more widespread than some historians give credit for.[33] Women were not only ignorant about sex, but pled ignorance for their moral identity. Fisher concludes: 'Being ignorant was a key element of female identity, closely connected to women's respectability and in particular their avoidance of illicit sexual behaviour prior to marriage.'[34]

---

[32] *Ibid.*, p. 79.
[33] Kate Fisher, *Birth control, sex and marriage in Britain 1918–1960* (Oxford: Oxford University Press, 2006), pp. 48–50.
[34] *Ibid.*, pp. 67–8. For autobiographers feeling the same mixture of religion and sexual guilt being imposed in the 1950s and early 1960s, see Jenni Murray, *Memoirs of a not so dutiful daughter* (London: Bantham, 2008), pp. 13, 19, 73 19, 304; Julie Walters, *That's another story: the autobiography* (London: Orion, 2008), pp. 69–76; Karen Armstrong, *Through the narrow gate: a nun's story* (London: Planigo, 1995), p. xiv.

The post-war years of rationing, utility furniture and dull clothing make an easy backdrop to this. The culture of constant moral censure seems to provide an explanation for the detection in recollection of a sense of female subordination. But Ina Zweiniger-Bargielowska has argued that women should not be seen as submitting docilely in the 1940s and 1950s. Women had a principal role in implementing government austerity policy – because it was about food, clothing and all things female. As a result, she says, 'domesticity became a site of political and economic power and a basis of female citizenship. Housewives became a major political force after the war and their discontent with the continuation of austerity had important political and electoral consequences.' Women's votes mattered, she argues, more and more at this time because of women's revolts against austerity measures. She shows how women and housewives were monitored by the state during the war. And women had low morale about food after the war, which inculcated a general pessimism.[35] This is an important censure against the casting of women as purely victims, but the pessimism detected by Zweiniger-Bargielowska helps explain the weight of autobiographical evidence concerning the way in which women and young girls experienced a culture in the late 1940s and 1950s that seemed to them to be a distinctive fortification of traditional roles, representations and expectations of the morally pure female in British life, and a suppression of openness about sexual desire and social experimentation.

How the religious mould was broken

By contrast to the remembrance of adult female sexual knowledge in the 1950s, much of the literature from the pens of 1960s' feminists gives the strong impression of the importance of sexual experimentation as the first bold step to breaking this mould, to shattering the encasement in discourses in which their mothers had been 'trapped'.

However, this was not straightforward. Sheila Rowbotham recalls that life at university revealed some differences, but not in the discursive sexual oppression. She recalled:

By the end of my first year I had grasped that beneath the superficial resemblances between Methodist Hunmanby [boarding school] and life in an Oxford women's college there were very significant differences. Methodist Hunmanby, preparing us for a life of moral witness had instilled the virtues of honesty: regardless of the consequences, you answered to your inner conscience.

[35] I. Zweiniger-Bargielowska, *Austerity in Britain: rationing, control and consumption, 1939–1955* (Oxford: Oxford University Press, 2000), pp. 100, 124.

Ruling-class Oxford, in contrast, was based on getting round the rules; the crime was to be found out – especially if you were female.[36]

So, even here, the freedoms had not yet emerged. Bakewell presents Cambridge as, if anything, more libertarian than Rowbotham recalled Oxford. There was constant challenging of the rules there in the early 1950s, pushing back the boundaries of the permissible in women's roles on (and behind) the theatre stage, in sexual freedom, as well as in censorship, blasphemy and so on. Oxford and Cambridge universities seem to have been extremely important centres of sexual learning and experimentation in the 1950s, and students like Rowbotham and Bakewell coming from the north of England found it to be a wholly different cultural environment for sex. This helps to explain the highly unusual evidence from Girton College, Cambridge, where in 1950–4, 33 per cent of female students claimed to have had pre-marital sex (and 57 per cent by 1960–1).[37]

It seems unlikely, were similar evidence to be available from outside the 'golden triangle', that sexual activity on that scale would have been reported by unmarried female students in the 1950s and early 1960s. Evidence from students at other colleges and universities is not only of there being less sexual experimentation, but less opportunity for it, as most British students in the 1950s still lived at home with parents and the overall moral environment was oppressive. At the Royal College of Glasgow, rules made it like school; in some classes students sat alphabetically, while political campaigning was forbidden, and swearing was only allowed in the male-only beer bar of the Union. This set the tone. The small numbers of women students neither challenged the men nor sought sexual liaisons. Pat McCudden, a student there in the late 1950s, recalls: 'We were very accepting. We were there to be prepared for the world of work. And you work hard and then you get on with it and that was it. It would never have entered our head to kick and want to be with the boys, would it?' Sex might be on their minds, but there it stayed. Elizabeth McCudden remembered that 'we did go down to the refectory a lot and that was where the talent was usually eyed up. The guys would eye you up, and then when it came to the dances it would be that they danced with you and make a bee line for you and that was how it all worked. Nothing was said.' University social life was often tame. Jeannette Smith, who was a student in Glasgow during 1951–5, reviled the refectory as 'a grubby, smelly hole where we could get dubious food

[36] Rowbotham, *Promise*, pp. 48–9.
[37] Hugh McLeod, *The religious crisis of the 1960s* (Oxford: Oxford University Press, 2007), p. 165.

and coffee ... Social life was much more sedate then.' Old-world cour-
tesies were in their prime in the 1950s; women students got the front seat
in the lectures, and were allowed to the front of the queues for student
refectory food.[38] With no sense of breaking the mould for most female
students, male–female student cohabitation was, with few exceptions, in
the 1950s out of the question, and pregnancy out of wedlock ended
student careers.

The freedom of sexual liberation appears from the sheer weight of
personal testimony to have come for most much later – in the years from
1963 to 1970, with the arrival of pop culture, and for many with
the arrival of the oral contraceptive pill for single women in 1968.[39]
Autobiography and oral testimony on the 1960s, certainly in published
form, gives an impression of a massive outburst of sexual freedom – of
multiple sexual partners, nudity in public, accompanied by drugs, popular music and 'dropping out' from conventional lifestyle. Certainly this
literature is dominated by those who were members of the London-
based 'scene', as Richard Neville has written: 'The concept of "swinging
London" caught on because the rest of the country was a graveyard.'[40]
Yet there is plenty of evidence of the bohemian youth culture of the early
1960s having already taken a firm hold amongst some young people.
Donovan Leitch, born and brought up in Glasgow and Welwyn Garden
City, recalls that before he broke through into the pop music world he
journeyed in 1961 to St Ives in Cornwall to join a small but highly
developed centre of young people, where sexual promiscuity was rife,
and based around a world of music and carefree lifestyle – what was to
become Britain's hippie centre.[41] But this may have been highly localised. In Liverpool, Paul McCartney makes it clear that he had not
developed what he calls 'much practical knowledge' of sex until 1960,
when the Beatles moved to Hamburg and the 'red light' district in which
they started to become famous, and on their return to England in 1962
sexual freedom was starting to become more perceptible.[42]

The place of religion in all this was critical. It was central to the
remembrance of the decision to commence, or resist, sexual

[38] Quotes in Brown, McIvor and Rafeek, *University experience*, pp. 99–101.
[39] H. Cook, *The long sexual revolution: English women, sex and contraception 1800–1975* (Oxford: Oxford University Press, 2004).
[40] R. Neville, *Hippie hippie shake: the dreams, the trips, the trials, the love-ins, the screw-ups. ...: the sixties* (London: Bloomsbury, 1995), p. 71.
[41] Donovan Leitch, *The hurdy gurdy man: the autobiography of Donovan* (London: Century, 2005), pp. 27–58.
[42] Barry Miles, *Paul McCartney: many years from now* (London: Vintage, 1997), pp. 70, 142.

experimentation for both young women and young men in the 1960s. One woman recalled her early sexual encounters, and how it began with lengthy 'snogging' sessions in groups at parties or youth clubs, and how one encounter led from snogging to groping, only to be stopped by her sense of Christian guilt: 'I was racked with guilt and I went off to confession and felt I'd really sinned.' Another woman remembered: 'In my teens I didn't have sex. I took the Catholic faith very seriously, and decided that for me it was sex within marriage – and I didn't want to get married – and that was it. So I'd go out with boys, but not go too far. Then at seventeen, when I was going to be confirmed, I fell in love.'[43] This changed her attitude, and she lost her virginity. For some, sexual experimentation was delayed by a mixture of religion and fear of loss of female respectability. The pop singer Lulu attained national stardom at the age of sixteen years, but she was just over twenty years of age in 1970 and still a virgin – despite what she described as 'obstacles, temptations and some marathon kissing sessions'.[44]

Sexual experimentation was also delayed by men for religious considerations. For pop singer Cliff Richard, religious faith became a central motif of his private life. Richard is widely seen as unusual in the pop world – both for his faith and what is believed to be his sexual abstinence. Richard is interesting, though, in revealing the place of the minority committed Christian. He recalled in the 1950s not being especially religious in home or school life. Religious education at school 'meant absolutely nothing', and he failed his O-level religious education. When he attained fame in the late 1950s, he was branded by the *Daily Mirror* as 'Britain's bad boy of pop', and was alleged to be 'too sexy' to appear on television. Interestingly, he recalled that one of the frequent questions asked by the press in the oppressive moral atmosphere of the 1950s was what his religion was – and he would reply Church of England and that he believed in God. 'Theoretically I wasn't an atheist but in practice there wasn't much difference.' It was the death of his father that started a process of religious inquiry – starting with him thinking about holding a séance, and then being dissuaded by a Jehovah's Witness (JW). His mother as well as Hank Marvin and Brian Bennett of his backing band The Shadows joined JW, with which Cliff also flirted. But he turned elsewhere, struggled for many months, attending Bible classes and a Christian camp at Lewes in Sussex, before finally experiencing his conversion whilst making one of his films. Cliff Richard was and remains

[43] Quoted in J. Green, *IT: sex since the sixties* (London: Secker & Warburg, 1993), pp. 60–1, 63, 266.
[44] Lulu, *I don't want to fight* (London: TimeWarner, 2002), p. 123.

seen as one of the exceptions of the sixties cultural revolution. Indeed, he became an object of attack for student campaigning groups in the later 1960s – including the Gay Liberation Movement, which lobbied the Christian Student Union meetings he held at Lancaster University.[45] Yet Richard was far from being a Christian conservative, despite the attitude of some left-wing movements. He did not join the charismatic Christian movement, and unlike many he saw his pop music work as separate from his Christian activity.[46]

In many ways, Cliff Richard's autobiographies are the exceptions to a very widespread rule. Whilst religion is central to his autobiographies (particularly his second, which has strong affinities with the traditional type of evangelising biography), the autobiographies generated by both men and women of the 1960s are almost always stories in which conventional Christian religion is marginalised, ignored or appears at the outset as the starting point that dominated and oppressed the individual in childhood and teenage years. The journey from staidness and conformity that is an important motif in Rowbotham and many others seems also a journey from organised religion. This story of a journey away from religion is one that continued to appear in British culture in the latter part of the twentieth century. Comedian Jimmy Carr, born in 1972, was a student at Cambridge University but was a virgin until the age of twenty-six, which he attributed to 'partly religion'. He said: 'I was a Christian. I didn't want to have sex before marriage.' His loss of faith occurred around the same time as his loss of virginity, though he says it was not clear-cut 'that as my religious beliefs changed I therefore felt able to have sex'. Nonetheless, he emerged in more sexually active middle age as being 'fundamentally an atheist'.[47]

In a minority of autobiographies, there are clear signs of the emergence of the New Age in the 1960s. The Glasgow-born singer Lulu was introduced to readings about eastern mysticism by Ringo Starr's wife, and when the Beatles returned from their spiritual quest in India in 1968 she was advised by John Lennon to meditate and became a devotee of Gurumayi Chidvilasananda, the spiritual head of the Siddha Yoga Foundation.[48] For Donovan and George Harrison, who had been along the same spiritual path already, the related movements of transcendental meditation, yoga and eastern mysticism became central to life.

---

[45] Cliff Richard, *Which one's Cliff? The autobiography of Cliff Richard* (London: Coronet, 1981), pp. 32–3, 53, 64–74, 93.
[46] Cliff Richard, *Single-minded* (London: Hodder & Stoughton, 1988), p. 71.
[47] *Observer Woman Magazine*, no. 27 (March 2007), p. 9.
[48] Lulu, *Fight*, pp. 218–19.

Donovan claims that he, along with Mia Farrow, was a critical figure in introducing western pop stars to eastern mysticism, and he was part of the Beatles' party at the Maharishi Mahesh Yogi's retreat in India in 1968.[49] Initially, such new religious ideas were the subject of press 'scandal'. The embryonic Findhorn Community, which was by the 1990s Britain's largest residential training centre for New Age religion, was born out of a newspaper frenzy in the 1960s. The *Daily Express*, the self-appointed centre of moral rectitude of the period, made it its special purpose to demonise Findhorn's founders, Sheena Govan and Peter Caddy, pursuing them across Scotland as they sought a permanent home, turning their journey, their camping lifestyle and even their vegetarianism into sensationalist newspaper copy that had all the hallmarks of seeking to cause a moral panic.[50] But the press furore over new spiritualities was to settle down as they became both widespread and widely influential. Through combining eastern and western religious ideas in a decentred holistic milieu of the 'mind, body, spirit', New Age religion acquired its distinctive and influential position in both British and western culture development of the later twentieth century.[51]

Autobiographies recalling the 1960s reflect a deep transformation of the way in which British culture imagined the place of religion in the life of the individual. They invariably tackle, in some way or other, the collapse of the hegemonic dominance of traditional Christian discourse about the interlinking of femininity, social respectability and piety. The collapse they record is invariably one of the 1960s, not the 1940s or 1950s. With few exceptions, the personnel who tried to liberalise British art and culture in the 1950s struggled to compete with the increasing conservatism of an invigorated 'establishment'. The religious part of this establishment was liberal over race, nuclear disarmament and the Vietnam War, but its liberalism was far outshone by the conservatism of the churches as a whole on sexual matters. In its death throes between 1957 and 1974, the religious establishment fought back against the liberalisation of popular culture – through the use of censorship in theatres, Moral Rearmament campaigning in the guise of Mary Whitehouse's National Viewers' and Listeners' Association, the constant television appearances of Christian conservatives like Malcolm Muggeridge and in the Festival of Light in the early 1970s.[52]

---

[49] Leitch, *Hurdy gurdy man*, pp. 211–52.
[50] J. Campbell, *A word for Scotland* (Edinburgh: Luath Press, 1998), pp. 113–16.
[51] S. Sutcliffe, *Children of the new age: a history of spiritual practices* (London: Routledge, 2003).
[52] Brown, *Religion and society*, pp. 177–277; R. Hewison, *Too much: art and society in the sixties, 1960–75* (London: Methuen, 1987).

This campaigning of Christian conservatives failed, heralding the continuous and massive shift in British moral culture in the final three decades of the century.

The sexual revolution in the 1960s is central to the secularisation of Britain; it may well also extend further into Europe and other European-influenced places. The battle lines were drawn by the British Christian churches over the female body in the 1950s and 1960s, making sexual liberation of women the key issue. In 1966, the Anglican Church once again rejected the ordination of women, with an official report claiming that the 'erotic facts' were that a woman in the pulpit would seduce both fellow male clergy and the laity.[53] The Church of Scotland in 1970 identified the key to the sexual revolution and the alienation of the young from the churches: 'It is the promiscuous girl who is the real problem here.'[54] The church actually understood that the 'moral turn' was in female permissiveness, not in men's, and that the churches were losing their central paradigm of Christian behaviour – the respectable and sexually abstinent single woman.

The regendering of British Christianity

This leads to the issue of men and what has happened to British religion since the 1960s. There is evidence emerging of a change to the nature of the religious element within male identity. Where men in the first three-quarters of the twentieth century represented at most a third of church-goers (and in some cases much less than that), the later twentieth century shows evidence of a growth in the proportion of churchgoers who are men. In Scotland, between 1984 and 2002 there was a net loss of 168,560 churchgoers over fifteen years of age, of whom 129,040 (or 77 per cent) were female.[55] In England, the evidence is a little slimmer at present, but still interesting. Between 1979 and 1989, more men than women stopped going to church, but not amongst fifteen to twenty-nine year-olds. In the Church of England and the Free Churches, there was a loss of 96,100 churchgoers aged fifteen to twenty-nine years in those ten years, of whom only 36,900 (or 38 per cent) were male, but 59,200 (62 per cent) of whom were female.[56]

---

[53] 'Women in holy orders', quoted in *The Times*, 15 December 1966.
[54] *Reports to the General Assembly of the Church of Scotland*, 1970, pp. 399–410.
[55] Calculated from data in P. Brierley, *Turning the tide: the challenge ahead* (London: Christian Research, 2003), p. 53, table 4.4.
[56] Statistics calculated from data in P. Brierley, *'Christian' England: what the English church census reveals* (London: MARC, 1991), pp. 88–9, tables 35 and 36.

Meanwhile, the abandonment of Christianity by women seems to have been greatest in Greater London where, with a population of 7.5 million in 2005, the proportion of church participants that was female fell very significantly during 1979–2005 from 57 to 52 per cent. Moreover, in England the highest levels of male participation were amongst the growing and least declining denominations: new churches were 50 per cent male, Pentecostal churches 49 per cent, independent churches 48 per cent and Roman Catholic Church 45 per cent. Meanwhile, the lowest male participation was in the most crisis-ridden denominations: the United Reformed Church was only 35 per cent, the Methodist Church 36 per cent, and the Church of England 41 per cent.[57] What is also interesting is that London, experiencing growth in male participation, used to be the most secularised part of Great Britain, but is the part where the high-growth churches, notably the Pentecostal churches, are now the most vigorous and important elements of organised Christianity.

In other words, though more research needs to be conducted on this, it is now clear that the notion of a fixed female dominance of churchgoing has been destabilised since 1970 by significant evidence of greater female alienation from active Christian church connection. This may be a small piece of evidence of the increasing role for men within remnant Christian church culture in Britain. With the rise of issue-based Christian campaigning (as distinct from traditional evangelising), it is evident that an increasing part has been played by men. In organisations fighting gay liberation, in the struggle of the Society for Protection of the Unborn Child, and in the Pro-Choice movement, there is a strong lead role being played by men. Some of these are prominent figures and wealthy business figures – such as Brian Souter, associated with the Stagecoach bus company, and Sir Peter Vardy, associated with the car dealership chain – who have played a part with others in funding activities ranging from the Scottish referendum on Clause 28 to the foundation of supposedly evangelical-aligned city academies. In the Alpha Course, in the charismatic renewal movement, in the House Church movement and in the increasingly extra-ecclesiastical development of conservative Christianity in Britain, it seems that men are finding a greater role to develop organising skills, to express their Christianity in a modern and unstuffy manner, and to enter the public sphere as campaigning Christians. This development is, of course, shared with the rise of militancy and influence of conservatism in other religious traditions both in Britain and in the wider world – in Islam, Sikhism and

[57] P. Brierley (ed.), *UKCH Religious Trends No. 6 2006/2007: Analyses of the 2005 English church census* (London, 2007), 5.8, 12.3, 12.47.

Judaism.[58] Certainly, the Christian discourse on the obedient male, sub-servient to the greater purity of the category woman, is being subverted.

By contrast, the link between New Age religion and women is also becoming more widely acknowledged.[59] Women are the leading con-sumers and practitioners of New Age activity in Britain, and both within and outwith the conventional churches they have been developing a mixing of spiritual practices drawn from eastern and western traditions, from religions and from body and health techniques. In the process, the discourse on the pure woman has been under considerable challenge – acknowledged in part in the Purity Ring movement imported from the USA, but which has had little apparent success in Europe. The spiritual woman is now perceived differently – sometimes in the press, as with Cherie Blair's former personal advisor, as being 'flaky'.[60] The hege-monic, unforgiving sexual purity required in discourse of the respectable woman in the 1950s has disappeared from British culture. In its place has come a discursive framework of a much more sexually liberated, spiritually experimental and career-minded woman.

The full ramifications of the regendering of religion in Britain since the 1960s have still to be explored. But enough is now apparent to be fairly confident that woman's changing gender in the 1960s was central to the collapse of the Christian-centred culture of Britain, leading to the freefall in churchgoing and adherence statistics. In 1960, the Church of England, the Church of Scotland and the Methodist Church claimed 4,212,382 members; by 2000, against a modest population rise, their membership had halved to 2,106,281. In 1979, more than 11 per cent of the population of England went to Sunday worship; by 2005, the figure was down to only 6.3 per cent.[61] The change to women's lives, and to their perception of their 'self', was central to that transformation.

---

[58] See the argument in Callum Brown, 'Secularisation, the growth of militancy and the spiritual revolution: religious change and gender power in Britain, 1901–2001', *Historical Research* 80/209 (2007), 393–418.

[59] Woodhead and Heelas, *Spiritual revolution*.

[60] C. G. Brown, '"Best not to take it too far": how the British cut religion down to size', www.opendemocracy.net, March 2006.

[61] Figures calculated from data in Brown, *Religion in twentieth century*, p. 25, and from www.christian-research.org.uk.

14 Does constitutionalisation lead to secularisation?

The case law of the European Court of Human Rights and its effect on European secularisation

Anat Scolnicov

In this chapter I enquire, what role does constitutionalisation play in secularisation? In particular, I will ask whether the constitutionalisation of a European legal order plays a role in secularisation. By 'constitutionalisation' I do not mean necessarily the adoption of a document entitled 'constitution', but rather a fundamental legal ordering, underpinning the state or a supra-state entity. All European states are based on a constitutional order, including the UK, which does not have a written constitution. The secular or religious nature of each European state is formulated by its constitution, but also by European regional treaties, which have constitutional implications for their member states.

The status of religion within constitutions is interesting and unique, because of the primordial character of religion as a social and political institution. In the emergence of modernity, constitutionality of states has superseded religion (or divine authority) as the fundamental legitimate source of authority. But this is by no means a completed or irreversible process. Even within the modern nation state, including in European states, remnants of an earlier order remain. Any national or international legal regulation necessarily operates over these underlying historical layers.

I will look at one important example of constitutional change: the role played by the European Convention on Human Rights, a fundamental legal document of the Council of Europe, in changing the legal landscape of Europe, and ask whether it led to secularisation in European states.

It is particularly interesting to examine the effects of transnational constitutionalisation on secularisation in Europe. Western European

I benefited from long discussions with Emile Perreau-Saussine on the topics reflected in this chapter before his untimely death.

states (and now Eastern European states as well) have accepted liberal political ideals, including religious freedom. That has not meant, however, a uniform principle of state secularity. In fact, a variety of legal relationships between state and religion has emerged in Europe, and different social levels of religiousness prevail in the region.

Of course, the European Convention is not an isolated cause. Other social orders, and other legal orders, have caused secularisation in Europe or have hindered it. A note on the difference between legal secularity and social secularity is in order. Constitutional secularity can have very different social outcomes. A state that is constitutionally not religious can foster a society which is not religious. But, conversely, a state that is not religious can lead to the flourishing of religions in a society that is free from interference of the state (as occurred in the United States). Therefore, although it is important to understand the legal status of religion in Europe, this is by no means the only analysis needed in order to understand its social role.

This chapter will examine whether, since the adoption of the Convention in 1950, the case law of the European Court of Human Rights (and previously also the European Commission of Human Rights, which decided admissibility of cases prior to 1999), has meant that the Convention has played a role in secularising Europe.

It will be shown that the answer to this question is complex. The Court has played a role in secularisation in specific issues relating to individual rights, in particular in the field of family and sexuality, but has steered clear of pronouncing upon the fundamental question of the legitimate place of religion (or, conversely, a principle of secularity) in the states, under the Convention.

Neither the European Court nor the European Commission has ever considered in a coherent manner whether the institutional aspect of establishment, the granting of official status to one or more religions in the state, constitutes an interference with religious freedom. I will argue that, therefore, the effect of the European human rights system on secularisation has been less pronounced than might have been expected. However, despite a lack of fundamental pronunciation on the permissible status of religion within the state, in some areas the Court has played a role in secularising law in Europe.

While playing an actual role in delimiting the boundaries of permissible involvement of the state within the religious or secular social ordering in the state, and furthering secularisation in the most intimate areas of an individual's Convention rights, the Court has not directly or comprehensively pronounced on the role of the state in this field.

The European Convention on Human Rights

The European Convention on Human Rights (ECHR) is a major legal instrument of the Council of Europe and applies to all its member states. The Council of Europe is an organisation of European states, which is wider, and much looser, than the European Union. It includes all EU members as well as many other European states.

The ECHR guarantees religious freedom in article 9[1] and non-discrimination on the basis of religion in protection of Convention rights, in article 14.[2] A general obligation of non-discrimination, not limited to protection of Convention rights, is included only in an additional Protocol to the European Convention – Protocol 12 – which state parties are not obliged to join.

An important doctrine employed by the European Court in enforcing these Convention rights is that of a principled deference to the states, under the doctrine it developed of respect for the margin of appreciation of state discretion. This has been particularly pronounced in matters of the relationship between state and religion,[3] although the Court has also employed the margin of appreciation as a general principle in a variety of matters.[4] The Court explained that:

Where questions concerning the relationship between state and religions are at stake, on which opinion in a democratic society may reasonably differ widely, the role of the national decision-making body must be given special importance.[5]

---

[1] Article 9:

   (1) 'Everyone has the right to freedom of thought, conscience and religion; this right includes freedom to change his religion or belief and freedom, either alone or in community with others and in public or private, to manifest his religion or belief, in worship, teaching, practice and observance.'

   (2) 'Freedom to manifest one's religion or beliefs shall be subject only to such limitations as are prescribed by law and are necessary in a democratic society in the interests of public safety, for the protection of public order, health or morals, or for the protection of the rights and freedoms of others.'

[2] Article 14:'The enjoyment of the rights and freedoms set forth in this Convention shall be secured without discrimination on any ground such as sex, race, colour, language, religion, political or other opinion, national or social origin, association with a national minority, property, birth or other status.'

[3] *Wingrove* v. *UK* (1996) 24 EHRR 1; *Campbell and Cousins* v. *UK* (1982) 4 EHRR 293

[4] See Y. Arai-Takahashi, *The margin of appreciation doctrine and the principle of proportionality in the jurisprudence of the ECHR* (Antwerp: Oxford Intersentia, 2002).

[5] *Sahin* v. *Turkey* (2007) 44 EHRR 5.

The implications of this 'hands-off' approach will become clear in the ensuing discussion of particular problems that arose regarding religion and the state, and the way the Court dealt with them.

Church and state – the legal relationship

In its rulings on matters relating to the relationship between state and church, a distinction can be seen in the European Court of Human Rights' approach between two types of claims: claims of infringement of specific rights of religious freedom, and claims that the institutionalisation of religion *in itself* constitutes a breach of religious freedom. The main aspect of religion to which the Court has taken a 'hands-off' approach is that of the institutional relationship between the state and religions operating within it, as such. This, in contrast to the more interventionary approach taken to claims that raise specific rights which were injured by state policy predicated on certain historical underlying moral or religious underpinnings.

Some European states (such as the UK and Greece) retain state churches to this day. The Court has never directly pronounced whether such an establishment – or indeed any type of establishment of religion within the state constitutional structure – is a breach of religious freedom. The Court has had opportunities to engage with this question, but preferred not to do so. In cases in which this question could have been raised, the Court decided the outcome on other issues. Different facets of the establishment of religion were at issue in cases before the Court, in cases in which the Court avoided principled pronouncement on the legality of such status.

A primary way in which states establish the state religion is by according them legal status or legal capacity that is not accorded to other religions. In *Canea Catholic Church v. Greece*,[6] legal personality, which is needed for the capacity to perform legal acts, was granted to one religion that was not the state religion, but not to another. The Court viewed this as discrimination on religious grounds of other religions, those not recognised as possessing legal personality. The Court was able to circumvent the question of the legitimacy of a privileged status of a state church, because it could point to discrimination between two religions that were not the state church. The Court avoided discussion of the underlying question, whether the legal status of a state

[6] (1999) 27 EHRR 21.

religion in itself is, or might be, in breach of the Convention right to non-discrimination on the basis of religion.

Another way in which states favour an established religion is by supporting it, but not other religions, with state funding obtained through compulsory taxation. The conformity of this practice with individual religious freedom under the ECHR was challenged in *Darby* v. *Sweden*,[7] but was left undecided, as the Court found a breach of the Convention on other grounds. The fundamental question that might have been raised here, but was not, whether the state could legitimately levy a tax in favour of the state church or if this contravened article 9 of the Convention, was left unexamined. The ECHR, however, had decided in *Iglesia Bautista* v. *Spain*[8] that the state could give special tax status to a religion with which it has formal links. The reasoning of the Commission was that different treatment is permitted if justified, for instance, by an additional burden placed on the established religion – in this an undertaking by the established (Catholic) church to put its historical heritage at the service of the Catholic people. This seems a rather non-rigorous analysis of the justification for departing from equality in treatment, as the obligation on the established religion seems quite ethereal, while the benefit conferred upon it, financial benefit, is quite real. The closest the Court has come to a demand that states maintain neutrality in the public sphere and refrain from showing preference for a state religion above other religions or non-religious beliefs has been in the recent case *Lautsi* v. *Italy*.[9] In this case the Court determined that crucifixes in state schools infringe Italy's obligations under the Convention.

This question of the legitimate role of state involvement with religion has gained added urgency with the break-up of the Soviet Union and the emergence of post-Communist states. These have given new importance to autocephalous churches, which have played an important role in the formation of national identity in new Eastern European states. At the same time, post-Communist states have maintained, and sometimes have tightened, their regulation of minority religions. Thus it appears that there is a more pressing need for a clear pronouncement of the Court on the legitimate role of religion in member states, a need which seemed to have lessened over the past three decades with the secularisation of older member states.

One of the main issues of contention in the European Court in regard to post-Communist states' approach to minority religions has been that

---

[7] (1991) 13 EHRR 774.   [8] App. no. 17522/90   [9] App. no. 30814/06.

of registration requirements imposed by states on religious organisations. This requirement impacts on both article 9 and article 11 of the Convention (protecting freedom of association). In several cases the Court has declared the refusal of states to register minority religions unlawful, as it deemed the specific decisions arbitrary or ill founded. It has not, until recently, pronounced on the legitimacy of the registration requirements as such.

In *Moscow branch of the Salvation Army* v. *Russia*,[10] the Court decided that freedom of association of the Salvation Army had been breached where its registration had been denied despite lack of evidence that it had any intention of breaching the law, as claimed by Russia. However, the Court did not pronounce on the legitimacy of such registration requirements for minority religions (as it might have done had it examined the alternative argument of the applicants under article 14, the non-discrimination article of the Convention). Likewise, in *Biserica Adevărat Ortodoxă din Moldova* v. *Moldova*[11] the Court decided that Moldova's refusal to register the applicant church ostensibly for failure to submit required documents was factually ill-based, and therefore a breach of the applicants' religious freedom. Again, the Court did not examine the registration requirement itself. In the recent decision in the case of the *Church of Scientology* v. *Russia*,[12] although it highlighted the connection between freedom of association and freedom of religion, the Court viewed the refusal of Russia to register the church as arbitrary and unlawful in the particular instance, without examining the registration requirement.

Thus, the Court has carefully tiptoed, protecting Convention rights, in this case those of minority religions, from state encroachment, without pronouncing on limitations on the ability of states to define the constitutional status of religions within the state.

Recently, in *Religionsgemeinschaft der Zeugen Jehovas* v. *Austria*,[13] the denial of registration of Jehovah's Witnesses was determined to breach Austria's obligations. However, in marked contrast to the cases previously cited, the Court stressed that being placed in an inferior status was in itself a violation of the rights of the applicant religious organisation. The fact that it could achieve most of the advantages of being a 'religious community' through other means did not change that. That Court decided that refusal to give the applicant religious organisation the same

---

[10] App. no. 72881/01.   [11] App. no. 952/03.   [12] App. no. 18147/02
[13] App. no. 40825/98, *Religionsgemeinschaft der Zeugen Jehovas* v. *Austria*, ECtHR (decided 31 July 2008).

status as other religions without justifiable reasons constituted discrimination in the protection of religious freedom.[14]

Some states have gone further than instituting registration requirements, but have tried to intervene in the appointment of clergy of minority religions. In *Hassan and Chaush v. Bulgaria*,[15] the appointment of such ministers by the state was at issue. The Court accepted the applicants' argument that Bulgaria had misused its discretion granted by law in the appointment of Muslim clergymen in that particular case, contravening the right to freedom of religion. The Court preferred to resolve the dispute regarding the particular facts rather than the general question. The Court did not examine the underlying question – whether the state can legitimately appoint religious ministers of a minority religion rather than leaving the choice to the members of the religion involved.

On some issues, however, the Court has inched towards greater intervention concerning the status of religion in the state. In *Supreme Holy Council of the Muslim Community v. Bulgaria*,[16] the Court decided that a state may not force factions of a minority religion to have one unified organisation, and must remain neutral on religious matters. In a further case it decided that, even regarding the state church, a state could not compel a splinter faction to remain within the state church, despite the social cohesion which the state may claim to be dependent on maintaining a unified church.[17]

Does religious freedom demand state neutrality on religious matters?

Although, as has been seen, the Court was reluctant to question the legitimacy of establishment, in a rare case, the Court did approach this issue, where it impinged upon another principle – democratic participation in the state. In *Buscarini v. San Marino*,[18] the applicant members of the Parliament of San Marino complained that they had to 'swear on the Holy Gospels' their oath of office. The Court found a

---

[14] This decision was followed by other decisions on religious discrimination: App. no. 76581/01, *Verein der Freunde der Christengemeinschaft v. Austria*, App. no. 42967/98, *Löffelmann v. Austria*; App. no. 49686/99, *Gütl v. Austria*.
[15] (2002) 34 EHRR 1339.   [16] App. no. 39023/97.
[17] *Metropolitan Church of Bessarabia v. Moldova* (2002) 35 EHRR 13.
[18] (2000) 30 EHRR 208.

prohibited interference with article 9, since it required them to swear allegiance to a particular religion or forfeit their parliamentary seats. The Court went on to quote approvingly the European Commission on Human Rights, stating that 'it would be contradictory to make the exercise of a mandate intended to represent different views of society within Parliament subject to a prior declaration of commitment to a particular set of beliefs'.[19] So, it appears that where lack of religious neutrality of the state impinges upon the democratic political process, the Court might intervene to prevent such a restriction.

In light of the *Buscarini* decision, it is hard to explain the decision in *McGuiness* v. *UK*,[20] which rejected the application of MPs from Northern Ireland, who claimed that swearing allegiance to the Queen infringed their rights under article 9. The factual difference between the cases was that in *McGuiness,* Parliament members did not have to swear allegiance to a certain religion, but they had to swear allegiance to the Queen who is the head of the state church. The commission saw this distinction as determinative, deciding that there was no infringement of article 9, as MPs were not required to affirm allegiance to a particular religion. The objection of the Northern Irish Republican MPs was nationally as well as religiously motivated. An argument of Republicans who simply object to a monarchy would not give rise to an argument under article 9. But the religious objection in this case, as is evident from Irish and English history, is an important aspect of the objection to the monarchy. By having to swear allegiance to the head of a church to which they object, the applicants had to accept the institutional position of the state church to which they object both politically and doctrinally. The Commission seems to have dismissed this argument too lightly. Indeed, this case (which never reached the European Court) suggests that not every lack of state religious neutrality, even if it impinges upon democratic participation, will be seen to infringe upon the religious freedom of the participants.

This case echoes a much earlier episode in English history: the refusal of an atheist MP to take a parliamentary oath on the Bible. The MP, Charles Bradlaugh, was elected in 1880, but was therefore unable to take his seat in Parliament. This lead to great controversy, which was settled only in 1886, when legislation permitted MPs to affirm rather than swear an oath.[21] There are important differences between the cases, of course (not least that

[19] *Ibid.*, para. 39.   [20] App. no. 39511/1998.
[21] See Paul Thompson, 'Liberals, Radicals and Labour in London 1880–1900', *Past and Present* 27/1 (1964), 73–101; Walter L. Arnstein, *The Bradlaugh case: a study in late-Victorian opinion and politics* (Oxford: Clarendon Press, 1965).

the applicants in *McGuiness* were members of another religion, rather than atheists). But it is interesting to note the historical political significance of the religious oath in light of the easy dismissal of the religious significance of the oath by the European Commission.

The state and the internal organisation of the state church

The degree of separation or entanglement between state and church created by the European Convention, as interpreted by the Court and the Commission, is determined not only by the decisions as to the legitimacy of according constitutional status to institutions of a state church. A different but related issue is whether such status entails obligations of the state church under the Convention. In a case which centred on the status of members of its clergy, the Commission again avoided ruling upon the constitutional question involved: if state churches are accepted as legitimate under the Convention, is the Convention applicable to them? In what way are those subject to acts and decisions of the state church, particularly clergy, subject to the protection of the Convention?

In *Tyler* v. *UK*,[22] an Anglican minister argued that article 6 of the European Convention, which guarantees an 'independent and impartial tribunal' in any determination of 'civil rights and obligations', should apply to disciplinary proceedings against him in ecclesiastical courts.[23] The Commission did not rule on this argument, as it decided that, whether the provision applied or not, the ecclesiastical court did constitute an independent and impartial tribunal, as required by this provision. So, there was no legal determination by the Strasbourg court as to the applicability of the Convention right.

Were the disciplinary proceedings in state churches to be regarded as subject to the provisions of article 6(1), this would affect the status of religion in the states in two opposing ways: the state church would be subject to further external, secular law (the European Convention), but, at the same time, this would add to the entrenchment of religion in the state. This aspect of the legal relationship between church and state is also, at present, left unexamined.

---

[22] (1994) 77 DR 81.
[23] Article 6(1): 'In the determination of his civil rights and obligations or of any criminal charge against him, everyone is entitled to a fair and public hearing within a reasonable time by an independent and impartial tribunal established by law. . .'

A constitutional principle of secularism

The European Court has been reluctant to intervene not only in the choice of those states which chose to establish a state church, but was also reluctant to intervene in the opposite constitutional stance, that of states with a constitutional principle of secularism. Although different states, in Europe and elsewhere, have variations of a principle of secularism,[24] it is concerning Turkey that the question of secularism has come repeatedly to the fore in the European Court. At first, in cases such as *Kalac* v. *Turkey*,[25] the Court (and, in *Karaduman* v. *Turkey*,[26] the Commission) tended to accept the mere fact that the state adopted a principle of secularism as legitimate justification for the state's interference in religious freedom. This principle was seen as part of the constitutional order of the state, which the state could legitimately fashion and uphold. Thus the adoption of this principle in the state's constitution served to justify restrictions on the religious affiliation of an army judge,[27] and the religious dress of a university student.[28]

Later, however, in a more recent case, *Sahin* v. *Turkey*,[29] dealing with prohibition on the wearing of headscarves, the Court looked beyond the principle of secularism. The Court did not accept the principle, in itself, as a justification of the state's restrictions on religious expression, but enquired whether a separate legitimate justification existed which required this principle to be upheld, such as whether the expression would disrupt public order. Although the Court accepted the state's position in *Sahin* itself, this may be seen as a turn in the Court's direction, a new willingness to subject the principle of secularism itself to scrutiny.

Legislation based on religious precepts

Religion plays a role in the constitution of the state not just through legal recognition of religious institutions, but also through legal endorsement of religious norms. Discussion of this aspect of the constitutional status of religion as well was avoided. The question whether basing a law on religious precepts is in itself a contravention of the right to freedom of conscience guaranteed by the Convention was not discussed by the Court, although it had the opportunity to do so.

In *Johnston* v. *Ireland*[30] the lack of a legal possibility of divorce in Ireland was argued to be in breach of article 9. The applicant argued that his inability to live with his partner other than in an extramarital

---

[24] For instance, the principle of *laïcité* in France.
[25] *Kalac* v. *Turkey* (1997) 27 EHRR 552.   [26] App. no. 16278/90.   [27] In *Kalac*.
[28] In *Karaduman*.   [29] App. no. 44774/98.   [30] (1986) 9 EHRR 203.

relationship was contrary to his conscience and therefore he was the victim of a violation of his freedom of religion and conscience.

After dealing with arguments based on other Convention articles, the Court summarily dismissed the article 9 argument, stating that: 'Roy Johnston's freedom to have and manifest his convictions is not in issue. His complaint derives, in essence, from the non-availability of divorce under Irish law, a matter to which, in the Court's view, article 9 cannot, in its ordinary meaning, be taken to extend.'

The non-availability of divorce was a product of state legislation. This legislation was a product of a particular religious outlook (although, of course, there might be additional reasons for non-availability of divorce). The Court did not consider, as it might have done, whether legislation, which, in fact, enforced a religious norm, was an illegitimate infringement of religious freedom. While the specific issue discussed (availability of divorce in Ireland) is now moot, the general question relating to law based on religious norms remains pertinent.

In *Refah Partisi* v. *Turkey*,[31] however, the Court did discuss the case of a party, whose aims were to be democratically elected, and thereafter to introduce religious legislation in the area of family law. The European Court decided that the order of the Turkish Constitutional Court, which dissolved the Refah political party, on the ground that it had become a 'centre of activities contrary to the principle of secularism', was not in breach of the Convention. The Court relied on two reasons for its ruling: the first, what it saw as an ambiguous stance of the party towards usurpation of power by force; the second, its proposed introduction of a religious family law system, which would apply to citizens according to the religion to which they belong. This could signal that the Court will now be prepared to view religious legislation, as such, as a breach of religious freedom, even without a specific claim of an individual whose rights are curtailed by it. It could be, however, that the Court viewed this as proposed legislation which will necessarily infringe individual rights, for example, of those who wish to belong to no religion, and would not apply the same ruling to other cases of legislation based on religious norms. A significant point highlighted by the case of Turkey, but true also elsewhere, is that family law is typically the last bastion of religious law remaining as state law in a process of secularisation and the first to emerge in a process of resacralisation.

In the next two sections, the rulings of the European Court and Commission on two specific issues of gender and family law, which have been pivotal in the secularisation of Europe in the past half century, will

---

[31] (2004) 37 EHRR 1 (Grand Chamber decision).

be briefly examined: the right to equality of treatment of sexual minorities and the right to abortion.

Contribution of the European Court to secularisation – family and sexuality

In some aspects of its jurisprudence, the European Court has contributed to secularisation of Europe. Most notable of these is its case law dealing with sexuality and family relationships, especially, but not exclusively, in matters relating to rights of homosexuals and transsexuals. These cases, some of which are discussed below, do not directly raise matters of religion, indeed they raised arguments of infringement of the rights to private and family life and non-discrimination in the protection of private and family life (article 14 and article 8 of the Convention). But the historical reasons for the legal recognition of particular types of family life, against which these applications were directed, often had their roots in religious precepts.

As will be seen, in some cases the rulings of the Court preceded social change and even precipitated it. However, in other cases the Court waited for a degree of European consensus to emerge before pronouncing on the rights of sexual minorities. Until then, it deferred to the state under the doctrine of the margin of appreciation.

An early case is *Marckx* v. *Belgium*,[32] in which the Court found discrimination in inheritance rights based on a status of illegitimacy to be unlawful. The Court's decision in *Marckx* was based on the explicit inclusion of 'birth or other status' amongst prohibited grounds of discrimination in Convention rights, in article 14. The Court was faced with a bigger challenge when dealing with claims of discrimination based on grounds not explicitly mentioned in the Convention, such as sexual orientation.

The status of 'illegitimacy' in the family, like the assignation of gender roles that led to legal discrimination of homosexuals and transsexuals, exists in secular state law, but has religious roots. Similarly, law in European states, which discriminates against these sexual minorities, has various roots, but religious perceptions of gender and sexual roles played an important part in their creation.

A decision which preceded social change was *Smith and Grady* v. *UK*,[33] mandating that homosexuals not be discriminated against in army recruitment. It brought about a change in British armed forces recruitment directly mandated by the case. Further decisions outlawing

---

[32] (1972) 2 EHRR 330.   [33] (2000) 29 EHRR 493.

discrimination against homosexuals followed: in *Sutherland* v. *UK*[34] the Commission determined that the higher age of consent for sexual relations between same-sex partners than that for opposite-sex partners infringed the requirement of non-discrimination in the protection of private life (included in article 8 in conjunction with article 14 of the Convention). At this point UK law was changed.[35]

The legal decisions of the European Court were also followed by a series of policy and legislative reforms in the UK (culminating in the Civil Partnerships Act 2004 which allows same-sex couples to register legally their partnership). These were part of a social and political change driven by many factors, but to which the decisions contributed at least in part.

In *Da Silva Mouta* v. *Portugal*[36] the same approach of the Court was applied to an issue even more intimately linked to the religious underpinnings of the state – the right to family life. In this case the state was not permitted to discriminate against a father in determining custody of his child because of his sexual orientation.

However, there was no uniform approach to issues of discrimination against homosexuals' right to family life. In *Fretté* v. *France*,[37] a case in which adoption, rather than custody, of the applicant's own child was at issue, the Court, relying on the margin of appreciation, deferred to the decision of the state, which did not allow the applicant to adopt a child because of his sexual orientation. While the state decisions in *Fretté* did not rely on religious reasons, it relied on traditional normative approaches to the family, based, among other reasons, on religious tradition. It is pertinent to note that the Court did not attempt to explain why the policy of the state might be rationally justified, thus strengthening the conclusion that deference to the state was indirectly deference to its religious traditions. Finally in a recent development, however, the Court decided that a state could not consider the homosexuality of a prospective adoptive parent as a reason for denying adoption.[38]

In the case law on recognition of the right of transsexuals to their new identity, the second type of process is evident: social change in the European states influenced a change in the judicial policy of the Court. The Court initially had not recognised the right of transsexuals

---

[34] (1997) 24 EHRR CD22.
[35] By the Sexual Offences (Amendment) Act 2000. This was passed using a procedure to by-pass the veto of the House of Lords (using the Parliament Acts of 1911 and 1949), a complication which further highlights the political change prompted by the Court in the face of remaining resistence in some quarters of society.
[36] (2001) 31 EHRR 47.   [37] (2004) 38 EHRR 438.
[38] App. no. 43546/02 *E.B.* v. *France.*

to be registered according to their new sex.[39] It only accepted this right at a later stage, in *Goodwin* v. *UK*,[40] after noting that some social perceptions on this matter, in Europe and elsewhere, had changed in the meantime.

Both perceptions of sexuality and perceptions of family life in Europe have origins in religious teachings. It is therefore interesting that the Court has increasingly accepted the new social reality of the family as worthy of protection, over the state's legal definition of family, a definition often historically rooted in religious teachings. This is true not just in relation to sexual minorities. In *Keegan* v. *Ireland*[41] the state was ordered to provide the same rights to an unmarried father in relation to paternity as those of a married father. The Court had accepted the new secular social definition of 'family life' over the state's legal definition, rooted in historical religious perceptions.

Abortion

One of the main points of contention regarding secularisation of society in Europe in the past half century is the question of a right to abortion.[42] In contrast to their pronouncements on other issues of family and sexuality, the European Court and, previously, the Commission, have so far avoided making any major determinations.

It is surprising, but no substantial determination as to the existence of a right to abortion has been made under the European Convention. In *Bruggemann and Scheuten* v. *Germany*[43] the Commission (by majority vote) found that pregnancy is not exclusively part of a woman's 'private life', and therefore is not protected by article 8 of the Convention, which mandates that states respect everyone's private life. In a later case, *H* v. *Norway*,[44] the Commission, asked to rule on a potential father's rights in connection with an abortion, left broad discretion to the state on this issue, avoiding again a clear statement on the existence of a woman's

---

[39] *Rees* v. *UK* (1986) EHRR 56; *Sheffield and Horsham* v. *UK* (1988) 27 EHRR 163. But see the different approach on the somewhat different facts of *B* v. *France* (1992) 16 EHRR 1.
[40] (2002) 35 EHRR 524. Subsequently, in *Van Kück* v. *Germany* (2003) 37 EHRR 973 the Court even imposed, in certain situations, a positive obligation on states to finance a sex-change operation for transgendered individuals.
[41] (1994) 18 EHRR 342.
[42] Indeed, and in testament to the ongoing controversy in European states on this issue, only recently, in 2007, Portugal's Parliament passed a new law liberalising abortion, despite the failure of a referendum on the matter.
[43] (1977) 10 DR 100.   [44] (1992) 73 DR 155.

right to abortion and permissible limitations upon it by others, in this case the father.

The issue was raised indirectly in *Open Door and Dublin Well Woman* v. *Ireland*,[45] which dealt with an application against an injunction banning dissemination of information in Ireland on abortion clinics outside Ireland. The Court decided the case on the issue of freedom of expression and made no determination as to whether a right of access to abortion is included within Convention rights. In *Tokarczyk* v. *Poland*,[46] the Court decided that the conviction of the applicant for arranging abortions did not infringe his right to freedom of expression under article 10 of the Convention. Thus the question of whether women had a right of access to abortions again remained unanswered.

Even in the very recent case *Tysiąc* v. *Poland*,[47] the Court accepted that an applicant who suffered severe myopia due to childbirth due to a lack of available legal abortion, article 8 (the right to protection of private life) had been breached, but only because there was no clear legal mechanism to determine the right already available in Polish law to termination because of medical considerations. The Court did not pronounce on the existence of such a right independently of the law of the member state.

Although these decisions do not explicitly deal with religion, as commentators have noted, the Court was probably guided in its deferential approach by the existence of a diversity of national moral, social and religious approaches to abortion.[48] But why should the diversity of national social and religious approaches to this issue matter? Either there is a violation of rights or there is none. If there is no violation, there is no role for the Court (or Commission), but if there is a violation, its victims should be protected, particularly where their choices run against the views of the majority.

But the Court and Commission have shied away from making a determination on the matter. On this subject, the right to abortion, it is social and political changes, not decisions of the Court, which have led the way to an increasingly secular European stance.

Secularisation, the family and the European Union

What does the future bode for the prospect of the constitutional secularisation of Europe? An important avenue of development will come not

[45] (1992) EHRR 244.   [46] App. no. 51792/99.   [47] App. no. 5410/03.
[48] A. Mowbray, *Cases and materials on the European Convention on Human Rights*, 1st edition (Oxford: Oxford University Press, 2004) p. 359.

from the ECHR mechanism, but from the other European regional mechanism – that of the EU.

Progress towards the constitutionalisation of the EU unsurprisingly raised religion as one point of contention. The negotiations on the draft Treaty Establishing a Constitution for Europe[49] exposed deep divisions regarding the inclusion of a mention of Christianity, mostly between Catholic states such as Poland, which demanded it, and secular states such as France, which opposed it. In the end no mention was made of Christianity, the Preamble referring only to the 'spiritual and moral heritage' of the European Union. Indeed, such divisions were exposed again, at least in statements of European politicians, regarding the possibility of admission of the first predominantly Muslim (although constitutionally secular) state of Turkey.

Under the Lisbon Treaty, which entered into force in 2009, the Charter of Fundamental Rights of the European Union now has legal force. This includes the right to freedom of thought, conscience and religion,[50] a general non-discrimination provision on grounds that include religion,[51] and a provision that 'the Union shall respect cultural, religious and linguistic diversity'.[52]

It is notable that the right to marry and found a family[53] a right related to religion, is made subordinate to national legislation. Although subordination to national legislation is not exclusive to rights concerning religion,[54] it is notable that such deference to national law is present regarding family life, seen as a deeply cultural choice, which religion underlies.

It was seen in the discussion of the case law of the European Court of Human Rights, that secularisation is intimately connected with the disentanglement of religious perceptions from legal regulation of family

---

[49] OJ C169, 18 July 2003.
[50] Article 10

    (1) 'Everyone has the right to freedom of thought, conscience and religion. This right includes freedom to change religion or belief and freedom, either alone or in community with others and in public or in private, to manifest religion or belief, in worship, teaching, practice and observance.'
    (2) 'The right to conscientious objection is recognised, in accordance with the national laws governing the exercise of this right.'

[51] Article 21: 'Any discrimination based on any ground such as sex, race, colour, ethnic or social origin, genetic features, language, religion or belief, political or any other opinion, membership of a national minority, property, birth, disability, age or sexual orientation shall be prohibited.'
[52] Article 22.   [53] Article 9.
[54] See Article II–27 (workers' right to information and consultation).

life. But this new regional European document, which creates a uniform baseline of religious equality and religious freedom, shows deference to member states, precisely in those areas that religion already underlies.[55]

Conclusion

The new European legal order of human rights formed by the ECHR has brought about secularisation in some areas, but has left some major areas untouched. Some of the contentions raised in applications to the Court stemmed from the underlying constitutional status of religion in the state. Whenever possible, the Court preferred an ad hoc solution, rather than an analysis of this underlying problem. Why is this so, and why have some important questions in this field been left unasked and unanswered?

The Court has shied away from any pronouncements on the legitimate status of religion – or secular ideology – in the states. The simple explanation for this is the language of article 9 itself. Differently from the First Amendment to the US Constitution, which prohibits any establishment of religion, the article does not mention establishment of religion at all. But there appears to be a deeper reason for this avoidance. Perhaps religious identity is so deeply embedded in the perception of national identity that interference in its manifestations by an external judicial agency is considered by the Court to be out of bounds.

Historically, religion has been a building block of the European nation states. Is the emergence of a supra-national Europe a reason to move away from such identity? Perhaps. Is it the role of the European Court of Human Rights to make this happen? Or should the Court see itself as occupying a traditional judicial role, that of merely settling disputes? This last approach was taken by the Court in many 'status of religion' cases. It took the 'path of least resistance' and handed decisions limited as closely as possible to the facts of the case, basing its intervention on abuse of governmental discretion in the particular case. It might instead have seen its role as setting down constitutional principles which will

---

[55] EU law has entered the field of family law, at least to a procedural extent. EU regulations (Council Regulation (EC) no. 2201/2003, OJ 338, 23 Dec. 203, p. 1–29) now allow a couple from any member state to obtain a divorce in a new country of residence, thus overcoming lack of national divorce provisions (currently a problem only in Malta). See A. Scolnicov, 'Multi-religious societies and state legal systems: religious marriages, the state and implications for human rights', in T. Wilhelmsson, E. Paunio and A. Pohjolainen (eds.), *Private law and the many legal cultures of Europe* (Frederick, MD: Kluwer International, 2007).

maintain a positive framework for the protection of human rights in this field. It could have done so by examining the state constitutional principles on which government actions are based. Indeed, some tendency to do this is seen in the latest decisions of the courts. New, and some old, developments in Europe may signal that the Court will have no choice but to engage in this broader role in the future if it is to maintain its pre-eminent role in this field.

The lack of engagement with the establishment question is obvious in comparison to the extensive discussion of this question by the US Supreme Court.[56] But does judicially maintained separation of state and church lead to a more secularised society? Not necessarily. American society is more religious than might be assumed from a strictly legal analysis of the American Constitution and the jurisprudence of US Supreme Court on establishment.[57] Conversely, European society has secularised to some extent since the adoption of the European Convention,[58] often without preceding legal secularisation.

Not only is it the case that the European Court has not dealt with the establishment question, it seems that not many applicants have raised it, at least not directly. This could support the argument that the prevailing European approach has succeeded in guaranteeing religious freedom without accepting the other component of the liberal project, commitment to separation of church and state. There is simply no public appetite in Europe for American-style battles over separation of state and church, because the European Convention as interpreted by the Court provides ample other ways for individuals to guarantee their rights. However, as analysis of cases has shown, nascent and emerging conflicts, whose underlying roots are related to state separation or identification with religion, exist and need to be addressed by the European Court.

Transnational constitutionalisation, as enacted by the European Court of Human Rights in its application of the European Convention, has played a role in the secularisation of Europe, albeit a limited role. Concurrently, national constitutional change in individual European states has also taken place. Significantly, in those areas in which the Court has had a secularising influence, it has been able to achieve

---

[56] The US Supreme Court has dealt with this issue over a long list of cases. Some milestones in the discussion of establishment of religion in the context of education are: *Pierce* v. *Society of Sisters*, 268 US 510; *Everson* v. *Board of Education*, 330 US 1; *Waltz* v. *Tax Commission*, 397 US 664; *Aguilar* v. *Felton*, 473 US 402; *Lee* v. *Weisman*, 505 US 577.

[57] See the data analysed in O'Brien's contribution to this volume.

[58] See the critical discussion in Klausen's contribution to this volume.

a common denominator, bringing more religious states in line with others. It has done so by looking to European standards, but has also looked to external, non-European standards.

It may have been expected that, in Europe, religion would recede into the state as a secular entity. But an examination of the cases coming before the Court shows that religion, both that mandated by the state and that confronting the state, is still a social force in Europe as elsewhere. Several factors that are changing the face of Europe today will be likely to make it harder for the European Court to continue avoiding playing a direct role in determining the level of permitted state interference in religious social manifestations. Currently, religious and national identity is being re-examined in new member states in post-Communist eastern Europe, which are according renewed national prominence to their own autocephalous churches, and redefining the role of religion in the state. Older member states are also facing new challenges to their religious and national identity. Western European states are facing these challenges to their predetermined identity from growing immigrant communities, particularly Muslim ones.[59] National identities are thus being re-formed and re-examined by the states in which religion plays a greater, rather than lesser role. These pose distinct human rights concern, which the Court, among other European institutions, will need to confront.

The European Convention promotes toleration towards all religions and beliefs by protecting individual liberty, while, as has been seen, it remains silent on the question of the religious or non-religious affiliation of the member states. The Court has explicated in recent case law pluralism as a different value of the Convention. This is different from state neutrality, secularity or separation, and presupposes none of these.

But claims regarding enforcement of Convention articles are related to underlying fundamental claims about the nature of the state – as a neutral entity which must be committed to no religion or as a social institution which can choose religious characteristics as part of its defining constitution. The legitimate constitutional role of religion in the state is an issue that will remain an eventually inescapable question for the Court to decide in the years to come.

---

[59] For instance, see the decision of the Court regarding the wearing of a headscarf by a Muslim school teacher in a predominantly Christian state: App. no. 42393/98 *Dahlab* v. *Switzerland*.

15 Europe's uneasy marriage of secularism and Christianity since 1945 and the challenge of contemporary religious pluralism

Jytte Klausen

Europeans pay little heed to the requirements of religious observance. In that sense, they deserve to be characterised as 'post-Christian'. Yet, the integration of Islam and Muslims has proven surprisingly difficult for a public that claims to care little about faith. Governments and courts have only recently begun to puzzle out the meaning of state neutrality in newly multi-religious societies while faced with assertive political voices reiterating the importance of Christianity to the European identity.[1]

Many subjects of European states – residents and citizens – no longer adhere to the official state Churches. Muslims comprise between 2 and 8 per cent, about fifteen million people, of the populations of the dozen west European countries with significant immigrant-origin minorities. Scientologists, Hassidim, Mormons, Catholics hewing to the Latin mass, Hindus, and many other groups, new and old, immigrant-origin or old European, are a growing presence. The European Evangelical Alliance, a lobbying organisation for the Evangelical churches in Brussels, claims fifteen million members. Born-again Christians adhere to the same Bible as Europe's Christians but the American-style Evangelical churches share with Muslims the status of outsider and the lack of official recognition. Their demands for accommodation strain the institutional habits of states sanctioned by Europe's national confessions, Protestant or Roman Catholic. Some European cities now face the prospect of becoming minority

The author thanks the Carnegie Corporation for supporting the research for this chapter. An earlier version was presented at workshop on Religion and the Political Imagination at the Centre for History and Economics, King's College, Cambridge, and the 2nd Galilee Colloquium on Religion and Public Space: Cross-Cultural Dimensions in Kibbutz Kfar Blum. The author gratefully acknowledges the contributions of the participants at these meetings.
[1] Brian C. Anderson, 'Secular Europe, religious America', *The Public Interest* (Spring 2004), 143–58; Robert Kagan, 'Power and weakness', *Policy Review* 113 (2002); Robert Cooper, 'The next empire', *Prospect* 67 (October 2001).

Christian and the need to adjust public calendars, municipal and social services, and consultation practices to reflect this fact. Change is invariably accompanied by squawking from the losers. Religion has once again become a highly salient matter in European politics and public policy making.

In the context of the long history of European secularisation and liberalisation, how is the return of heated controversy over religion and Christian identity in present-day Europe to be understood? 1968 is widely credited with having secularised Europe, but Church–state reform pre-dated 1968. Viewed this way, the importance of 1968 recedes and post-war liberalisation assumes the character of a protracted reform movement, rather than a revolution. It also set the stage for today's contest over the meaning of secularism and the role of religious state institutions in multi-religious societies. Freedom of choice was celebrated, but the constitutional reforms pluralism necessitates did not occur. The emergence of a new religious demography and new global religious movements pose analogous but different challenges to Europe's constitutional preference for a merger of Church and state and the corporatist post-war institutions sustaining the societal compromise between reformers and traditionalists.

This chapter pursues two trains of thought. The first focuses on the institutional foundations for state sponsorship of religion in Europe. The second traces the consequence of the Europe path to secularisation for immigrant religious minorities. I shall start with a discussion of the failure of the behavioural approach to secularisation to appreciate the long-lasting effects of the historical role of Churches in European state-formation processes and the consequences for contemporary religious dilemmas.

Secularisation and social science

The distinguished lineage of the secularisation thesis goes back to Weber and Comte. 'Secularism' was taken to mean the waning of belief in God and 'secularisation' was understood as the decline of overt demonstrations of religiosity and religious values in personal and public life. At the macro-level, religiosity correlates with insufficient modernisation and is associated with backward societies.[2] It followed that progressive secularisation would take place when affluence and education eliminates the need for religion. After the events of 1968 and three decades of changes to family structures and social mores, sociologists convinced themselves that the waning of religion was an inevitable sociological process.

---

[2] Pippa Norris and Ronald Inglehart, *Sacred and secular: religion and politics worldwide* (Cambridge: Cambridge University Press, 2004).

Sometimes belief is regarded as a threat to democracy, or rather certain beliefs and certain theologies are considered incompatible with modernity. Ernest Gellner, who wrote about the clash of civilisations in very difference cadencies than those used by Samuel Huntington, viewed the subordination of religion to nationalism as a critical turn in the road to the democratic mass society. His view of the threat presented by religion to the state project is widely shared by contemporary Europeans, as is also his view that Islam is particularly 'secularisation-resistant'.[3]

The secularisation thesis conflates personal behaviour with institutional change. Religious commitments are expressions of transcendental belief, personal identity, and adherence to national and group identities. Cracks show up in the theoretical argument in a number of places. No clear correlation exists between GDP and the propensity to support secular constitutional arrangements.[4] What are we to make of the 52 per cent of Israelis who live in a theocratic state and describe themselves as not religious?[5] Germany was among the countries (together with Venezuela and Tanzania) that reported the highest increase in the number of people who regarded faith as a precondition for morality.

In a recent reformulation of the thesis, Pippa Norris and Ronald Inglehart argued that the welfare state was a motor of secularisation. By the law of averages, Europe is in this view considered secular and the United States exceptional because Americans are affluent and 'religious'.[6] Norris and Inglehart rely on the World Values Survey, but a second, even larger, worldwide survey of 45,000 people, conducted by Pew, also found religious norms to decline with growing affluence, if allowances are made for Kuwait and the United States. The higher GDP per capita, the less inclined people are to express views associated with religious beliefs.[7] Nevertheless, no corresponding correlation exists between GDP and the propensity to support secular constitutional arrangements.

Measurements of religiosity do not capture the institutional aspects of faith issues. Pew used three questions to measure religiosity: do you need

[3] Ernest Gellner, 'Islam and Marxism: Some Comparison', *International Affairs* 67 (1991), 1–6.
[4] Robert J. Barro and Rachael M. McCleary, 'Which countries have state religions?' *National Bureau of Economic Research, Working Paper no. W10438* (April 2004). At http://ssrn.com/abstract=532997.
[5] Gallup International, *Voice of the people. religiosity around the World* (16 November 2005).
[6] *Ibid.*, p. 224.
[7] *47-Nation Pew Global Attitudes Survey* (4 October 2007), pp. 3 and 34. There is no correlation between theology and popular views on the legitimacy of religion in politics. Pew found that majorities in 46 out of 47 countries thought that religion is 'a private matter'. One exception was China, a highly secular country, where people thought perhaps a little religion in matters of government might help, see p. 37.

to believe in God to be a good person? Is religion very important to your personal life? How often do you pray? The first question conflates belief with prejudice and intolerance. The second makes assumptions about identity and faith that cannot be taken to apply in equal measure to Jews, Muslims, and Christianity's denominations and sects. The prayer measure fails to take into account the varying role of ritual in Judaism and Islam (and even within Islam's schools) and Roman Catholicism and Lutheranism, and Confucianism, the least ritualistic religions. The importance of praying as a sign of belief varies widely across religions and even between denominations and sects of Christianity, Judaism and Islam.

Another issue is that religious people are not necessarily conservatives, and vice versa. The political correlates of theology are uncertain. The political radicalism of 'liberation theology' is a case in point. The fact that ethno-religious minorities – Jews and Muslims in Europe, Copts in Egypt – adhere to faith as a marker of identity in addition to personal belief complicates the relationship between religions and political identities. Complex faith, identity and secular allegiances often leave little room for minorities in party systems created upon a coalition matrix of interest representation set by the majority faith. That religious Muslims are often attracted to the human rights agenda of Europe's highly secular Green parties is a recent example of the unpredictability of the correlates of faith and partisanship. Social scientists are well advised to be cautious about quick generalisations about the political stances of believers.[8]

From the viewpoint of theories of the state and the theoretical vantage point concerned with how institutions shape political action, the secularisation thesis puts the cart before the horse. Secularism is here understood not as an attribute of behaviour or psychology but as a product of the institutional principles guiding the state. The institutional literature too suffers from blind spots. In *A theory of justice* John Rawls promoted American constitutionalism to high theory: 'The state can favour no particular religion and no penalties or disabilities may be attached to any religious affiliation or lack thereof.'[9] By this definition Europe, with all its established and 'recognised' state confessions, hardly qualifies as 'secular'. France and Holland may qualify, but neither is a comfortable fit. France's list of prohibited sects and the Dutch proclivity for denominational delivery of welfare state services – schools and universities, hospitals, childcare and nursing homes, trade unions, employers, newspapers – hardly make the two countries ideal examples of

---

[8] Scott Appleby, *The ambivalence of the sacred: religion, violence, and reconciliation* (Lanham, MD: Rowman & Littlefield, 2000).
[9] John Rawls, *A theory of justice* (Cambridge, MA: Harvard University Press, 1971), p. 212.

Rawlsian neutrality. In the United States, the neutrality principle has historically faltered when confronted with the harsher aspects of religious exercise, and on particular issues the distance narrows. Satanists or parents who refuse medical treatment for their children in God's name get little respect on either continent.[10]

A strict legal separation of faith institutions and the state is hardly the only way to satisfy the neutrality criteria. A more nuanced understanding of secularisation as a result of distinct sociological, historical and ideational processes is required. The difficult transatlantic conversation about religion is in part due to a semantic confusion over the meaning of 'secular' and in part a reflection of divergent histories of national identity and constitutional principles. Most Europeans consider 'secular' to mean the absence of ardent displays of belief, and insist that religious values are permissible in politics only to the extent they can be voted on.[11] The twentieth-century European states modernised religion, but never embraced constitutional principles about the separation of state and Church.

The Augsburg legacy

Secularisation in Europe was achieved by means of pacts between Church and state, which tamed clerical influence on political matters but also protected the Church's status. The 1555 Augsburg Treaty brought 'religious peace', *Religionsfriede*, to Europe by creating an inflexible map of stable national religious affiliations, the *cuius regio, eius religio* principle. Roughly translated it means 'his region, his faith' and implied that the regent decided the faith of the realm. The map created by the principle of state religion has held for centuries, and for the most part survived even the upheavals of the twentieth century. The exception is eastern Europe, where forced secularisation severed the link between Church and state. Yet in some respects the imprint of the Augsburg map outlived even communism.

The legacy of the Augsburg compromise for modern states was twofold: it established state Churches as the normal template for conflict resolution between altar and throne, and the state-building process induced faith conformity among subjects. Only the two main parties to the schism in the Christian Church – Lutheranism and the Holy See – were recognised by the Augsburg compromise. Henceforth, treatment of

---

[10] Marci A. Hamilton, *God vs. the gavel: religion and the rule of law* (Cambridge and New York: Cambridge University Press, 2005).

[11] Oddbjørn Knutsen, 'Religious denomination and party choice in western Europe: a comparative longitudinal study from eight countries, 1970–97', *International Political Science Review* 25/1 (2004), 97–128.

nonconforming religious groups – Jews, Anabaptists, Quakers, Calvinists – was a matter of 'toleration'.

The state-centred denominational paradigm was created half a millennium ago, when the dust from the Protestant secessions settled, and the Counter-Reformation reasserted the Vatican's control in the remnants of Catholic Europe. It survived the class wars of the twentieth century, and even in some measure withstood the forced secularisation imposed by communism, but then crumbled in response to choice and individualism, and migration and a growing non-Christian population. Its terminology, the expectations, the conformism and the curious merger of national identity and religious belief still influence the laws and the norms Europeans use when thinking about the role of religion in the public realm.

The sixteenth-century schism created two models for Church–state relations in Europe that lasted, with modifications, to the twenty-first century. Both models ushered in a measure of state control over the clerical power structure by fusing secular and clerical spheres of interest.

The Catholic model was based upon bilateral treaties between the rulers of the realm and the Vatican, which usually ceded ecclesiastical self-governance to the Church and the curia in Rome in exchange for restrictions on the Church's legitimate political activities.

In the Protestant model, in contrast, the Prince was head of the state and of the Church. Church properties were confiscated by the state and left under state control, ecclesiastical government was merged with that of the state, and the clergy subordinated to the crown. Scandinavia and the patchwork of German principalities remained intact examples of the model until the nineteenth century. Over time, convergence set in as rulers reined in the power of the Catholic Church by means of ever-more restrictive treaties and the Protestant monarchies returned a measure of self-government to the bishops. In both models, religious conformism became a vehicle of societal integration and assimilation to the nation state.[12]

The comparative literature on Church–state relations focuses upon constitutional-legal arrangements, but fiscal relations are important signifiers of power relations in modern states. State funding of national Churches sometimes keeps intact a marriage that has ended on paper. In Poland, the constitution asserts principles of separation of Church and state and equal treatment of all religions, but the Catholic Church is the beneficiary of subsidies and privileges not available to other groups.

[12] Aage B. Sørensen, 'On kings, pietism and rent-seeking in Scandinavian welfare states', *Acta Sociologica* 41 (1998), 363–75.

Spain's 1978 constitution, created after the overthrow of the Franco regime, declared the state to be secular and ended the Roman Catholic Church's long-standing association with the state. Yet the government continued to fund the Catholic Church following an informal agreement reached in 1979 and still in effect.

Classification schemes invariably fail to capture the ambiguity of legal and fiscal arrangements, and the many national idiosyncrasies. Barrett's *World Christian Encyclopaedia* is the most common source for classifying states but few authors use it without second-guessing some of the classifications.[13] Useful typologies of constitutional variations in Church–state matters are hardly of interest to sociologists in the absence of attention to the economic reality of fiscal establishment or policies that grant national Churches a *de facto* veto right.

Countries that have both constitutionally established confessions *and* directly subsidised faiths include Denmark, Croatia, Bulgaria, Norway, Finland, Greece, Iceland, Italy and Portugal.[14] (Europe's very small states – Liechtenstein, Luxembourg, Monaco, Malta – also have state Churches.) Spain is an ambiguous case because the Catholic Church is the only religion that remains fully funded by the state, even though the 1978 constitution separated Church and state. The Church of England is an established Church, but receives few direct subsidies. If we count funding for faith-based educational institutions, the education of Christian clergy at the theological faculties at public universities, and publicly funded Christian social and health services as examples of public support for religion, the self-portrayal of Europe as deeply committed to secular values and state neutrality crumbles even further.

Austria, Belgium, Germany and Sweden, are constitutionally secular states but provide direct or indirect subsidies for institutions associated with *recognised* faiths, e.g. religious schools or social and health services. In Sweden, Belgium and Austria funding opportunities are *de jure* available to all religions but parity and state neutrality remain elusive and not fully accepted goals.

The Concordat model

Napoleon's 1801 Concordat and subsequent agreements between states and the Holy See about the regulation of Church affairs set a milestone in the forward march of secularism. But even so, a comparison to

---

[13] David Barrett, George Kurian and Todd Johnson, *World Christian Encyclopaedia*, 2nd edition (New York: Oxford University Press, 2001).

[14] In Malta, the High Court stopped deconfessionalisation in 1987.

US constitutional First Amendment principles casts a different light on the laws and associated practical arrangements created by the Concordat model. The French Revolution nationalised Church property and proclaimed a civil constitution for the clergy, and the Concordat gave little back to the Church that was of interest to the state. The act of devolution meant that ecclesiastical authority was recognised but subordinated to the rule of the state and the civil constitution. The Church's role vis-à-vis civil society was reinstated, however. Roman Catholicism was declared the faith of the French and the Vatican's authority over the clergy restored. The Christian calendar was brought back. (The secular calendar introduced by the Jacobins was used for thirteen years.) Catholic control of education was continued until the establishment of secular public education in the 1880s during the Third Republic. Civil marriage was required but canon law retained its authority over what we today classify as personal law matters.

Subsequent legislation concerning the status of Catholicism and Protestantism in France, the so-called 'organic articles', affirmed a measure of parity between the confessions. Confiscated church property remained in the hands of the state but the state assumed financial responsibility for seminaries and clerical salaries, and parishes reassumed control of schools, hospitals, churches, cemeteries and other parish real estate. Other control measures included a state-issued uniform catechism and a clerical dress code requiring priests to dress in the 'French manner' in black.

A hundred years later, the Law of 1905 arranged for what is often described as 'the strict separation' of church and state. The law applied the plural – *Loi du 9 décembre 1905 concernant la séparation des églises et de l'état* – because it applied in equal measure to Roman Catholicism and Protestantism. The law famously states that 'the Republic neither recognises, nor salaries, nor subsidises any religion'. Aspects of the Concordat nonetheless continued in part as a reflection of the 'stakeholder' privileges of Catholics.

The Concordat model has been replicated across Europe over the past two centuries. The essential elements are public financing of clerical salaries, seminaries, churches and cemeteries and other diocesan property, self-government in ecclesiastical affairs, including the appointment of clergy, and public funding for general education and social services provided by the Church, and grants to the Catholic media and recognition of the Church's standing as a national confession and a right to have a say in certain policy matters. Civil marriages are recent additions in most countries, and the Church generally was given the right to determine and adjudicate personal law issues – marriage, divorce, baptism and burial, paternal rights over children and women, etc. Papal decrees, clerical dress, the management of the Church foundations, the estates, and the clergy's influence on the public imagination through the pulpit, schools and the catechism, were subjected to bilateral diplomatic negotiation.

In Europe's multi-confessional countries, the Concordat model established a 'pillared' system of legal and administrative devolution that gave the Church significant power over the lives of Catholics. Key examples are Austria, Belgium and the Netherlands. Austria provides an interesting instance of the dissemination of the Concordat model. The Austrian Empire included parts of contemporary Germany, the Czech Republic, Hungary, Poland, Ukraine, Slovenia, Croatia, Serbia, Italy and Romania. Its subjects included adherents of Islam, Judaism, Eastern Orthodoxy and various Protestant groups.

The 1855 Concordat between the Austrian Empire (1804–67) and the Vatican was more generous to the Church than Napoleon's 1801 Concordat. It gave the Church jurisdiction over education and family law for Catholics, and control over educational and religious foundations and estates. The constitutional monarchy (1867) revoked the Concordat and established state control (and taxation) of Church foundations and a universal civil code. The reforms also created a separate parish tax to meet the expenses of worship and clerical salaries. The new constitution in 1920, after the collapse of the empire, reiterated the elements of the 1870s reforms and in 1934 a new Concordat was made with the Vatican. German occupation in 1938 voided the Concordat, which nonetheless was renewed in 1957. (Austria was put under Allied administration in 1945 and carved into four occupation zones. Soviet withdrawal took place only in 1955.)

Germany is another example of the updating of the Concordat model to provide a framework for a system of national confessions. The parity compromise combined with substantial devolution to the state level worked as long as the overwhelming majority of German subjects comfortably fit within the two Christian denominations, the Protestant *Landeskirche* (the Evangelical Church of Germany, EKD) and the German Roman Catholic Church. Today, the Protestant and Roman Catholic Churches, as well as Judaism, but not Islam, the third largest faith, are entitled to federally collected church taxes and the right to run state-subsidised religious social services and hospitals.

Regime change and continuity

In the 'long duration' sketched in the above, revolution and occupation stand out as the causes of regime change in Church–state relations. The 1789 French Revolution, the 1848 Revolution and the 1917

Russian Revolution loom large as secularising events. Yet the forced secularisation produced by revolutions was partially reversed during subsequent movements of restoration or moderated by concessions.

The frequent reshuffling of the country's borders makes Germany a complicated case to describe, but if one keeps in mind the basic maps of religious adherence created by the Reformation, the continuity of confessional arrangements becomes clear. Until 1918, German principalities had established religions. The king of Prussia was also the head of the Church. In Trier, Cologne and Mainz, the archbishops combined the offices of head of state and head of the Church in another perfect merger of pulpit and throne.

The Weimar constitution (1919) declared Germany a secular state, but created a compromise between separation and state confessionalism by declaring the two main confessions public corporations and making treaties with each. The arrangement in effect extended the Concordat model to both confessions, with the associated privileges regarding Church self-governance and state subsidies for educational and religious activities. The national state and the local states negotiated bilateral treaties with the two confessions but the negotiating partners varied. In the case of the Catholic Church, all treaties were negotiated with the Vatican, whereas the Protestant counterparts were the local bishoprics. The content consequently varied. In 1933, Hitler made a new concordat with the Vatican, which required the clergy to swear an oath of allegiance to the state, and consolidated the Protestant Church under a *Reichsbischof*.

In reaction, the new federal constitution of 1949 asserted the principle of state neutrality in religious matters and parity for all religions, but in practical terms for the most part reverted to the Weimar model of two national confessions organised as public entities. The federal government collects a tax on behalf of the two confessions, but jurisdiction over religious affairs is located with the states. Matters were further complicated when the constitutional court in 1957 ruled that the 1933 Concordat still had legal force.

State governments (*Länder*) have since entered into individual concordats with the Vatican on a range of matters, including confessional religious education in public schools. About a dozen agreements between states and the Vatican exist, many of which are routinely renegotiated to reflect state interests with respect to confessional social services and education. The decentralisation enabled the old confessional map to reassert itself. Hesse, a predominantly Protestant state, has no treaty with the Vatican, and Bremen and Hamburg negotiated concordats only in 2003 and 2005. After 1989, all five new states formerly comprising the DDR entered into concordats with the Vatican (Saxony 1996, Thuringia 1997, Mecklenburg-Pomerania 1997, Saxony-Anhalt 1998, Brandenburg 2003).[15]

The Netherlands and Sweden 'privatised' but fully funded clergy salaries and pensions in 1983 and 2000 respectively. Even in France, where the law of 1905 and the principle of *laïcité* has been invoked to prohibit Muslim girls from covering their heads in school, churches are municipal properties and are lent free of charge to parishes, and cemeteries are owned by municipalities but run by parish councils.

The forced resettlement and ethnic cleansing in the former Yugoslavia are sometimes taken as paradigmatic examples of the violence released by the return of 'primordial' religious attachments, but some post-Communist countries embrace state neutrality (the Czech Republic, Hungary and Latvia) while others returned to a state faith (Bulgaria: Eastern Orthodox; Croatia: Roman Catholic). Church–state relations are often ambiguous or still under negotiation.

Church–state relations after 1945

Europeans do not think the Church should decide their values for them but are behaviourally Christian even if they are reticent or lazy about it. With the exception of Scandinavia, where the Church's institutional position was little affected by the personal beliefs of adherents, belief in God has been stubbornly resistant to expectations of the 'waning of faith'.[16] Europeans did not banish faith but narrowed the room for considerations of 'sacred values' and the continuation of a public ethics and public policies while assigning a privileged position to Christianity. The twentieth-century 'stability pacts' between Church and state assured the national confessions of financial security and cast religion in a supporting role in the development of national cohesion. Tamed religion remained part of the nation state's arsenal of means for national integration.

The continued ability of the Church to influence codes regulating sexual relations, education and the family could be ascribed to the electoral influence of religion and the veto power of the conservative and clerical parties. However, Protestant Scandinavia similarly showed

---

[15] Concordat agreements are listed on the website of the German Foreign Ministry; see www.auswaertiges-amt.de/diplo/de/Laenderinformationen/HeiligerStuhlVatikan/Bilateral.html.

[16] Pippa Norris and Ronald Inglehart, 'God, guns and gays: supply and demand of religion in the US and western Europe', *Public Policy Research* 12/4 (2006), 224–33, table 1 on 226.

no inclination to banish the Church from the foundations of the state. The large Christian democratic parties in the Netherlands, Germany and Italy were electoral conduits for social conservatism, as were the French Gaullists, who after De Gaulle's return in 1944 merged Republicanism and Catholicism. But the European left also found ways to accommodate religion. The prospects of power made the socialists moderate their views on how to deal with the church. The Danish Social Democrats abandoned all ideas of church reform in the 1930s and accepted the idea of the 'People's Church', which informed a 1907 reform that established general elections to parish councils and made all pastors civil servants, a system that continues to be regarded by left and right as 'foundational' to the Danish identity. In Sweden, the Social Democrats were deeply divided over the 'People's Church' concept, which originated among German Protestants and paved the road for Nazification of the Protestant Church in 1936. The promise to disestablish the church, which was part of the Social Democrats' platform when first elected to power in 1933, was removed. On 1 January 2000, Sweden became the first – and only – Nordic country to disestablish the state church.

The loss of the predominantly Protestant eastern territory after 1945 altered the balance between Roman Catholics and Protestants in the Federal Republic of Germany. The social fact of religious parity between Catholics and Protestants was reflected in the 1949 Basic Law's equal treatment of two national Churches. The post-war reorganisation of the old conservative parties into the Christian Democratic Party under the leadership of Konrad Adenauer meant that religious values became deeply entrenched in the Federal Republic. During the war, Nazi family law had reversed many reforms from the Weimar period, and returned the regulation of family law and women's status to the old nineteenth-century civil code. The 1949 Basic Law mandated the replacement of the old pre-Weimar code, but the Christian Democrats allowed the old laws to continue. Legal patriarchy existed until 1959, when a new family and equality law was finally passed after the Constitutional Court intervened. A husband's statutory right to decide over children was also eliminated. Other changes ensured that wives no longer needed their husbands' permission to work and that female civil servants could no longer be automatically dismissed when they married.

The German Social Democrats moderated their views on the Church question much later as part of the new centrism ushered in by the Willy Brandt era. In the 1959 Bad Godesberg programme, the *Sozialistische Partei Dentschlands* (SPD) abandoned old socialist ideas about the 'socialisation' of the family, and in a nod to Catholic values affirmed

that the family was a fundamental unit of society – 'Die Familie ist als
ursprüngliche Einheit eine Grundform der Gesellschaft' – and declared
motherly love to be essential to the raising of children.[17] Expecting that
religion would wilt on its own, as educational reform and social security
progressed, the left chose to avoid a confrontation with the national
Churches and saw benefit in the ability to control sectarianism through
enhanced 'supply-side' regulation of the Church's activities.

Shifting boundaries: speech, sex and education

In theory, ecumenical speech protection against defamation of religion is
quite possible. The reality is that judges find it very difficult to define
blasphemy as an offence outside the Christian religious imagination.
There is the practical difficulty of defining what might constitute
blasphemy in a faith with which one is unfamiliar. A more important
constraint is the unpopularity of expansion of curbs on free speech
with respect to minority faiths. By definition it is the majority who will
have to curb the tongue or hand.

Blasphemy laws are secular expressions of the prohibition in Mark 3:29:
'But whoever blasphemes against the Holy Spirit never has forgiveness,
but is guilty of an eternal sin.' Prohibition against blasphemy remains
entrenched in the penal code in a majority of European countries.
Austria, Denmark, Finland, Germany, Ireland, the Netherlands, Spain,
Switzerland, Poland and the UK all prohibit blasphemy. In the UK, only
the Anglican Church was protected against blasphemy until the House
of Lords abolished the law in 2008. Blasphemy protection was successfully invoked in Germany in 1994 against a musical comedy that crucified
pigs to ridicule the doctrine of the Immaculate Conception.

Some countries have in recent years amended the laws to include
Judaism or rephrased the laws as protection against various forms
for group defamation. The result has been an expansion of speech
codes on identity grounds ranging from racialist speech to incitement
to religious hatred and Holocaust denial, which has left many legal
scholars uneasy. Muslim associations attempted to use blasphemy laws
against Salman Rushdie's *Satanic verses* and the Danish Muhammad
cartoons, but were universally unsuccessful. (A case against *Jyllands-
Posten*, the newspaper that published the cartoons, filed by Danish
Muslim associations, is pending before the European Court of
Human Rights.)

---

[17] SPD, *Jahrbuch 1960/1961*, p. 467.

Clerical strictures on sexuality were most effectively challenged when issues became framed as matters of science. The first Kinsey Report, *Sexual behavior in the human male* (1948), had tremendous impact on public policy on sodomy in Europe. The second report, *Sexual behavior in the human female* (1953), had hardly any. The UK eliminated the prohibition on consensual homosexual sex in 1955. Other countries followed suit significantly later, West Germany in 1969, Finland and Austria in 1971. The German Constitutional Court reaffirmed that homosexuality was a crime as late as 1957 but in 1968 consensual relationships were decriminalised. In 1984, the European Court of Human Rights declared the criminalisation of homosexuality contrary to human rights.

In France, where the Vichy government had instituted the death penalty for carrying out an abortion, special courts outside the judicial system were set up after the war charged with the task of balancing punishment to the circumstances of the crime. Abortion was not made legal until 1975.

Divorce and birth control were extracted from the grip of clerical control late and with great difficulty, and only with partial success. One exception to the general picture of the relatively recent elimination of the Church's control over women's sexuality is Sweden, where eugenicists made abortion available for 'damaged foetuses' as early as 1938, and socio-economic hardship was added as a legitimate indicator for legal abortion in 1944.

On 25 July 1968, Pope Paul VI disappointed Catholics across the US and Europe by declaring the contraceptive pill a sin in his encyclical, *Humanae Vitae*. The decision was a surprise. It was widely expected that the Church would accept the pill as a lesser evil compared to abortion, and it is perhaps today surprising that so many Catholics cared about what the Church said. Most Catholic countries gradually extracted policy with respect to divorce, abortion and birth control from ecclesiastical authority.

In Ireland, Italy and Spain, the Roman Catholic Church prevented reform. (Legalisation failed as recently as 2002 in Ireland.) In the Federal Republic of Germany, the two Christian Churches invoked the right to life clause in the German constitution (Basic law, art. 1, par 1) and jointly prevented direct legalisation.

In 1967, when the UK legalised abortion, an uproar resulted and conservatives predicted the collapse of marriage and social order. Arguably, they were proven right. Feminists started 'underground railroads' getting women in need of abortions onto the ferries to England. In the following ten years, most European countries legalised abortion, although not without sometimes debilitating political conflicts with conservatives, the clergy and the national Churches.

The sexual revolution is conventionally dated to the sixties. As Philip Larkin famously wrote in his poem:

> Sexual intercourse began
> in nineteen sixty-three
> (which was rather late for me)
> between the end of the Chatterley ban
> and the Beatles' first LP.

Poems speak to our subjective understanding of events, but the reality is that the 'freedom to choose' in matters of morals was wrested from the Church's control gradually and through the disjointed progress of constitutional secularisation and legal reform. Sometimes secularisation in one arena brings analogous changes in another, as in the case of the sexual deregulation after 1968, but there is hardly a firm chain of causation between the waning of religious belief and the secularisation of the civil code or of public education, both important areas of clerical influence.

The liberalisation of sexual codes took place in a more incremental fashion than those of us who enjoyed what at the time seemed like a sudden flowering of transgression in the sixties. The revolution was also incomplete. Religion was not banished from the institutions of the state. The ambiguous compromises that entered into the stability pacts between Church and state ceded territory in education and in areas of speech regulation, to mention some examples, to the Church in order to appease still important public sentiments about the bedrock importance of Christianity in European society and the state.

In some respects the interpenetration of church and state deepened as the state's mission expanded in the 1960s. Religious schools were guaranteed students and public funding in exchange for teaching secular syllabi and accepting a prohibition on proselytising. The education of Christian clergy at the theological faculties at fast-growing public universities (Protestant countries) or at private but publicly funded seminaries (the Catholic countries) installed civic values in the clergy's mission. The social institutions of the church – hospitals, schools, nursing homes – are examples of the meshing of social and religious services in the lives of citizens. It is why we today have difficult discussions about the provision of halal food in hospitals and crucifixes on the walls of public schools that do not allow teachers to wear the headscarf.

Education remained an ecclesiastic stronghold, in part due to parent demand and in part because faith-based schools are convenient for governments. Typically, European governments fund religious schools, maintain church property and cemeteries, and educate the clergy at public universities. Often, states could not provide adequate educational services in the absence of collaboration with the Church. The curious result is that in secular Europe religious education is promoted by the state. However, Christian insistence that religious schools be continued has had the unintended consequence of leaving a window open for the creation of Muslim schools.

Following a 1917 law, the Dutch government has continued to pay for religious schools and religious institutions, contributing in equal measure to each of the religious 'pillars'. Parents have a constitutional right to create their own school and to follow a religious curriculum. Efforts to deny Muslim parents the same right were met by resistance from Christians who feared anti-clerical sentiments might spread to them.

Since 1959, the French state has paid the salaries of teachers in religious schools. About 20 per cent of French students go to religious schools, which are mostly Catholic. The schools receive about 80 per cent of their budgets (teachers' salaries and some operating costs) from the government. In the case of special contract schools, those on a *contrat d'association*, public funding is set at 105 per cent of the cost per student in public schools. Catholic schools are private schools and exempt from the sumptuary rules introduced by what is popularly referred to as the 'headscarf law', technically is called the 'Law of 15 March 2004, concerning, as an application of the principle of the separation of church and state, the wearing of symbols or garb which show religious affiliation in public primary and secondary schools'. The law did not affect private schools. The consequence is that many headscarf-wearing Muslim girls now attend Catholic schools. One Muslim girls' school receives public funding but several other Muslim schools are seeking recognition.

Britain started funding Muslim public schools – or state schools as they are called in Britain – only recently, but in addition to the religiously managed state schools there exist a large number of independent – or private – religious schools. Public funding currently covers 85 per cent of voluntary-aided schools' costs, and it has been proposed that it should be set at 100 per cent. The so-called 'voluntary Church-aided' schools are state schools managed by the Church. 'Church foundation' schools are owned by the Church but public education authorities pay teacher salaries and other operating expenses. Another way of describing the difference is to say that the first category refers to religious state schools and the second to publicly funded private religious schools. The independent schools are not government funded but must teach to a national curriculum. By 2004, five Muslim state schools were established and over eighty independent private schools accredited. In comparison, there are over 2,000 Roman Catholic voluntary (or public) and 160 independent (or private but publicly supported) schools in England and Wales. The Church of England manages a quarter of all state schools.

When Baden-Württemberg passed a law in 2004, which prohibits teachers from wearing the headscarf in the classroom, it was justified with the argument that the headscarf is a threat to fundamental 'occidental' norms and the values expressed in the state constitution. The state constitution says that public education must be 'value neutral'. Nonetheless, the crucifix is by law displayed in public classrooms. The argument for the inequity in the treatment of Christianity and Islam is that Christian symbols are regarded as universal and 'democratic', whereas Muslim women wearing the headscarf are accused of 'prosely-tising'. The state's culture minister, Annette Schavan, a Christian Democrat who became a federal minister for education, warned against value neutrality. 'We cannot allow a spiritual vacuum to emerge that would leave our society without guidance', she said, 'we must stand by our cultural and religious traditions as they are expressed in our Constitution'.[18] The accommodation of new non-Christian religions invariably involves a discussion of the place of Christianity in what Europeans paradoxically have thought of as secularised institutions.

State neutrality may take many forms. The Rawlsian agnostic state is a beautiful but a politically complicated ideal. The Dutch and the Belgian adjustments to multi-confessional societies and mass democracy involved a more messy approximation to equal treatment of confessional groups. Another approach is to deny a conflict exists. A majority of Danish parties – including the social democrats – have explicitly or tacitly decided that Denmark is essentially Christian and that no conflict of basic principles exists when minority faiths and denomin-ations are denied equal treatment.

The return to a culturalist conception of nationhood is not a promis-ing strategy. Social and political exclusion breeds resistance and conflict, which do not necessarily assume political forms but create internal pressures for normalisation. International organisations and courts – the foremost are the European Court of Human Rights and

---

[18] My translation from the original, 'Wir dürfen kein geistiges Vakuum entstehen lassen, das unsere Gesellschaft orientierungslos werden lässt. Wir müssen zu unseren kulturellen und religiösen Traditionen stehen, die Eingang in unsere Verfassung gefunden haben.' Land Baden-Württemberg, announcement on 1 April 2004.

the European Union's Court of Justice – exercise considerable pressure on states to accept the devolution of the universalist principles of international human rights commitments into national legal and policy frameworks. In sum, as religious pluralism increases, we should expect European states to secularise Church–state relations to a point where the difference between recognised confessions and minority religions is minimised.

A study by Jonathan Fox of trends in religious discrimination between 1990 and 2002 suggests that the expectation that states will respond by promoting neutrality or anti-discrimination norms is overly optimistic. Fox defines discrimination as 'restrictions placed on the religious practices or organisations of a religious minority in a state that are not placed on those of the majority religion' and breaks the measure down to sixteen common types of discriminatory treatment. These range from restrictions on proselytising and conversion to restrictions on worship, the construction and maintenance of buildings for worship, and personal observance (marriage, burial, rituals). By the standards of American norms with respect to equal treatment the standard is low. Discriminatory funding practices are not included in the measures, and no concessions are made to multi-culturalist norms regarding the obligations of liberal states to provide compensatory support for exposed minorities.

Fox found that 55 states out of 175 increased the level of discrimination against minorities over the period. The average increase in discrimination was modest, 11.4 per cent. Discrimination decreased in 17 states.[19] Contrary to public assumptions, only the Middle East did not increase discrimination. The greatest increase took place in the former Soviet states and in Africa. Broken down by majority religion, the Islamic countries showed the smallest increase and the predominantly Orthodox and Catholic countries led the way.[20] Western democracies placed hindrances in particular on proselytising and access to registration and construction of places of worship.[21]

Civic religion vs national identity

Institutions and public norms change over time in response to social facts, but often at a snail's pace. In 1958, Reinhold Niebuhr, an American Lutheran theologian, reached a conclusion about Christians' obligations to Jews. Judaism had to be accepted on its own grounds, and

---

[19] Jonathan Fox, 'Religious discrimination: a world survey', *Journal of International Affairs* 61 (2007), 47–67.
[20] *Ibid.*, 52, table 1.   [21] *Ibid.*, 56, table 4a.

the Christian desire to convert Jews had to be recognised as 'an impossible task'. The fact that the Jew could not be separated from his community without committing an assault on the community compelled Niebuhr to reconsider the theological absolute of the true faith. The internalisation of a *de jure* recognition of the coexistence of multiple religions in the modern public sphere in Niebuhr's revision became internalised into his theology as a recognition of the multiplicity of faiths. 'By "converting" to civil religion', wrote John Murray Cuddihy, 'Niebuhr saw all denominational religions – including Judaism – as group and ethnic religions, as henotheisms, coexisting tolerantly in a religious détente.'[22] (Henotheism accepts the existence of gods other than one's own.)

Niebuhr's intellectual breakthrough was motivated by the Holocaust, but the position he articulated forms the basis for the articulation of contemporary civic religion in the United States. Mayors hold prayer breakfasts with civic prayers performed by clergy from every faith group in town. Public schools put up the menorah next to the lamb and pictures of the baby Jesus, or any other symbol the teacher can invent, to reflect the demography of the class. Europe is mid-stream in a cultural revolution on such matters.

Multi-religious societies compel believers to make choices between the demands of civic religion and the one true faith. The paradox of the liberal paradigm is that whatever constitutional compromises are made they need to be sufficiently commodious to allow the faithful to refuse theological revision. In the early years of the twenty-first century, Pope Benedict has been a learned and insistent spokesman for the essential Christian-ness of Europe. Echoing Huntington, the Pope has argued that Europe is not primarily a geographical but a cultural and historical concept. The title of his 2006 book says it all, *Without roots: the West, relativism, Christianity, Islam.*[23] Pope Benedict has condemned forms of multiculturalism that fall into what he has described as western self-hatred. The message is that Europe's dialogue with other 'cultures' (i.e. Islam) must proceed on the bedrock of the Christian faith, if we are to avoid falling into value relativism and reawaken the spectre of totalitarianism. This of course is fine from the viewpoint of theology, but from the viewpoint of the state the more the Church insists on Christian primacy the less the state can grant the Church its wishes.

---

[22] John Murray Cuddihy, *No offense: civil religion and Protestant taste* (New York: Seabury Press, 1978), p. 44.

[23] Joseph Ratzinger (Pope Benedict XVI) and Marcello Pera, *Without roots: the West, relativism, Christianity, Islam* (New York: Basic Books, 2006).

Civility demands that you no longer accuse believers of religions other than your own of being infidels. Questioning the secular loyalty of non-Christians is another matter. In the April 2008 general election, Italian voters switched in large numbers to the parties that campaigned on 'values', the *Italia dei Valori* and the *Lega Nord*. No longer just simply anti-immigrant, the agendas of the 'values' parties invariably now also have a religious aspect propelled by resistance to Muslims. These are themes that have sustained the decade-long rise of the Danish Peoples' Party and the *Vlaams Belang*, and in barely moderated tones informed Nicolas Sarkozy's 2007 presidential campaign in France and Roland Koch's struggling campaign to retain the CDU's control of the premiership in the German state of Hesse in early 2008.

The European tradition of assimilating religious and national identities has always played a central role in anti-Semitic narratives. Religion acts in this respect much the same way as race or ethnicity as a source of exclusion in certain kinds of nationalisms. The old Protestant tropes about 'papists' as the fifth-column representatives of the Pope invoked doubts about Catholics' loyalty to the nation in a manner comparable to anti-Semitic complaints about Jewish international conspiracies.[24] The anti-Catholic and anti-Semitic rants are strikingly similar to things said today about Muslims in Europe, who also are presumed to be remote-controlled by their faith to seek the 'Islamisation' of Europe and to want to impose the caliphate.

Much of the ongoing debate about the integration of Islam has focused upon the incompatibility between religious fundamentalism and secularism. Fundamentalism poses a particular difficulty for liberal society because it rejects secularism as the source of evil and regards scriptural literalism and proselytising as civic virtues. But most religious people are not fundamentalists and are perfectly capable of distinguishing between their religious selves and their secular and public selves. Nor is fundamentalism a 'Muslim problem'.[25]

Can you, as has been the custom, ask religious minorities to identify with the state over their group? A Pew Survey that intended to study how Muslims and Christians balance secular and religious identities set off alarms in the editorial pages of European papers when it was reported that Christians overwhelmingly see themselves as citizens of their country first and Christians second, but Muslims describe themselves as Muslims first and citizens of their countries second. The results were

---

[24] Anthony W. Marx, 'The nation state and its exclusions', *Political Science Quarterly* 117 (2002), 103–26.
[25] David Zeidan, 'A comparative study of selected themes in Christian and Islamic fundamentalist discourses', *British Journal of Middle Eastern Studies* 30 (2003), 43–80.

taken to provide support for the 'clash of civilisations' argument that Muslims are 'secularisation-resistant'.

Among British Muslims, 81 per cent said they were Muslims first. In Spain and Germany, 69 and 66 per cent respectively said 'Muslims first'. France was the exception with only 46 per cent saying Muslims first, a number not unlike that provided by Christians in the US. How should we interpret such numbers? The easy thing is to say that the statistics show the importance of secularist values and Muslims are on balance deficient in this respect. But what is the meaning of this test?

Members of minority religions cannot easily discard religious affiliation. Faith is in such cases frequently not simply an expression of belief but also of tradition, belonging and identity. When, as is the case for Jews in general and increasingly for Muslims in Europe, discarding the faith becomes synonymous with assimilation, the expression of religious affiliation turns into a political statement.

Researchers would be reluctant to ask Jews if they were Jewish or German first. Minorities who have a sense of being endangered cannot agree to the assimilationist implication of such questions without questioning their allegiance to their family and history. A subsequent survey conducted by the Gallup World Poll challenged the Pew results when it showed that European Muslims were extremely supportive of national institutions, when given the opportunity to express support for God and country simultaneously.

Sexuality and abortion, education, blasphemy and artistic expression are issues that may well return to the forefront of Europe's religion wars. Evangelicals and Muslim clerics have little in common, and even less commonality with Pope Benedict's defence of the Catholic Church's social conservatism. But these groups may yet join forces against gay rights and civil libertarians.

In January 2008, after years of deliberation, a new European association of religious organisations unveiled a charter that stipulated the political values they derived from their faith. One article listed the importance of religious values for the groups' view on the family:

[...] considers that a family based on the bonds of marriage between a man and a woman is the natural and necessary environment for the raising of future generations. The family is an indispensable condition for the happiness of the individual and stability of society. Thus, [...] emphasises the significance of taking all measures in order to reinforce the family and protect it from all things that will weaken or marginalise its role.[26]

---

[26] Federation of Islamic Organisations in Europe, *European Muslim Charter* (10 January 2008).

Table 1 *Percentage who say they believe in God (selected countries)*

	Change +/−	1990	1995	2001
Sweden	8–10%	38	48	46
Netherlands	−3%	61		58
Norway	7%	58	65	
Denmark	3%	59		62
GB	−9%	72		61
W. Germany	6–8%	63	71	69
Canada	3%	85		88
Austria	5%	78		83
Italy	6%	82		88

Source: World Values Survey. Results from the fourth wave from 2005 not posted.

The manifesto could have been written by Europe's Christian Democratic parties but it was issued by the Federation of Islamic Organisations in Europe (FIOE), an umbrella group for the Muslim Brotherhood in Europe, and 'Islam' is the word missing in the brackets. The possibility of the emergence of an alliance between religious parties spanning Protestant, Roman Catholics and Muslims is in some respects the best harbinger of the final secularisation of European politics. To work together in a partnership of civic religious, the faiths concede that conversion is not on the agenda. A state of mutual recognition is implied if not publicly acknowledged. Nevertheless, the prospect that the Vatican will ride back into power on the coat-tails of the black-robed imams to control sex and women, as a new generation of anti-clerical writers imagine, are slim.[27] Few Muslims – or Catholics – want to curtail the freedom to choose in lifestyle matters in any case, and religiously conservative Muslims will hesitate to enter into an alliance with a Pope who considers them infidels and questions their place in Europe. The freedom to express one's religion now also includes the freedom not to be religious, and to vote for something else.

[27] Christopher Hitchen, *God is not great: how religion poisons everything* (New York: Warner, 2006).

16   On thick and thin religion: some critical reflections on secularisation theory

Sudipta Kaviraj

Secularisation theory – analysis of the role of religion under modern conditions – has been thrown into confusion by some baffling historical developments. Writing about 'secularisation' as a subject involves a paradox: it pre-commits us to write about the 'decline' of religion, although the entire point of the analysis should be to ascertain whether religion has suffered a decline or not. Conceiving the subject that way presupposes an answer to a question still under analysis. History appeared to be obediently following the logic of rationalisation detected by modern social theory, until the revolution by Ayatollah Khomeini unreasonably upset its rhythms and confused its directions. After a time, it was clear that the Iranian Revolution was not an isolated incident, which could be treated as an anomaly. A revivalist Taliban successfully destroyed Afghanistan's modernist communist regime, supported by Soviet arms – though, in this startling achievement the US policies contributed more generously than is normally admitted. Western governments sought simply to use these medieval fanatics, incongruously placed in a modern world, for their own geopolitical strategy, and intended to offer them strictly temporary support. After their victory over communism, the fundamentalist army refused to melt into oblivion, and on the contrary, started spreading influence in surrounding regions. Even in the enlightened continent of Europe, where government policies implicitly assumed that immigrants, stepping on these enlightened shores, would be instantly converted to secular rationalism, surprising developments happened. Contrary to the theory of instant enlightenment, immigrants settled into a sullen refusal to convert to secular rationalism. Revival of religion was restricted not to Islam. An unprecedented revival of Christian fundamentalism occurred in the US. Remarkably, the most theatrical protagonists in the modern political struggle, George W. Bush and Osama Bin Laden, had guns in their hands and an intensely parochial god on their side. After the fall of communism, eastern Europe witnessed a wave of Christian revival. In India, comfortably secular and democratic, a Hindu nationalist party surged to electoral power. What, one could ask from the point of view of social theory, was happening to the world?

There is a widespread sense that this is not supposed to have happened. Yet, oddly, there is clearly strangeness in this way of describing the matter. Why should events not have happened? How can we accuse historical events of unreasonableness? This illustrates the immense power theory exerts over our immediate perceptions of the world.[1] Thinking *historically*, it should not be surprising that a period in which religious culture declines is followed by one in which it undergoes a revival. Strange things happen in history. But thinking *theoretically*, the 'decline of religion' is seen as teleological and terminal, not to be reversed without the collapse of all the reliable laws of history. A theory so spectacularly at odds with the facts of history is obviously in need of some re-examination.

On the theory of secularisation

Revising the theory of secularisation could be attempted in two ways: the first is to assess if the claims of the theory, taken as a whole, are justified. A second method might be to examine closely the kind of claims which constitute the theory, and decide whether these can be disaggregated, prior to an appraisal of their correctness. Weber's theory of secularisation draws upon two somewhat contradictory prior intellectual sources. On one side, Weber drew on the methodological apparatus of historicism fashioned by neo-Kantians like Dilthey and Rickert.[2] Historicism was committed to a thick historical description of peculiarities of and human experience internal to specific social forms. On the other hand, Weber is also drawn towards another impulse, attempting to bring social structures under large-scale functional generalisations, particularly evident in his strong theory about the functional cross-generation of different processes of modernity.[3]

Two features of this sociology of religion require close critical analysis. In Weber's sociology there is a clear understanding of the plurality of

---

[1] Charles Taylor claimed that in the modern world we live theoretically. This is one possible gloss on that claim, and an illustration of its truth in modern history. See Charles Taylor, 'Social theory as practice', in *Philosophical papers: philosophy and the human sciences philosophical papers* (Cambridge: Cambridge University Press, 1985), vol. II.
[2] H. P. Rickman (ed.), *Dilthey: selected writings* (Cambridge: Cambridge University Press, 1979).
[3] Although it is true that this functionalist impulse is not the only or probably even the dominant one in Weber's sociology, Talcott Parsons picked up a significant strand of his thought, though he undoubtedly developed it rather one-sidedly. See Max Weber, *The sociology of religion*, introduction by Talcott Parsons (London: Methuen, 1965).

religious institutions, a keen perception of the fact that what we generally call 'religion' is actually a combination of many institutional and ideational structures.[4] In Weber's own work, this perception of internal complexity of the social fact of religion is at times masked by his emphasis on the functional integration of the reality of 'religion'. Subsequently, social science analyses have tended to take for granted this overly functional view of religion as a *single* phenomenon. This inattention has large negative consequences. This is particularly true of discussions about contemporary history, partly because the primary commentators are students of politics and history, who are often not specialists in rigorous examination of religious phenomena. They fall more easily to the temptation of speaking of 'religion' at an excessively high level of abstraction and generality.

Modern social theory has habituated us to the expectation that through evolution of modernity 'religion' would inevitably decline; and what startles us is the apparently contradictory historical perception that while the processes of modernity have constantly advanced across the world, 'religion' has refused to decline. Indeed, against this historical grammar, it has tended to become stronger. What I wish to criticise in this chapter is this general, vague, indiscriminate use of two linguistic elements crucial to a history of the present – the singular concept of *religion*, and the *bivalent* judgement about its becoming either 'weaker' or 'stronger'.

The primary cognitive and linguistic conventions of our thinking about religion were formed implicitly through Weber's classical secularisation thesis, which explains the manner in which the development of the capitalist economy and its logic of rationality works as the fundamental causal process behind secularisation.[5] This process is assisted by the spread of rationalisation from the economic to the political sphere, through the extension of calculative rationality of capitalist economic

---

[4] This is particularly true of the treatment of ideas, ideals, institutions and common practices Weber offers in such detail in his *Sociology of religion*.

[5] It can be argued that Weber's original conception of 'rationalisation' has two distinct meanings in his detailed sociology of religion, carrying a terminal and a non-terminal meaning of the process. Rationalisation can mean a process through which rationally untenable beliefs about the world are gradually undermined and rejected, leading eventually to a terminal process of 'disenchantment': without this meaning of the term, disenchantment cannot occur. The other meaning of the term rationalisation can indicate a tendency towards a greater elaboration and analytic systematisation of ideas, without an entailment of a teleological movement towards disenchantment. It can be suggested, for instance, that in the great period of philosophical reflection and elaboration on religious ideas by the Kashmir Saivas in the eighth to the tenth centuries in India, there was a rationalisation of religious ideas in the second sense, but not in the first.

action to the political rationality of the modern bureaucracy. The conventional theory left some room for internal complexity – but that complexity was conceived in a specific fashion. Lags could develop between various sectors of social institutions leading to a process of 'catching up'. It is even conceivable that the dark forces of tradition might overcome the processes of rational secularisation and lead to a defeat of modernity. But, within the terms of that theory, it is hard to conceive of a state of affairs in which some parts of a society seem to move in one direction and others in another. The fluvial dynamics of historical forces disallow such radical complexity: everything must 'turn' or 'move' in a single direction. The primary task is to modify the theory in a manner that it can admit such contrary motions of historical possibility.

The internal complexity of religion

Phenomenally what strikes us about religion is that it is many different things, leading therefore to an indeterminacy of reference when the concept is used generally. It always represents a complex combination of various elements: an intellectual system – sometimes more than one; a set of authoritative institutions – which can be many and contested; a range of social practices; a set of ritual observances. Religion refers to a whole range of distinct institutional fields – an ethical order, a social order, philosophical systems, political institutions. Secularisation theory expects that, under historical conditions of modernity, these elements will move symmetrically in the same direction – of stability or decline.

Additionally, secularisation theory conceives of this historical 'decline' in a manner that is not sufficiently *strategic* – in case of either religious beliefs, or religious practices or the capacity of historical self-maintenance of religious institutions. The theory encourages us to forget what beliefs, practices and institutions really are: these are believed, observed and maintained by real human beings, and these processes are intimately linked to their individual and group interests. It is an excessively rationalistic notion that if a group of intellectuals, Group A, produce rationally compelling arguments that undercut the primary beliefs of another, Group B, the second group would simply hang their heads in shame, and abandon their ideas. Outcomes of historical disputes are rarely so decisive and one-sided; and this picture also underrates the human capacity for self-righteousness. Usually Group B will go home and try to come back with better arguments next time, and try to keep it from themselves that they have lost the argument. In addition, most of the

central points of dispute are not like questions of natural science, capable
of clear proof or disproof. Interpretative ideas rarely admit of such
decisive destruction. Viewed sociologically, it appears as a field of strategic action regarding both the reliability of beliefs and self-sustaining
power of institutions. In conflicts over the 'truth' of religion, groups and
individuals who constitute the other side of the rationalists seek ways of
holding on to their ideas and ideals; and in some cases, where historical
change becomes undeniable or institutionally irresistible, they try out
adaptation strategies, which involve some concession to change, but not
a comprehensive surrender. In the late eighteenth century, Christian
missionaries campaigned for large-scale conversion of Indians from
Hinduism to Christianity. They tirelessly pointed out that remaining a
Hindu involved being mired in superstition, belief in the supernatural,
and other disreputably irrational ideas. They placed what they considered an unavoidable choice before educated Indians: they must either
admit to being irrational and Hindu, or convert to Christianity and enjoy
the epistemic privileges of rationalism. Contemporary Hindus refused
the way the choice was structured, and decided instead, as Ram Mohan
Roy's work shows, to re-form their Hindu beliefs according to rationalistic principles, dropping their commitment to the supernatural and the
socially repugnant, to continue to remain Hindu, rejecting the offer of
Christian rationalism. In fact, Ram Mohan Roy wickedly provoked his
missionary interlocutors by asserting that his rationalist commitments
prevented him from becoming a Christian, as that would involve admission of irrational beliefs in the Immaculate Conception, and the godliness of Christ.[6] Given the choice between terminal decline of their
religious beliefs and doctrinal adaptation, nineteenth-century Hindus
chose to adapt their religious beliefs to new cognitive procedures and
intellectual styles. It is possible to generalise from such instances and to
assert that when faced with the challenges of modernity, traditional
forms (but these really are people) do not drop their weapons and die.
Some of these groups ignore their historical duty to decline and find
unreasonable ways of adapting and even flourishing in the new cultural
ecology. We need a more complex and supple theory which allows
different elements of religious life to move, at least temporarily, in
contrary directions, for some parts of religion to become weak, and
others strong.

[6] Raja Rammohan Ray, *The essential writings of Raja Rammohan Ray*, ed. Bruce Carlisle
Robertson (Delhi: Oxford University Press, 1999).

Weberian sociology and Indian politics

Political sociology in India faced a problem in the 1980s which was directly parallel to this general difficulty with secularisation theory. The rise of Hindu nationalism in India from the mid 1980s could be viewed as a part of this troubling 'desecularisation of the world'. Viewed according to received theory, Indian society was going through a conventional secularisation process since the nineteenth century, with a steady decline of religion both in social conduct and in political institutions. The sudden irruption of religious politics in the 1940s leading to partition was viewed as an 'aberration'.[7] After partition, insistent secularisation resumed, driven by three distinct, mutually reinforcing causal mechanisms. Economic industrialisation, driven by both market and state, was supposed to lead to secularisation by transmission and extension of rational calculative behaviour. Second, the quotidian working of the democratic state, in which institutional devices of constantly recurring electoral choice interpellated the citizen to act individualistically,[8] was meant to dissolve attachment to primary religious communities. Indian political leaders could not be indifferent to the continuing presence of Hindu nationalist political opinion which demanded that people should act politically on the basis of their religious affiliations. But the constitutional mechanisms of state secularism and the vigilance of the major political parties were expected to ensure that such ideas did not acquire enough strength to dominate political life. Industrialisation and electoral democracy were long-term processes working *indirectly* for secularisation, and state secularism was a *direct* institutional expedient; but these produced convergent results. The rapid urbanisation processes, large-scale migration of people from more community-oriented villages to cities fostering sociability among strangers, produced intermixture and social individuation. This theoretical picture was Weberian in two senses: in terms of its content of ideas, and the logical form in which these ideas were arranged. Once a society went through a phase of secularisation, they believed further, it could not regress.

Indian intellectuals did not entertain excessively simple empirical understandings of the place of religion in Indian life. Foremost among

---

[7] However, political forces which supported partition, like the Muslim League led by M. A. Jinnah, obviously viewed this history differently, and saw modern Indian history as deeply influenced by religion. The 'two-nation theory' was a view which implicitly asserted the continued effectiveness of religion.

[8] I am using interpellation in the sense used by Louis Althusser, *Lenin and philosophy and other essays*, trans. Ben Brewster (London: NLB, 1971).

modernist secularists, Nehru remarked that Hinduism had two contradictory aspects – a body of deep philosophical reflection which could attract modern rationalists, but also a social system based on the caste order wholly repugnant to the intellectual spirit of modernity and institutions of democracy.[9] In their actual analysis of religion, therefore, Indian intellectuals acknowledged the internal complexity of religion. Second, the very fact that their political efforts – in both constitution-building and everyday political campaigns – focused so heavily on the problem of 'communalism' admitted implicitly the existence of a significant body of political opinion which believed that the state should be based on Hindu rather than secular principles. Third, the more astute observers noted that political Hinduism was quite different from everyday Hindu religious belief, and while the state should explicitly oppose the first, it should not try to eradicate the second.[10] Secularisation lay in 'the logic of history': thus what began to happen in Indian politics from the mid 1970s appeared not as a historical curiosity, but as a strange and inexplicable transgression of historical norms.

On thick and thin religion

Thickness and tolerance   Accordingly, the rise of Hindu nationalism was widely interpreted in startled language as 'a revival of religion'. Yet, on closer inspection, this might not be seen as a comprehensive reversal of secularity; and the 'religion' that the Bharatiya Janata Party (BJP) invoked was, again, quite distinct from traditional forms of religious practice. To capture this essential distinction I shall use a distinction between *thick* and *thin* religion.

Let me explain what I mean by *thickness* and *thinness* of religion by a commonplace personal experience.[11] I shall recount two conversations with my grandfather about *his religion*, as they reveal some important characteristics of his beliefs, and show, by implication, not merely what his religious beliefs were, but more importantly, what it meant to him to have a religious belief. Hindu society in Bengal is divided primarily

---

[9] J. Nehru, *The discovery of India* (Delhi: Oxford University Press, 1998).

[10] For a detailed analysis of the implications of this distinction, see Rajeev Bhargava, 'On the distinctiveness of Indian secularism', in T. N. Srinivasan (ed.), *Future of secularism* (Delhi: Oxford University Press, 2007).

[11] My father was a Marxist historian and an appropriately fierce atheist; but I was brought up partly by my grandfather who, by contrast, was a deeply religious individual, and an observant Vaishnava. I saw the functioning of religion from close quarters by observing his practice and general social life in the religious town where I grew up – a major place of Vaishnava pilgrimage.

between two sects, Vaishnavas[12] and Shaktas.[13] Although our town was a major holy place for the Vaishnavas, it had a large segment of Shakta inhabitants – a common pattern in Bengal. The two sects lived side by side in apparently tolerant neighbourliness, though there were some paradoxes of traditional tolerance. Shakta ceremonies were held in our locality in which there was ritual sacrifice of animals; but by my time, actual slaughter of a buffalo or a goat was considered distasteful, and in many instances, the priest, after appropriately violent invocations of the goddess Kali, usually sacrificed a vegetable substitute like cucumber or marrow. My grandfather disapproved of these ceremonies deeply, because he thought it was aesthetically and morally repugnant to associate the worship of the creator with wanton destruction of life of his creatures. If I pointed out the slaughter of vegetables, instead of real animals, as an extenuation, to him this meant that in addition to being violent in principle, they were also weak-willed in practice. It compounded his distaste, instead of mitigating it. His belief in religion involved not merely a deep and vivid faith in the ideas and observances of his own Vaishnava sect, but also *a sharp differentiation from others* – though, paradoxically, this did not come in the way of settled habits of religious tolerance. Curiously, sharp diversity of religious beliefs was a condition for the practice of tolerance: if religious beliefs of all people were identical or similar, that would represent consensus rather than tolerance. Someone with strong religious faith had to face the question: what should be his attitude to religious practices other than his own?

There can be a simple route from perception of religious diversity to intolerance. If a religious person believed that his own religion was the right one, and worshipping God in other ways inappropriate, did this not imply that other forms of religious practice should be suppressed? To this, my grandfather returned an interesting and careful response. Although he found some Shakta religious practices repulsive, it was inappropriate to obstruct them by law or by social pressure. As a human being, he possessed finite cognitive powers, seriously limited by space, time, capacity and opportunity for knowledge, and above all by the finite character of individual experience; while God and his creation were infinite. So it was quite possible that finite human minds were only impressed by what they could grasp of this infinite being and his infinite

---

[12] Vaisnavas are the worshippers of Visnu, and a major sect of Hinduism; but there are major variations of the Vaisnava faith between its south Indian and east Indian forms. My grandfather practised the eastern, Gaudiya Vaisnava form of this doctrine.

[13] Shaktas are the worshippers of the Hindu goddess Shakti, who is commonly worshipped in the benign, invincible, ten-armed form of Durga, or the dark, destructive and equally invincible form of Kali.

creation. Each group accordingly built their conception of God and what was morally worthy from that circle of finite and partial experience and capacity. As a practising Hindu, it was important for him to hold on firmly to his beliefs, as he had strong moral and intellectual reasons for them; but equally, he had no moral or cognitive authority to impose his ideas on others. The diversity of forms in which God can be worshipped within Hinduism captured this perspective perfectly, and could be extended, by implication, to other faiths like Islam and Christianity. This stylised picture of his beliefs captures its attractive combination of firm religious belief, attentive ritualistic observance, cognitive modesty, recognition of religious pluralism and social tolerance.[14]

This set of core beliefs was connected to other significant ones. On another occasion, I went to a local fair and found a charming image of Radha and Krishna – the form in which my grandfather worshipped God. I bought it for him with my pocket money, hoping that he would install it in his prayer room in place of the wooden image he worshipped – which I found unnaturally shaped, and did not call ugly only out of politeness. Though touched by my gesture, he said he could not worship the image; he would keep it along with other *aesthetically* valued objects. This, he explained, was because it was a porcelain statue, made by man, in a shape and material that were both man-made. Images made of clay, wood or stone could be worshipped – because worship of god must contain within itself an anamnetic reference to the bounteousness of his created nature. There are certain structures which god had put in place, and worship was essentially remembering to respect those things. So the *times* of worship, the *material* for image-making, etc. were all governed by a system of acceptance of divine dispensations. The statue I bought was to be classified and valued as aesthetic, but not treated as being linked to the divine, which was a value of a different order. In time I found many of his conclusions unconvincing, and in matters of ethics sided more with secularists; but what I found particularly attractive was its paradoxical combination of deep faith and an ethic of tolerance drawn out of an acceptance of cognitive finitude and partiality of human vision.

Evidently, it is remarkably inappropriate to claim that my grandfather's kind of religion was in linear decline since the mid nineteenth century, and has been suddenly revived by the political initiatives of

---

[14] Incidentally, this also captures a side of tolerance which is often erased in modern liberal discussions, and the modern embrace of diversity. The word tolerance, in many languages, is connected to the sense of 'bearing' something annoying, irritating or repugnant.

the BJP. The BJP's rise in electoral politics had certainly brought religious ideas into play in the political public sphere, and some observers began to view this as a 'return of religion'. But, even impressionistically, the content, purposes and implications of these new religious ideas are entirely different from those conventional ideas of religiosity.[15] Clearly, this political religion was not what my grandfather meant by religion. It is genetically connected to it historically, because it comes out of the general field of Hinduism, but also something doctrinally and functionally distinct: so that it becomes essential to stop speaking vaguely about 'religion' in the abstract, and to attentively scrutinise this difference.[16]

On thick religion   A religious believer's identity was anchored in beliefs that were spread across a wide variety of religious themes, which can be arranged at different levels of generality. These included metaphysical beliefs about the nature of existence, the nature of God and his relation to the created world, epistemological theories about the nature, limits and trustworthiness of human cognition, sociological perceptions about the basis and boundaries of community, ritual observances in practical situations of worship, minutely detailed paraphernalia about everyday religious practice – how to determine the days of worship, to decorate the place, what to offer to the deity, physical comportment in prayer, the exact chants specific to occasions, and even where to place holy objects like a coconut, a mass of flowers or a banana plant. This religion is *thick* in the sense that its internal contents are a vast, but not disorderly, catalogue of beliefs about large and small things, but all of them are crucial to the practice of this particular faith. These are what make the faith what it is.

Sociologically, his religion comprised of metaphysical beliefs, religious customs, beliefs governing social conduct and regarding ethical life. Crucially, for him, religious ideas had very little relevance for

---

[15] In Indian political sociology, Ashis Nandy was the first observer to notice the deep difference between traditional and modern religiosity and try to theorise it. He suggested a distinction between 'religion and faith' and 'religion as ideology' in a paper that exerted a vast influence on the analysis of political religion in India. Ashis Nandy, 'The politics of secularism and return of religious tolerance', in R. Bhargava (ed.) *Secularism and its critics* (Delhi: Oxford University Press, 1998). I attempted a preliminary elaboration of the implications of this distinction as 'thick and thin' in a paper, 'Religion, politics and modernity in India', in Bhikhu Parekh and Upendra Baxi (eds.), *Crisis and change in contemporary India* (New Delhi: Sage, 1994).

[16] For a much earlier and sketchier approach to these issues, see my 'Religion, politics and modernity in India', in Parekh and Baxi (eds.) *Crisis and change.*

political life.[17] My grandfather would have thought that it was unlikely that God was deeply involved in judgements about how the Congress government ruled, or what the constitution should be like. His religion was indifferent to political affairs; though individually he was not. He took his duties of voting during elections with utmost seriousness, and though he took the secretness of the ballot rather too seriously and never divulged his choice, I suspect he kept on voting for the Congress with a kind of despairing and increasingly disenchanted loyalty common to Indian nationalists of his generation. To him, the most serious value of religion was in determining social conduct and ethical problems, not in political life. It is because of the vast range of issues that religion covered in his mind that I call his religion thick: to state it differently, if he was asked who practised the same religion as his own, he would have laid down a long list of criteria – starting from metaphysical beliefs to ritual observances – and claimed that only someone who satisfied *all* these criteria of religious sameness practised the same religion.

Religious militants are often regarded with a perverse admiration because of the supposed intensity of their convictions, with an unintended implication that others, with politically gentler ideas, lack strong religious belief. This, again, is untrue. My grandfather, and traditional religious people, had a fervent belief in his God, and tried to lead his life, as far as possible, the way he thought his God would approve; though it appeared that God also held some ideas about caste which were, strictly speaking, unconstitutional.[18] Traditional believers were willing to make significant sacrifices for such beliefs, sometimes at great cost to their personal lives.

These criteria, applied in deciding an individual's religious identity, also linked his individual identity to a larger collective religious group. By consequence, this kind of religiosity produces a map of highly segmented identities of social groups. The logic of this form of sectarian

---

[17] Caitanya, the great saint founder of his sect, the Gaudiya Vaisnavas, had enjoined a practice of unconditional humility to his followers:

trnadapi sunicena taroriva sahisnuna
amanina manadena kirtaniya sada harih

Vaisnavas should be humble like the grass, tolerant like the tree, they should honour others, but not seek honour for themselves, and constantly chant Hari's name. This can be decoded as advice not to tangle with political authority, and to seek a religious life unconnected with political power. It is a plausible surmise that Muslim rulers of Bengal gave significant patronage to Vaisnava sects to reward them for their political quietism. But my argument is that the marginality of political life is a general condition of traditional religiosity, not a peculiar feature of the Gaudiya Vaisnava faith.

[18] He believed in, and practised, caste, with the evident belief that though some of these practices were odious from a modern point of view, they were evidently endorsed by God.

differentiation produces highly defined, but *small communities* in large numbers. If differences between Bengali and Southern Vaishnavism were important, the individual religious communities would be comparatively small; if these were disregarded, then the 'Indian' Vaishnava community would be a vast body. If aggregation is taken a step further and all Hindus were included in one single religious community, that would comprise an alarming 80 per cent of the entire body of Indian citizens. My grandfather would have been perplexed by the suggestion that he belonged to such an abstract 'Hindu' community of immense magnitude, and by the idea that it was vital that he recognised that he belonged to it *politically*.

Thick religion, collective identity and collective action   A first politically significant implication of this analysis is that there exists an inverse relation between *thickness* of religious beliefs and the *size* of religious communities. Second, in the Indian context, the search for a large community – moving from a thick to a thin form – is linked to a highly significant substitution of functions. The reason for the 'production' of the religious community for traditionalists – common beliefs and proper conduct regarding the nature of god, nature, society, man and offering a conception of goodness – is substituted by the reason for the production of a comprehensive Hindu community – the application of force on or through the state – mainly in distribution of political rights and benefits. To the practitioners of thick religion, this is an application of religion to an illegitimate field or function.

On thin religion and political intolerance   We now turn the argument towards politics. The most significant implication of thick religion was its effect on the calculus of identity. Thick religion necessarily produces relatively small worship communities – due to the social segmentation of Hindu religion.[19] This meant that if members of a particular religious community decided to make a demand on the state, or on other social groups – for turning the arrangements of the secular world to their advantage – to demand reservation of jobs, to secure a legal immunity, or some other mundane political advantage, the community of mobilisation would be relatively small. A small group does not have the electoral power to force a decision on a democratic state.

[19] My example is drawn from a single Hindu religious sect; but the property I am referring to is a relational one, which would be exhibited to all groups belonging to this religion. But I am sure this will be true of other religions: this is certainly true of south Asian Islam and Christianity.

Neither does a small group carry the same menace of violence – to threaten other communities or the state with their numbers. It is important to recognise that the force of numbers is a crucial resource in modern states – irrespective of whether these are democratic or not.

Origins of thin religion: enumeration processes and religious commu-
nities   The religion that attracts contemporary Hindu nationalists is the exact opposite of this thick religion, and its functions and purposes are correspondently different. Schematically, the religion of Hindu nationalists is *thin*, because it is entirely indifferent to the sectarian practices of everyday worship; indeed, its primary purpose is to make them redundant. The criteria it uses for inclusion of groups into a vast, *loosely defined* Hindu religion, consequently, are sketchy and few. By reducing the number of criteria, and additionally making them quite vague, they make for easy inclusion, and a vast expansion of numbers belonging to this unified religious identity. For the BJP, belonging to various worship sects within Hinduism is of little consequence, just as their attitude towards ritual observances is derisory.[20] In fact, on the BJP's reckoning, the Hindu community would encompass not merely Shaktas, Vaishnavas, Saivas and other traditional Hindu sects, but also Buddhists, Jains and Sikhs, and, troublingly, even people who are from a Hindu background but suffer from a secularist 'false consciousness'. Demands on behalf of this incongruously expansive Hinduism have become increasingly broad, strident, intolerant and, in cases like Gujarat in 2002, its political actions murderous. There is a certain paradox in the way it orders the world: it uses a broad and inclusive movement for all Hindus, and groups linked to Hinduism by their origin; but the entire purpose is to harden and inflame the boundary between this expansive Hinduism and other selected adversaries, particularly Muslims.[21] Ironically, the primary purpose of this inclusion is exclusion of other communities from a sense of participating in a historically common and interactive religious culture. In sum, traditional religion and the new form are opposed in fundamental ways: it is thin, not thick; political, not ethical; intolerant, not accommodating; interested in this world, not

---

[20] It is an interesting fact however that much of the fierce opposition to recent Hindu nationalist politics has come from a secular intelligentsia who would be regarded from their point of view as 'self-hating Hindus'.

[21] The clearest exposition of this form of political Hinduism, which is inclusive towards the Hindus and irreconcilably hostile towards Muslims, comes in the work of the founder of this political tendency in modern India, V. D. Savarkar's *Hindutva: who is a Hindu?* (New Delhi: Hindi Sahitya Sadan, 2005).

in the next; its main purpose is to control mundane power, not to inspire indifference towards it. It is very odd to view this phenomenon as a *return* of the religion of my grandfather.

How do these paradoxical facts affect the secularisation thesis? First, this recent eruption of religious identity in the politics of a democratic state has often been attributed to a recidivist power of tradition.[22] The rise of Hindu nationalism in India since the 1980s is first assimilated with Islamic fundamentalism, and this is then advanced as an illustration of a *general* desecularisation thesis – that instead of becoming weaker with modernity, religious identity is becoming stronger in all parts of the world. My suggestion is that this is not a traditional form of religion, (thick religion) that is becoming increasingly assertive, but a new thin form – a form which adherents of thick religion would regard with perplexity if not revulsion. Ashis Nandy suggested insightfully that this religion effects a great substitution of the primary function of the religious community, by turning its attention from God to the state, Hobbes's mortal God.[23] A sociological argument requires some further explanatory device to account for its development. Of the various fields of social life in which the secularisation thesis leads us to expect a decline of religion, this pertains to only one – the political order; and even in that sphere it works with some peculiarities. In all other spheres of life – the economic sphere of livelihoods, the social sphere of everyday interaction, and even in the ethical sphere of selecting standards for making binding moral decisions – the authority of religion in contemporary India appears to be in decline. No one, for instance, advocates a return to the traditional link between birth and hereditary occupation. Uninterrupted growth of the modern economy continues unchallenged by religious objections or scruples. Religiously observant people happily adapt to capitalism as an economic form. Caste-based religiously sanctioned partitioning of social life – which placed barriers in the conduct of marriage, commensality and social intercourse – is becoming distinctly less common.[24] Even political groups like the BJP, the party of Hindu communalism itself, cannot seriously advocate a return to a caste social

---

[22] Conventional social science argument would view the BJP as a 'traditionalist' force.

[23] Ashis Nandy, who distinguished between religion as faith and as ideology, characterises the rise of this politics as a pathology of modernity, not of tradition. 'Politics of secularism and the recovery of religious tolerance', in Bhargava (ed.), *Secularism and its critics*, p. 322.

[24] India is a big and complex place, and counter-examples are often offered from brutal incidents of communal punishment against couples who married across caste lines. But the correct historical reading of such incidents is to see in them the desperation of conservatives rather than a general retrogressive trend.

order, or a formally subordinate status for women and lower castes. Ironically, they often join in the competition to appear more 'progressive' on these questions.[25] The overall political presentation of the party is not anti-modernist. The Indian case, therefore, can be treated as an example of the thesis that religion is becoming stronger again in the contemporary world, only if we entirely ignore these parallel trends – a paradoxical state in which a depletion of religious authority in social life is accompanied by a strident revival of Hindu identity in the political public sphere. It is an irruption of a political demand based on religious/communal identity in a partial, restricted, though admittedly vital domain of social life. Additionally, this revival is elicited by the power of democratic aggregative politics, not a returning power of traditional conduct. Thus it is misleading to hold that in India either religion is becoming stronger, or the secularisation thesis is disconfirmed.

Modernity and collective identity: enumeration of communities   Did peculiar features of modern politics bring this religion into existence? I suggested in some earlier work that two essential constituents of modern politics contributed to this specific transformation in religious beliefs and their worldly use. Intellectual practices of the colonial state were drawn from western rationalist cognitive techniques. Colonial administrators had to administer a society fundamentally different in its constructive principles from their own. The first step in ruling the country was therefore to understand the subjects they were to rule: successful use of power depended crucially on reliable knowledge.[26] Initially, the colonial state adapted to its specific needs the vast mechanisms of information collection existing from Mughal times. Later, the British colonial state initiated a vast enterprise of enumeration of Indian society through modern census and mapping, producing a vast process of cognitive 'objectification' of space and populations.[27] Cognitive

---

[25] The BJP has not seriously suggested that women should retreat from either the public sphere of political contestation or from modern occupations, though some of their women leaders exhibit a more traditional cultural comportment. On the question of caste subordination, it can truthfully claim that at least one strand of Hindu nationalism has demanded equality among all castes, for instance, Savarkar.

[26] For a detailed and insightful analysis of the emergence of this cognitive process, stressing particularly the continuities between pre-British and British systems of information gathering, C. A. Bayly, *Empire and information: intelligence gathering and social communication in India, 1780–1870* (Cambridge: Cambridge University Press, 1996).

[27] For the primary argument on the 'objectification process', see Bernard Cohn in *An anthropologist among the historians and other essays* (Delhi: Oxford University Press, 1990) and his later *Colonialism and its forms of knowledge: the British in India* (Princeton: Princeton University Press), 1996.

processes of everyday administration led to a fundamental transformation of not merely the epistemic techniques applied to think about
religious communities by insiders and outsiders, but to their ontological
character. Being a Hindu or a Muslim was of course an important part
of the traditional social world, but this changed what being a Hindu
or a Muslim involved.[28] Several far-reaching practical consequences
followed from the processes of colonial enumeration. First, the *aggregate*
outline of the community became objectified and numerically defined:
everybody knew how many Muslims and Hindus there were – both
in the world, and its small localities – so that there could be precise
calculations of potential for political acts and mobilisation. For the first
time, the ideas of *ethnic* majority/minority became really meaningful.[29]
I wish to suggest that formerly communities were dominant and subordinate, or superior and inferior, but not majorities and minorities.[30]
Second, these communities became *abstract*: the Hindu community
referred to *all* Hindus who existed in India, irrespective of the fact that
these people would never come to have any vivid or even real interrela-
tions among them, unless rendered possible precisely by this imaginative
inclusion.[31] Finally, these abstract communities were seen as increasingly *agentive* in character: they were viewed as gigantic collective
actors, involving all their innumerable constituent members, such that
an act of an individual or a group of Muslims came to be regarded as
an 'act of Muslims' as a putative group in which all inacting members were
in some sense involved, or at least implicitly subsumed. Cognitive processes
associated with mundane everyday administration thus made possible an
entirely new kind of conflict between new kinds of communities.

Enumeration processes had a strong connection with representative politics – both in its pre-democratic and democratic forms.[32]

---

[28] I make the argument in greater detail in 'The imaginary institution of India', in Partha
Chatterjee and Gyan Pandey (eds.), *Subaltern studies VII* (New Delhi: Oxford University
Press, 1994).

[29] It is essential to note that ideas of majority/minority became relevant in discussions about
democratic decision-making; using the concepts of majority and minority in terms of
identities is a new, and quite different kind of political argument. In Indian debates about
political institutions, the argument turned quite early from decisional to identity majorities.

[30] Kaviraj, *Imaginary institution*; also Rashmi Pant, 'The cognitive status of caste in colonial
ethnography: a review of some literature on the north west provinces and Oudh', *IESHR*
24/2 (1987) and Arjun Appadurai, 'Number in the colonial imagination', in Carol
Breckenridge and Peter van der Veer (eds.), *Orientalism and the colonial predicament*
(Philadelphia: University of Pennsylvania Press, 1993).

[31] This is also the sense in which Anderson speaks of nations as imagined communities: to
call them abstract is not to underestimate their political efficacy.

[32] Enumerated identities affect not merely democratic forms of politics, but also others.
Political life in modern times is affected not merely by democracy, but by a more general

Aggregate, abstract, agentive communities based on religious identity continue to be used as resources in modern politics. These might become subdued, and seem to fade during particular periods of political life; but they remain hidden until drawn out by interpellative acts of political groups. In a very odd fashion, democratic politics began to invoke these abstract identities in everyday electoral politics. As democracy is a politics of numbers, introduction of electoral democracy sets off a contest amongst political groups in finding the largest possible aggregative principle, a majority which can defeat all possible competitors.[33] The desperate democratic search for ever larger majorities contributed partly to the eventual invocation of the majority of Hindus, because, if Hindus can be persuaded to view themselves as a single permanent interest group, and induced to vote collectively, that majority will be simply impossible to defeat. To be effectively mobilised in democratic politics, religion must bear the thin form, as the thinness of the definition can produce an immense numerical combine.

Effects of modernity on individual and collective identities Historical processes of modernity, it is generally acknowledged, affect perceptions of identity and actions stemming from them in fundamental ways. In the existing sociological literature, however, an overwhelming emphasis has been placed on one side of this process – chronicling in careful and subtle detail the movements towards individuation. There is obviously a strong connection between Weber's ideas about secularisation and Ferdinand Toennies's parallel theory of individuation of communities and similar explorations in theorists like Simmel. Modernity is claimed to encourage individuation in many different but mutually reinforcing ways: through the rise of social individuation, the logic of capitalist labour processes, the establishment of subjectivist ethics, significantly individualistic conceptions of cultural production and appreciation. In order to understand the complexity of modern identity it is necessary to supplement the theory of *individuation* by theorising patterns by which introduction of enumeration, the subsequent entry of representational politics (not necessarily its democratic form) create new forms of *collective* identity-formation. Modernity offers the enticements not merely of new kinds of individual identity, but equally of new forms

---

form of representation. The Muslim League argued that after independence the Muslims would be reduced to a minority, implicitly claiming that democratic institutions are ineffective against agentive identities.

[33] Kaviraj in Baxi and Parekh (eds.), *Crisis and change.*

of collective ones which have particularly significant effects on political life. In his recent work, *Identity and violence*,[34] Amartya Sen has forcefully insisted on the many-sidedness of the identity of modern individuals – the plurality of identity – attributes that each individual carries. It is important to supplement this insight by two further arguments. First, modernity creates conditions which highlight to modern persons a function or a choice they exercise in arranging their identity-attributes in a particular order or configuration, responding to their perceptions of social circumstances. All human beings have *constituents* of identity that are plural, drawn from the many social settings in which their lives are involved. An individual's identity, in social or political action, is determined by the particular arrangement in which these constituents or attributes are ordered; how exactly, depending on his or her political circumstances, the individual stresses or fades these attributes. Let me use an example of two women from the same family in England. A young woman in a London University college wore the *hijab* to cover her hair; but mentioned that her mother, a modernist woman who migrated from Pakistan, never wore it, and considered it oppressive. It is true that the older woman's rejection of the veil and the younger woman's re-adoption confounds the regular expectations of a simple secularisation theory, but these decisions are not difficult to understand historically. In fact, these two cases of decision about dress are in one sense quite similar. An assertive individual, the mother showed her defiance of patriarchy in south Asian society by refusing the veil. The daughter reacted to her perception of neglect and hostility in British society by defiantly adopting a mark of Islamic identity. Out of the cluster of identity-attributes that the two women possessed, which were quite similar, each chose to foreground a particular one in response to her environment. Individuals possess this cluster of social characteristics: the exact arrangement of these attributes is achieved by the use of a *function*, or a verb. The specific identity of any one individual, at any particular time, is what this *identity-function* selects out of his or her *identity-attributes*. In an ideal language, identity should be a verb rather than a noun; or, there is an adjectival aspect of identity and a verb aspect.

Evidently, there are highly significant connections between these choices of individual identity and the collective processes of identity-formation that require closer analysis. For instance, some of these choices involve attributes which are collective in a strong sense: these

---

[34] Amartya Sen, *Identity and violence: the illusion of destiny* (London: Allen Lane, 2006).

attributes – like being Muslim or a Communist or belonging to an Indian nation – can exist only if there are large collective bodies which commonly share and historically produce them through repetitive and convergent patterns of conduct. Second, collective identities themselves are significantly reformed by processes of modernity– particularly by the exigencies of the modern state and the devices of mobilisation. It appears that there are some general processes of identity – formations which occur invariably with the entry of modernity. Cognitive techniques of modernity – objectification of populations and space – have produced, irreversibly, new formations of identity. The connection between enumerated identities and the instrumentalities of the modern state is similarly printed indelibly into the history of modern politics. Yet historically contingent causalities decide how specific groups and individuals are going to choose between these identities and what they do with them. Historically, segmentation of religious groups in India led to tolerance and pluralism in many cases. But there is no historical rule that segmented religious communities would necessarily be tolerant; though segmentation will necessarily limit the size of the groups which act as unified political agents. The story of Indian modernity, particularly of the Hindu religion, shows a process in which a thin Hindu identity seeks to overcome segmentation and produce a collective agency to menace minorities and demand a homogenising and intolerant version of nationalism. Obviously, this is not a general or universal rule: there exist numerous examples of intolerant politics practised by groups which wish to create large religious identities, but whose religious commitments are not thin in this sense. But what appears to be a constant in the diversity of all such historically local narratives is the constant factor of the great seduction of the modern state as an apparatus of reflexive power. The modern state is a peculiarly powerful device of reflexive organisation of society: an instrument by which a society acts upon itself, and conserves, transforms or decides about its own organisation. Political groups appear intent on the control of the modern state: because whoever lays hold of the power of the state captures this reflexive power of self-organisation. The exact form of religiosity differs contingently from one historical example to another: but all these stories are narratives of political action which swirl round the modern political imaginary.

To make sense of what is happening around us, we need a theory of religion and secularisation that has the capacity to deal with the complexity of the historical interaction between religion and the modern political world. It should not, first of all, unreasonably, exalt the experience of a part of western Europe into a universal norm, and then, more unreasonably, try to disqualify any evidence of difference as a lag or an exception. If there are more exceptions than instances confirming the rule, we need to look more closely at the putative rule itself. We need a theory which should try to plot adequately the cognitive and agentive transformations in identities of religious groups. Finally, we need a theory which can coherently join an analysis of the historical constitution of collective identities with the adventitious, exigent formation of individual selves.

Index

radicals and conservatives, split
between, 268
Vatican II, 255, 256, 259, 268
change in, nature, causes, and
chronology of, 254
church-state relations in, 269
decline in church affiliation and
attendance, 258–60, 276, 288–90,
292–4
eastern and New Age religions,
interest in, 259, 264, 290
economic affluence affecting, 255,
256, 261–3, 264
European focus of secularisation of, 19
family and neighborhood, role of,
262, 263
individual belief, changes in, 269
liberalising legal reforms of, 271–3
'long sixties,' concept of, 261
1950s, religious observance and
involvement in, 256–7
political radicalisation in, 255, 256,
266–9
as revolutionary decade, 254
secularisation, attribution of changes
to, 269
sexual revolution of, 255, 256, 257,
264–5, 276, 286–92, 328
subcultures, confessional and
ideological, waning of, 263
theological radicalisation in, 255, 266–9
Vatican II and change in, 16, 255, 256,
259, 268
women and. *See* entries at women
youth culture of, 261, 262
Nocedal, Cándido, 198
Noll, Mark, 85
non-Christian populations.
See under Europe, religious pluralism
in; Hinduism; Islam; Jews and
Judaism
nonconformist politics in 19th century
Britain, 214
depression of 1829–30 to elections of 1847,
215–19, 223, 229, 230
1853 to elections of 1873, 219–22,
223–4, 229, 230, 231
1880s to 1910, 226–9, 231–3
Anti-Corn Law League, 216, 218
anti-slavery movement, 216
Catholicism
alliance with, 87
dislike of, 227
Contagious Diseases Acts, efforts to
repeal, 222

Cromwell and Commonwealth,
views on, 224
disestablishment movement, 13
elections of 1847, 219
1853–1873, 219–21
1880s, as declining priority in, 226–9
American separation of church and
state as aspiration of, 86
Church of Ireland, disestablishment
of, 220, 228
church rates, struggle against, 217,
218, 219, 220,
Conservative party identified
with maintenance of Anglican
privilege, 230
educational voluntaryism policies,
217–19, 221, 224, 227–9, 231
societies formed to promote, 217,
219–20
economic depressions, effects of, 216,
integration of religious motives into
political party system, 233–4
Liberal Party and
elections of 1847, 219, 229
elections of 1868, 220
1870–1873 revolt against, 221, 222,
229, 231
1880s, nonconformist acceptance of
Whig position by, 227–8, 231–3
alliance between, 229–33
Gladstone, admiration for, 225
manly earnestness, cult of, 224–6
moral fervour for political reform, 215
nationalism of, 224
Radical critique of the state
nonconformist use of, 218
waning of, 222–9
reforms of 1828–1832 providing
national political presence, 214
temperance/prohibition movement,
219, 222, 230, 232
non-discrimination on basis of religion,
297, 330–1
Norris, Pippa, 316
Northern Ireland. *See also* Britain
religious objection of MPs to
swearing oath of allegiance to
Queen, 302
religious observance and affiliation,
drop in, 276
sexual revolution in, 276
Norway
abortion law in, 308
both established confessions and directly
subsidized faiths in, 320

For EU product safety concerns, contact us at Calle de José Abascal, 56–1°,
28003 Madrid, Spain or eugpsr@cambridge.org.

www.ingramcontent.com/pod-product-compliance
Ingram Content Group UK Ltd.
Pitfield, Milton Keynes, MK11 3LW, UK
UKHW020343140625
459647UK00018B/2280